CORNEILLE AND RACINE

PROBLEMS OF TRAGIC FORM

GORDON POCOCK

CAMBRIDGE
AT THE UNIVERSITY PRESS
1973

Published by the Syndics of the Cambridge University Press
Bentley House, 200 Euston Road, London NW1 2DB
American Branch: 32 East 57th Street, New York, N.Y. 10022

Library of Congress Catalogue Card Number: 72–97886

ISBN 0 521 20197 7

Printed in Great Britain
by W & J Mackay Limited, Chatham

CONTENTS

ACKNOWLEDGMENTS

I am grateful for their advice and encouragement to Dr Denys C. Potts, of Keble College, Oxford, and Dr C. J. Betts, of Warwick University, who read an earlier version of this book and made many helpful criticisms. This final version owes much to the scholarship and critical acumen of Mr Michael Black, of the Cambridge University Press. Their advice has helped me to avoid many faults. Those that remain are my own.

INTRODUCTION

I

This book is concerned with the formal aspects of French classical tragedy in a particular sense. It discusses only incidentally such matters as the three unities, the five-act convention, or the use of soliloquies and asides. Its concern is with the formal principles underlying the play-wrights' techniques. Its theme is that the form of French classical tragedy can be considered as a stage in that evolution from a poetic to a natural-istic drama which characterised the European theatre from the Renais-sance until the late nineteeth century. It argues that Corneille's tragedies show a progressive adoption of naturalistic techniques, and that this helps to explain not only the form they take, but also why they are rarely tragic in the modern sense. It argues that Racine was a partial exception to this trend towards naturalism, and that his plays are more strictly poetic and tragic.

In this summary form, the argument may seem another example of the familiar exercise of contrasting Corneille and Racine. The layout of the chapters may seem to support this, in that those in the first half of the book discuss mainly Corneille, and the later ones mainly Racine. This layout has been dictated by the need to trace the development of each dramatist. The argument concerns a contrast of modes apparent within their work as well as between them. Indeed, my contention will be that this contrast underlies the development of seventeeth-century tragedy generally.

My concern is primarily with literary criticism, and in this first chap-ter I shall discuss the critical terms to be used. This is not to imply that the discussion of literary terms and criteria can be divorced from more general social and cultural questions. Such terms as 'poetry', 'natural-ism' or 'tragedy' are borderline concepts, which from one aspect are purely literary, but from another are linked to wider questions. There has been much discussion of social and intellectual developments in seventeenth-century Europe, and of their relationship with the rise of naturalism and the decline of poetry. These issues are fascinating and important, but outside the focus of our present concern. I shall pursue the argument in literary terms, and content myself with noting where connections with these wider questions may be relevant.

2

'Naturalism' is a term in which the literary and historical aspects are not easy to separate. Its most obvious use is in connection with the nineteenth-century dramatic movement exemplified in the middle and late works of Ibsen. It was these works which were immediately and widely influential, and which have since been the main object of attack by critics opposed to naturalism. The general line of attack – and the way in which naturalism is sometimes seen to be linked with wider cultural questions – is well shown by the following passage from a Shakespearean critic:

The Renaissance gave rise to rationalism and to experimental science . . . The eighteenth century saw the growth of materialism, in which the function of reason became limited to the ordering of physical fact. And later, in the same way, that movement in dramatic criticism, which began with the exaltation of reason, ended in submission to the dictatorship of meaningless physical phenomena. For in the nineteenth century philosophical naturalism reached its consummation in the work of Darwin and the popular writings of Spencer and Huxley; and, corresponding to this, the so-called 'realistic' drama of the school of Ibsen usurped the serious theatre.[1]

I leave on one side the implied assessment of Ibsen, and consider the more general issues. In this simple form, the account of the development of science and philosophy is clearly inadequate, and needs to be supplemented by the results of more recent work on the history of ideas. On the one hand, scholars such as Clagett, Dijksterhuis and Lynn White Jr have demonstrated the continuity of the new science of the seventeenth-century with intellectual and technological developments in the Middle Ages. On the other, Garin, Yates and Rossi, for example, have emphasised the rôle of the Renaissance revival of magical Hermetism in stimulating the scientific movement. In the sphere of religion, there has been a similar breaking down of the crude nineteenth-century antithesis between rationalism and religion. Popper and others have stressed the influence of mediaeval scholasticism on rationalist philosophies such as Cartesianism, and scholars such as Adam and Spink have shown the diversity of the strands in seventeenth-century free thought, some of which are far removed from scientific rationalism.

Nevertheless, there is clearly something in the views stated by Bethell, and this is related in some way to the rise of naturalism in literature. We might, as a more recent critic has done, distinguish between naturalism in the sense of the imitation of the surfaces of life ('representational form') and the view of life which assumes that the

2

material is all, and hence implies naturalistic form ('the naturalistic vision').[2] But this distinction also leads to difficulties. A dramatist like Brecht may accept the naturalistic vision (and be, as Gaskell contends, a naturalistic playwright), and yet adopt non-representational conventions. Similarly, a writer like Beckett may accept much of the naturalistic vision, yet be classified (again rightly) as a poetic dramatist. A borderline case might be Chekhov, an agnostic who was educated as a nineteenth-century materialist clinician, whose work is cast in a mainly representational form, and yet has elements we might call poetic. Nor does it follow that all naturalist writers accept the naturalistic vision. Ibsen might plausibly be considered a Romantic Idealist, and his plays are largely concerned with vocation as a transcendental rather than psychological concept. Yet Ibsen is one of the masters of modern naturalism.

We may gain clarity (and come closer to the argument on seventeenth-century tragedy) if we consider the history of naturalism in the theatre. Traces of naturalism, in the sense of representational form, can be found in works of almost any era. Nevertheless, the end of the sixteenth and the beginning of the seventeenth centuries clearly mark a period of poetic drama. In England, we have the great age of Elizabethan and Jacobean drama; in France, the not negligible works of Garnier and Montchrestien. Leaving aside for the moment Corneille and Racine, however, we can see in seventeenth-century France the development of naturalism in at least one sense. In Molière, for instance, we can see two strands developing. On the one hand, we have the puppet-like energy of the farces and the theatrical verve of the *comédies-ballets* – not the literary Molière, but perhaps the most Molièresque part of his work, the spirit of which was to survive into Feydeau, or even Jarry and Ionesco. On the other hand, we have a more rationalised drama, with a social and intellectual slant: *Le Misanthrope*, or *Les Femmes Savantes*. Although in verse, these plays are more representational, closer to social realities. Although comic, they are sometimes close to being serious in the nineteenth-century sense of serious drama.

In the eighteenth century, it is this second line of development which becomes dominant. In both France and England, we have a movement at once towards an intermediate form of drama blurring the division of tragedy and comedy into something closer to the amorphousness of life (the sentimental comedy of Steele or Nivelle de la Chaussée) and towards a form avowedly nearer to representing middle-class life (the bourgeois tragedy of Moore and Lillo, the *drame* of Diderot). Here, naturalism as representational form may be linked with the development of the naturalistic vision. But another aspect of the matter is perhaps more interesting. What may strike us about the *drame* is not so much its form or the philosophic ideas of its authors as the simplification of attitudes which lies behind it. Representation of the surfaces of life is seen as desirable in itself, as though only a simple one-to-one relationship between reality and its representation were admissible. The choice of a middle level of sentiment is not a unification of tragedy and comedy so much as a splitting of the components of each. The complexities of the tragic emotion are reduced to simple pathos or blame. The cathartic joy of comedy is separated into sympathy or disapproval. And the separating goes further than this. Tragedy and comedy both admit thought, in the sense of a constant meditation on human nature and the place of mankind in the scheme of things, but in sixteenth- and seventeenth-century plays this element is usually implicit, and can rarely be separated out as a 'message' or 'ideas'. In the *drame* and *comédie larmoyante*, the message is more overt. Diderot went further in this cultivation of thought as a separate element, and envisaged a discussion-play on the death of Socrates.[3] These developments are clearly in the line which leads to nineteenth-century naturalism. As Beuchat remarked in his *Histoire du Naturalisme Français*, 'L'originalité divinatrice de Diderot montre le chemin à Zola'.[4]

Before following this development further, however, let us consider for a moment eighteenth-century neo-classical tragedy, which descends in direct line from its seventeenth-century predecessors. From one angle, the tragedies of Crébillon or Voltaire are anachronisms, repeating seventeenth-century routines long after they had lost their freshness. Nevertheless, these writers were to some extent innovators. Crébillon flouted the moral conventions of neo-classical drama and refurbished over-used classical stories by ingeniously reconstructing them with minor or invented characters as the main focus of interest. Voltaire experimented with new themes and settings, and took liberties with the unities. More significantly, certain changes reflected the more naturalistic developments: more pathos, greater closeness to the externals of life (in the sense of local colour in manners and costumes), and the exploitation of ideas for didactic purposes. This suggests that some of the changes in the direction of naturalism which appeared in eighteenth-century drama were not so much in opposition to formal neo-classicism as a development of tendencies inherent in it.

This thought is perhaps not so strange if we consider some principles proclaimed by neo-classical critics in the formative years of French classical drama. Among the guiding ideas in the development of naturalism in the eighteenth century, two must at least be considered important: the impulse towards a more exact representation of reality, and didacticism (Diderot's proposal for the arts of 'un commun objet . . . pour nous faire aimer la vertu et haïr le vice'.)[5] Both these elements are strongly present in seventeenth-century critical doctrine, the first as a insistence on *vraisemblance*, the second as a concern with the moral aim of poetry.

We shall discuss in connection with Corneille the neo-classical insistence on *le vraisemblable* and its relation to *le vrai*. Here, it may suffice to make two points. First, *vraisemblance* is sometimes meant literally, as the most truthful possible representation of reality. This is so not only in the pronouncement of Corneille as a tyro:

La comédie n'est qu'un portrait de nos actions et de nos discours, et la perfection des portraits consiste en la ressemblance. Sur cette maxime je tâche de ne mettre en la bouche de mes acteurs que ce que diraient vraisemblablement en leur place ceux qu'ils représentent, et de les faire discourir en honnêtes gens, et non pas en auteurs.[6]

It comes out strongly in Chapelain, in a statement which comes astonishingly close to demanding the most exact, slice-of-life realism:

Je pose donc pour fondement que l'imitation en tous poèmes doit être si parfaite qu'il ne paraisse aucune différence entre la chose imitée et celle qui imite, car le principal effet de celle-ci consiste à proposer à l'esprit . . . les objets comme vrais et comme présents . . . le tout pour rendre la feinte pareille à la vérité même et faire la même impression sur l'esprit des assistants par l'expression qu'aurait la chose exprimée sur ceux qui en auraient vu le véritable succès.[7]

More usually, of course this demand is transmuted into one that poetry should imitate a stylised and carefully-selected reality in accordance with a generalised idea of plausibility: neo-classical art rarely (though more often than is sometimes supposed) aims at realism in the sense Chapelain is here recommending. This brings us to our second point: the generalisation is at least partly recommended for didactic purposes. The particular, perhaps untypical, case cannot provide a convincing *exemplum*. Only the generally plausible type can form a firm basis for a moral art: 'la fonction moralisatrice de la poésie est la base la plus sûre que puisse trouver Chapelain pour établir l'omnipotence du vraisemblable'.[8] Verisimilitude is thus linked on one side with representational accuracy, and on the other with didactic purpose. In this sense, it is central to neo-classical theory.

If we now return to the eighteenth century, we can see similar factors at work as the trend towards naturalism gathers strength. We can, in fact, leap forward to the fully-fledged naturalism of the nineteenth century and trace similar factors at work there.

Insofar as modern dramatic naturalism can be said to have been developed as a mature form by any one man, Ibsen is the crucial figure, and the critical part of his career for this purpose is that interesting middle period – from *The League of Youth* to *The Pillars of Society* – in which he was struggling to work out the basis of his new form. The crucial work of these years is his vast double play, the 'World-Historic Drama' *Emperor and Galilean*.

This play is of interest here in two ways. The first is its form. Ibsen explained this in a letter to Gosse:

You think my play should have been in verse, and that it would have gained by this. On that point I must contradict you, for the play is – as you will have noted – cast in a form as realistic as possible; it was the illusion of reality I wanted to produce. I wanted to evoke in the reader the impression that what he was reading really happened. If I had used verse, I would have run counter to my own intentions and to the task I had set myself.[9]

The emphasis on representational form is not far from what we meet in Chapelain and Diderot.

The second point is the means by which the play's seriousness is to be achieved. Partly, Ibsen implies that the decision to imitate reality is a guarantee of seriousness. But the real seriousness comes from the content. In a letter to Frederik Hegel, Ibsen said: 'The positive "Weltanschauung" which the critics have long demanded of me will be found here'.[10]

This demand (and Ibsen's acceptance of its validity) is not far from Diderot's concern with the moral aim of drama. It looks forward to another characteristic of the naturalism of the nineteenth century and later: a concern with social, political or philosophical problems.

These two points – the demand for representational form and for a didactic content – are connected, but for a moment we will discuss them separately.

The requirement that the dramatist should aim at the 'illusion of reality' has often been criticised. Clearly, the purpose is self-defeating: if the illusion were successful, the play would be no different from life itself, and it would be hard to see any reason for the exercise. In practice, however, the purpose is virtually never achieved. When we see a play, we experience a curious doubleness of response. However stylised the play or production, there seems to be an irresistible tendency to take the figures acted on the stage as real people. Even Brecht, for all his distancing devices, was unable to overcome this. At the same time, however carefully illusionistic the play or production, we are aware that it is a play. While reacting as though it were real life, we are appraising the text, the acting, the costumes, the lighting, and so on. However deeply stirred, we do not forget that we are in a theatre.[11]

If we keep in mind this doubleness of the dramatic experience, we can formulate the naturalist demand for the 'illusion of reality' in another way. It is a demand for a singleness of response, based on the assumption that we do in fact accept the illusion. This, implies in turn, a particular set of critical values. Many of the traditional features of drama – verse soliloquies, emblematic action and characters – are proscribed as unrealistic. The way in which we are to evaluate what happens on the stage is to be exactly as if it were real life. If a character says or does something, we are to infer his purposes and motives, exactly as we do with a real person. This is less normal in drama than it may seem, and leads to one of the most difficult issues in dramatic criticism. Dramatists over the centuries have varied greatly in their attitudes to characterisation. Good Deeds in *Everyman* or Mr and Mrs Smith in *La Cantatrice Chauve* are not characters in the sense of Miss Julie or Rebecca West. In most sixteenth and seventeenth century drama, and some modern drama, there is liberal use of soliloquy, chorus and direct statements about the characters and their motivation which seem from their tone and context to be intended to be taken at their face value by the audience. When Shakespeare's Richard III says, 'I am determined to prove a villain', or Molière's Sosie, 'Que son bonheur est extrême | De ce que je suis poltron', or Eliot's Thomas, 'Now is my way clear, now is the meaning plain', we are presumably to accept these statements and to evaluate them as elements in the play as a whole, rather than to ponder why the characters utter them. In eschewing such devices because they are unrealistic, naturalism forfeits valuable means of clarifying and developing the meaning of a play. In theory (though not in the practice of the greatest naturalists), this abandonment of articulate means of expression and insistence on the illusion of reality leads to a total disintegration of dramatic form. A play ceases to have any standing as a statement in its own right, and becomes nothing but a vehicle for actors and directors. It is not simply that inarticulate speech and unemphatic events do not impose their own meaning on a performance: they often require the addition of the actors' and directors' interpretation before they have any meaning at all.

It is here that we come to Ibsen's second requirement: that serious drama must present a philosophy of life. This again brings us to one of the great critical problems. When we say that the great poetic dramatists are concerned with profound issues, we are not usually crediting them with preaching any particular doctrine or philosophy. Shakespeare is only the most notorious example of a dramatist from whom it is possible to extract any – and, therefore, no – moral lesson. If great drama teaches (as in some sense it surely does) it does not teach in the same way as a sermon or a text-book. Nor does it do so in exactly the same way as real life does. The moral and emotional education we go through when we see *Oedipus* or *Hamlet* is not what we should experience by watching similar events in real life: the psychological circumstances are too different.

Critics have long tried to define the sense in which these dramatic representations (which are not necessarily trying to represent events realistically) can teach without teaching in the normal sense. One class of explanation is that artistic presentation is a sort of sweetening to make a lesson palatable. This is a very ancient view, but it does not seem to take account of the complexity of the process: sometimes the sweetening is bitter, and very often there is no message which can be separated out and made explicit. At the other extreme is Shelley's claim that poets are the unacknowledged legislators of mankind, which seems hardly more acceptable. We might get nearer a consensus by saying that by embodying and making concrete the dramatist's deepest perceptions, a good play enables us to deepen and extend our own. Whatever our critical views, I think we must all admit that there remains something in good drama, as in other good works of art, that is stubbornly irreducible to any statement in discursive terms. If drama communicates, it does so in a special sense.

In the history of naturalism, however, we can trace a growing willingness among playwrights and novelists to be more explicit about the criteria by which their art is to be measured. In Aeschylus or Shakespeare we find a cavalier attitude to the representation of everyday reality, both in terms of their use of unrealistic conventions and their disregard of common knowledge: the Strymon will freeze and thaw suddenly, or Bohemia acquire a sea-coast. It is difficult to be so precise about their treatment of accepted religious or political doctrine, but it seems unlikely that the *Oresteia* merely exemplifies the traditional view of Zeus, or that *King Lear* is simply a celebration of Jacobean ideas on religious and political order. The same is true of some of the naturalists. Despite his attempts to express a 'positive "Weltanschauung"' and his references to contemporary ideas, Ibsen is not the propagandist his admirers once made out. In Chekhov, despite his materialistic view of life, there is little trace of ideology. But other naturalists adopted a more rigorous line. Zola took up with enthusiasm the ideas of Bernard on physiology and Lucas on heredity. In his critical jottings, he points to Bernard's *Introduction à l'Etude de la Médecine Expérimentale* as a book which will provide the novel with its proper method,[12] and there is little doubt that for much of his career he regarded Bernard's conclusions as objective truth, to which his novels should conform. Nor is this a quirk of Zola's. It is one example of a common naturalist attitude. Brecht, for instance, takes a similar line, only for him the prophet is Marx.[13]

A typical naturalistic attitude of this type is implied in Shaw's complaint about Shakespeare's failure to provide psychological and sociological notes on his characters: 'For want of this elaboration . . . Shakespeare, unsurpassed as poet, story-teller, character draughtsman, humorist and rhetorician, has left us no intellectually coherent drama, and could not afford to pursue a genuinely scientific method in his studies of character, and society.'[14]

To discuss this would take us far afield, but I think we can make a connection between this second demand of naturalism (the appeal to the authority of some scientific or other interpretation of experience, rather than experience itself) and the first demand (that for realistic imitation of the surfaces of everyday life). If the great dramatists of the past had paid relatively little attention to representing everyday behaviour or reflecting contemporary knowledge, this was not necessarily through incompetence or ignorance. Rather, it was a sign of their concentration on achieving by means as powerful and precise as possible that special form of communication we have tried to describe. Somewhere between the sixteenth and seventeenth centuries, dramatists radically changed these priorities. Emphasis on the independent importance of that form of communication made possible by artistic representation became muted. The emphasis on validation by the two types of external criteria which we have discussed became enormously increased. Some critics, such as Bethell, would see this change as due to the growing prestige of science and materialistic philosophy. I think the matter is more complicated than that, as the remainder of this book will show. We may concede, however, that for the nineteenth century at least, the point seems to have substance.

We have reached a boundary at which literary criticism comes up against much wider questions, and at this we must turn back. The discussion has, however, brought us towards a definition which is crucial for the argument of this book. 'Naturalism' is used here in two senses. The narrower sense is that of common usage: the style derived from Ibsen's *Doll's House* period and still current in the normal Broadway or West End straight play or light comedy.

I also use the term in a wider sense implied in the preceding discussion. Surface style is clearly not a sufficient criterion for what is naturalism and what is not: *A Doll's House, Death of a Salesman* and the latest light comedy are all naturalistic, yet differ considerably in style. Nor is it satisfactory, as some critics do, to define naturalistic drama by contrast with conventional drama. All drama is wholly conventional. In one play, the actors may move on a lighted platform in a dark hall and pretend they are living their lives there for two hours without noticing the presence of the audience. In another, they may represent God or Satan on a platform in the street and speak directly to the audience. If we call the second play more conventional than the first, this merely means that its convention is the one we are less used to.

A more satisfactory differentiation between naturalistic and other conventions would be the degree of articulacy they permit. But this itself needs clarifying. A play such as *Pillars of Society* may be as explicit as *Everyman*, in that a character explicitly tells the audience what to think. The important criterion is the type of articulacy. One is the articulacy of prose discourse, which any type of play can accommodate; another is the articulacy which is made possible only by the full complexity of the play – that is, the 'meaning' which the play itself is. Here we come to our fundamental point. In theory, at least, we can set up a distinction between two types of drama. In the first, the meaning is that special kind which is by definition inherent in the play itself: the seriousness or truth or meaning (whichever word we like to use) is not reducible to other terms. In the second type, the seriousness or truth or meaning (if the play aspires to one, and is not content to be simply amusement) is determined by reference to some criterion which is not dependent on our attempt to grapple with any inner meaning of the sort aimed at in the first type. The focus of concern may be whether life outside the play is credibly represented (the 'illusion of reality'). Alternatively, it may be the truth of the ideas expressed, judged by the formulations of some philosophical or other discipline (the 'positive "Weltanschauung"').

Of these two types of drama, I call the first poetic and the second naturalistic. On the whole, plays which are towards the poetic end of the spectrum will tend to use verse, emblematic action, and a method of characterisation which is not mainly intended to create the illusion of real people. Towards the other end of the spectrum, there will normally be a tendency towards realistic representation (although a dramatist like Brecht may regard the expression of a 'true' philosophy as more important, and use non-representational conventions to achieve this aim more effectively). But in neither case does the classification depend mainly on surface style or arbitrary notions of what is conventional. A play is poetic if its prime purpose is to express a meaning which can be expressed only in that form, and which (being inexpressible in the language of any other discipline) cannot be validated by the criterion of any other discipline. Its appeal is direct to the audience's experience, at a level deeper than that of their perception of everyday behaviour. I call a play naturalistic if two criteria are satisfied: first, that the implied standards of truth are of the type described ('illusion of reality' or 'positive "Weltanschauung"'); second, that the articulacy of which the play is capable is in principle that of prose discourse, rather than that special type which is attainable only through the complexity of dramatic form.

There are a number of reasons for feeling unhappy with extending in this way the use of terms like 'poetic' and 'naturalistic', which are already sufficiently vague. Most obviously, there is the objection that they represent theoretical extremes, rather than totally distinct types of drama. In practice, most playwrights operate in a middle area, though Aeschylus and Shakespeare are clearly towards the 'poetic' extreme, and the early Strindberg or Gorky towards the other. The distinction is also open to some criticism because it does not correspond exactly to distinctions made entirely on stylistic criteria. Many plays in verse are not primarily poetic in method, and some which are in prose are based on the poetic principle which puts in first place the overall pattern of meaning.

Nevertheless, it is not easy to find more appropriate terms, and those chosen correspond broadly to categories apparent in the history of Western drama. In particular, the extension of the meaning of naturalism seems justified for two reasons. First, the term has little explanatory power if confined to the narrower sense. Second, the narrower and wider senses are connected historically. The history of Western drama since the Renaissance is of the gradual replacement of the poetic by the naturalistic mode, and then of attempts to reverse the process. It is in this historical perspective that the wider sense of the term shows its value. In much of this book I shall be concerned with close analysis of selected plays to locate their fluctuations on the scale I have posited. This is an essential method, because generalities are of little use when we come to the complexities of a living work of art. But I hope the result of these analyses will be to locate the tragedies of seventeenth-century France in the historical development from poetic to naturalistic drama.

It is here that we come to the question posed by our third term: 'tragedy'. It is frequently implied that the decline of poetic drama and the rise of naturalism are connected with the decline of tragedy. Tragedy is thus a critical term which often assumes a special importance in discussions of the change of direction of European civilisation in the seventeenth century. It is a concept which is elusive in itself, and properly only exists in the works which embody it. Nevertheless, it is an important term in our argument, and I shall end this chapter with a brief discussion of it.

3

'Tragedy' is used in two senses in this book, neither of which corresponds exactly to the use of *tragédie* in seventeenth-century France.

First, it is used to mean any play coming within such general categories as 'Greek tragedy', 'Elizabethan tragedy', 'French classical tragedy'. In this last case, it includes *tragi-comédies* and *comédies héroïques*. This is common usage, and unlikely to cause confusion.

The second sense is more elusive, and more modern: it refers to any work which evokes the tragic emotion. As such, it is both narrower and wider than the first sense. Only a few of the plays which come under the first definition come also under the second. On the other hand, some non-dramatic works may be tragic in this second sense.

Tragedy in this second sense is indefinable, but we can at least list some characteristics which may show what is meant by it here. It is always felt as serious: not in the sense that it deals with social or philosophical problems (in my view it shuns them) but that we feel it as immediately and deeply important. Its endings are always sad and painful, but in a special way – not depressing, nor quite exhilarating, but impressive in a way that defies description yet is unmistakable. Finally, the progress of tragic events is felt to be inevitable, not only in the literal sense of unavoidable but in the aesthetic sense that their results are fitting, and could not decently be otherwise: 'More pliant divorce laws could not alter the fate of Agamemnon; social psychiatry is no answer to "Oedipus" . . . Tragedy is irreparable. It cannot lead to just and material compensation for past suffering.'[15]

The relation between 'tragedy' in this sense and *tragédie* in the normal seventeenth-century sense is not easy to define. The modern conception was not commonly in the minds of seventeenth-century critics and audiences, as far as we can tell. To them, a play was a *tragédie* if it dealt with eminent persons in peril of losing their lives or states, or of being banished.[16] It was expected to be moving, but its ending might be happy, and often was. If a play was attacked as not a proper *tragédie* (as some of Racine's were), the grounds would be that it did not treat of sufficiently lofty subjects, or show its characters behaving with the dignity and virtue proper to their high rank.

Corneille and Racine, however, do not always share these views. Corneille will not accept that the rank of the participants is a criterion: kings may appear in a comedy,[17] 'ce n'est pas une nécessité de ne mettre que les infortunes des rois sur le théâtre', and a peasant's misfortune may be a proper tragic theme.[18] His criterion of tragedy is the type of incidents treated, which must be illustrious and extraordinary, so that they may strongly interest.[19] Like Aristotle, he admits of tragedy with a happy ending, although he acknowledges as a rule that it should aim to arouse pity for the hero 'par l'excès de ses infortunes'.[20] He himself, however, thinks it reasonable to seek to arouse other emotions, such as admiration.[21] Clearly, he is concerned with aesthetic effect, not with the mechanical criteria laid down by some other theoreticians, but the type of aesthetic effect is not always what we regard as tragic today.

With Racine, the position is different. Although some of his plays end happily, in his critical discussions he seems always to be concerned with the tragic emotion. This he defines either in terms of the traditional pity and terror, 'qui sont les véritables effets de la tragédie',[22] or (in a phrase which shows that he meant something very close to our modern concept) 'cette tristesse majestueuse qui fait tout le plaisir de la tragédie'.[23] Nor is this a matter of prefatorial polemics. In his private notes on Aristotle he is almost alone among seventeenth-century critics in viewing catharsis as an emotional rather than a moral purgation.[24]

However we regard these historical questions, we are left with a serious critical issue. The special quality we now regard as tragic is certainly present in many of Racine's plays, in some of Corneille's, and occasionally in those of their contemporaries. One of the reasons why the *tragédies* of the period seem so significant today is precisely that they represent one of those rare moments at which true tragedy was achieved. It is therefore legitimate to inquire how far the plays possess this elusive but important quality, especially as this question is related to that of the dramatic techniques used.

On the modern view, tragedy as a dramatic form presupposes a particular attitude to experience (in the sense, not of a conscious philo-sophy, but of a characteristic pattern of thought and feeling). As such, we might expect it to require a particular approach to dramatic technique, and perhaps particular formal characteristics. A *tragédie* in the normal seventeenth-century sense might not make the same demands, and might allow different approaches and techniques. If my critical approach is valid, it is necessary to examine both of these interacting variables: the playwright's technical procedures and the content they are designed to express. It is in terms of this dual requirement that I shall pursue my discussion of French classical tragedy, beginning with Corneille.

2

CORNEILLE AND THE CRITICS

I

Corneille's dramatic career from *Mélite* (1629/30) to *Suréna* (1674) was extremely long, and marked by extreme variations in the styles, contemporary success and critical reception of his plays. His early comedies were well received, but fell rapidly from favour. He later heavily revised them, and they have only recently received much critical esteem (largely because of renewed study of the unrevised texts). His experiments outside social comedy – the *tragédies* of *Clitandre* (1630/1) and *Médée* (1635), the fantastic comedy *L'Illusion Comique* (1635/6) – suggest a concern with effects far different from those of later neo-classical plays.

His reputation has long rested mainly on the four great tragedies – *Le Cid* (1636/7), *Horace* (1640), *Cinna* (1640/1) and *Polyeucte* (1641/2) – in which he seemed to bring to perfection an austere form of classical tragedy. But even these four plays have suffered vicissitudes. *Le Cid*, though enormously successful with the public, was on the whole harshly judged by contemporary critics, and during the heyday of neo-classicism the critics were never quite happy with it. *Horace* seems to have failed at first, and in his later *Examen* Corneille tries to explain its 'chute'. *Cinna* was highly regarded in the seventeenth and eighteenth centuries, but nineteenth-century critics tended to be less enthusiastic. By contrast, *Polyeucte*, the favourite of nineteenth- and twentieth-century critics, did not much please the critics at the time or in the eighteenth century, despite its success in the theatre. These masterpieces were followed by a group of very varied plays which met equally varied fates. *Théodore* (1645/6) and *Pertharite* (1651) found little favour, at the time or since. *Pompée* (1643), *Rodogune* (1644/5) and *Héraclius* (1647) were greatly successful at the time and later, and fell from critical and popular favour only after the triumph of Romanticism. Of the *tragédies* of this period, only *Nicomède* (1651) has maintained and increased its reputation, and is now regarded as one of Corneille's undoubted masterpieces. Some of the most interesting plays of these years are those in which Corneille experimented outside formal tragedy: the comedy *Le Menteur* (1643), the machine-play *Andromède* (1650) and the *comédie héroïque* of *Don Sanche* (1649).

After a seven-year retirement from the theatre, Corneille returned in 1659 with *Oedipe*, and the fate of the last group of plays was as varied as those of the earlier period. It is certainly not true that they were all contemporary failures: *Oedipe*, *La Toison d'Or* (1660), *Sertorius* (1662) and his collaboration with Molière and Quinault on *Psyché* (1671) were all triumphs; *Attila* (1667), *Tite et Bérénice* (1670) and perhaps *Pulchérie* (1672) had some success. *Sertorius* at least has always enjoyed critical esteem, and modern critics have done much to rescue the other late plays from the discredit into which they had fallen.

Although even this rapid survey may suggest that the matter is rather complex, by the end of the nineteenth century critics had settled on a quite simple consensus: Corneille's work was astonishingly uneven in quality, beginning with feeble comedies and a couple of romantic plays, flaring out in four masterpieces, then dying away in a long line of failures which finally reached the depths of ineptitude.

As many modern critics have seen, this view is unjust. But even if we accept the general revaluation by twentieth-century critics – which seems right, though not yet confirmed in the theatre – Corneille's career still seems a strange patchwork. The older view had behind it the simple (if misleading) biological pattern of growth, maturity and decay. Despite brilliant rehabilitations of individual plays, and much illuminating exposition of their background, the modern view seems to lack any such unifying principle – one which makes sense of the apparent variations of tone and quality in the plays, and the diversity of reactions to them. I shall try to develop such a principle, making use of the concepts discussed in the first chapter, and taking my as point of entry the critical doctrines of the seventeenth century, and in particular Corneille's treatment of them in 1656–60.

2

In seventeenth-century France, criticism was articulate and influential. A set of critical precepts became generally accepted as 'the Rules'. Why did a set of doctrines acquire such importance as to supply the framework, or at least the language, of so much critical discussion for a century-and-a-half, despite considerable changes in literary tastes and great changes in other intellectual spheres?

To pose the question in these terms is to go against a major trend in modern criticism. In a justified reaction against the over-schematic views of nineteenth- and early twentieth-century critics, the tendency has been to play down the significance of the rules. They are now sometimes seen as a more or less unrelated group of ideas, deriving variously from a taste for concentrated and orderly aesthetic forms, from empirical observation of what pleased seventeenth-century playgoers and readers, and from the material conditions of the theatres. Clearly, the rules were never as monolithic or as binding as used to be supposed, and my discussion will confirm what complexities lie behind them.

Nevertheless, the modern emphasis can perhaps be carried too far. The extent to which seventeenth-century discussion focussed on the rules, and the frequently dogmatic tone of that discussion, do not suggest that they were thought as inessential as some modern scholars imply. Secondly, the close study which has dissolved 'the rules' as an entity can produce its own error of perspective. If we stand back and compare neo-classical France with other great ages of Western literature, we can see how extraordinary it was that the question of rules should have been taken so seriously for so long in this one case and not in the others. Finally, the older views, mistaken though they were, had one great merit: they attempted to relate the influence of the rules to wider social and ideological developments.

From his *Examen* to *Clitandre* it is clear that at the outset of his career Corneille hardly knew that the rules were beginning to be debated, and despite such superficial gestures as bringing *Clitandre* nominally within the unity of time his early plays do not show him in the vanguard of those who espoused them. At moments in the quarrel over *Le Cid*, he showed himself openly intransigent. Nevertheless, he subsequently accepted the rules, and achieved his best work after he had done so. We cannot easily claim that he accepted them against his creative instincts. This suggests that there were valid artistic reasons for their acceptance.

In the years 1656–60 – two-thirds of the way through his career, and perhaps partly prompted by the slighting remarks of d'Aubignac – Corneille set down in his *Examens* and *Discours* his attitudes on the great critical questions of the day. These statements differ from some earlier ones made in the heat of controversy over *Le Cid*, and condemn explicitly or implicitly much of his earlier practice. They are not, however, mere expositions of the received critical wisdom. They show a fascinating mixture of orthodoxy and independence.

Even at this late stage of his career, indications of revolt are fairly common. In introducing *Nicomède* and *Agésilas*, he insists on his right to innovate. In the *Discours* he flatly disagrees with Aristotle's view of comedy: 'Quoi qu'il en soit, cette définition avait du rapport à l'usage de son temps . . . mais elle n'a pas une entière justesse pour le nôtre',[1] and gives short shrift to the idea of catharsis: 'j'ai bien peur que le raisonnement d'Aristote sur ce point ne soit qu'une belle idée qui n'ait jamais son effet dans la vérité.'[2]

Nevertheless, his *Discours* are full of respectful, even worshipping, references to Aristotle. Some are ironical, but by no means all. In itself the critical sifting of Aristotle's theories shows an involvement that goes beyond lip-service, and beyond the attention most contemporary authors felt it necessary to show. Aristotle is 'notre docteur.'[3] Agreement with him is the touchstone of truth ('il est aisé de nous accommoder avec Aristote. Nous n'avons qu'à dire que . . .').[4] He is even assumed to have foreknowledge of French dramatic forms ('Je réduis ce pro-logue à notre premier acte, suivant l'intention d'Aristote.').[5] It would be a bold critic who would undertake to assign to each of these utterances the exact degree of irony intended.

This mixture of plainness and irony should warn us against any ten-dency to regard Corneille as simple, even when he presents himself as such:

Je tâche de suivre toujours le sentiment d'Aristote dans les matières qu'il a traitées, et comme peut-être je l'entends à ma mode, je ne suis point jaloux qu'un autre l'entende à la sienne . . . J'ai pris pour m'expliquer un style simple, et me contente d'une expression nue de mes opinions, bonnes ou mauvaises, sans y rechercher aucun enrichissement d'éloquence.[6]

The *Discours* are not as clear as Corneille would have us believe: their honesty conceals deep ambiguities. In examining them, we will con-centrate on his uncertainties on two topics: the relation of poetry to morality; and the relation of poetry to truth. Corneille is far from evad-ing the great issues. The large questions are there, and some of his answers – but usually only between the lines.

First, his attitude to morals. At first glance, nothing could be clearer. He enumerates four ways in which poetry (for which we can usually read 'tragedy') can have a moral effect. The first is by moral maxims – 'sentences'. As he says, their effect can be overrated, and he counsels moderation in their use. Secondly, we have 'la naïve' (natural, lifelike, untendentious) 'peinture des vertus et des vices'. This is the most original of the four methods, as though Corneille, realising the futility of the others, was stimulated to find a better one. His reasoning is interesting:

La naïve peinture des vices et des vertus . . . ne manque jamais à faire son effet, quand elle est bien achevée, et que les traits en sont si reconnaissables qu'on ne les peut confondre l'un dans l'autre, ni prendre le vice pour vertu. Celle-ci se fait alors toujours aimer, quoique malheureuse; et celui-là se fait toujours haïr, bien que triomphant. Les anciens se sont fort souvent contentés de cette peinture, sans se mettre en peine de faire récompenser les bonnes actions et punir les mauvaises.[7]

This has far-reaching implications, but Corneille hastens on to his third method: the mechanical poetic justice which does what the Ancients did not put themselves to the trouble of doing, i.e. punish the wicked and reward the righteous.

The fourth method is the most famous and hallowed by classical tradition: the Aristotelian catharsis. In the *Deuxième Discours* Corneille discusses this at length, with much reference to the commentators. We need not take much account of his view of what catharsis means, though we have already mentioned his unorthodox opinion on its effectiveness. We shall come in a moment to some of the peculiarities of his arguments. For the present, the interesting point is that, like his contemporaries, he sees catharsis in terms of moral rectification. This ties in with the first part of the first *Discours*: the purpose of poetry is to teach moral virtue as well as to please, and the means by which it teaches are neatly listed and discussed.

But things are not so straightforward as they seem. When it comes down to brass tacks, Corneille cannot reconcile his four methods with the practice of the Ancients, the precepts of Aristotle, or the success of his own plays. After a struggle, he avows the first two difficulties. It is his treatment of the third – the relation of his principles to his own plays – which is of the greatest interest.

His aim, naturally, is to defend his own successful use of exciting but either monstrous or totally heroic characters as the chief figures in many of his plays.[8] This is clearly at odds with Aristotle, and difficult to reconcile with the moralistic prescriptions of neo-classical criticism. He tries to achieve his aim in three ways. First, in a long discussion of Aristotle's theory of tragedy, he is at pains to separate catharsis by pity from catharsis by fear:

Nous n'avons qu'à dire que par cette façon de s'énoncer il [Aristotle] n'a pas entendu que ces deux moyens y servissent toujours ensemble et qu'il suffit selon lui de l'un des deux pour faire cette purgation . . . L'auditeur peut avoir de la commisération pour Antiochus, pour Nicomède, pour Héraclius; mais, s'il en demeure là et qu'il ne puisse craindre de tomber dans un pareil malheur, il ne guérira d'aucune passion. Au contraire, il n'en a point pour Cléopâtre, ni pour Prusias, ni pour Phocas; mais la crainte d'une infortune semblable ou approchante peut purger en une mère l'opiniâtreté à ne se point dessaisir du bien de ses enfants, en un mari le trop de déférence à une seconde femme au préjudice de ceux de son premier lit, en tout le monde l'avidité d'usurper le bien ou la dignité d'autrui par violence; et tout cela proportionnément à la condition d'un chacun et à ce qu'il est capable d'entreprendre.[9]

The argument is ingenious, but it clearly allows every form of melodrama to be brought within the tragic formula.

Secondly, Corneille claims that we may be 'purged' by 'passions semblables' in a character who has the same faults as we, but in a more exaggerated form:

Il est peu de mères qui voulussent assassiner ou empoisonner leurs enfants, de peur de leur rendre leur bien, comme Cléopâtre dans 'Rodogune'; mais il en est assez qui prennent goût à en jouir et ne s'en dessaisissent qu'à regret et le plus tard qu'il leur est possible. Bien qu'elles ne soient pas capables d'une action si noire et si denaturée que celle de cette reine de Syrie, elles ont en elles quelque teinture du principe qui l'y porta, et la vue de la juste punition qu'elle en reçoit leur peut faire craindre, non pas un pareil malheur, mais une infortune proportionnée à ce qu'elles sont capables de commettre.[10]

Thirdly, he is willing to reinterpret drastically Aristotle's precept that tragic characters should be 'good'. Not to put too fine a point upon it, he is willing to argue that 'good' can mean 'extreme':

s'il m'est permis de dire mes conjectures sur ce qu'Aristote nous demande par là, je crois que c'est le caractère brillant et élevé d'une habitude vertueuse ou criminelle, selon qu'elle est propre et convenable à la personne qu'on introduit. Cléopâtre, dans 'Rodogune', est tres méchante . . . mais tous ses crimes sont accommpagnés d'une grandeur, d'âme qui a quelquechose de si haut, qu'en même temps qu'on déteste ses actions, on admire la source dont elles partent.[11]

Alternatively, he is attracted by Castelvetro's view:

Je trouve dans Castelvetro une troisième explication qui pourrait ne déplaire pas, qui est que cette bonté de moeurs ne regarde que le premier personnage, qui doit toujours se faire aimer, et par conséquent être vertueux, et non pas ceux qui le persécutent ou le font périr.[12]

We need not discuss how far he succeeded in these efforts to reconcile his practice with the precepts of Aristotle. But there can be no doubt about the total effect of his glosses. What starts as a demand that tragedy should teach a moral lesson soon becomes a licence for abandoning moral purposes altogether. A character need not be good, as long as he is impressive (or, alternatively, as long as the hero is good). The only moral requirement is that 'poetic justice' should be enforced, but even here Corneille is half of a mind to let admiration for a determined criminal override moral judgments. Finally, we should note the implications of his praise of 'la naïve peinture'. Although he brings this forward as a means of inculcating morality, he is in fact withdrawing responsibility for moral teaching from the playwright and leaving the spectator to draw what lessons he can. Accurate presentation of facts is neither moral nor immoral. However 'immoral' his subject, the artist can disclaim responsibility: his answer to critics is simply, 'This is true.' The attitude is now familiar; but it does not fit very well the moral rules of French classicism.

This brings us to our second topic – Corneille's treatment of the relation of poetry to truth. Corneille and his contemporaries wrote plays in a very formal style: a play was a *poème dramatique,* or simply a *poème.* A major source of the audience's pleasure was the beauty of the verse, and the verse was highly stylised in form and subject-matter. In general, critics had not yet objected to this. We might therefore have expected from Corneille a ringing assertion of the independent rights of poetry. We get nothing of the sort: his attitude wobbles. He does defend the right of the poet to create, but on very strange grounds. In essence, his attitude is the same as the one that led him to advocate 'la naïve peinture': he defends the status of poetry by stressing its fidelity to fact:

les grands sujets qui remuent fortement les passions, et en opposent l'impétuosité aux lois du devoir ou aux tendresses du sang, doivent toujours aller au-delà du vraisemblable, et ne trouveraient aucune croyance parmi les auditeurs s'ils n'étaient soutenus, ou par l'autorité de l'histoire qui persuade avec empire, ou par la préoccupation de l'opinion commune qui nous donne ces mêmes auditeurs déjà tous persuadés.[13]

The further implications of this passage will be discussed below, but it clearly embodies that appeal to fact which we find elsewhere in Corneille's criticism.

Corneille's literal-minded attitude goes a good deal further than a mere willingness to shelter behind the facts of history when convenient. Of 'sentences' he remarks:

il faut en user sobrement . . . surtout quand on fait parler un homme passionné, ou qu'on lui fait répondre par un autre; car il ne doit avoir non plus de patience pour les entendre, que de quiétude d'esprit pour les concevoir et les dire . . . Dans le quatrième acte de 'Mélite', la joie qu'elle a d'être aimée de Tircis lui fait souffrir sans chagrin la remontrance de sa nourrice, . . . mais, si elle savait que Tircis la crût infidèle et qu'il en fût au désespoir . . . elle n'en souffrirait pas quatre vers.[14]

He does not always follow his own precepts on this, but the intention is clear: he advises against too many 'sentences' because people do not talk like this in real life.[15] This attitude is found in other seventeenth-century critics such as d'Aubignac, but it would have seemed inexplicable, for instance, to the French sixteenth-century tragic poets. What Corneille is beginning to do, in fact, is to cast doubt on the convention that tragedy is in verse, on the grounds that really people do not talk in verse.

His discussion of this point in the *Examen* to *Andromède* is illuminating, because it shows him hesitating between two possible views. He begins to defend verse (even 'stances') on the grounds that they give pleasure, and calls on that element in neo-classicism which, if taken seriously, would subvert its doctrine: the imitation of the Ancients. But then he recoils, and rests on a very different argument:

> les vers de stances sont moins vers que les alexandrins, parce que parmi notre langage commun il se coule plus de ces vers inégaux . . . que de ceux dont la mesure est toujours égale, et les rimes toujours mariées . . . il serait bon de ne régler point toutes les strophes sur la même mesure, ni sur les mêmes croisures des rimes, ni sur le même nombre de vers. Leur inégalité en ces trois articles approcherait davantage du discours ordinaire, et sentirait l'emportement et les élans d'un esprit qui n'a que sa passion pour guide, et non pas la régularité d'un auteur qui les arrondit sur le même tour.[16]

To us, who are used to naturalistic assumptions in drama, this seems plausible, but clearly Corneille, as a poetic dramatist, is on dangerous ground. Chapelain in his *Lettre sur la Règle des Vingt-Quatre Heures* (1630) had already attacked the use of verse in plays, and the days are not far off when serious critics will demand that tragedies be written in prose. The appeal to 'truth' – in the sense of the literal facts of behaviour – can serve as a defence for the poet against charges of extravagance or immorality, but leads logically to the abandonment of poetry.

Corneille's attitude to the relation of poetry to truth is as ambiguous as his attitude to the relation of poetry to morals, and has the same implications. On the one hand, he defends the poet's freedom by appealing to historical fact or received opinion. Part of the significance of the passage from the first *Discours* about 'les grands sujets' and their relation to *vraisemblance* is to shelter poetic extravagance under the umbrella of history: it is a way of escape from the *vraisemblable* in the sense of humdrum. But many of his remarks have a different implication: they reproach poetry with a lack of fidelity to fact in the sense of observed behaviour. It is a commonplace that the neo-classical defence of the unities on the grounds that they favour a greater fidelity to fact leads logically to Ibsenite prose drama.[17] It is not always sufficiently stressed, however, that in Corneille the process is already far advanced. We may point to a significant detail in the third *Discours*:

Ainsi, je serais d'avis que le poète prît grand soin de marquer à la marge les menues actions qui ne méritent pas qu'il en charge ses vers, et qui leur ôteraient même quelquechose de leur dignité, s'il se ravalait à les exprimer. Le comédien y supplée aisément sur le théâtre; mais sur le livre on serait assez souvent réduit à deviner.[18]

This is the first sign of a tendency which has reduced verse to prose, then to inarticulate prose, and which has inflated stage directions into the main repositories of a play's significance. Corneille's further remark that the plays of the Greeks are often obscure for lack of stage directions, though true in a minor way, implies a similar concern with physical action on the stage rather than with a reading of experience mediated primarily by the verse. As we shall see, Corneille's remark is not without significance for an understanding of his later verse-technique.

Before we sum up the basic trends in Corneille's criticism, there is one further topic to mention. It has long been recognised that seventeenth-century French tragedy differs from its classical and Renaissance ancestors by its use of a formal intrigue making large use of suspense and surprise. Corneille assumes this as basic to his art, as his discussion of the fifth act shows:

Je n'y ajouterai que ce mot: qu'il faut, s'il se peut, lui réserver toute la catastrophe, et même la reculer vers la fin, autant qu'il est possible. Plus on la diffère, plus les esprits demeurent suspendus, et l'impatience qu'ils ont de savoir de quelle côté elle tournera est cause qu'ils la reçoivent avec plus de plaisir: ce qui n'arrive pas quand elle commence avec cet acte. L'auditeur qui la sait trop tôt n'a plus de curiosité, et son attention languit durant tout le reste, qui ne lui apprend rien de nouveau.[19]

This assumption is his starting-point for a discussion of the unity of action: 'Il n'y doit avoir qu'une action complète, qui laisse l'esprit de l'auditeur dans le calme; mais elle ne peut le devenir que par plusieurs autres imparfaites, qui lui servent d'acheminements, et tiennent cet auditeur dans une agréable suspension.'[20]

In other words, it is this 'agréable suspension' which links the parts of the play together. Corneille returns again and again to this idea: for him, it is essential that there are no gaps. There are many manifestations of this in his advice on details. He demands very strict care for the 'liaison des scènes', and for the motivation of characters's entrances and exits. In many ways he goes as far as the most severe contemporary critics – for instance, he endorses d'Aubignac's 'nouvelle et assez sévère' requirement that the first act should contain the beginnings of all that is to come later.[21] The trend of his prescriptions is unmistakable, and is brought out clearly in his recommendations to the dramatist near the beginning of the third *Discours*: 'Surtout il doit se souvenir que les unes et les autres [the actions which make up the plot] doivent avoir une telle liaison ensemble, que les dernières soient produites par celles qui les précèdent, et que toutes aient leur source dans la protase que doit fermer le premier acte.'[22]

The aim is to give a play a formal mechanical structure which leaves no gaps which can be attributed to fantasy: the construction must be logically water-tight. This is one reason for the rules: they are a suit of armour, not a strait-jacket.

It seems to me that we only begin to see the significance of Corneille's long preoccupation with the rules if we emphasise two trends in his criticism.

The first is the marked trend towards naturalism. Neo-classical critical dogmas commonly rest on an implied basis of realism (hence the stress on the unities), but this is usually overlaid by an emphasis on formal and moral values and respect for the example of the Ancients. Corneille carries this naturalistic trend further than his contemporaries in several ways. His stress on 'la naïve peinture' as a form of moral justification; his tendency to appeal to fidelity to fact as a guarantee of moral or aesthetic value; his advocacy of the formal concatenation of the well-made play; his assumption that the poetic text is not self-sufficient but needs to be supplemented by stage-directions; his argument that people do not talk in verse, or listen to narratives at moments of stress, and therefore should do so as unobtrusively as possible in plays: all these attitudes leave behind the ambiguities of most neo-classical criticism and point clearly to Scribe, Zola, Ibsen, and the modern naturalistic theatre.

The second trend runs counter to this, and counter to neo-classical doctrine. We have seen that on many points Corneille's practice differs from his theory: this is a commonplace of Cornelian criticism. It is not, however, a sign that he is trying to evade the rules or the critics as such: he often lays extra obligations on himself. It is rather the struggle of a poet to escape from the logical results of the naturalistic bias in his (and their) assumptions: an attempt to escape the drabness which naturalism imposes on drama. Hence the prominence in Corneille of what is violent, extraordinary, or frankly immoral. We may think here of some aspects of the work of Ibsen, who stands at the culmination of the main naturalistic tradition, just as Corneille stands at its beginning. Ibsen, too, was a poet who accepted the logic of naturalism, and whose work shows the struggle to express meaning through the forms permitted by this logic. In Ibsen's case, attempts to express a meaning were made more difficult by the strict commitment to a prose imitation of reality. The resulting attempts at poetic heightening often seems at the same time obtrusive and inadequate: ghost horses, harps in the air, the 'danse macabre'. The heightening, in fact, is often the heightening of Romantic melodrama. Nor is the association surprising. Naturalism is logically committed to the humdrum and the inarticulate. If the naturalist tries to introduce excitement, his method gives little scope for subtlety. He is therefore driven to use crude romantic effects, without any means of endowing them with real significance. And melodrama is precisely the employment of strong effects without giving them significance. If Corneille's work frequently tends towards melodrama, this tendency is at the same time a result of, and an attempt to evade the consequences of, his accceptance of naturalistic assumptions. In this, as in so much else, he is one of the forerunners of naturalism.

3

Corneille's acceptance of the rules – or, more precisely, his acceptance of many of the premises of neo-classic doctrine – naturally entailed some disadvantages. These go beyond the constraints on the use of violent events, comic relief, scene-changes, or long lapses of time. These constraints were in practice fairly elastic, and Corneille was adept at stretching them. The serious implications of neo-classicism are more fundamental, and I will recapitulate those which arise from my survey of Corneille's criticism.

The first is the basic problem of truth or verisimilitude. Corneille is very anxious to avoid being tied to the verisimilar (in the sense of the everyday) by making use of events which are true, but violent and extraordinary. But he is also worried by the whole question of realism: whether verse is really permissible; whether dramatic use can be made of such poetic devices as 'les narrations ornées et pathétiques', or whether his business is not rather to reproduce behaviour.

Secondly, there is the other basic element in naturalism in our wider sense: the demand that poetry should be submitted to some external philosophic or other criterion. Here a discussion of factors favouring neo-classicism would be in point. Some would claim that the factor influencing the acceptance of the rules was the power of the Counter-

Reformation Church, which achieved its greatest triumphs in France at this period.[23] It would be fascinating to explore the connections between the Counter-Reformation and neo-classicism and baroque in the arts. From one aspect, Corneille is a baroque poet, just as from another he is a naturalist. The two are perhaps not as far apart as they might seem. From both the baroque and neo-classical viewpoints there is agreement on at least one point: that the purpose of poetry is to teach (Christian) morality. It is precisely this fundamental demand that Corneille seems most concerned to avoid. But his main device for doing so – 'la naïve peinture' – logically throws him back on a literal imitation of behaviour which not only conflicts with the requirements of the poetic form but also implies a renunciation of the effort to express a meaning.

Against this, we can set some gains. The first is speculative, but psychologically may have been vital. Corneille was a deeply religious man, and in the age of the great Counter-Reformation saints and 'la crise du libertinage' many may have suspected that poetry was in essence frivolous or worse. In these circumstances, we should not overlook the possibility that the apparent solidity of the neo-classical position was itself an attraction. A set of rules founded on authority and reason, demonstrating poetry to be a serious and highly moral discipline, might well be a comfort to poets and critics alike.

Secondly, (and here we regain the evidence of the *Discours*), one ambiguity at the heart of neo-classicism had a special value for the tragic poet. The logic of neo-classicism leads to didactic realism. But the doctrine had another aspect: imitation of the Ancients. Poetry and tragedy had behind them the prestige and example of the classical poets, which sanctioned the most elaborate and unnaturalistic poetic forms. For all his questioning, this tradition enabled Corneille to retain the use of verse. More important still, it preserved the possibility of that special type of meaning which we call tragic, and which has nothing in common with the inculcation of morality. The Ancients chose for their tragedies subjects far removed from the verisimilar, and did not trouble to observe poetic justice – and Aristotle's theory of catharsis, which might have saved the moral appearances, did not correspond to the facts. The example of the Ancients could be used polemically to justify all sorts of audacities.

In the next eight chapters I will present an argument which may be summarised as follows. Corneille's basic dilemma was how to satisfy his impulse towards a poetic drama embodying its own meaning and yet comply with the neo-classic trend towards naturalism. In his early tragedies, the meaning he had in mind was at least akin to tragedy in the modern sense. In these plays – long before he reached a conscious formulation of his difficulties in the *Examens* and *Discours* – the result of his dilemma is a confusion of aims which flaws some of his greatest achievements. Only in *Cinna* does he achieve a consistent poetic form; and it is in this play that the meaning is especially far removed from the tragic. In his later plays, he usually abandons the attempt to express a meaning. He builds up the best play he can by exploiting its separate elements for their own sake. That is, he takes a story or situation and endows it with significance by elaborating it, filling in its background, drawing out the interest in its events and characters, using heightened language as an extra resource. In doing so, he moves away from tragedy and the poetic method towards a subtle mixture of poetry and naturalism. In many of his later plays – after the *Examens* and *Discours* – he accepts the implications of naturalism very boldly, producing some unexpected, sophisticated, and even bizarre effects.

I hope this approach can throw light on Corneille's historical importance, the constant shifts and experiments that mark his career, the varied reception of his works by contemporaries and later critics. It will also lead to evaluations of the individual plays in some respects different from those commonly accepted.

3

'LE CID'

The appearance of *Le Cid* put Corneille at the centre of the French dramatic movement. Contemporaries realised that here was a play of undoubted stature, and one that raised issues of fundamental importance: it became the battleground on which the new critics affirmed their conquests. Time has endorsed the verdict of contemporaries: *Le Cid* is the earliest French play that has been accepted as a masterpiece. It is the most immediately attractive of Corneille's plays, and the most unfailingly successful on the stage.

Despite its powerful emotional appeal, however, there has always been dispute about its status as a tragedy. To ask whether it is tragic is to frame the question in modern terms, but this does not mean that the question is irrelevant. Few could deny that the play catches something of the strict tragic quality, and many have accorded it the full status of tragedy. It is with this question that we shall start our examination; and particularly with that problem which has been much discussed, the ambiguity of the ending.

Many critics have mocked the Academy's description of Chimène as 'une fille dénaturée', and its desire that the count should be found to be still alive, or not her father. The Academy perhaps chose the wrong grounds for its criticism; the criticism itself is not frivolous. We need not debate whether a young lady should agree to marry her father's murderer, especially on the day of the murder, but we can ask a more purely aesthetic question. Does Corneille hesitate between different approaches to his material? If so, is his ambiguity over the ending a sign of his hesitation?

The action depends for its effect on an inescapable dilemma: Rodrigue must kill Chimène's father, Chimène must seek Rodrigue's death. To make this situation affect us powerfully, Corneille has to convince us, during most of the play, that the dilemma is indeed inescapable. We must not think, as we might in a comedy, that Chimène is making a fuss for the sake of appearances, and will come round as soon as she decently can. Nor must we think (as we might in real life) that Rodrigue should not have killed the count but have sought redress in some other way. To feel the situation not simply as moving but as tragic, we must believe that Rodrigue has to kill the count, not just because of social pressures, but because he realises his conception of his honour demands it, and that unless he fulfils this conception he cannot deserve Chimène. Similarly, we must feel that Chimène must demand his death. Nadal[1] argues strongly along these lines, and his reading, if correct, would confirm the play's tragic status. But, as we shall see, there is difficulty in reconciling this reading with the text, which supports at least as strongly the untragic interpretation: that Corneille meant Rodrigue to marry Chimène, and that only the unity of time prevented him from showing us the wedding. The final words of the king (which leave the matter in doubt) then appear merely as a concession to decorum: Chimène cannot be harried into marrying immediately. If Rodrigue and Chimène are irrevocably parted, and we feel it, the play is indeed tragic. But if they are to marry after all, Corneille has built a high wall between them only to let them walk through it, and we may find something in the Academy's suggestion (inept as it is in detail) that he should first have demolished it in some way.

As the text is ambiguous, it may help if we look at other ambiguous endings in Corneille's tragedies. A surprising number end on points of doubt: notably *Nicomède*, *Sophonisbe*, *Othon*, *Tite et Bérénice* and *Pulchérie*.[2]

In *Sophonisbe*, Massinisse is the problem. He has encouraged Sophonisbe to die, rather than defend her, and to make a neat ending the least he could do would be to despair and die. Historically, however, he did not, and soon found himself other women. As Corneille explains in his foreword, the ambiguity of the ending is intended to get over this difficulty: it allows the audience to believe either that Massinisse died or that he lived on and consoled himself.

In *Othon*, *Tite et Bérénice* and *Pulchérie*, the case is different. In *Othon*, Camille is a forceful character who loves her uncle, wants to be empress, and adores Othon. By the end of Act V, her uncle is dead, she is not going to be empress, and Othon is to marry Plautine. The play ends uncertainly. In *Tite et Bérénice*, similarly, there is some difficulty in believing that Domitie, who is presented as a strong character devoured by ambition, will accept the deferment of her hopes of becoming empress. *Pulchérie* also ends with a reference to an ambitious character (Aspar) whose ambitions have been thwarted, and the last lines leave his fate open.

In *Sophonisbe*, the ambiguous ending is clearly intended to reconcile dramatic effect with historic truth. This has little to do with tragedy, but much to do with the naturalism implicit in Corneille's criticism.

The endings of *Othon*, *Tite et Bérénice* and *Pulchérie* confirm this view. A playwright concerned with the 'illusion of reality' cannot avoid one special difficulty. If his play is to move us, his characters must be shown to be strongly moved. But this brings him up against the problem which caused more modern naturalistic dramatists such difficulties with their last acts:

> We have agreed to regard a play as essentially a crisis in the lives of one or more persons . . . But how few crises come to a definite or dramatic conclusion! Nine times out of ten, they end in some petty compromise, or do not end at all, but simply subside . . . It is the playwright's chief difficulty to find a crisis with an ending which satisfies at once his artistic conscience and the requirements of dramatic effect.[3]

If a play contains serious elements but cannot reasonably end in wholesale murder or suicide (and *Othon*, *Tite et Bérénice* and *Pulchérie* are of this type) the naturalistic playwright is virtually forced to end on a note of ambiguity, or more accurately uncertainty: the indeterminate ending is a compromise between the need to end a play somehow and the recognition that in real life there are rarely clear endings.

But matters are not always as simple as this with Corneille. We have the case of *Nicomède*, which Prusias ends thus:

> Préparons à demain de justes sacrifices;
> Et demandons aux Dieux, nos dignes souverains,
> Pour comble de bonheur, l'amitié des Romains.

Nineteenth-century critics called this ending comic, but it seems rather to be ambiguous in a particular way. Nicomède is undoubtedly the hero of the play, but the context which Corneille has devised raises some disturbing questions. Corneille tells us that his 'principal but a été de peindre la politique des Romains au dehors, et comme ils agissaient impérieusement avec les rois leurs alliés; leurs maximes pour les empêcher à s'accroître, et les soins qu'ils prenaient de traverser leur grandeur quand elle commençait à leur devenir suspecte.'[4] Against this background, which is amply depicted in the play, Prusias's concluding line is more than comic. It tries to deny a conflict on which the play is founded. Rome will not tolerate a proud and strong power in the East: the ascendancy of Nicomède and 'l'amitié des Romains' are not compatible. The references to Hannibal are a further clue: if this greatest of Rome's enemies had failed, how could Nicomède succeed? It is likely that Nicomède is modelled on Condé, and that the play refers to the imprisonment of the rebel princes. But Corneille was a declared partisan of Mazarin, and when the princes were released their influence was to lose him a post which Mazarin had given him. The irony in *Nicomède* goes very deep. It is not introduced simply to give scope for a few scathing remarks. If our view is correct, the ambiguous ending has an aesthetic purpose. The emotional effect at which the play aims is truly ambiguous, and this is what the ending expresses.

These considerations prompt a number of questions about *Le Cid*. Is Corneille aiming at a tragic effect, which requires that the ending should be unambiguous? Or is he aiming at a new (non-tragic) effect, to which an ambiguous ending is appropriate? Or does he find it difficult to achieve a clear ending because he is preoccupied with naturalistic criteria such as verisimilitude or historical accuracy? It is with these questions in mind that we will examine the text.

The first point to be settled is whether the barriers between Rodrigue and Chimène are, in true tragic fashion, insuperable. There is much to suggest that they are. Rodrigue sums up the position thus in I. vi:

> Il faut venger un père, et perdre une maîtresse . . .
> Allons, mon bras, sauvons du moins l'honneur,
> Puisqu'après tout il faut perdre Chimène.

Chimène is equally convincing:

> Je ne consulte point pour suivre mon devoir:
> Je cours sans balancer où mon honneur m'oblige.
> Rodrigue m'est bien cher, son intérêt m'afflge;
> Mone coeur prend son parti; mais malgré son effort,
> Je sais ce que je suis, et que mon père est mort.
>
> (III. iii)

> Après mon père mort, je n'ai point à choisir.
>
> (IV. ii)

> Quand il [Rodrigue] sera vainqueur, crois-tu que je me rende?
> Mon devoir est trop fort, et me perte trop grande.
>
> (V. iv)

Her last words are a refusal:

> Si Rodrigue à l'Etat devient si nécessaire,
> De ce qu'il fait pour vous dois-je être le salaire,
> Et me livrer moi-même au reproche éternel
> D'avoir trempé mes mains dans le sang paternel?
>
> (V. vii)

All this might lead us to accept the separation of the lovers as inevitable, and therefore tragic. But three considerations should give us pause.

First, Corneille leads us to believe from time to time that Chimène's resolve is maintained only by an effort of will, and that it will weaken and allow her to marry Rodrigue. This is difficult to demonstrate by formal citation: her self-revelations are made by her actions, rather than by direct statement. When Elvire describes the defeat of the Moors (IV.i), Chimène's first thought is for Rodrigue – 'Et la main de Rodrigue a fait tous ces miracles? . . . Mais n'est-il point blessé?' In IV.v, there is the king's ruse: he tells her that Rodrigue is dead, and she faints. Finally, she cannot bring herself in V.i to avoid encouraging Rodrigue:

> Sors vainqueur d'un combat dont Chimène est le prix.

The second consideration is more fundamental. Many of the characters, far from sharing Chimène's tragic view of honour, take a realistic, even cynical, line. Elvire is quite matter-of-fact:

> Madame, croyez-moi, vous serez excusable
> D'avoir moins de chaleur contre un objet aimable,
> Contre un amant si cher: vous avez assez fait,
> Vous avez vu le Roi; n'en pressez point l'effet,
> Ne vous obstinez point en cette humeur étrange.
>
> (III. iii)

Don Diègue (in III.vi) is just as realistic and Léonor (in V.iii) assumes that Chimène's demand for a duel is merely a trick to save appearances.

The clearest indication comes from the king, whose comment when Chimène comes to demand vengeance puts the unheroic interpretation of the position succinctly:

> La fâcheuse nouvelle, et l'importun devoir!
>
> (IV. iv)

Our third consideration follows from this. Corneille not only scatters his play with unheroic remarks which make a happy ending seem plausible: he appears deliberately from time to time to lighten the tone when it is becoming too tragic. The cynical remarks are only one example. He also adopts the devices of trickery (the king's ruse in IV.v), misunderstanding (Don Sanche's appearance in Act V), and transparently unreal gestures (the repeated offers by Rodrigue – in III.iv, V.i, and V.vii – and Don Diègue – in II.viii – to die to expiate the count's death). These flourishes belong to a lighter and more romantic world than tragedy. Finally, there is the tone of the love-scenes between Rodrigue and Chimène. They are tender and lyrical, but they are not for that reason tragic. Indeed, this type of scene belongs to romance rather than tragedy. The first scene (III.iv) might be taken as a grace-note before the action builds up to a more austere climax, but this is not so: the second scene (V.i) is far from austere. It seems, rather, that Corneille adopts a strategy of steering the tone away from austerity. The attitudes implicit in Rodrigue's repeated offers to die and in Chimène's final avowal are untragic, and the verse aims at an emotional effect a good deal less hard and vigorous than that of tragedy. Rodrigue's speeches take on a languorous, almost lachrymose softness, enhanced by a sentimental use of the third person:

> On dira seulement: 'Il adorait Chimène;
> Il n'a pas voulu vivre et mériter sa haine;
> Il a cédé lui-même à la rigueur du sort
> Qui forçait sa maîtresse à poursuivre sa mort.
> Elle voulait sa tête; et son cœur magnanime,
> S'il l'en eût refusée, eût pensé faire un crime.
> Pour venger son honneur il perdit son amour,
> Pour venger sa maîtresse il a quitté le jour,
> Préférant, quelque espoir qu'eût son âme asservie,
> Son honneur à Chimène, et Chimène à sa vie.'

And the resolution of the scene, after Chimène's avowal, has a straightforward high-spiritedness far removed from tragedy:

> Paraissez, Navarrois, Mores et Castillans . . .

All these considerations seem to me to lead inevitably to a reading of the play different both from Nadal's and those of most earlier critics. It is certainly impossible to accept Nadal's view of the play as tragic, and recent critics have emphasised this.[5] Nevertheless, the play has some tragic features, and it is impossible to dismiss Nadal's view entirely. Neither view is right, because both are right: there is a confusion at the heart of the play.

Le Cid is a powerful work, but it lacks what the clumsiest sixteenth-century tragedy had: concentration on a single tragic meaning. We have, instead, a play which (for the first time in French drama) success-fully attains seriousness by means of a clearly articulated plot arousing suspense and surprise and resting on the psychological conflicts of characters portrayed as human beings. This method is one reason for the varying valuations which Corneille has to put on Chimène's desire for vengeance at different points in the play. It looks forward to the see-sawing emotional effects of much of later drama, through the *pièce bien faite* to Ibsen and beyond. That is, *Le Cid* points forward (in this, and in its use of realistic and non-tragic elements) to a more naturalistic type of drama. It marks the beginning of something new: but this new element has little to do with the methods of the Greek and Latin dramatists, and still less to do with tragedy. *Le Cid* marks the beginning of a form of the naturalistic *pièce bien faite* whose ghost still haunts our stages. It marks a break from the efforts in France to continue the classical tradition of tragedy.

The play is not, however, a whole-hearted application of the new formula. In some respects it still harks back to the older tradition. We see Corneille struggling with a problem which is at the heart of his work: how to write serious drama in an age which does not grant full seriousness to poetry. Those features of *Le Cid* we have just singled out point to one solution, which many later dramatists were to take up. But *Le Cid* still shows clear traces of a tragic conception, as Nadal has emphasised: one in which the barriers to the hero's happiness are not those built by society or pig-headedness (which time and reason can wear down) but the unreasoning powers of the universe. This conception was more obvious in the original text. Corneille revised *Le Cid* more radically than any of his other tragedies, and it is noteworthy how often he diluted statements which made the separation of the lovers appear inevitable. Chimène's original complaint to the king in II.viii contained these emphatic lines (referring to her father's blood):

> Rodrigue en votre cour vient d'en couvrir la terre,
> Et pour son coup d'essai son indigne attentat
> D'un si ferme soutien a privé votre Etat,
> De vos meilleurs soldats abattu l'assurance,
> Et de vos ennemis relevé l'espérance.
> J'arrivai sur le lieu sans force et sans couleur:
> Je le trouvai sans vie. Excusez me douleur.

All but the first and the (modified) last of these lines were later omitted.

In III.iii, 'Je sais que je suis fille, et que mon père est mort', with its brutal insistence on 'père' and 'fille', is softened to the more appealing but ambiguous 'Je sais ce que je suis, et que mon père est mort'. Similarly, the straightforward 'Quoi! j'aurai *vu* mourir mon père entre mes bras' becomes the less emphatic 'Quoi! mon père etant mort, et *presque* entre mes bras'. Finally, in the original text Chimène's last refusal to marry Rodrigue was more explicit and emphatic:

> Sire, quelle apparence, à ce triste hyménée,
> Qu'un même jour commence et finisse mon deuil,
> Mette en mon lit Rodrigue et mon père au cercueil.

C'est trop d'intelligence avec son homicide,
Vers ses mânes sacrés c'est me rendre perfide,
Et souiller mon honneur d'un reproche éternel.

The significance of this change has been much discussed, but only one
interpretation seems feasible: that the first version, with its firm anti-
theses and concrete language, stressed only too effectively the barriers
between Rodrigue and Chimène, and that Corneille, meaning to make
plain they would marry, replaced it by the final version, with its more
abstract language, its use of the interrogative and the conditional, its
stress on Rodrigue's importance to the state, and its deference to the
king. If he really intended us to think that the lovers are parted for ever
(which is hard enough to read into the original text), it is strange that
when he revised the play he made his intention even harder to
recognise.

What the textual evidence does confirm is that Corneille had difficulty in deciding whether or not he was writing tragedy. In my view,
his dilemma went deeper still: *Le Cid*, as first written, embodied two
incompatible approaches to drama. At one level, he was striving towards a poetic tragedy resting on an insoluble conflict; at another, he
was reaching forward to a new type of play, more serious and rigorous
than tragi-comedy, but making use of suspense, realism, and even
comedy. In his revisions, he tried to remedy this basic confusion by
toning down the vestigial tragic elements. This is in line with his later
development, which tends more and more towards naturalism.

2

Before *Le Cid*, Corneille had made one serious attempt at tragedy.
Médée (1634/5) is obviously inferior to *Le Cid*, but remains a strangely
powerful work. If we could see its significance in the evolution of
Corneille's dramatic method, and of French tragedy as a whole, we
might be able, while still judging it a failure, to appreciate better its
real interest and merits.

Lanson put forward the view that in France two forms of tragedy
were developed, one after the other. The first type is the tragedy of
suffering. Its emphasis is on the misfortunes of the hero, who is often
seen as passive. Its method is poetic and lyrical. It needs little in the way
of plot or well-defined characters. The second type is active: it is a
drama of struggle, with a well-developed plot producing surprise and
suspense, and characters in conflict with each other and themselves. The
first type is that of the sixteenth-century tragic poets, the second that

of the writers of tragi-comedy in the early part of the seventeenth
century. The first attempts at tragedy of Mairet, Tristan and Rotrou
show a confusion between the two types, as does Corneille's *Médée*.
Only with *Le Cid* are the two fused into one coherent and powerful
form: 'En un mot, la tragédie, tiraillée en deux sens, s'arrêtait dans un
mélange incohérent es confus. Le *Cid* fit la lumière, ce qu'on cherchait
à tâtons apparut à tous les yeux.'[6]

We cannot accept Lanson's judgment of *Le Cid*, and his theory will
not do as it stands, but it has obvious importance for *Médée*. For much
of the play, Corneille concentrates attention on the image of the
heroine, a woman of supernatural powers who has given up everything
for her faithless lover and is now determined on a horrible revenge.
Much of the action – her soliloquy (I.iv), her famous colloquy with
Nérine (I.v), her interview with Creon (II.ii) – is hardly 'plot' at all,
but a sustained poetic development of this central image. These Senecan
parts of the play are often turgid, but they have a force and impressiveness different in kind from anything in *Le Cid*. They are clearly related
to tragedy as understood by the sixteenth-century poets. But this
'pathetic' element is mixed up with clumsy attempts (mainly in the
Créuse–Médée–Egée episodes) to introduce a plot. The mixture of
modes is disconcerting: the horrors and supernatural elements, which
might be impressive in a tragedy or exciting in a melodrama, are here
merely grotesque.

When we read *Médée*, we can hardly fail to be struck by the violence
of the heroine's tirades. Critical attention has been mainly directed to
the famous 'Moi' as showing the development of the Cornelian hero.
But much more interesting is the way in which the verse takes on an
incantatory quality, a life of its own which transcends the immediate
situation:

> Souverains protecteurs des lois de l'hyménée,
> Dieux garants de la foi que Jason m'a donnée...
> Tu t'abuses, Jason, je suis encor moi-même.
> Tout ce qu'en ta faveur fit mon amour extrême,
> Je le ferai par haine; et je veux pour le moins
> Qu'un forfait nous sépare, ainsi qu'il nous a joints;
> Que mon sanglant divorce, en meurtres, en carnage,
> S'égale aux premiers jours de notre mariage...
> Est-ce assez, ma vengeance, est-ce assez de deux morts?

Alone among Corneille's plays, *Médée* uses a Greek myth in a way
which exploits to the full its irrational splendour. As Bellessort pointed
out, Racine must have studied *Médée* carefully. There are echoes of it in

Andromaque[7] and *Bajazet*,[8] and resemblances in atmosphere, and often in the use of words, between *Médée* and *Phèdre*.[9]

Médée dates from 1634/5. The *Examen*, which appeard in 1660, concentrates almost exclusively on the 'plot' element. Corneille plumes himself on the ways in which he made his action more logical and realistic than in Euripides or Seneca. He discusses at length how to make expositions and narratives 'vraisemblables': it is not easy to find for expositions characters who can realistically appear to be ignorant of public events preceding the tragedy, and 'les narrations ornées et pathétiques' must not be brought in unless the characters who listen to them can realistically be supposed to have the time and patience. The difference between the play and the critique written many years later shows clearly how in the interval Corneille has evolved away from the poetic and towards the naturalistic mode.

We can now perhaps see better the relationship of *Médée* to *Le Cid*, and of *Le Cid* to the development of French tragedy. Both plays – the later as well as the earlier – show the dis-articulation which Lanson describes, though *Médée* shows it in a more extreme form. But *Médée* also shows in its 'pathetic' elements a more whole-hearted use of the poetic method, and at least the potential of tragedy in the narrower sense. In *Le Cid*, Corneille may have achieved (especially after his revisions) a greater degree of harmony. But he did so by moving further away from the poetic and potentially tragic method.

3

We can confirm our view of the direction in which Corneille was moving if we look at a play which appeared after *Médée* and before *Le Cid*: Tristan's *La Mariane*. This play has a strong tragic quality, and Adam has remarked that it might have encouraged a new fashion for tragedy if *Le Cid* had not led to a revival of tragi-comedy.[10]

From the point of view of technique, the difference between Tristan's practice and Corneille's later precepts in the *Examens* and *Discours* is striking. Tristan is little concerned to construct a formal plot, and his play proceeds openly according to the logic of its theme. Mariane does not appear in the first act, which is occupied by a presentation of Hérode's peculiar mental states: it includes a discussion of the significance of dreams, which are linked with the idea of fate – 'Ce qu'écrit le Destin ne peut être effacé' (l. 146). Corneille was to note with disapproval that Mariane dies between Acts IV and V, leaving the last act to be filled entirely with Hérode's remorse and despair.[11] At the emotional climax of his play, Tristan violates in advance one of Corneille's most typical injunctions,[12] and brings on unannounced a new character at the end of Act IV. Mariane has been condemned to death. Her mother Alexandra appears, grieving for her daughter, but more frightened for herself:

> O grand Dieu! je t'invoque au fort de ma misère;
> Veuille prendre la fille et conserver la mère.

She urges her companion not to show grief at Mariane's fate:

> Prends garde seulement que tes yeux ne produisent,
> Voyant ce triste objet, des larmes qui me nuisent;
> Ayons à sa rencontre un visage assuré,
> Et qui ne montre pas que nous ayons pleuré.
> Car il faut aujourd'hui pour éviter l'orage
> Trahir ses sentiments, et cacher son courage.

Mariane appears, led to execution. She addresses her mother with touching dignity:

> Madame, on me contraint de changer de demeure;
> Mais j'en vais habiter une beaucoup meilleure . . .
> Consolez-vous en donc, et veuillez m'embrasser.

Alexandra denounces her:

> Achève tes destins, méchante et malheureuse;
> Cette mort pour ton crime est trop peu rigoureuse:
> Il fallait que la flamme expiât ton péché,
> Ou que sur une croix ton corps fût attaché . . .
> Je ne te connais point, tu ne viens pas de moi,
> Car de ces trahisons je ne suis pas capable.

Mariane answers, with heart-breaking simplicity:

> Vous vivrez innocente, et je mourrai coupable.

Mariane is led out to die, and Alexandra baldly states that her own attitude was wrong:

> O lâche stratagème! ô cruel artifice!
> Je devais bien plutôt passer pour sa complice.

There is little preparation for this episode, no attempt to work up any previous relationship between Mariane and her mother, no attempt to elaborate the psychological factors which might motivate Alexandra to react to the situation in this way. Tristan obtains the emotional effect he requires, just at the point he requires it, and wastes no time on irrelevancies. His technique is not more primitive than Corneille's: it is different.

We may reflect again on Lanson's theory of the two types of French tragedy. On this view, *La Mariane*, like *Médée*, is a work from that period of uncertainty before *Le Cid* showed the true path. In fact, *La Mariane* is remarkably sure in its technique: it shows none of the uncertainty of *Médée* or *Le Cid*. Like many nineteenth-century critics, Lanson was influenced by a simplist view of evolution: the second type of tragedy comes after, and therefore supersedes and is superior to the first type. If we adopt a less linear model, we can avoid this error and still make use of what is valid in his insight. We can construct an interpretation of French serious drama based on two differing approaches to playwriting. We can perhaps call them two traditions, provided we take tradition in the sense, not of a body of doctrine handed down from master to disciple, but of a similarity of basic attitude (which may, indeed, be accompanied at the conscious level by disagreements or misunderstanding between those who share the same basic attitude). The first tradition, which is inherently naturalistic (in our wider sense) would include Corneille, Voltaire, Hugo, Scribe, and all writers of *pièces bien faites* or social plays: it is the central tradition of European drama from about the fourth decade of the seventeenth century until a change becomes evident at the end of the nineteenth century in Jarry and the later Strindberg. The other, which is poetic, starts in the efforts of the sixteenth-century dramatists: it has affinities with, and sometimes consciously looks back to, the tragedies of the Greeks and Seneca. *La Mariane* belongs to this tradition. The work of Corneille on the whole marks an increasing divergence from it. I shall argue later that the work of Racine marks an isolated return to it. But by the time Racine began to write, the idea of drama implicit in *La Mariane* had been lost sight of, and he had to rediscover and recreate it in a new and unfavourable literary context.

This new context was partly shaped by the success of Corneille in creating a more naturalistic drama. Whatever his reasons, after *Le Cid* Corneille moved on the whole towards acceptance of neo-classical attitudes to playwriting. In *Horace*, he adopted the full rigour of the unity of place – the first established poet to do so. But the conflict between naturalism and poetry remained active. In *Cinna* it was to take a new turn.

4
'CINNA'

Cinna has always been recognised as one of Corneille's masterpieces, but since at least the beginning of the eighteenth century it has attracted severe criticism. The points selected for attack are in themselves interesting. In the later stages of neo-classicism, *Cinna* was criticised for its *enflure*, its exaggerated grandiloquence, and at the same time for the lapses from decorum in some of the more domestic passages (especially in the rôle of Livie, who then is given in Act V the task of uttering a prophecy). From the beginnings of Romanticism, critics complained of the inhumanity of the characters and the subordination of love to politics. The later nineteenth-century added complaints about the feebleness (even the incoherence) of the plot and emphasised the inconsistencies in the character-drawing (especially of Cinna and Maxime).

All these features are certainly present in the play, and require some explanation. More important still, there are the difficulties which modern critics have found in trying to appreciate the overall effect of the play. There is general agreement that it is not the tragic purgation by pity and terror. Is it then admiration – that is, is Auguste a superman in whom we admire the triumph of will-power? If so, why are we led along with superfluous melodramatic effects like the feigned suicide and reappearance of Maxime? Why is Cinna given such prominence, and why is Livie set beside Auguste to make such disabused comments?

These difficulties also are real. But – despite them, and despite the faults pointed out by earlier critics – there is no doubt that *Cinna* makes a majestically unified impression in which these separate points of difficulty are forgotten. I shall therefore try and find a way of looking at the play – and at the environment in which it was written – in which all these points fall into place as valid parts of a coherent whole. In doing so, my study of *Le Cid* will not be much help: *Cinna* is very different in texture and method, and requires a less piecemeal approach.

2

We will start by a careful scrutiny of the text, considered as an acting script which is a poem, a pattern of words into which the meaning and experience implicit in the play are concentrated, and from which we can draw out what is needed for a full understanding and for the basis of an adequate performance. In doing so, we shall have to try and bear in mind the probable standard reactions of a seventeenth-century spectator as well as our own, but the effort to do so may be a check on our modern prejudices.

The play starts with a monologue of 52 lines by Emilie, from which we gather that in order to avenge her father, whom Auguste murdered, she has made her lover, Cinna, plot to murder Auguste. Fulvie, her confidante, arrives, and they discuss the situation. Cinna enters, and in a speech of 114 lines describes his preparations. Emilie urges him on, but his freedman Evandre arrives with the news that Auguste has sent for him and Maxime, the other leader of the plot. Emilie is sure the plot is discovered, and urges Cinna to save himself. Cinna, however, keeps his head. He goes off to see Auguste, leaving Emilie slightly recovered.

In the bulk of this act, virtually nothing happens, and the time is passed in long and elaborate speeches. Only with the entrance of Evandre does the mode change. Curiosity and suspense are aroused: is the conspiracy discovered? what will happen to Cinna? how will Emilie react?

Before we try and grasp the significance of this change, let us go back and look at the text in detail. It begins thus:

> Impatients désirs d'une illustre vengeance
> Dont la mort de mon père a formé la naissance,
> Enfants impétueux de mon ressentiment,
> Que ma douleur séduite embrasse aveuglément,
> Vous prenez sur mon âme un trop puissant empire:
> Durant quelques moments souffrez que je respire,
> Et que je considère, en l'état ou je suis,
> Et ce que je hasarde, et ce que je poursuis.

This monologue forms a sort of prelude to the play. As the alexandrines drive forward, they bring before us two things. First, their meaning is clearly that tumultuous passions are overpowering Emilie and clouding her judgment – something which does not, perhaps, make Emilie quite sympathetic to us (or even less to the original audience). Secondly, they convey an impression of exaggeration by the very emphasis of the style. Of course, seventeenth-century audiences and authors expected tragedy to be much larger and more ornate than life. But, even if we make full allowance for this, we may still believe that in this monologue Corneille is deliberately over-inflating the verse. In the first line, the stress falls on 'illustre' rather than 'vengeance', which suggests a slightly false concern with effect. Emilie's wish to avenge her father – which might be made very touching – is somewhat distanced by the prolonged conceit that her desires for vengeance are her children.[1] Finally, the emphatic, gasping divisions of 'Et que je considère, | en l'état où je suis, | Et ce que je hasarde, | et ce que je poursuis' present an almost grotesque contrast in their determination to be sensible. The movement from excitement to further excitement, then back to an attempt at calm, is repeated in the next few lines. The firm rhythm of 'Quand je regarde Auguste au milieu de sa gloire' is broken into by the rising clamour for vengeance, and mounts to another climax of exaggeration ('Je m'abandonne toute à vos ardents transports, | Et crois, pour une mort, lui devoir mille morts') only to descend abruptly to a more matter-of-fact tone in which the reality of her situation and her love for Cinna are expressed: 'je sens refroidir ce bouillant mouvement | Quand il faut, pour le suivre, exposer mon amant'.

She now addresses the absent Cinna directly:

> Oui, Cinna, contre moi moi-même je m'irrite,
> Quand je songe aux dangers où je te précipite.
> Quoique pour me servir tu n'appréhendes rien,
> Te demander du sang, c'est exposer le tien.

This, with its caressing rhythm and informal *tutoiement*, contrasts with the invocation of 'Impatients désirs' and 'enfants impétueux': the verse conveys love as a more real presence than the desire for revenge. But this personal interlude does not last. After realistic reflections on the danger of betrayal, and another passionate revelation of the overriding importance of her love for Cinna, the exaggerated world of vengeance is reintroduced, with its characteristic trappings of invocations and abstractions ('Cessez, vaines frayeurs, cessez, lâches tendresses'), and the monologue ends with a flourish which applies the second person singular, not to Cinna, but to the abstract 'Amour', which is to be subordinate to her 'devoir':

> Lui céder, c'est ta gloire, et le vaincre, ta honte:
> Montre-toi généreux, souffrant qu'il te surmonte;
> Plus tu lui donneras, plus il va te donner,
> Et ne triomphera que pour te couronner.[2]

This tone comes out still more strongly when Fulvie enters: repetitions, parallel phrases, heavily stressed verbs, emphatic caesuras, under-

line the mood. But then, as in the opening monologue, Corneille sets
against this heroism a mundane realism:

> Mais encore une fois souffrez que je vous die
> Qu'une si juste ardeur devrait être attiédie.
> Auguste, chaque jour, à force de bienfaits,
> Semble assez réparer les maux qu'il vous a faits;
> Sa faveur envers vous paraît si déclarée
> Que vous êtes chez lui la plus considérée.

The prosaic rhythm and 'seems' verbs contrast markedly with
Emilie's heroic verse. The ensuing dialogue does not advance the action,
in the sense of 'plot'. What it does advance is the action in the sense of
the development of opposed views of the situation in the minds of the
audience. If we react to each piece of evidence as it is enunciated on the
stage, our understanding moves forward; the meaning of the play takes
shape with each added detail and suggested point of view. Fulvie's
verse is neat and prosaic, its subject-matter shrewd:

> Quel besoin toutefois de passer pour ingrate?
> Ne pouvez-vous haïr sans que la haine éclate?

She knows how to expose the folly of Emilie's actions:

> Votre amour à ce prix n'est qu'un présent funeste
> Qui porte à votre amant sa perte manifeste . . .
> Pensez mieux, Emilie, à quoi vous l'exposez.

Though spoken by a mere confidante, this has authority. Against it,
Corneille makes Emilie's verse rise in quality. Her lines take on a fresh
appealing ring:

> Toute cette faveur [d'Auguste] ne me rend pas mon père;
> Et de quelque façon que l'on me considère,
> Abondante en richesse, ou puissante en crédit,
> Je demeure toujours la fille d'un proscrit.

This personal tone is maintained to the end of the scene:

> Aux mânes paternels je dois ce sacrifice;
> Cinna me l'a promis en recevant ma foi,
> Et ce coup seul aussi le rend digne de moi.
> Il est tard, après tout, de m'en vouloir dédire.
> Aujourd'hui l'on s'assemble, aujourd'hui l'on conspire;
> L'heure, le lieu, le bras se choisit aujourd'hui,
> Et c'est à faire enfin à mourir après lui.

These lines draw together contrasting feelings important to the play.
The pompous 'sacrifice to the paternal manes' is followed by the naive

'anyway, Cinna promised'; the romantic 'only this exploit makes him
worthy of me' is cut across by the prosaic 'anyway, it's too late to stop
him'; the emphasis of 'today . . . today . . . today' peters out in the
touching but pessimistic conclusion of 'I can always kill myself after he
is dead.' In other words, Corneille is presenting Emilie's values as
muddled, and this muddle is conveyed by the controlled variations of
the verse.

The next scene is taken up mainly with Cinna's magnificent speech
about the conspiracy. I would make only two points about it. The first
is that its length, and the quality of the verse, mark it out as an important element in the play: the long recital of Auguste's crimes means
something, and we are meant to see behind the play (even behind the
majestic tableau of Auguste's forgiveness) this vista of treachery and
massacre:

> . . . ce tigre altéré de tout le sang romain . . .
> Tantôt ami d'Antoine, et tantot ennemi,
> Et jamais insolent ni cruel à demi! . . .
> . . . ces tristes batailles
> Où Rome par ses mains déchirait ses entrailles . . .
> Rome entière noyée au sang de ses enfants:
> Les uns assassinés dans les places publiques,
> Les autres dans le sein de leurs dieux domestiques;
> Le méchant par le prix au crime encouragé;
> Le mari par sa femme en son lit égorgé;
> Le fils tout dégouttant du meurtre de son père,
> Et sa tête à la main demandant son salaire . . .
> La perte de nos biens et de nos libertés,
> Le ravage des champs, le pillage des villes,
> Et les proscriptions, et les guerres civiles,
> Sont les degrés sanglants dont Auguste a fait choix
> Pour monter dans le trône et nous donner des lois.

The second point is that the speech is deliberately presented with a
certain irony. Our attention is also specifically drawn to the rhetorical
arts by which the picture is presented:

> *Je leur fais des tableaux* de ces tristes batailles . . .
> J'ajoute à *ces tableaux* la *peinture* effroyable . . .
> Mais je ne trouve point de *couleurs* assez noires . . .
> Je les *peins* dans le meurtre à l'envi triomphants . . .
> Sans pouvoir *exprimer* par tant d'horribles traits
> Qu'un *crayon* imparfait de leur sanglante paix . . .
> . . . les noms de ces grands personnages

Dont j'ai *dépeint* les morts pour aigrir les courages
Ces indignes trépas, quoique mal *figurés* . . .

We might say (misleadingly, in my opinion) that this is because Cinna is given to exaggeration and self-dramatisation. But if we look at the references in context they are primarily distancing devices. They prevent us from becoming too uncritically committed to Cinna's viewpoint, and remind us that we are in a theatre listening to a speech: that is, we are listening to a feigned speech referring to feigned events, not listening to a real man talking about real events. Some of the effects have a very piquant ambiguity. 'Quoique mal figurés' – what is badly portrayed? The crimes of Auguste in Cinna's speech? Or Cinna's speech to the conspirators in Cinna's speech to Emilie? Or Cinna's speech to Emilie in the speech Corneille has written? The conception of the report has a hall-of-mirrors quality that is important to the play: it is not just a speech, but a speech about a speech. As so often when this sort of device is used, its effect (and therefore, in the hands of a good dramatist, its purpose) is to induce reflection about the reality of the different planes represented. Here we have a key theme in *Cinna*: there is an ambiguity about the idealism of the conspirators, and a suggestion that the reality of the situation is not objective, but dependent on the subjective wishes and efforts of the characters. Specifically, this speech of Cinna's again suggests what the overinflation and variations of tone of Emilie's speeches so far have indicated: the conspirators are presented with sympathy, but at the same time with a certain ironical detachment.

The irony becomes plain when we proceed from the description of Auguste's wickedness to a description of the plotters' plans:

> Demain, au Capitole, il fait un sacrifice;
> Qu'il en soit la victime, et faisons en ces lieux
> Justice à tout le monde, à la face des dieux:
> Là presque pour sa suite il n'a que notre troupe;
> C'est de ma main qu'il prend et l'encens et la coupe;
> Et je veux pour signal que cette même main
> Lui donne, au lieu d'encens, d'un poignard dans le sein.

This comes 25 lines after the virtuous complaint that some of the proscribed were 'sacrifiés jusque sur les autels'. Lest we should miss the irony, it is strengthened by some delicate ambiguities in the wording: 'à la face des dieux' ('before the gods' – in the temple, openly – or 'in the face of the gods' – in defiance of them); 'au lieu d'encens' ('instead of the incense I was to hand him' – but also 'instead of the flattery I usually render him').

Finally, the speech sets out formally the moral ambiguity of the contrast between Auguste and the plotters:

> Demain j'attends la haine ou la faveur des hommes,
> Le nom de parricide ou de libérateur . . .
> *Du succès qu'on obtienne* contre la tyrannie
> *Dépend* ou *notre gloire* ou *notre ignominie*.

The relativity of moral values could hardly be put more plainly; and this moral chaos is appropriately ushered in by a line of incongruous banality:

> Voilà, belle Emilie, à quel point nous en sommes.

Eighteenth- and nineteenth-century critics usually assumed that Corneille mingled such banal lines with his rhetoric from simple incapacity. But here Corneille has a specific purpose for his bathetic line: it points up the contrast between the megalomaniac fantasies of the conspirators and their less impressive selves.

It is against this background of uncertain values that Evandre comes with his chilling message. The pace immediately changes. For the first time in the play, we have short speeches and broken lines. We also have a *volte-face* by Emilie, whose only thought is for Cinna's safety: 'Ah! Cinna, je te perds!' Reality has broken in. We are not to think of the lovers as merely foolish. The dangers they run are real, and the power of Auguste is all around:

> Tu voudrais fuir en vain, Cinna, je le confesse:
> Si tout est découvert, Auguste a su pourvoir
> A ne te laisser pas ta fuite en ton pouvoir.

And behind their bravado, the verse speaks of a real heroism and tenderness:

> S'il faut subir le coup d'un destin rigoureux,
> Je mourrai tout ensemble heureux et malheureux:
> Heureux pour vous servir de perdre ainsi la vie,
> Malheureux de mourir sans vous avoir servie.

What are we to make, then, of this first act? If we attend to the verse, our impression is surely something like this: a group of slightly hysterical young people (two of them sincerely in love) are conspiring to kill the emperor; although their motives are muddled and their gestures have a touch of play-acting, their reasons seem real enough – Auguste is a monster who has waded through blood to the throne; we cannot laugh at them, because their actions are presented in convincing verse as noble; their danger is real, because behind their gestures we see the power of Auguste's police state; and yet the verse (especially in Fulvie's common-sense tone and in the deliberate hollowness of much of Cinna's recital) has implanted in us some uncertainty about the moral rights and wrongs of the piece – indeed, about the validity of absolute standards of any sort; and the summons to Auguste has brought us up against the uncertainty of what the tyrant will do next. We might perhaps sum up by saying that this act presents in exciting terms a chaos of moral values.

Act II presents us with the tyrant. He has sent for the plotters, not because he knows of their plot, but because he wants their advice on whether to abdicate. Maxime urges him to do so, but Cinna dissuades him. Maxime, left alone with Cinna, is astounded, and Cinna tries to justify his action.

This act is famous for the strength and beauty of its verse, and also for the difficulties it presents. Why does Corneille spend nearly 300 lines (a sixth of the play) on a debate which leads nowhere? Is it in fact a debate which leads nowhere? Is it a debate on politics which we are meant to savour for its own sake, or do the ideas have some specific function in the play? Why does Auguste, whom the first act presented as odious, here seem almost sympathetic compared with Cinna? Why does Cinna (who is supposed to be an honest man) equivocate so shamefully, while Maxime (whom Corneille is to use as a villain) behaves honestly and bravely? And why, this being so, is Cinna's dishonesty expressed in verse as firm and beautiful as Maxime's?

The only answers are to be found in the text, if we read it in the light of what we have learned during the first act.

Act I ended with the real power of Auguste cutting across the fantasy world of the conspirators. Act II opens with an enactment of this power:

> Que chacun se retire et qu'aucun n'entre ici.
> Vous, Cinna, demeurez, et vous, Maxime, aussi.
>
> (*Tous se retirent, à la réserve de Cinna et de Maxime.*)
>
> Cet empire absolu sur la terre et sur l'onde,
> Ce pouvoir souverain que j'ai sur tout le monde,
> Cette grandeur sans borne et cet illustre rang,
> Qui m'a jadis coûté tant de peine et de sang,
> Enfin tout ce qu'adore en ma haute fortune
> D'un courtisan flatteur la présence importune . . .

These lines, like those of the opening monologue, were soon to be attacked for overemphasis. But Fénelon's criticisms were made from the characteristic naturalistic viewpoint of neo-classicism: the style of Auguste does not agree with the moderation of the historical Augustus. The real point is the function of the lines in the pattern of the play: they express the facts of Auguste's power. The solemn amplitude of the verse – so different from the hysterical assertiveness of Emilie's mono-logue and Cinna's report – confirms the solidity of the power. Auguste can even refer – and this self-knowledge is another important *motif* in the play – to the crimes by which he attained his power ('Qui m'a jadis coûté tant de peine et de sang'). At this stage we know him only as a tyrant, and we expect him to denounce Maxime and Cinna. But to our surprise he takes up another theme:

> Enfin tout ce qu'adore en ma haute fortune
> D'un courtisan flatteur la présence importune,
> N'est que de ces beautés dont l'éclat éblouit,
> Et qu'on cesse d'aimer sitôt qu'on en jouit.

We have to revise our ideas quickly; and in this moment of disarray we may absorb the suggestion that there is a contrast between reality and appearance – a suggestion for which the hollowness of much of the conspirators' verse in Act I has already prepared us.[3]

Auguste goes on to develop this theme in full, rich verse marked with the sadness of experience:

> L'ambition déplaît quand elle est assouvie . . .
> J'ai souhaité l'empire, et j'y suis parvenu;
> Mais en le souhaitant, je ne l'ai pas connu:
> Dans sa possession j'ai trouvé pour tous charmes
> D'effroyables soucis, d'éternelles alarmes,
> Mille ennemis secrets, la mort à tous propos,
> Point de plaisir sans trouble, et jamais de repos.

Voltaire (taking up the other, formalistic, trend in neo-classicism) was to attack these lines as too familiar. The point is that they are familiar for a purpose: we are meant to feel the contrast in tone be-tween this and the verse of Emilie and Cinna; it marks not only the difference between experience and immaturity but also the difference between disillusion and enthusiasm. Auguste's disenchantment is a very human feeling, based on experience, not theory.

To underline this, we then have another evocation of the recent past, but very different from that by Cinna: Auguste shows, quite simply, from the examples of Sulla and Julius Caesar, that there is no stability in life, and that virtue or vice may each be lucky or unlucky. This takes up, with a deeper note, Cinna's theme in Act I.[4]

After this, the tension raised at the end of Act I is relaxed: Auguste has not discovered the plot. The relief is tempered by a new feeling, however:

> Voilà, mes chers amis, ce qui me met en peine.
> Vous, qui me tenez lieu d'Agrippe et de Mécène . . .

After the statement of the moral ambiguity of the world comes this demonstration of it: the tyrant begins to draw our sympathy when he takes his would-be murderers for his friends. The ambiguity is emphasised by the phrasing: '*Vous, qui me tenez lieu*'.

Now comes the passage which has disquieted so many critics: Cinna flatters Auguste and begs him not to abdicate, whereas Maxime urges him to carry out his intention. For a moment, let us leave on one side the question of Corneille's characterisation here, and concentrate on the verse without too much regard for the presumed motives of the speakers.

The first lines spoken by Cinna in response to Auguste are lies, and this is made more obvious to us by their exaggerated sycophancy. (There is also – though this was less obvious given seventeenth-century usage – another subtle ambiguity: Cinna has indeed 'un esprit jaloux de votre gloire'.) The rest of the speech mounts in energy and conviction, and the beauty of the lines forces them into our minds:

> N'en craignez point, Seigneur, les tristes destinées;
> Un plus puissant démon veille sur vos années . . .
> On entreprend assez, mais aucun exécute;
> Il est des assassins, mais il n'est plus de Brute:
> Enfin, s'il faut attendre un semblable revers,
> Il est beau de mourir maître de l'univers.

Then Maxime speaks. What he says also rings true and extends our vision further:

> Rome, est à vous, Seigneur, l'empire est votre bien;
> Chacun en liberté peut disposer du sien . . .
> Le bonheur peut conduire à la grandeur suprême;
> Mais pour y renoncer il faut la vertu même.

The next speech can cap this: it defends eloquently the virtues of absolute monarchy, and even more eloquently denounces the failings of the alternative:

> Mais quand le peuple est maître, on n'agit qu'en tumulte:
> La voix de la raison jamais ne se consulte . . .
> Le pire des Etats, c'est l'Etat populaire.

Let us forget that this is spoken by Cinna: the verse rings true, and the sentiments would have seemed to a seventeenth-century audience more obviously sensible than they do now. After this, Maxime again defends the republic, but the temperature falls in the middle part of the scene (ll. 522–570). Nevertheless, the topic in this less splendid passage is noteworthy: it is the relativity of political ideals:

> J'ose dire, Seigneur, que par tous les climats
> Ne sont pas bien reçus toutes sortes d'Etats;
> Chaque peuple a le sien conforme à sa nature.
>
> Il est vrai que du ciel la prudence infinie
> Départ a chaque peuple un différent génie;
> Mais il n'est pas moins vrai que cet ordre des cieux
> Change selon les temps comme selon les lieux.

Then the tone rises again, and the verse reaches its greatest intensity in Cinna's final appeal to Auguste. He attacks the ideal of Rome's liberty:

> Ce nom depuis longtemps ne sert qu'à éblouir,
> Et sa propre grandeur l'empêche d'en jouir.
> Depuis qu'elle se voit la maîtresse du monde,
> Depuis que la richesse entre ses murs abonde,
> Et que son sein, fécond en glorieux exploits,
> Produit des citoyens plus puissants que des rois,
> Les grands, pour s'affermir achetant les suffrages,
> Tiennent pompeusement leurs maîtres à leurs gages,
> Qui, par des fers dorés se laissant enchaîner,
> Reçoivent d'eux les lois qu'ils pensent leur donner.

There is no mistaking the authority of this verse. The full, easy rhythm, the criss-cross of irony, the insistence on concrete facts, the scornful imaging of topsy-turveydom, all stick in the heart and mind. This sense of turmoil is crucial to the play: the vitality of the verse proves it. And it is followed immediately by the remedy:

> Seigneur, pour sauver Rome, il faut qu'elle s'unisse
> En la main d'un bon chef à qui tout obéisse . . .
> Conservez-vous, Seigneur, en lui laissant un maître
> Sous qui son vrai bonheur commence de renaître.

This appeal brings a temporary resolution – the first appearance of a pattern to be repeated on a higher level in Act V. Auguste agrees to remain emperor, and proceeds (as in Act V) to overwhelm his treacherous friends with favours. The verse still has a ring about it, but the tone is firmly grounded in reality, and is even familiar in places:

> Pour épouse, Cinna, je vous donne Emilie . . .
> Et que si nos malheurs et la nécessité
> M'ont fait traiter son père avec sévérité
> Mon épargne depuis en sa faveur ouverte
> Doit avoir adouci l'aigreur de cette perte.

Here the moral ambiguity is powerful in its effect: Auguste is behaving with simplicity and sincerity:

> Je vois trop que vos coeurs n'ont point pour moi de fard . . .
> Adieu: j'en veux porter la nouvelle à Livie.

I have dwelt on this scene to emphasise how the quality of the verse should control our responses. If we attend to the verse, our experience of the play is continually widened: cogent argument succeeds argument, dazzling image succeeds image. And this succession of experiences does two things. First, it enforces the realisation that the range of political action is infinite, that there are no easy answers. Secondly, the shifts in the verse and the subtle suggestions within it emphasise the relativity, the untrustworthy nature, of apparent moral absolutes.

We can now see something of the purpose of the inconsistency of Cinna's and Maxime's characters and the shift of interest from the conspirators to the emperor. Corneille is not presenting us with life-like portraits of politicians. He is enacting for us in language, and forcing us to enact in our minds, the imposition of order in a chaotic universe. The bewildering shifts of viewpoint have a multiple purpose and effect. They stop us from taking too myopic an interest in the characters to the exclusion of the larger pattern; they emphasise the kaleidoscopic shifting of the moral universe, and thus actualise for us the chaos on which order is to be imposed; and they administer a series of shocks to our tendency to slip into stereotyped reactions. By jolting us out of the 'Roman hero/tyrant' set of stock reactions without allowing us to slip into the 'wicked plotters/ wronged monarch' set of stock reactions, they make us ready to share the full experience of the play. If we try to examine in isolation those elements – e.g. characterisation – which we happen to find most interesting, and if we attempt to apply naturalistic criteria to them, we get nowhere. Corneille's method in *Cinna* is not naturalistic, but poetic. He is using all the elements of drama – action, character, thought, diction and spectacle – to express the inner experience of the play at every level at which we are capable of experiencing it; the elements are means of achieving the total effect, not developed for their own sake.

Auguste's exit at l. 646 brings the first movement of the play to an end. There follows the very confusing middle section, which extends from l. 647 to the end of Act IV. It is concerned mainly with the conspirators, though it includes Auguste's self-debate in Act IV, in which the final resolution of the play is foreshadowed.

In Act II, Scene ii, and in Act III, the conspirators hold the stage, but they can undertake no vital action. Their apparently idealistic world of Act I has vanished, and they wander in limbo, their large gestures ever more divorced from reality, their emotions zigzagging unpredictably. It is not that Emilie and Cinna, or even Maxime, are ridiculous. There are honest and tender passages in the verse. But the heroic tone is forced, and when Cinna rises to his grand decision in Act III the verse becomes almost parody:

> Il faut sur un tyran porter de justes coups;
> Mais apprenez qu'Auguste est moins tyran que vous:
> S'il nous ôte à son gré nos biens, nos jours, nos femmes,
> Il n'a point jusqu'ici tyrannisé nos âmes;
> Mais l'empire inhumain qu'exercent vos beautés
> Force jusqu'aux esprits et jusqu'aux volontés.
> Vous me faites priser ce qui me déshonore;
> Vous me faites haïr ce que mon âme adore.

This is nonsense: the absurd comparison of Emilie's tyranny with that of Auguste; the assumption that to deprive a man of his wife is not to tyrannise over his desires; the emphatic repetitions; the revelation that Auguste is what Cinna's soul adores (if this is what is meant); all this leads up to the exaggeration of:

> Vous me faites répandre un sang pour qui je dois
> Exposer tout le mien et mille et mille fols.

The conclusion which Cinna draws from his strange reasoning expresses as plainly as possible the conspirators' confusion:

> Vous le voulez, j'y cours, ma parole est donnée;
> Mais ma main, aussitôt contre mon sein tournée,
> Aux mânes d'un tel prince immolant votre amant,
> A mon crime forcé joindra mon châtiment
> Et, par cette action dans l'autre confondue,
> Recouvrera ma gloire aussitôt que perdue.

Nevertheless, through all this unreal posturing, we can hear the verse transmitting its powerful ground-note, at once expressing and ordering the moral confusion:

> Nous sommes encor loin de mettre en evidence
> Si nous nous conduirons avec plus de prudence.
> Auguste s'est lassé d'être si rigoureux.
> Envers nos citoyens je sais quelle est ma faute.

It is by listening to this undertone, not by puzzling about the psychology of the characters, that we can understand this middle section of the play for what it mainly is: an enactment of confusion in a world where values have lost their meaning, and where the people are too weak and conventional to create their values anew.

This theme is most completely expressed in Act IV, which presents the chaos and prepares the way for reconstruction. The act falls clearly into two halves – the first concentrates on Auguste, the second on the conspirators. As Corneille admitted, this is a blemish from the limited point of view of neatness of construction. Nevertheless, as we shall see, this divided structure has its significance.

We start with Auguste, and with unwonted bustle. In one short scene, Euphorbe reveals the plot, a new minor character is introduced and sent about his business, guards are sent to arrest the conspirators, and Euphorbe is taken into custody. This is rapid motion indeed in a play with little external action. In the midst of this, the verse dwells on Auguste's grief:

> Quoi? mes plus chers amis? quoi? Cinna! quoi? Maxime!
> O trop sensible coup d'une main si chérie!
> Cinna, tu me trahis!

Then the scene clears: Auguste is alone. The theme of grief is taken up:

> Ciel, à qui voulez-vous désormais que je fie
> Les secrets de mon âme et le soin de ma vie?
> Reprenez le pouvoir que vous m'avez commis
> Si donnant des sujets il ôte les amis;
> Si tel est le destin des grandeurs souveraines
> Que leurs plus grands bienfaits n'attirent que des haines,
> Et si votre rigueur les condamne à chérir
> Ceux que vous animez à les faire périr.
> Pour elles rien n'est sûr; qui peut tout doit tout craindre.

'Pour elles rien n'est sûr': power, cruelty, success, have all come to this. But the world-weariness is not religious in spirit. The 'ciel' is an alien entity. Corneille's choice of 'rigueur' and 'animez' instead of 'justice' and 'inspirez' shows he is not referring to a supernatural judiciary.

We now approach the heart of the play: the centre at which the destructive forces collect and begin to be transformed. The verse re-enacts the physical movement we have just seen. Physically, Auguste has been left to commune with himself; the verse takes up the theme of withdrawal into the self:

> Rentre en toi-même, Octave, et cesse de te plaindre.

Auguste invokes his old self and his crimes:

> Songe aux fleuves de sang où ton bras s'est baigné,
> De combien ont rougi les champs de Macédoine.
> Combien en a versé la défaite d'Antoine . . .
> Pérouse au sien noyée, et tous ses habitants.

The language echoes that of Cinna's recital in Act I, but here the sombre rhythm chastens the effect. What was before external is here internalised: Auguste accuses himself; responsibility is not evaded. The paradoxes of an uncertain universe are given form in the emphatic antitheses:

> Rends un sang infidèle à l'infidélité
>
> Toi, dont la trahison . . .
> Me traite en criminel et fait seule mon crime,
> Relève pour l'abattre un trône illégitime.

The remedy of violent action in the external world ('Punissons l'assassin, proscrivons les complices') is proposed, only to be followed by the realisation of futility, the sense so often invoked in the play of endless, meaningless repetition:

> Mais quoi? tuojours du sang, et toujours des supplices!

Yet Corneille's creative search goes deeper still. He seeks and tracks down to its inner root the paradox of man turned against himself:

> Ma cruauté se lasse et ne peut s'arrêter.

This profound and terrible verse is at the heart of Corneille's insight: it expresses with an almost physical sense of constriction this intransi-gent compulsion to destroy, which is part of the mind but not con-trollable by it. This recognition that the evil is within, and therefore cannot be shrugged aside or blamed on external forces, delivers the mind helpless to the death-wish. The rest of the soliloquy again struggles to externalise the conflict by violent action:

> Mais jouissons plutôt nous-mêmes de sa peine,
> Et si Rome nous hait, triomphons de sa haine.

but behind this bravado is the fascination of death, of weariness and self-destruction:

> Meurs, et dérobe-lui la gloire de ta chute;
> Meurs: tu ferais pour vivre un lâche et vain effort.
>
> Meurs, puisque c'est un mal que tu ne peux guérir;
> Meurs enfin, puisqu'il faut ou tout perdre, ou mourir.
> La vie est peu de chose, et le peu qui t'en reste
> Ne vaut pas l'acheter par un prix si funeste.
> Meurs . . .

The solution is not yet near, and Auguste can only end with the dilemma sharply realised:

> Qui des deux dois-je suivre, et duquel m'éloigner?
> Ou laissez-moi périr, ou laissez-moi régner.

It is the glory of *Cinna* that the whole play is devoted to the enactment of its central experience; the themes are enunciated, developed, repeated and varied, so that we may realise this experience at every level. After Auguste's soliloquy, Corneille yet again varies the tone and multiplies his means of expression. Livie arrives (in contradiction to his later demand that in a well-made play all the characters should be introduced in the first act). With her entrance, the verse changes: here, as throughout the play, it follows with extraordinary variety and suppleness the twists and turns of the emotion. Livie's speeches are matter-of-fact and sensible, and the verse matches them:

> Votre sévérité, sans produire aucun fruit,
> Seigneur, jusqu'à présent fait beaucoup de bruit.

She urges clemency in the most level-headed way possible:

> Essayez sur Cinna ce que peut la clémence . . .
> Son pardon peut servir à votre renommée.

Beside hers, Auguste's verse loses timbre and takes on a shriller tone:

> J'ai trop par vos avis consulté là-dessus;
> Ne m'en parlez jamais, je ne consulte plus.

The heroic moment is succeeded by petulance:

> Vous m'aviez bien promis des conseils d'une femme :
> Vous me tenez parole, et c'en sont là, Madame.

and above all by weariness:

> J'abandonne mon sang à qui voudra l'épandre.
> Après un long orage il faut trouver un port;
> Et je n'en vois que deux, le repos ou la mort.
> De tout ce qu'eut Sylla de puissance et d'honneur,
> Lassé comme il en fut, j'aspire à son bonheur.

This last couplet recalls Auguste's first speech in Act II. Livie's reply here anchors it to earth:

> Assez et trop longtemps son exemple vous flatte.

As Corneille does not blench at grandiloquence, so here he does not blench at comedy. The most important point about the 'Auguste' expression of the meaning which the play embodies is that it is firmly grounded in reality: it is not unballasted excitement of the kind we meet in Cinna's speeches. Corneille underlines this relation to reality at the end of the scene with Livie. For the only time in the play a character addresses the audience directly, in Livie's four candid lines:

> Il m'échappe: suivons, et forçons-le de voir
> Qu'il peut, en faisant grâce, affermir son pouvoir,
> Et qu'enfin la clémence est la plus belle marque
> Qui fasse à l'univers connaître un vrai monarque.

This device is reminiscent of Corneille's bourgeois comedies. There is a similar movement in *La Veuve*, when Chrysante soliloquises about her son, who has left the stage refusing to be guided by her realistic common-sense:

> Dieux! que cet obstiné me donne de tourment!
> Que je te plains, ma fille! Hélas, pour ta misère
> Les destins ennemis t'ont fait naître ce frère.
> Déplorable! le ciel te veut favoriser
> D'une bonne fortune, et tu n'en peux user.
> Rejoignons toutes deux ce naturel sauvage,
> Et tâchons par nos pleurs d'amollir son courage.[5]

And now, again for the only time in *Cinna*, the 'liaison des scènes' is broken in mid-act. The scene changes (or, as originally, a different part of the décor is used). Emilie enters with Fulvie, and at once the theme of unreality reappears:

> D'où me vient cette joie? et que mal à propos
> Mon esprit malgré moi goûte un entier repos!

The banal verse of Fulvie's reply supplies the background of realism, but makes no contact with Emilie, who is baffled by her own sense of unreality:

> Que de sujets de craindre et de désespérer,
> Sans que mon triste coeur en daigne murmurer!
> A chaque occasion le ciel y fait descendre
> Un sentiment contraire à celui qu'il doit prendre.

This impression of unreality is heightened when Maxime reappears:

> Mais je vous vois, Maxime, et l'on vous faisait mort!

The scene between them is full of falsehood and references to falsehood. The verse, with its lurchings between the insipid ('La plus belle moitié qui reste de lui-même') and the false sublime ('Rappelez, rappelez cette vertu sublime') conveys the lack of liaison between reality and the sentiments expressed. Emilie is given stronger lines, and her instinct to confess and go to Auguste with Cinna is right and noble, but, despite her denials, it is blind. Like Auguste, she is drawn by thoughts of death:

> Viens mourir avec moi pour te justifier.

– but she has not achieved Auguste's lucidity; she acts energetically, but without comprehension:

> Ma vertu tout entière agit sans s'émouvoir,
> Et je vois malgré moi plus que je ne veux voir.

The lucidity of Auguste was followed by the realism of Livie. Here, Maxime is left with only confusion and despair. Auguste had faced his own evil, but Maxime can only blame someone else:

> Euphorbe, c'est l'effet de tes lâches conseils.

Auguste's facing of the darkness brought him firm contact with reality. Maxime's evasions have brought him to this half-world: he is disgraced, in his own eyes and those of Emilie, and officially he has no existence at all.

The contrast between the unreal world of the conspirators and the firmly-grounded world of Auguste is brought out strongly by the beginning of Act V. Cinna is humbled before Auguste, who confronts him with calm authority:

> Prends un siège, Cinna, prends, et sur toute chose
> Observe exactement la loi que je t'impose.

Then, except for two small interruptions by Cinna (one humble, one falsely indignant), Auguste draws up the indictment. It is useless for Cinna to burst out in denials: behind the verse of Auguste – so clear, so full, so firm – lies the inexorable strength of fact:

> Tu veux m'assassiner demain, au Capitole,
> Pendant le sacrifice, et ta main pour signal
> Me doit, au lieu d'encens, donner le coup fatal;
> La moitié de tes gens doit occuper la porte,
> L'autre moitié te suivre et te prêter main-forte.
> Ai-je de bons avis, ou de mauvais soupçons?

Auguste appeals to Cinna to face the pain of self-knowledge:

> Apprends à te connaître, et descends en toi-même.

Against this enactment of authority, Cinna's lines are confused and his attitudes false (his excuse, though an attempt to shield Emilie, is a lie). Auguste can truly dismiss his courage as bravado.

The play so far has shown a continual shifting between different levels and viewpoints, between appearance and the presumed reality, which is again distanced or contradicted by the verse. Now, as the climax approaches, Corneille increases his pace, bringing his themes forward in rapid alternation. Livie enters with her news: 'Vous ne connaissez pas encor tous les complices.' Auguste's control is shaken; Cinna's lie is exposed. Auguste tries to find an escape in constructing a false reality:

> Quoi? l'amour qu'en ton coeur j'a fait naître aujourd'hui
> T'emporte-t-il déjà jusqu'à mourir pour lui?

– but Emilie's frankness again forces him to accept his misdeeds:

> Songe avec quel amour j'élevai ta jeunesse.
>
> Il éleva la vôtre avec même tendresse;
> Il fut votre tuteur, et vous son assassin;
> Et vous m'avez au crime enseigné le chemin.

Livie breaks in with a surprising speech. She distinguishes between 'Octave' and 'l'Empereur', and argues that the monarch is absolute and absolved from his crimes. We need not argue whether this is appropriate to her character: Corneille is expressing an element of his theme, not giving us a character-sketch of an old empress. Nor need we be shocked by the cynicism expressed. What Livie says is that when a man changes his social rôle his past crimes cease to exist, and that if he succeeds in attaining the highest point of manhood (as absolute monarch) he can manipulate the moral facts of both past and future ('Le passé devient juste et l'avenir permis'). The point is – and this is the central theme in *Cinna* – that man, by changing himself, can change the moral universe.

Livie's speech shows the subtlety of Corneille's technique and the traps to avoid in discussing his ideas. It has significance as one indication of the play's theme, and he must make sure we take it as authoritative. Livie's address to the audience in Act IV has established her as the author's mouthpiece. She has also been established as Emilie's friend and Auguste's impartial (even unwelcome) counsellor. We therefore accept her as an arbitrator, and will take from her a correction of Emilie's attitude. The content of the speech might appear daringly immoral, but Corneille makes it acceptable by expressing it in terms of two ideas (a beneficent providence and the divine right of kings) accepted by, or at least familiar to, his audience. So much for technique. What of the ideas? There are two traps to avoid. First, we should not assume that Corneille is merely echoing contemporary beliefs. Virtually all his contemporaries believed in divine providence; by no means all would in 1641 have subscribed to an absolutist view of monarchy. Yet in Livie's speech the most extreme view of monarchy is unequivocally supported, and the idea of providence is so devalued that it seems dependent on human will. The elements in Livie's speech refer in large part to values built up by the play itself. Much of *Cinna* elaborates the theme of Auguste's progress from crime to moral awareness to the imposition of moral order on the universe: this is why Livie's speech refers to monarchy in such absolute terms. The play has also strongly suggested the relativity of moral values: hence the relative weakness of the idea of 'le ciel' in the speech.

Second, we need not think that Corneille is consciously preaching amorality: all we know of him shows that he was sincerely orthodox in his views. Primarily, it is the values which the play creates which are expressed in this speech. The play creates its own meaning. This meaning is not a preconceived message which the playwright wants to propagate: it is a meaning of the special type which results from the use of the poetic method. This, by its nature, goes beyond any conscious intention of the author, and is not expressible by any means other than the play. If Corneille were expressing in *Cinna* merely his consciously-held views, he would not have needed poetry to do so.

Against this preparation in Livie's speech for the play's resolution he sets the posturing of Cinna and Emilie. It is touching, but their gestures are ill-adapted to reality. The hollowness is emphasised by the way in which Cinna affects frankness when telling what we know to be lies:

> Seigneur, la vérité doit ici s'exprimer.

Into this charade of falsity comes Maxime, to reinforce the theme of deception. Auguste thinks him a friend, but Maxime confesses his treacheries. Just as in Act IV his confusion contrasted with Auguste's lucidity, so here his dispirited facing of facts contrasts with the positive response which Auguste will enact for us. The verse is flat and dogged:

> Pour perdre mon rival j'ai découvert sa trame.
> Euphorbe vous a feint que je m'étais noyé,
> De crainte qu'après moi vous n'eussiez envoyé.

The insistence on Euphorbe's punishment completes the unflattering contrast.

Having exposed in all its dinginess one side of the coin, Corneille can now dazzle us by displaying the other. From Maxime's hangdog lines Auguste rebounds with the most famous demonstration of resilience in Corneille:

> En est-ce assez, ô ciel! et le sort, pour me nuire,
> A-t-il quelqu'un des miens qu'il veuille encor séduire?
> Qu'il joigne à ses efforts le secours des enfers:
> Je suis maître de moi comme de l'univers;
> Je le suis, je veux l'être.

Let us not worry about whether this is an act of will (Auguste is not a real man): it is a poetic reversal, an assertion of creative energy. The lines bound forward, then check at the famous 'je veux', then again go forward. And at 'l'être' the tension is released in the creative act. The climax is savoured ('O siècles, ô mémoire, | Conservez à jamais ma dernière victoire') and then comes the full flow of creative spirit:

> Soyons amis, Cinna, c'est moi qui t'en convie:
> Comme à mon ennemi je t'ai donné la vie,
> Et malgré la fureur de ton lâche destin,
> Je te la donne encor comme à mon assassin.
> Commençons un combat qui montre par l'issue
> Qui l'aura mieux de nous ou donnée ou reçue.
> Tu trahis mes bienfaits, je les veux redoubler;

Je t'en avais comblé, je t'en veux accabler:
Avec cette beauté que je t'avais donnée,
Reçois le consulat pour la prochaine année.

The key-note is of human effort overcoming fate ('malgré la fureur de ton lâche destin'). The effect is immediate, and twofold. It is a revelation ('Je recouvre la *vue* auprès de leurs clartés:|Je *connais* mon forfait, qui me *semblait* justice'), and it is a revelation of order ('Je n'en murmure point, *il a trop de justice*' – 'De votre heureux destin c'est l'immuable loi'). In this consummation the tone is joyful, like the end of a Shakespearean comedy:

Cesse d'en retarder un oubli magnanime,
Et tous deux avec moi faites grâce a Maxime:
Il nous a trahi tous; mais ce qu'il a commis
Vous conserve innocents et me rend mes amis.

(*A Maxime*)

Reprends auprès de moi ta place accoutumée;
Rentre dans ton crédit et dans ta renommée;
Qu'Euphorbe de tous trois ait sa grâce à son tour;
Et que demain l'hymen couronne leur amour.
Si tu l'aimes encor ce sera ton supplice.[6]

Then the way in which we are intended to interpret this resolution is confirmed by Livie. It is a commonplace that in poetic drama a character may be 'depersonalised' for a specific purpose. This happens with Livie here. In the general resolution of discord it is irrelevant whether what she says is 'in character': it is enough that the verse proclaims convincingly that the order now achieved is lasting. But here again the reference to 'le ciel' is not given much weight. The emphasis is on Auguste and his triumphant recognition as a worthy ruler after 'cette action'. Among those who ratify his triumph, 'le ciel' has a pointedly less prominent place than 'les indomptés', 'Rome', and 'la postérité'.

Finally, it is Auguste who takes responsibility for the future:

J'en *accepte* l'augure, et j'*ose* l'espérer

and ends the play with two lines which firmly link the public effect with the complete knowledge and moral exertion by which order was achieved:

Et que vos conjurés entendent *publier*
Qu'Auguste *a tout appris* et *veut* tout oublier.

3

I have examined and quoted the text of *Cinna* at length for two reasons. The first is that in my view *Cinna* is Corneille's greatest achievement, and of a kind unique in his work. The second is to try and show how much we gain if we approach a poetic play through the words of the text, taking it as a sequence of lines which builds up a pattern, rather than examining as separate entities the plot, characters and verse. Attempts to sum up this pattern in a few words are hopeless with a play of the stature of *Cinna*: like every great poetic play, it is its own meaning.

This use of the poetic method is remarkable in the context: it is opposed to the naturalism implicit in neo-classicism and the critical position to which Corneille was evolving. It is more characteristic of the Renaissance, and *Cinna*, with its clear reliance on poetic speech and its relative neglect of plot and characterisation, is reminiscent of some types of Renaissance play.

This brings us to the crucial question of what kind of pattern the play embodies. *Cinna* is exceptionally stately, yet contains much that is earthy or undignified. It has an almost overpowering seriousness, yet it ends happily – and not just in the sense that no-one dies: Auguste's decision to pardon the conspirators releases a flow of benevolent energy. Finally, there is the strangeness of its moral atmosphere: the usual baroque background of divine justice plays no part in the moral resolution of the play; there is an ironical undercutting of heroic postures and their conventional motives; there is the phantasmagoric effect of the conspirators in limbo in Acts III and IV; and there is the forcefulness with which Auguste is presented as facing himself fully before he can impose his order on the world.

These features make it impossible to regard the play as tragedy in the strict sense. Yet *Cinna*, though non-tragic, is not serious in the usual naturalistic sense of dealing with social problems or individual psychology. The usual critical terms do not help us to define the quality of its seriousness.

The reference to its Renaissance quality, however, perhaps provides a clue. We have emphasised in *Cinna* the importance of the idea that the world is in a sense created by men as they go along, that it is human striving which creates the moral universe and expands its limits. This is in line with the view of Corneille as a dramatist of heroism and will-power. But it is also a theme characteristic of the Renaissance, rather than of the Counter-Reformation, with its reassertion of the stable mediaeval world-order based on theology. However we regard the transition from the Middle Ages to the Renaissance, there can be no doubt that one element is the appearance of a new mood of confidence in human endeavour, a sense that the traditional limits of the human condition can be expanded: the movement from 'un univers clos, anhistorique, intemporel et immobile' to 'un univers sans limites, ouvert, où tout est possible'.[7] This mood is echoed in a play like *Tamburlaine*, with its image of the amoral conqueror endlessly inflating himself to dominate the world. *Cinna* is much more controlled and mature, but a similar energy impels it.

This Renaissance quality is unexpected in the context of the sober moralism of most neo-classicism, especially if we regard this as largely influenced by Counter-Reformation ideals. Equally, the whole-hearted application of the poetic method in *Cinna* is out of harmony with the naturalism implicit in neo-classicism. How far Corneille was conscious of the heterodox implications of what he was doing – heterodox from the point of view of both religious and literary doctrine – we cannot know. Nevertheless, it is interesting that in his next play he not only chose an edifying religious subject but also returned to something nearer the orthodox literary form.

5

'POLYEUCTE'

I

I shall examine *Polyeucte* mainly from the point of view of its formal qualities. Before doing so, however, we should look briefly at the questions posed by its subtitle: *tragédie chrétienne*.

Whether Christian tragedy is possible has often been debated. Most critics have concluded it is not, which seems reasonable enough if we take tragedy in its strict modern sense. Christianity posits a beneficient order in the universe. A happy outcome is therefore assured in the larger sense; and in the specific case of the Christian hero, however dreadful his sufferings, the end for him is a happy ending.

There is, however, another aspect of the matter which is relevant here, and which is implicit in our discussion of neo-classical criticism. Although the concept of tragedy eludes precise definition, we may agree that tragedy in the strict sense depends on a recognition that absolute and inscrutable forces dominate man's fate. This idea can be linked with my discussion of the poetic method – that is, the realisation in expressive form of an unknown meaning which cannot be expressed in discourse. If we put this in another way, we may say that poetry – and especially tragic poetry – depends on a relationship with forces which may be felt as numinous but not necessarily as supernatural in the conventional sense. These forces may be impossible to seize conceptually, but capable of being embodied in symbolic imitations. On this view, poetry – especially tragic poetry – can claim to be a direct means of apprehending and making tangible what is deeply sensed to be true and important. The reverse of this is any view by which truth is apprehended only by non-poetic means and then becomes the raw material of poetry, which dresses it up in 'agreeable fictions'. At best, poetry is then a secondary activity.

It is here that the poet who chooses to write on a religious theme comes up against a special difficulty. To the extent that he feels he must conform to truths already set by an external authority – a dogma, a piece of sacred history, or a set of moral precepts – he is in much the same position as the naturalist who must submit his imagination to the representation of behaviour or the expression of political or scientific doctrines. However we regard the intellectual milieu in which Corneille worked, I think we must agree that the Counter-Reformation Church (like the neo-classical criticism it helped to foster) laid much emphasis on obedience to external authority. In taking a religious subject for *Polyeucte*, Corneille was therefore not necessarily taking a more poetic basis for his art than the Roman politics of *Horace* and *Cinna*. In some ways he was setting himself on a course which made the use of the poetic method more difficult.

2

A point of difficulty in *Polyeucte* has always been the conversions at the end. Pauline is a carefully-drawn character whom it is easy to take as a real (and lovable) human being. Critics have been eager to grant her eternal bliss, and have thought up reasons why Corneille was right to arrange it. Félix, however, is not so attractive, and it has often been argued that his conversion is unconvincing.

If we approach the text with the aim of inferring subtleties of character which lie behind the actual words, we can certainly find evidence that Pauline's conversion is the result of her love for her husband. She has first tried to love him because her duty required it. Then she finds she really loves him, and uses her duty as a rationalisation and excuse. She then follows him into Christianity, but the operation of grace is the explanation she gives herself for what is really her discovery of the depth of her love, and is just as much a rationalisation as the operation of duty was earlier. This view reduces the play to human terms, but only by disintegrating it. An interpretation in terms of human love reduces Corneille's insistence on the importance of grace to a mere pious excrescence, and makes the conversion of Félix an arbitrary appendage.

But if we look at *Polyeucte* as a poetic play, with a central meaning which plot, character and verse combine to express, another interpretation is possible. On this view, the rôle of grace is central. The play shows two worlds: the everyday world of fallen man, and the metaphysical world which can redeem man, and of which he can be made a part by grace. The action of the play is then how the second, divine, world erupts into the first, mundane, world and irradiates it.

This conception is strongly present in Corneille's text. The first scene brings before us Polyeucte and Néarque. The first words give the clue: the thoughts and emotions of Pauline and her world are presented as insignificant:

Quoi! vous vous arrêtez aux songes d'une femme!
De si faibles sujets troublent cette grande âme!
Et ce coeur tant de fois dans la guerre éprouvé
S'alarme d'un péril qu'une femme a rêvé!

If we take the tone and quality of the verse as our guide, the divergence between the world of grace and the mundane world is clearly
stated. Polyeucte's references to his love for Pauline are in conventional terms ('Sur mes pareils, Néarque, un bel oeil est bien fort').
This is the language of cultivated society – of 'the world' as opposed to
the religious order. To Corneille, this *beau monde* certainly has virtues,
including the virtue of elegance, but its perceptions are banal compared with those of religion. This is surely his point here: the earthly
world of Pauline is ruled by banal forms of thought and feeling, and he
uses the jargon of the 'beau monde' to express this. By contrast, the
vitality and importance of the world of grace are brought before us
unmistakably:

Et Dieu, qui tient votre âme et vos jours dans sa main,
Promet-il à vos voeux de le pouvoir demain?
Il est toujours tout juste et tout bon; mais sa grâce
Ne descend pas toujours avec même efficace . . .
Dieu ne veut point d'un coeur où le monde domine . . .

Enunciation of the rôle of divine grace takes up a large part of this
first scene, and the length, the placing and the forthright energy of these
passages leave no doubt that they carry the main dramatic accent.

When Pauline enters with her confidante, the tone changes. Critics
have indeed sometimes been surprised at her disillusioned attitude:

Tu vois, ma Stratonice, en quel siècle nous sommes:
Voilà notre pouvoir sur les esprits des hommes;
Voilà ce qui nous reste, et l'ordinaire effet
De l'amour qu'on nous offre, et des voeux qu'on nous fait.

But Pauline is not simply being presented as an adorable heroine, and
Corneille is here presenting a part of his theme. The substance of
Pauline's speech is that in the mundane world social conventions are
dishonest – insincere protestations which cover egoism; the speech
suggests peevishness and small-mindedness. This mundane tone is quite
in keeping with the rest of the scene.

Pauline's narration of her dream raises the tone a little, but there is
something arbitrary and confused about it. The only impressive line is
one that refers to Polyeucte's death:

Le sang de Polyeucte a satisfait leurs rages.

In contrast to the contrived horrors of the rest of the speech, this line has a mystical tone – though we do not yet grasp its significance.

With the entrance of Félix the tone is lowered still further. His dismay is frankly comic:

> Ah! regret qui me tue,
> De n'avoir pas aimé la vertu toute nue!
> Ah! Pauline, en effet, tu m'a trop obéi;
> Ton courage était bon, ton devoir l'a trahi.

This scene brings yet more narrative. Albin tells of Sévère's heroism and favour with the emperor. The whole tone of the speech is curiously banal. The repeated epithets ('cette grande journée'; 'ses hauts faits'; 'ce prince généreux'; 'l'âme ravie'; 'tant de beaux faits'; 'une amour infinie') are conventional. The constructions are vague and confused (Où l'Empereur captif, par sa main dégagé | Rassura son parti déjà découragé, | Tandis que sa vertu succomba sous le nombre'). The transitions are awkward ('Il en fit prendre soin, la cure en fut secrète; | Et comme au bout d'un mois sa santé fut parfaite'; 'La faveur de Décie en fut le digne prix. | De nouveau l'on combat, et nous sommes surpris'). But in *Polyeucte* Corneille is obviously at the height of his powers, and if we want to know why he is writing like this there is a simple explanation. In the first scene of the act, Polyeucte, though still hankering after the banal everyday world, is called to participate in the higher world of grace. The overwhelming élan and importance of this higher world are brought before us in the superior vitality of the verse. By contrast, Corneille goes on to show us what the everyday world is like: a world of disillusionment and cynical manoeuvring, where the elegancies of courtship mask lust and selfishness, where filial duty is an untrustworthy guide, and where even the heroism and success of Sévère seem lack-lustre. The tone and quality of the verse are pitched to express this. The only point where the higher, metaphysical, world breaks in is in Pauline's dream; but the lower world is not yet ready to receive it, and the dream appears an arbitrary riddle, illumined only by the (misunderstood) promise of redemption by blood.

This opposition of two worlds is forcibly represented by the structure of the act. Corneille does not start with a recital of past events, then go on to something more elevated: if he did, we should see only a normal progression of dramatic interest, and would not give due weight to the dullness of the one world and the vitality of the other. Instead, he starts with a forceful enactment of the vitality of the world of grace, then goes on to less intense scenes containing those recitals of the past that normally come first. This reversal of the usual order throws into prominence the pettiness of the mundane world. This interpretation is borne out by Act II. The act opens with Sévère, then goes on to his interview with Pauline. These scenes are written at fairly low pressure, and are full of this sort of thing:

> Pourrai-je voir Pauline, et rendre à ses beaux yeux
> L'hommage souverain que l'on va rendre aux Dieux?
>
> Adieu, trop vertueux objet, et trop charmant. –
> – Adieu, trop malheureux et trop parfait amant.

It is not enough to say that to Corneille and his first audiences these phrases were fresh and appealing (though this may be true). Corneille is presenting the attitude of Pauline and Sévère as touching and estimable, but only by worldly standards. In comparison with the higher world of grace, the lower world is at best insipid; and this is what the verse expresses.

The point is made sharply when Polyeucte returns from baptism. The verse takes on a confident vigour, and when Pauline has left the tone soars higher still: after the languors of the Pauline/Sévère scene, with its emphasis on 'soupir'/'mourir', we are swept forward by the vigour of the divine world. To arrange this, Corneille makes Néarque falter and have to be swept on by Polyeucte: the scene between them thus enacts the effect of divine grace on fallen man:

> Dieu fait part, au besoin, de sa force infinie . . .
> Abandonnons nos jours à cette ardeur céleste;
> Faisons triompher Dieu; qu'il dispose du reste!

In Act III, the emphasis is on the reaction of the mundane world to Polyeucte's act of faith. Stratonice is allowed to denounce Christianity, and Félix is shown in a more sordid and comical light than before:

> Que je suis malheureux! . . .
> J'entre en des sentiments qui ne sont pas croyables . . .
> J'en ai même de bas, et qui me font rougir.

The world of grace does not shine on this dark world, except in two places. Pauline reverts to her preoccupation with her dream, which keeps before us the idea of a second, supernatural, world which guides the first, and Stratonice reports Polyeucte's confession of faith. Here the opposition is at its most obvious. Stratonice has nothing but contempt for the Christians, but Polyeucte's reported words have a reso-

nance and energy which testify to the superior values which they
embody.

Act IV brings the most intense collision of the two worlds. Polyeucte's lyrical soliloquy specifically sets the divine world above and in
opposition to the other: this is at once its theme and purpose:

> Monde, pour moi tu n'as plus rien;
> Je porte en un coeur tout chrétien
> Une flamme toute divine;
> Et je ne regarde Pauline
> Que comme un obstacle à mon bien . . .
> Et mes yeux, éclairés des célestes lumières,
> Ne trouvent plus aux siens leurs grâces coutumières.

The confrontation with Pauline takes up this contrast between the
fallen and the divine worlds:

> J'ai de l'ambition, mais plus noble et plus belle:
> Cette grandeur périt, j'en veux une immortelle,
> Un bonheur assuré, sans mesure et sans fin,
> Au-dessus de l'envie, au-dessus du destin.

Polyeucte appeals again and again in grave and ringing verse to the
reality of this other, more vital, world overseeing the mundane world:

> Quel Dieu! –
>   – Tout, beau, Pauline, il entend vos paroles,
> Et ce n'est pas un Dieu comme vos Dieux frivoles . . .
>
> Mais si, dans ce séjour de gloire et de lumière,
> Ce Dieu tout juste et bon peut souffrir ma prière,
> S'il y daigne écouter un conjugal amour,
> Sur votre aveuglement il répandra le jour.

The climax comes in a sharp exchange which echoes the insipid anti-
phonies of Pauline and Sévère in Act II, but here the opposition is
between two sets of values, not two sets of phrases, and the verse is
more rapid and intense:

> Imaginations!
>   – Célestes vérités!
> – Etrange aveuglement!
>   – Eternelles clartés!
> – Tu préfères la mort à l'amour de Pauline!
> – Vous préférez le monde à la bonté divine!

Polyeucte refuses Pauline's pleas to him to recant, and even relinquishes her to Sévère. Félix still keeps to his cynical course, and in Act V Polyeucte goes to his death. But by his martyrdom the others are redeemed: Pauline and Félix are converted, and the conversion of Sévère is foreshadowed.

3

This reading of *Polyeucte* as a poetic play with an inner action – of the divine world bending to redeem the mundane world – is certainly justified by the text. In my view it not only explains much of the vitality of the play but also clears up several difficulties – notably the evident variations of tone and quality of the verse. Nevertheless, it does not clear up all the difficulties. My interpretation does not quite fit the text at all points – especially in the last part of Act IV and parts of Act V: the points at which the more naturalistic interpretation that Pauline is converted by her love for Polyeucte fits very well. This suggests that the play shows an unresolved discord not only in values but in technique. It raises again the problem present in *Le Cid*: whether Corneille has failed to resolve a contradiction between the poetic and naturalistic modes. To decide this, I will consider his presentation of the mundane world, particularly in the last part of Act IV and in Act V. This subject may be divided into three. First, there is the presentation of the values of the mundane world. Secondly, there is the method of characterisation, especially of the persons belonging to the mundane world. Thirdly, the point to which I finally return, there is the presentation of the conversions at the end.

Part of my argument has been that the values of Pauline and Sévère (and *a fortiori* of Félix) are presented as inferior, and that this is expressed largely in the changing quality of the verse. The characteristic of this mundane world is deceit. This is clearest in the self-deluding hypocrisy of Félix, which is contrasted with the directness of Polyeucte:

> N'en riez point, Félix, il sera votre juge.
> Un chrétien ne craint rien, ne dissimule rien:
> Aux yeux de tout le monde il est toujours chrétien.

But the deception goes further. Pauline is willing, for most of the play, to attribute her love for Polyeucte to duty. As the action progresses, she is brought to realise that her love is genuine. Nevertheless, she makes the same patently sophistical excuse for continuing to love him after his crime:

Je l'aimai par devoir: ce devoir dure encore . . .
Et si de tant d'amour tu peux être ébahie,
Apprends que mon devoir ne dépend point du sien:
Qu'il y manque, s'il veut, je dois faire le mien.

This lack of moral directness goes with a willingness to fall in with conventional manners and phraseology – as in most of her scenes with Sévère. This willingness veils the depths of emotion and suggests, not quite insincerity, but at least banality. Linked with this, again, is a tendency to small-mindedness. Corneille himself seems to have regarded Félix as short-sighted rather than wicked, and there is more than a trace of the pettiness of Félix in Pauline:

Vous n'avez point ici d'ennemi que vous-même.

Voilà de vos chrétiens les ridicules songes.

Est-ce là ce beau feu? Sont-ce là tes serments?
Témoignes-tu pour moi les moindres sentiments? . . .
Et ton coeur insensible à ces tristes appas,
Se figure un bonheur où je ne serais pas!

Corneille stresses another aspect of the philosophy of the mundane world, its tendency to think of pedestrian or over-cynical reasons for everything. The machiavellian subtleties of Félix and the sophistries of Pauline show this tendency. Polyeucte consistently opposes to this feeble and fallible power of reasoning the supra-rational power of grace:

Mais que sert de parler de ces trésors cachés
A des esprits que Dieu n'a pas encore touchés?

Elle est un don du ciel, et non de la raison.

So far, we may agree that Corneille has succeeded in presenting a convincing mundane world on which grace can act: the qualities of this world are not so much mistaken as limited. But in the second half of Act IV he veers; and here we approach the crux of any evaluation of the play. Polyeucte resigns Pauline to Sévère, and leaves them. Sévère can only embark on another round of gallantries:

Pour moi, si mes destins, un peu plus tôt propices,
Eussent de votre hymen honoré mes services,
Je n'aurais adoré que l'éclat de vos yeux,
J'en aurais fait mes rois, j'en aurais fait mes Dieux;
On m'aurait mis en poudre, on m'aurait mis en cendre,
Avant que . . .

This is insipid, and meant to be. Pauline brushes it aside, and her verse takes on a quite different intensity:

> Sévère, connaissez Pauline toute entière.
> Mon Polyeucte touche à son heure dernière . . .
> Vous en êtes la cause, encor qu'innocemment . . .
> Vous êtes généreux; soyez-le jusqu'au bout.
> Mon père est en état de vous accorder tout . . .
> Je sais que c'est beaucoup que ce que je demande . . .
> Souvenez-vous enfin que vous êtes Sévère.
> Adieu; résolvez seul ce que vous voulez faire;
> Si vous n'êtes pas tel que j'ose l'espérer,
> Pour vous priser encor je le veux ignorer.

This passage is remarkable in two ways. First, it shows an honesty of feeling new in Pauline, and appeals to a similar honesty in Sévère. This is far removed from the earlier presentation of worldly values as petty and limited: here, they appear valid in their own right. Secondly, the tone of the verse lacks the banality of the previous Sévère/ Pauline scenes, and has the firmness and energy which have up to now marked the presentation of the divine world.

Corneille goes further. In the last scene of the act Sévère presents his values at length. Its verse is clear and forceful: there is none of the languor of Sévère's earlier utterances. Furthermore, it repeats and amplifies the point that the despised mundane world has positive standards which in no way depend on divine grace. Finally, it implies a set of values not only opposed to, but incompatible with, those of the divine world of grace. Sévère is willing to defend Polyeucte for purely secular motives. His philosophy is tolerance. He defends the Christians on the grounds of their virtues, not their doctrines. The sceptical and urbane tone of the speech is far removed from Polyeucte's intransigence: we feel a breath of cool air from the eighteenth century, for which Christianity, with its fanaticism and dogmatism, was not so much untrue as inelegant. Sévère inhabits a world whose air is unfavourable to enthusiasm. This attitude is incompatible with the interaction between the fallen world and the world of grace underlying the play.

We may argue that Corneille is showing the true dramatic touch in giving each side its due. But a dramatist is making a work of art which he has to bring to some form of unity, not arguing a case which can be left unresolved. He fails in craftsmanship if he introduces an element which he cannot assimilate into his pattern. Corneille is in fact moving towards the fragmented naturalist method, which insists that each component should be developed independently of the whole; but, for the moment, our concern is simply to establish that he has here admitted, even emphasised, an element that cannot be assimilated.

This brings us to Corneille's treatment of character. In general, he follows the common poetic method of making what we need to know explicit in the verse, but he clearly departs somewhat from this norm in characterising Pauline: when we consider her lines we are often drawn into deducing what are her personal attitudes behind them. Indeed, there is a difference between the characterisation of those belonging to the higher world (Polyeucte and Néarque) and those belonging to the lower world (Pauline in particular, but also Félix and Sévère). The representatives of the higher world, especially Polyeucte, bear the main accent of the play, and are given the most positive verse. Polyeucte is a poetic creation, full of human interest because of the profound human experience which he embodies, but he is not the most fully-developed figure in the play, in the sense of being a 'fully-rounded character', as the phrase goes. The development of his rôle is not to be thought of in terms of individual psychology, but as a progressive revelation of the power of the world of grace. The treatment of the mundane characters is different: we are invited to see them as individuals and to be interested in their personal motives and difficulties, rather than in the aspect of the meaning expressed by the play which they as dramatic figures represent.

This difference is crucial. With Polyeucte, as in much poetic drama, the focus of interest is the part which his rôle embodies of the total pattern which the play exists to express. The values by which we judge him are those which our experience of the read or acted text enables us to appreciate. If we are invited to regard the characters as real people, however, we judge them not so much by what the text says as by what we think are their real motives; by our ideas of what is psychologically plausible in everyday life; and by the unmodified values we bring with us. By concentrating on realistic representation, and by leaving so much to inferences by us in terms of our habitual values whilst neglecting the expression of any overall meaning, the author is leaving us to alter the pattern of his play according to our own lights to an amazing extent. In this case, he is making it easy for us to sympathise with the charming Pauline and Sévère, and to find the fanatical Polyeucte tiresome.

Pauline's character in particular is presented in this naturalistic way. We are drawn into seeing things from her point of view by the urgency and conviction with which her grief is expressed, especially in the last half of Act IV. Much the same applies to Sévère, and again this is especially evident at the end of Act IV, where his decision to help Polyeucte is strongly presented to us as painful and noble. Félix is not so obviously sympathetic, but at several points Corneille goes out of his way to make us sympathise with him as well:

> J'aime ce malheureux que j'ai choisi pour gendre.
>
> Il y va de ma charge, il y va de ma vie:
> Ainsi tantôt pour lui je m'expose au trépas,
> Et tantôt je le perds pour en me perdre pas.

The question is not simply whether we find Pauline and Sévère (or even Félix) humanly appealing. The important points are that Corneille deliberately adopts a mode of presentation which draws our sympathy towards them; that this mode is antithetical to the predominantly poetic mode of the play; and that the sympathy he attracts to them runs counter to the poetic theme he is expressing.

We now come to the conversions in Act V. Pauline's is obviously the more important. I have already argued that it can easily be taken as psychologically plausible, but only at the risk of devaluing the importance of grace. It is here that Corneille's naturalistic treatment of Pauline has its unbalancing effect: it makes the natural explanation seem not only plausible but immediately appealing, and so works against the poetic pattern.

The case of Félix shows still more sharply the effects of the change of method. He announces his conversion baldly, and without preparation. As Corneille says in his *Examen*, this is a miracle – an intervention of the divine world in the mundane world. This is quite compatible with the poetic pattern, and in a consistently poetic play would seem a logical development. The difficulty is that the partially naturalistic treatment has prepared us to judge events by mundane standards. We perceive – quite correctly by these standards – that Pauline may be carried away by enthusiasm, but not the timid and cynical Félix.

Finally, what of Sévère? Corneille only hints at his conversion:

> Sans doutes vos chrétiens, qu'on persécute en vain,
> Ont quelque chose en eux qui surpasse l'humain . . .
> Et peut-être qu'un jour je les connaîtrai mieux.

If we could take this seriously, it would complete the underlying poetic pattern. Grace has irrupted into the mundane world, transfiguring first Polyeucte, then Pauline, then Félix, then Sévère. The trouble is that the lines are difficult to take seriously: Sévère has been presented to us as living in a noble and self-sufficient world quite removed from a martyr's enthusiasm. The tone ('Sans doute' . . . 'peut-être') is not enthusiastic, and is further modified by what follows:

> J'approuve cependant que chacun ait ses Dieux,
> Qu'il les serve à sa mode, et sans peur de la peine.

We are reminded that Sévère's attitude is one of urbane tolerance, and in this context his reference to his conversion is in danger of seeming no more than politeness.[1] Corneille has invited us to judge Sévère by these standards, and it is too late for us to change our viewpoint.

The crux, of course, is not whether we think Sévère is right and Polyeucte is wrong. It is that Corneille has written a play which in its values and method is centred round Polyeucte's world, and has then compromised by introducing (in Sévère, but also in Pauline and Félix) a different and incompatible viewpoint presented by a different method. The ending appears arbitrary because it cannot resolve this confusion.

4

This confusion of method and purpose makes it impossible to endorse the view that *Polyeucte* is Corneille's masterpiece. This title belongs to *Cinna*, as Corneille's contemporaries perceived. My argument has been that in *Polyeucte*, as in *Le Cid*, Corneille is hesitating between the poetic and naturalistic modes (in the senses which we discussed in chapter 1), and that this hesitation destroys the coherence of the plays. *Cinna* is very different. It is not tragic in the strict sense, because it lacks the sense we find so powerfully in tragedy that there are absolute limits which hedge in the human condition. On the contrary, it seems to centre on the theme that apparently unyielding limits can be pushed back by human effort. From the formal point of view, however, the important feature is that it is rigorously organised to express this central meaning, and the separate elements of plot and character are not developed for their own sakes. It is because of its perfect consistency that I consider it Corneille's masterpiece.

Wherever our preferences lie, there is no doubt that after *Cinna* and *Polyeucte* there is a change in the quality of Corneille's work. It has been suggested that Corneille, having found his formula of heroic drama, could only run through the four types of heroism that interested him – chivalrous, patriotic, political and religious – and then fall into self-parody. Maurens has claimed that from *Le Cid* to *Polyeucte* Corneille's sole aim was to express the neo-stoical ideal of *générosité* favoured by Richelieu, and that Richelieu's death made him change tack.[2] This seems very schematic. If we interpret the development of Corneille's drama in terms of the opposition between poetic and naturalistic techniques, a more complex, and I hope more credible, pattern emerges.

Corneille began with realistic comedies, and this vein of realism continues through his work. Nevertheless, a preoccupation with themes and images more appropriate to the poetic approach soon begins to emerge. With *Médée*, he turns to Senecan modes in his search for a form to embody these new preoccupations, but cannot reconcile the opposite impulses towards naturalism and poetry. In *Le Cid* this conflict is more nearly reconciled (largely by muting the tragic note) but the inner contradiction remains. In *Horace* Corneille achieves a more consistent poetic pattern,[3] but still has difficulty in reconciling his *action* (the poetic theme he is enacting) with his *intrigue* (the characters and incidents of the play and the inferences we draw from them as people and events). In *Cinna* he finally achieves a perfect expression: he finds a form which is poetic but untragic, and which enables him to write in the poetic mode with full conviction. But, as nineteenth-century critics complained, this rigour meant sacrificing some popular luxuries of plot and characterisation which are possible in the naturalistic mode. Very rarely, the poetic method may encompass some of these luxuries, and for a while Corneille pursues a double ideal: he wants to write a poetic play with the rigour of *Cinna* and the picturesque naturalness of *Le Cid*.

These two aims are obviously difficult to reconcile, and in *Polyeucte* they clash. The mainly poetic presentation of the Polyeucte/Néarque world is brought sharply up against the mainly naturalistic presentation of the Pauline/Sévère/Félix world, and in Act V their incompatibility is apparent.

Perhaps Corneille felt that he was pursuing impossibly divergent aims, for after *Polyeucte* he abandons the attempt to advance on all fronts at once. Instead, he embarks on a series of plays in which he exploits, more or less in isolation, one or two individual elements of the ideal dramatic totality, and does so with extraordinary thoroughness. *Pompée* is a magnificent play, but is quite different in feeling from *Polyeucte*. From the technical point of view, Corneille's strategy in it is fairly clear. Not only is there no attempt to express a central meaning, but there is little effort to provide an exciting plot or subtlety of characterisation. Everything is staked on a bravura display of speechmaking: deliberative, narrative and pathetic. In later plays, he develops other elements to virtuoso extremes. This change in aim is reflected in changes in the quality of the verse, which on the whole is markedly inferior in these middle-period works to that in the plays from *Le Cid* to *Polyeucte*. This brings us to a number of questions about Corneille's use of verse, and the use of verse in drama generally.

6

CORNEILLE'S VERSE

I

Although Corneille's verse has a wide range, there is one particular tone which we call 'Cornelian'. Some typical lines come to mind:

> Qu'importe de mon coeur, si je sais mon devoir.
>
> *(Sertorius, I.iii)*
>
> Et sur mes passions ma raison souveraine
>
> *(Polyeucte, II.ii)*
>
> Je suis maître de moi, comme de l'univers.
>
> *(Cinna, V.iii)*

This 'Cornelian' quality is not so much a quality of the style as of the attitude behind it. Corneille's verse is full of words like 'devoir' and 'raison', and we associate these abstractions with the subordination of impulse to reflection or will-power. It is true that the attitudes apparent in the above lines take on a more humane quality if we look at them in context. Nevertheless, the impression remains that these somewhat harsh attitudes and their embodiment in ringing but inhuman lines are typical of Corneille. It is but a step from these qualities to bravado, or to the unmoral display of sheer energy, in verse which, however exhilarating, has not quite the same resonance:

> Tombe sur moi le ciel, pourvu que je me venge!
>
> *(Rodogune, V.i)*
>
> Je suis maître, je parle; allez, obéissez.
>
> *(Sertorius, V.vi)*

From this it is not far to lines and gestures that are mere rant and attitudinising:

> Je sais qu'il m'appartient, ce trône où tu te sieds,
> Que c'est à moi d'y voir tout le monde à mes pieds;
> Mais comme il est encor teint du sang de mon pére,
> S'il n'est lavé du tien, il ne saurait me plaire;
> Et ta mort, que mes voeux s'efforcent de hâter,
> Est l'unique degré par où j'y veux monter:
> Voilà quelle je suis, et quelle je veux être.
> Qu'un autre t'aime en père, ou te redoute en maître,

78

Le coeur de Pulchérie est trop haut et trop franc
Pour craindre ou pour flatter le bourreau de son sang.

(Héraclius, I.ii)

It is too simple to define the 'Cornelian' quality by the simple criterion of the apparent values expressed. But the contrast between these good and bad 'Cornelian' lines does point to something – the different degrees of solidity which they express.

Turnell has finely said that in his best verse Corneille limits and defines: he sets a particular feeling firmly against its background. Turnell quotes some of the famous lines ('Il est doux de revoir les murs de la patrie'; 'Tous les monstres d'Egypte ont leurs temples dans Rome'.) and tellingly contrasts them with outwardly similar lines by Racine which show the Racinian (but quite un-Cornelian) allusiveness and sense of indefinite extension.[1] We may look more closely at the passage from which the line in *Sertorius* is quoted:

> Il est doux de revoir les murs de la patrie:
> C'est elle par ma voix, Seigneur, qui vous en prie;
> C'est Rome . . .
>   – Le séjour de votre potentat,
> Qui n'a que ses fureurs pour maximes d'Etat!
> Je n'appelle plus Rome un enclos de murailles,
> Que ses proscriptions comblent de funérailles;
> Ces murs, dont le destin fut autrefois si beau,
> N'en sont que la prison, ou plutôt le tombeau;
> Mais, pour revivre ailleurs dans sa première force,
> Avec les faux Romains elle a fait plein divorce;
> Et, comme autour de moi j'ai tout ces vrais appuis,
> Rome n'est plus dans Rome, elle est toute où je suis.

(Sertorius, III.i)

The lines are beautiful, but verse is more than that: it is a means of expressing what could not otherwise be expressed, and the whole movement and meaning of it are what decide its quality. Here the movement and meaning are part of a perfect and very Cornelian unity.

The passage starts with a definite statement. 'Patrie' has a precise geographical connotation. This is emphasised by the extreme concreteness of the idea: to see walls. The firm, clear words and rhythm underline the solidity of the statement: we feel a strong and stable world. Then, immediately, we get a veering towards inflation:

> C'est elle par ma voix, Seigneur, qui vous en prie;
> C'est Rome.

79

The excited rhythm, the repetition, the personification, give the lines a sensuous, slightly hysterical emphasis: there begins a seductive but tendentious turning away from reality.

The accent falls on 'Rome': a talisman of order and clarity in Corneille's world. The naming of the symbol of order at the climax of an appeal to a false order marks a turning-point; Sertorius breaks in with a blunt version of the truth which abruptly counteracts the inflation:

> Le séjour de votre potentat,
> Qui n'a que ses fureurs pour maximes d'Etat.

In four lines we have in rapid succession three versions of the truth: the sober idealism of a reliance on decent human feeling and civilised order; the politician's over-rhetorical gloss on it; and then the exposure of the sordid side of the politician's picture. The moral terms of reference have been explored and defined, and Sertorius is given eight lines which are among the summits of Corneille's poetry. They are built around two pairs of opposites: at the rhetorical level, 'elle' (the personified Rome of Pompée) and 'murs' (the 'murs de la patrie'), and at a deeper level the contrast between abstractness and concreteness, between appearance and reality.

> Je n'appelle plus Rome un enclos de murailles

Here the 'elle' (abstract) is balanced against the 'murs' (concrete), but the 'plus' suggests the movement in time – the balance is shifting.

> Que ses proscriptions comblent de funérailles

The abstract 'proscriptions' is represented concretely as 'filling up' the 'enclos de murailles'; 'combler', so frequently used in a vague sense, is here used with its full literal meaning.

> Ces murs, dont le destin fut autrefois si beau

Here again the balance shifts, and very markedly: the 'walls', hitherto concrete and presented as desirable adjuncts of Pompée's Rome, are linked with an abstraction – and a past abstraction at that.

> N'en sont que la prison, ou plutôt le tombeau

Here the emphasis again shifts to the concrete, but now the concrete objects are undesirable and are associated with Pompée and his party.

> Mais, pour revivre ailleurs dans sa première force,
> Avec les faux Romains elle a fait plein divorce

Here the swing is obvious. Rome ('elle') is now on the side of Sertorius. Pompée's party is reproached as being 'false'. The point is sharpened by the use of the sexual metaphor: Pompée has had to divorce his wife because of his political ambitions, and she has passed over to Sertorius's party. But these lines are not just a fierce indictment of Pompée; Corneille's awareness of the complexity of the situation is keener than that. The use of 'faux Romains' reminds us that Sertorius also has his false followers: Perpenna, sent to crush Sertorius, has been obliged to join him, but is even now plotting to kill him. This prepares us for the next two lines, which demonstrate both the superiority of Sertorius over Pompée and the weakness of Sertorius's position.

> Et, comme autour de moi j'ai tous ces vrais appuis

The reversal is now complete: Sertorius now has 'around him' (like an 'enclosure of walls') these 'supports' (a striking use of both the literal and metaphorical uses of 'appuis'). But these 'true' supports are not in fact 'true': they are as false as the 'faux Romains'.

Finally, the next line completes Sertorius's triumph and exposes its hollowness:

> Rome n'est plus dans Rome, elle est toute où je suis.

Rome has moved from Rome to Sertorius, and from the physical 'murs de la patrie' to a pure idealised Rome, remote from the rhetorically idealised Rome of Pompée. But at the same time there is a change in the way in which this concept of the Rome of Sertorius is validated. In the line before, Sertorius's Rome was the real Rome, because it possessed all the 'true supports'. But these 'true supports' are in fact false. The true validation and support of Sertorius's Rome is Sertorius himself: 'elle est toute où *je* suis'. The passage works at all levels, as drama and as poetry. It enacts the movement is describes: we feel, almost literally, that Rome is set before us concretely, then volatilised into an ideal, then transported to Sertorius's side, then made concrete again; but at the same time the undercurrents in the verse warn us of the weakness of Sertorius's position. The passage is not a statement of the situation but an enactment of it; and this enactment is achieved by a complex interweaving of the concrete and the abstract.

This brings us very near to an essential Cornelian quality: the abstract and the concrete are felt as equally real. Corneille's verse makes frequent use of antithesis, and he will often use to balance each other an emotion, or an abstract value, and a concrete reality; and in so doing he makes frequent use of words which bear at once a physical, concrete meaning and an extended or abstract meaning:

> Qu'importe de mon *coeur* si je sais mon *devoir*
>> (*Sertorius*, I.iii)
>
> S'il ne s'en fallait point l'*Arménie* et mon *coeur*
>> (*Nicomède*, III.ii)
>
> Avec tout son *orgueil* et sa *Lusitanie*
>> (*Sertorius*, V.vi)
>
> Prêtez-moi votre *main*, je vous donne l'*Empire*
>> (*Pulchérie*, V. iii)

The dangers of this method are obvious. The movement of the verse is extremely impressive when (as in the passage from *Sertorius*) it corresponds to the movement of the underlying situation. The abstract words are impressive as long as their solidity is demonstrated to us. But antithesis easily degenerates into a mannerism, and the manipulation of big words into rant. The typical 'Cornelian' line depends on our conviction that it represents real experience, really thought-out and felt intellectual and moral values. When Corneille's interest is concentrated less on communicating experience, and more on contriving strong theatrical effects, he rarely provides the substance to sustain this conviction. The temptation then is for him to use words like 'honneur' and 'devoir' as ready-made counters, which represented real values for contemporaries, but no longer have the same associations for us. This, I think, does much to explain the weakness of a good deal of his verse in the plays following *Polyeucte*.

There is, however, another possibility. In his later works at least, what we take to be bad 'Cornelian' verse may be good verse in a different mode. It is a reasonable supposition that the verse in a play will vary in its procedures and quality according to its functions. I will therefore pause to consider what the functions of verse in drama may be.

2

When we speak of the decline of poetic drama since the Renaissance, we need to distinguish between the decrease in the elaboration of dramatic dialogue and the decline of the poetic method. Verse is normally more 'ornamental' than prose, but the degree of the surface ornamentation has nothing to do with whether a play is poetic or not. The issue is not ornament but function: whether the function of the language is to carry and control the meaning of the play, or to represent what (according to the chosen level of convention) the characters might be presumed to say in similar situations in real life.

The decrease in literary elaboration is obvious, but so is the shift in the importance of the means of expression and of the contributions to the play as performed. In a Renaissance play, the verse not only conveys its meanings with precision, but also in a way which is controlled by the author rather than the actors, director or designer. In a modern naturalistic play, the language is primarily representational, and to that extent less precise. The significance of the words depends on careful placing – which is the playwright's business – but also very largely on the expressions of the actor and the context of sets, lighting, rhythm and movement in which they are set by the director and designer.

As an example of the poetic method, we will take a famous moment from *Le Cid*, Act IV, Scene ii. The Infanta asks Chimène no longer to seek vengeance on Rodrigue, whose exploits against the Moors have made him the hero of the hour. Chimène replies:

> Quoique pour ce vainqueur mon amour s'intéresse,
> Quoiqu'un peuple l'adore et qu'un roi le caresse,
> Qu'il soit environné des plus vaillants guerriers,
> J'irai sous mes cyprès accabler ses lauriers.

Whatever Corneille's hesitations in parts of *Le Cid*, these lines are a fine example of the poetic method. Even in isolation, they are splendid as poetry, but their value is not just that they entertain us with four lines of beautiful and appropriate verse. We can say that they tell us a good deal about what Corneille is presenting as Chimène's state of mind. The first three lines have a triumphant lilt and strong sexual undertones ('adore', 'caresse') which make them almost a panegyric by Chimène on her lover, and suggest that her love is in fact stronger than her desire for vengeance. We may even (though, in my view, this is unwise) claim that the antithesis in the fourth line indicates a frantic effort by Chimène to whip up her flagging enthusiasm for revenge. It is unwise because it would mean taking the lines too much as an expression of Chimène's 'character'. We often slip into the assumption that revealing character is the main purpose of drama. But character, like plot, is a means of expression; and the sixteenth- and seventeenth-century dramatists will usually, if they are choosing how to make an important point, choose to make it directly by means of a statement in the verse, because this is the most powerful and subtle means of expression they have. If we look at Chimène's speech from this point of view, we can see that these four lines do more than embody her presumed feelings. They crystallise the basic motif of the play: love and youthful élan brought up sharp against a strong barrier. Their rhythm itself does this: the first three lines surge forward and then culminate in a fourth line which tells us that this youthful passion is itself set against the satisfaction of that passion. The imagery (in the literal sense of the pictures evoked) sums up the situation: on the one hand, the king, courtiers and people crowding round Rodrigue; on the other, Chimène, alone (not only isolated from the crowd but also bereft of her father and cut off from Rodrigue). The victor's laurels are more than a pale figure of speech: conquerors actually wore them or were pictured wearing them. 'Cyprès' was also a concrete reality: the word denotes not only the tree (a classical symbol of mourning) but also a material of which mourning garments were made. We can imagine Rodrigue and Chimène as actually wearing 'laurels' and 'cypress'. The yoking of the two words sets the lovers before us, side by side, united but separated. These four lines express in small figure the action of the play.

A naturalistic playwright may, of course, use words with great skill and sensitivity, but typically he will rely not so much on what is actually said as on our inferences about the characters who say it, and to some extent on such extraneous factors as stage sets, lighting or sound-effects. The words themselves are no longer the prime carriers of the meaning, and no longer control the performance so exactly.

The basic difference in the function of language in poetic as distinct from naturalistic drama does not mean that there is only one form of poetic drama. To some extent, the poetic and naturalistic modes are often mixed, and there are some plays which are predominantly poetic in mode but which can be forced into naturalistic categories. There are poetic plays where the incidents are sufficiently plausible, the characters sufficiently lifelike and the verse sufficiently unemphatic to favour the illusion. We shall argue later, for instance, that Racine's *Bérénice* comes within this category.

On the other hand, there is a large group of poetic plays which cannot by any critical violence be understood in naturalistic terms. Examples would be the surviving plays of Aeschylus, the earlier plays of Marlowe, the plays of Montchrestien, and many modern works, such as *Calvary* or *Murder in the Cathedral*. In this form of drama, the primacy of the verse is unmistakable, often with a more or less complete disregard of what we understand as plot and character. Plays of this type often fall into a sequence of speeches, each precisely designed to make a separate and specific emotional effect. Sometimes the tendency is carried to the point where the emphasis seems to fall on the individual speech as a set-piece in its own right. Griffiths has demonstrated how this approach is at the basis of the plays of Montchrestien, and Clemen has shown how deeply it is embedded in Elizabethan drama.[2] We lack a term for this type of speech and for the type of drama in which the meaning is carried and controlled by the individual speeches and the relation between them, rather than a total pattern in which plot and character are also important. For convenience, I will use the term 'Senecan', partly because it seems to me that Seneca's plays display this method in its extreme form, partly because it was his example, rightly understood or not, which influenced Renaissance poets in their attempts at tragedy and encouraged them in their cultivation of the speech as set-piece.

I have argued that a relatively naturalistic surface does not make a play naturalistic in method, and it is clear enough (again, the verse of such a play as *Bérénice* comes to mind) that apparently prosaic verse may exemplify the poetic method. But here we must make a distinction. What are we to make of a passage like this from Racine?

> Madame, j'ai reçu des lettres de l'armée.
> De tout ce qui s'y passe êtes-vous informée?
> – On m'a dit que du camp un esclave est venu;
> Le reste est un secret qui ne m'est pas connu.
> – Amurat est heureux, la fortune est changée.
>
> (*Bajazet*, IV.iii)

These lines can tell us nothing about whether *Bajazet* is a poetic play. Though skilful, they are not in themselves great poetry. They are the kind of lines which any play in verse, whether poetic or naturalistic, must have: they convey information. They are what we may call 'business' lines.

This brings us to the question of how a naturalistic play can use language in a poetic or quasi-poetic way. A naturalistic playwright will have at least as much need of 'business' lines as any poetic dramatist, and if he uses verse, they may give him trouble. But we have to consider how far the naturalistic playwright (whether in prose or verse) can approach the poetic method in the higher levels of speech. What advantages does he have if he casts his play in verse? What nevertheless distinguishes his most 'poetic' speech from that of poetic drama?

The most obvious point is one I have made earlier: the assumptions on which even the most realistic drama rests are highly conventional. It is a shorter step from 'realistic' dialogue to the most high-flown poetry than from speech in real life to the most carefully realistic (even improvised) speech on a stage before an audience. Equally obviously, it is necessary to adopt highly explicit language from time to time in any play to convey the significance of the action. When a play is written in prose and not conceived in poetic terms, there will be occasions when its dialogue approaches the pitch of poetic speech. If the play is natural-istically-conceived but written in verse, the explicitness and elaboration of the language at the high points can be greater than in a play written in prose: the base-line of the convention is higher, as it were. But the heightened language is nevertheless conceived of as an acceptable intensification of the normal language of the character who speaks it: it is often referred to simply as 'heightened speech'. There is still a clear distinction between elaborate speech used poetically and elaborate speech used naturalistically. Poetic speech will express explicitly the emotion important at this point. If the character is confused and excited, he will say he is confused to express this. We may take an example from *Troilus and Cressida*:

> I am giddy; expectation whirls me round . . .
> My heart beats thicker than a feverous pulse;
> And all my powers do their bestowing lose,
> Like vassalage at unawares encountering
> The eye of majesty.

A naturalistic dramatist cannot approach this degree of expressive-ness, which requires a fully articulate use of language. However much he heightens his language, he must remember that the character must express himself naturally (within the limits of the chosen convention), and that if the character is confused the language must appear to some extent confused. The use of verse permits a higher degree of articulate-ness, because of the higher baseline of the convention, but as long as the mode is naturalistic the basic difficulty remains. The poet writing within the naturalistic mode must write at the presumed level of his characters' control of language, not at his own.

There is one type of speech in which this difficulty is partly relaxed: the set-piece speech which in poetic drama we have called Senecan. Even in the most realistic drama, it is easy to find a pretext – high emo-tion, drunkenness, a trial scene or a public meeting – which will justify the making of a speech which is elaborate and articulate far beyond what is normal in everyday life. In a naturalistic form which still operates within conventions framed for poetic drama, a speech of this kind is even more easily justified. In both cases a playwright may need a speech to develop and emphasise one of the ideas imported from out-side on which naturalistic drama has to rely to attain any sort of seriousness. And there is of course another function of a Senecan speech which only the most dour naturalist would refuse to admit: its value as decorative display. In plays lacking the seriousness of poetic drama but written in poetic form, the tendency to exploit the Senecan type of speech for its bravura qualities is naturally strong. (We may think of Rostand or Christopher Fry.) But a resourceful naturalist can exploit even in prose drama both the articulateness and the decorative qualities of a Senecan speech. In Shaw's *The Apple Cart*, Magnus makes a long, carefully-shaped speech warning his ministers not to undermine the monarchy. When he finishes, Lysistrata says, 'Splendid!', and Amanda says, 'You did speak that piece beautifully, sir.' When a speech is used as a set-piece in this way, elaboration and display are obviously required, and we should not be too ready to complain of artificiality or over-emphasis.

We can now look at some characteristic verses of Corneille in the light of this discussion. A trivial example first:

> Va, je reconnaîtrai ce service en son lieu.
>
> (*Rodogune*, III.i)

There is no difficulty about this. It is a straightforward 'business' line, and means no more than it says. But how does it differ in texture from this?

> Je vous en tirerai, Seigneur, dans peu de temps.

We should be hard put to it to judge the significance of this line in isolation, on literary grounds alone. It is, in fact, from one of the high points of *Héraclius*: it is spoken by Exupère in the middle of Act IV, and has very great relevance to the fabric of the play. If *Héraclius* were performed nowadays, this line would surely create a powerful effect in the theatre. But its power comes entirely from the situation. The tyrant Phocas has murdered the Emperor Maurice and usurped the throne. Léontine, faithful to the dead emperor, saves his son Héraclius and brings him up as her own son, under the name Léonce. Later, profiting from Phocas's favour, she substitutes Héraclius/Léonce for Phocas's son Martian. Héraclius/Léonce thus passes for Martian, and Martian passes for Léonce. In the scene in which this line comes, Phocas has been warned by Exupère that Léonce (the real Martian, Phocas's son) is really Héraclius (the son of Phocas's enemy). Phocas is about to kill his son when Héraclius (whom Phocas believes to be his son Martian) reveals his true identity. Phocas hesitates agonisingly, realising that whatever he does he risks killing his son and letting his enemy live. Léontine refuses to say which young man is which, and Exupère does not help. Exupère is in fact playing a double game: his real aim is to destroy Phocas and establish Héraclius on the throne. His interjections in the scene have a double purpose: he is both pretending to be perplexed and goading Phocas to his doom:

> PHOCAS
> Lequel croire, Exupère, et lequel démentir?
> Tombé-je dans l'erreur, ou si j'en vais sortir?
> Si ce billet est vrai, le reste est vraisemblable.
>
> EXUPERE
> Mais qui sait si ce reste est faux ou véritable?
>
> PHOCAS
> Léontine deux fois a pu tromper Phocas.
>
> EXUPERE
> Elle a pu les changer, et ne les changer pas. . . .
>
> PHOCAS
> Dis-moi, tout est-il prêt pour ce juste supplice?
>
> EXUPERE
> Oui, si nous connaissions le vrai fils de Maurice.

The passage is effective, but the effect does not depend on any literary complexity.

This might be dismissed as a use of bare language for a particular purpose at a moment of crisis. But this unsubtle type of verse pervades the play. Exupère plays a double game until almost the end, and for most of the time neither the audience nor the other characters know this. A typical example is at the end of Act III, when Exupère is high in Phocas's favour for his supposed betrayal of Héraclius:

> EXUPERE
> Nous sommes en faveur, ami, tout est à nous:
> L'heur de notre destin va faire des jaloux.
>
> AMINTAS
> Quelque allégresse ici que vous fassiez paraître,
> Trouvez-vous doux les noms de perfide et de traître?
>
> EXUPERE
> Je sais qu'aux généreux ils doivent faire horreur;
> Ils m'ont frappé l'oreille, ils m'ont blessé le coeur:
> Mais bientôt, par l'effet que nous devons attendre,
> Nous serons en état de ne les plus entendre.
> Allons; pour un moment qu'il faut les endurer,
> Ne fuyons pas les biens qu'ils nous font espérer.

These lines are complex in the simplest possible way: they bear two meanings, one of which we understand at the time (Exupère is a shameless traitor), the other of which we understand in retrospect (Exupère is tricking Phocas). This effect bears no relation to the traditional tragic irony: when we know the truth we do not see a deeper meaning in the lines, but merely a different one. This makes it virtually impossible for the verse to express any deep meaning at all: in order to express two simple but contradictory meanings it must be kept at the simple level of a riddle. The same goes for many of Exupère's speeches. He is sometimes given a noble, 'Cornelian' line:

> Je sers mon empereur, et je sais mon devoir.

> (III.ii)

If this sounds hollow, it is not because Corneille's inspiration has failed: it is because the verse has to tread with careful neutrality between its assumed meaning ('I am loyal to Phocas') and its real meaning ('I am loyal to Héraclius'). We can no longer say that the verse controls our response, and that we can elicit from the verse (as verse) its meaning for the play. Our attention has now to be directed away from the verse itself to the hypothetical purposes behind it. In *Héraclius* we infer the significance of large parts of the verse by relating it to the events of the plot; this is no different in principle from the case where we infer the meaning of a speech in itself vague or inarticulate from what we know of the character speaking it. If the play is produced, the director's task is not to bring out and project the reading of experience embodied in the verse (there is none) but to arrange the stage events so that we can interpret the lines correctly. *Héraclius* is an excellent play which contains not one line with the resonance of great poetry. Although it is written in verse, and with great verbal dexterity, the method behind it is that of modern prose drama.

This discussion of some of the uses of verse in drama may help us to understand the variations of Corneille's verse. Critics have often noted its decline in quality in the plays immediately following *Polyeucte*, and his increasing reliance on crude methods of achieving and appearance of vigour: invective, antithesis, conceits. Turnell well describes the reliance for 'poetry' on 'the drive of the alexandrine', and notes the 'loss of subtlety' and 'marked coarseness of texture' in Corneille's plays of this period.[3] Critics who pursue this line sometimes assume that the trouble with this verse is that it has become two-dimensional, or abstract, and that this is because Corneille has lost the knack of creating 'living people' and now creates only 'bloodless puppets'. Such explanations may have some truth in them, but they do not explain enough: there are types of verse which may be two-dimensional, or even abstract, and yet make precisely the effect required in a poetic play (we may think, for instance, of *Sweeney Agonistes*); and there are many great poetic plays (as various as *Prometheus Bound* and *Tamburlaine*) where the characters are not 'living people' in any naturalistic sense.

It is clear enough that in the later plays high poetry jostles with the prosaic, heroism with cynicism, dignity with bathos, fancifulness with sobriety, but it is sometimes difficult to make sense of the variations in the quality of the verse. The way out of this difficulty is to recognise that in different plays, and in different parts of the same play, Corneille is doing different things; and the only way of judging a play or a part of a play is to try and unravel what his aims are, and what means he is using to achieve them. This approach may be of particular help in evaluating the verse of the later plays.

3

Without doubt, the badness of some of the verse in Corneille's late plays does require explanation. We cannot say – as did so many critics from the end of the seventeenth century to the beginning of the twentieth – that with increasing age Corneille's powers deserted him. The later plays have excellences of plot, characterisation and verbal power that show a vigorous mind at work. It is not just a question of striking lines and individual felicities, though these abound. Corneille is able to write sustained passages of subtlety and power. Nor has his verse hardened into one mould. It can still encompass not only grandeur and passion but also more unexpected notes: delicacy of sentiment (as in the speeches of Martian in *Pulchérie*); charming comedy (as in much of *Agésilas*); or the striking mixture of sarcasm, passion and bravado that characterises much of Attila's utterance. It is certainly not true that his verse falls off in his last years. The verse of *Pulchérie* and *Suréna* is of consistently higher quality than that of *Héraclius*, *Oedipe* or *Sophonisbe*. His non-dramatic verse, which continues after 1674, shows little evidence of decline. His lines of thanks to the king for the representation of six of his plays at Court in 1676 are deservedly famous. Court poetry is not a genre in which to expect masterpieces, but even in the poem on Monseigneur's marriage in 1680 (three years after *Phèdre*) Corneille can command a fine vigour and flexibility.

Nevertheless, much of the verse in the late plays is disconcerting. Two features are particularly distressing. One is that the worst passages seem quite extraordinarily bad: confused, obscure and bathetic, or feeble and diffuse. The lines from *Tite et Bérénice* are notorious:

> Faut-il mourir, Madame? et si proche du terme,
> Votre illustre inconstance est-elle encor si ferme
> Que les restes d'un feu que j'avais cru si fort
> Puissent dans quatre jours se promettre ma mort?
>
> (I.ii)

Much verse is wretchedly flat. In *Agésilas*, Lysander addresses his prospective son-in-law thus:

> Quoique, en matière d'hyménée,
> L'importune longueur des affaires traînées
> Attire assez souvent de fâcheux embarras,
> J'ai voulu qu'à loisir vous puissiez voir mes filles
> Avant que demander l'aveu d'Agésilas
> Sur l'union de nos familles.
>
> (II.ii)

One passage from the same play is even more painful because it recalls a great moment from *Cinna*. Agésilas debates whether to forgive Lysander, who has plotted against him. After a struggle, he decides on forgiveness:

> Mais enfin il est beau de triompher de soi,
> Et de s'accorder ce miracle,
> Quand on peut hautement donner à tous la loi,
> Et que le juste soin de combler notre gloire
> Demande notre coeur pour dernière victoire.
> Un roi né pour l'éclat des grandes actions
> Dompte jusqu'à ses passions,
> Et ne se croit point roi, s'il ne fait sur lui-même
> Le plus illustre essai de son pouvoir suprême.
>
> (V.vi)

The second distressing feature is disconcerting change in tone and quality; we are for ever being picked up and then suddenly dropped. As an example, we may take *Attila*, Act III, Scene ii. The conception is strong and dramatic. Attila is a striking figure: ferocious, wily and sarcastic, he rejoices in his ability to divide and destroy his enemies without resorting to force. He pursues his policy by appearing to hesitate between two princesses, Ildione of Gaul and Honorie of Rome, and by playing off against each other two vassal kings, Ardaric and Valamir, each of whom loves one of the princesses. Corneille has made his tyrant more arresting still by making him in love; in spite of his boastful sarcasms, Attila finds his cynical policy traversed by his unwilling passion for Ildione. For this reason he refuses to marry her; if he did, she would have power over him and prevent him from following his policy. In this scene, shot through with passion and irony, he tells the proud Ildione.

At first the verse is firm and strong, with ironic undertones:

> Venir jusqu'en ma tente enlever mes hommages,
> Madame, c'est trop lion pousser vos avantages;
> Ne vous suffit-il point que le coeur soit à vous?

Then Attila confesses his love and refuses to give way to it. The verse rises in intensity:

> Ah! vous me charmez trop, moi, de qui l'âme altière
> Cherche à voir sous mes pieds trembler la terre entière:
> Moi, qui veux pouvoir tout, sitôt que je vous voi,
> Malgré tout cet orgueil, je ne puis rien sur moi.
> Je veux, je tâche en vain d'éviter par la fuite
> Ce charme dominant qui marche à votre suite . . .
> Il s'empare et du coeur et des soins les plus doux;
> Et j'oublie Attila dès que je pense a vous.

By any standard, the scene up to now is in fine dramatic verse. Attila's tirade is magnificent, its climax discordant with the intensity of conflicting passions. Then disaster: Ildione replies, in dudgeon:

> L'aurait-on jamais cru qu'un Attila pût craindre,
> Qu'un si léger éclat eût de quoi l'y contraindre,
> Et que de ce grand nom qui remplit tout d'effroi
> Il n'osât hasarder tout l'orgueil contre moi?
> Avant qu'il porte ailleurs ces timides hommages
> Que jusqu'ici j'enlève avec tant d'avantages,
> Apprenez-moi, Seigneur, pour suivre vos desseins,
> Comme il faut dédaigner le plus grand des humains.

The scene rises again at the end with Attila's resolute paradoxes, so dramatic in their grandeur, absurdity and pathos:

> Quoi! vous pourriez m'aimer, Madame, à votre tour?
> Qui sème tant d'horreurs fait naître peu d'amour.
> Qu'aimeriez-vous en moi? Je suis cruel, barbare;
> Je n'ai que ma fierté, que ma fureur de rare;
> On me craint, on me hait; on me nomme en tout lieu
> La terreur des mortels, et le fléau de Dieu.

How, then, do we explain that dead patch in the middle? We cannot attribute it to Corneille's inability to keep going for long stretches: when he wants to, as in the political debate in Act I, he can easily sustain his chosen level for hundreds of lines. Moreover, some of his other late plays clearly show him choosing and sustaining a consistent tone and quality. The verse of *Othon* has a distinctive character – clear, neat, and slightly abstract – which is maintained throughout. In *Suréna*, the verse has a soft, sad, rather overripe texture which expresses the essential feeling of the play: the variations, which range from reasonable political discussion to the proud desire for vengeance, are carefully modulated to fit in with this overall impression.

The answer seems to lie in this very concern to adjust the verse exactly to the way in which each play is conceived. The editor of the *Classiques Larousse* edition of *Attila* asks *à propos* of Ildione's speech what game she is playing and what feeling inspires her. Such questions, irrelevant in normal poetic drama, are here in place. Ildione's feelings are extremely complex. She loves Ardaric and hates Attila; nevertheless, she feels it her duty to marry him, for political reasons. She is proud of her charms and her position, and fiercely jealous of her rival, Honorie. If Attila does marry her, she will be pleased, because then she will have opportunities to kill him. Although *Attila* draws much of its force from the poetic pattern it expresses, at this particular point we are indeed concerned with the supposed feelings of Ildione. We are also concerned with the complexities of the plot, which her conflicting emotions are to further. If her verse at this point is confused and obscure, it is because her feelings are confused and her intentions must be kept obscure from Attila. And there is no need for the verse to be explicit: at this point there is no underlying poetic pattern for it to be explicit about. Corneille therefore writes a passage which is clumsy as verse but which fits in with the plot and with what the audience (but not Attila) know of Ildione's intentions. If the verse is bad, it is bad for the same reasons as much of the verse in *Héraclius*.

But what of those stretches in the late plays where the verse seems unusually bad? Let us examine, as an example, Act I of *Tite et Bérénice*. In the first scene, Domitie explains to her confidante that although she loves Domitian she will marry his brother Tite to satisfy her ambition. The construction here seems maladroit, in that she is unashamedly explaining herself to someone who knows it all already, and much of the verse is astonishingly clumsy:

> Ce pompeux appareil, où sans cesse il ajoute,
> Recule chaque jour un noeud qui le dégoûte.
> Il souffre chaque jour que le gouvernement

Vole ce qu'à me plaire il doit d'attachement . . .
Il vint, mais d'un esprit à nos voeux si contraire.
Que, quoi qu'on lui pût dire, on n'en pût arracher
Ce qu'attendait un feu qui nous était si cher.

In Scene ii, Domitian comes in, talking nonsense ('Faut-il mourir, Madame? et si proche du terme . . .'), and aske her to marry him after all: he is sure that Tite will agree. Domitie evades his proposal: she still loves him, but she loves the empire more, and if he wants to marry her his best plan is to become emperor. The verse again lapses into bathos:

Durant un déplaisir si long et si sensible,
De voir toujours un père à nos voeux inflexible,
Ai-je écouté quelqu'un de tant de soupirants
Qui m'accablaient partout de leurs regards mourants?

In Scene iii, Domitian is left with his confidant Albin, who explains, not very tragically, that his love for Domitie is really self-love. When Domitian refuses to be consoled, Albin advises him to bring Bérénice to Rome so that Tite may return to her and abandon Domitie. Domitian objects that there is not time to fetch Bérénice before the wedding, whereupon Albin hints that she is in Rome already.

We might be tempted to write off the entire act as bathos. Before we do so, however, we may note that there are fine things in it – for instance, Albin's speech on self-love:

Seigneur, s'il m'est permis de parler librement,
Dans toute la nature aime-t-on autrement?
L'amour-propre est la source en nous de tous les autres;
C'en est le sentiment qui forme tous les nôtres;
Lui seul allume, éteint, ou change nos désirs:
Les objets de nos voeux le sont de nos plaisirs.
Vous-même, qui brûlez d'un ardeur si fidèle,
Aimez-vous Domitie, ou vos plaisirs en elle?
Et quand vous aspirez à des liens si doux,
Est-ce pour l'amour d'elle ou pour l'amour de vous?

This is light and relaxed, but shrewd; not tragic, but not negligible. The lines throw a light on the overblown preciosity of so much of the play.

Pursuing our search for merits in this act, what are we to make of this?

Non, Seigneur, je vous aime, et garde au fond de l'âme
Tout ce que j'eus pour vous de tendresse et de flamme:

L'effort que je me fais me tue autant que vous;
Mais enfin l'empereur veut être mon époux.

– Ah! si vous n'acceptez sa main qu'avec contrainte,
Venez, venez, Madame, autoriser ma plainte;
L'empereur m'aime assez pour quitter vos liens
Quand je lui porterai vos voeux avec les miens.
Dites que vous m'aimez, et que tout son empire . . .

– C'est ce qu'à dire vrai j'aurai peine à lui dire,
Seigneur.

Here we have the usual jargon of 'flamme' and 'tue' and 'liens', and then the exposure of the real feeling behind the solemn game. The tone is not tragic, but realistic and comic. The virtue of the verse is that it can hit off accurately a realistic view of the situation. Domitie explains her feelings to Domitian:

Je ne veux point, Seigneur, vous le dissimuler,
Mon coeur va tout à vous quand je le laisse aller:
Mais sans dissimuler j'ose aussi vous le dire,
Ce n'est pas mon dessein qu'il m'en coûte l'empire;
Et je n'ai point une âme à se laisser charmer
Du ridicule honneur de savoir bien aimer.

Even the paired names (Domitian/Domitie: Millamant/Mirabel) add to the lightness of the tone. In short, Corneille is moving towards a subtle and realistic comedy of sentiment, in which the frankly comic elements that appear from time to time in the Domitie/Domitian scenes balance against the more serious (but still untragic) sentiment and pride of the Tite/Bérénice scenes. The method does not allow of intense or harrowing emotion, but it extends easily to exact expression of emotional states:

Je m'emporte, et mes sens interdits
Impriment leur désordre en tout ce que je dis.
Comment saurai-je aussi ce que je te dois dire,
Si je ne sais pas même à quoi mon âme aspire?
Mon aveugle fureur s'égare à tout propos.
Allons penser à tout avec plus de repos.

(II.vii)

or even to plain statement of a more heroic kind:

Si de tels souvenirs ne me faisaient la guerre,
Serait-il potentat plus heureux sur la terre?
Mon nom par la victoire est si bien affermi,

Qu'on me croit dans la paix un lion endormi:
Mon réveil incertain du monde fait l'étude.

(II.i)

But the mode is essentially naturalistic comedy dressed as poetic tragedy. Apart from the comic tone, there is a tendency to use the little tricks of naturalism which goes admirably with the tone chosen: the play is full of broken sentences (e.g. ll. 44, 214, 247, 265, 349, 635, 1189, 1655, 1711, 1713) and speeches (such as that from II.vii just quoted) where the character is too confused or overcome with emotion to express himself articulately. It is easy enough to see that to treat a serio-comic subject in a naturalistic way within the conventions of French classical tragedy has its dangers. The tone is very hard to hit exactly. Very often, Corneille succeeds in both exploiting and delicately mocking the elegance of précieux jargon – as when Domitie expresses her exasperation at the 'soupirants | Qui m'accablaient partout de leurs regards mourants'; sometimes he just misses his tone, and falls into nonsense – as when Domitian makes his famous entrance speech. One problem is the characteristic naturalistic care that the speech must resemble what the character would say in real life: much of the time most of the characters are being insincere or divided in their emotions, and the verse expresses their confusion and embarrassment. An example is in III.i, when Domitian is preposterously pretending to love Bérénice. Bérénice naturally refuses to believe him, and demands a clear explanation. The best he can manage is this:

Il [Tite] vous respecte trop; c'est à vous qu'il me donne,
Et me fait la justice, en m'enlevant mon bien,
De vouloir que je tâche à m'enrichir du sien:
Mais à peine il le veut, qu'il craint pour moi la haine
Que Rome concevrait pour l'époux d'une reine.
C'est à vous de juger d'où part ce sentiment.
En vain, par politique, il fait ailleurs l'amant;
Il s'y réduit en vain par grandeur de courage:
A ces fausses clartés opposez quelque ombrage;
Et je renonce au jour, s'il ne revient à vous,
Pour peu que vous penchiez à le rendre jaloux.

This is wretched as verse, but not necessarily bad dialogue: Domitian is a pleasant fellow, and we can imagine him stumbling helplessly through this nonsense before the calm and ironical Bérénice. The scene is comic, and rather touching; and it is clinched by the next one, where Domitie catches him at it and rounds on him. He pleads in vain that she advised him to love someone else; she indignantly tells him that he should not have believed her, or at least not to the extent of offering himself to someone else in her presence.

The method has one other disadvantage, and one which produces verse which is risible in the wrong sense. The conventions of neo-classical verse can excellently encompass intense emotion or close-packed thought, and can serve well enough for conveying matter of lesser intensity, provided it can be reduced to a fairly abstract level. But naturalistic comedy requires a great deal to be expressed which is not dignified or intense, and a great deal to be conveyed in the way of sheer concrete information. Domitie's self-revelation in Act I, Scene i, suffers from this. The basic situation is that a woman is complaining about her love-life and thwarted ambitions, with much narrative of past events. Prose could manage this very well, but classical verse can only embarrass the expression of this prosaic substance. The same difficulty occurs wherever plain factual matter has to be expressed. At best, the flat statement can be stated flatly:

> Tite fit tôt après
> De Bérénice à Rome admirer les attraits.
> Pour elle avec Martie il avait fait divorce;
> Et cette belle reine eut sur lui tant de force
> Que, pour montrer à tous sa flamme, et hautement,
> Il lui fit au palais prendre un appartement.
>
> (I.i)

This is bad, but surely an attempt to drape plain facts in high-sounding diction betrays Corneille into worse:

> Irez-vous au sénat?
> – Non; il peut s'assembler
> Sur ce déluge ardent qui nous a fait trembler,
> Et pourvoir sous mon ordre aux affreuses ruines
> Dont ses feux ont couvert les campagnes voisines.
>
> (II.i)

What, then, do we make of the old charges that the verse of Corneille's later plays is very bad, or at least extraordinarily uneven? Taking for this purpose his last six plays, and ignoring the fact that Corneille, like all writers, has occasional lapses of detail, my view would be as follows. There is no truth in the view that his power of writing sustained and excellent verse failed him. The verse in *Othon* and *Suréna* (and most of *Attila*) is not only of very high quality but also consistent and skilfully adjusted to the tone and purpose of the play. In *Agésilas*, *Tite et Bérénice* and *Pulchérie*, he is writing sentimental comedy: much of the verse which has been criticised as unintentionally comic is comic by intention and excellently so, and in the more serious parts he deliberately avoids any forcing of the tone to a level which would be acceptable in tragedy but ridiculous in this context. In these plays (and in one or two passages in *Attila*) the verse (considered as verse) is often bad. This is sometimes because he is feeling his way towards a naturalistic form, in which the speech has to correspond to what the speaker might naturally say, in the light of his purpose, situation and character. In this case, the fact that the verse is bad as verse does not always mean that it would be ineffective on the stage. Sometimes the verse is bad by any criterion. This again is because Corneille is inclining towards naturalism in technique and subject-matter. In a naturalistic play there will usually be many things to be said that will not fit easily into verse, and especially the verse of neo-classical tragedy. The attempt to make them fit leads either to flatness, or to clumsiness, pomposity, obscurity and bathos.

7

'RODOGUNE'

I

Few critics have followed Corneille's tendency to regard *Rodogune* as his masterpiece. Voltaire criticised it mercilessly in his *Commentaires,* and in *L'Ingénu* insinuated it was of little value. Lessing made it the chief object of his attack on French tragedy, and Schlegel dismissed it as turgid melodrama. Although the twentieth-century revival of interest in Corneille has brought *Rodogune* some admirers, it has never risen very high in critical regard. Corneille's preference for it has been discounted as a sign of his admiration for his own power of inventing complications. This does not in itself seem sufficient reason: he speaks without much enthusiasm of *Héraclius,* which is just as original and twice as complicated, and was also a great success on the stage. But *Rodogune* has lasted, as *Héraclius* has not, and this gives some support to Corneille's opinion.

Admirers and detractors alike usually fasten on the plot. Admirers extol the firm construction, the controlled rise and fall of the tension.[1] Detractors attribute all the play's success to the merely nervous thrills engendered by the plot, and complain that everything is sacrificed to the needs of a striking last act. Let us therefore start by examining the plot, with the aim of finding out what sort of play *Rodogune* is.

The first act has been much criticised, and Corneille admits in his *Examen* that the criticisms are partly justified. Much of it is taken up with long conversations between two confidants on Syrian history, including Cléopâtre's murder of her husband, her hatred of her husband's fiancée Rodogune, the doubt about which of her twin sons Antiochus and Séleucus is the elder, and the political necessity that the elder must now displace Cléopâtre from power and marry Rodogune.

There is no denying the clumsiness with which this material is conveyed, but a more interesting point is the way in which it is used. Many great plays are much taken up with exposition of past facts. In Ibsen, it is often the stuff of the play: the past is a relentless power which informs and destroys the present. In *Agamemnon,* when the chorus sing of Iphigenia's death or the siege of Troy, we know that the ode is a further unfolding of the significance of the drama, not mere narration of antecedent facts. But narration of antecedent facts is just what the retrospection in *Rodogune* is: it is past history which we must learn before we can enjoy the plot. The events related are doom-laden enough – wars, falls of princes, near-incest, murderous enmity of kin against kin – but they form the background of the play in a mechanical sense only: there is little effort to develop their significance in any moral or metaphysical sense. Corneille skirts the tragic implications of his material. Believing her husband dead, Cléopâtre struggles to keep the empire together for her children, and takes her husband's brother as her second husband. But this second husband is defeated and killed. At this juncture, she finds that her first husband is not dead: enraged by her second marriage, he is returning to claim his throne, marry the daughter of her mortal enemy, and disinherit her children. Cléopâtre tries in vain to excuse herself:

> On a beau la défendre, on a beau le prier,
> On ne rencontre en lui qu'un juge inexorable,
> Et son amour nouveau la veut croire coupable:
> Son erreur est un crime.

This is tragic enough, and Cléopâtre's desperate reaction also is of the stuff of tragedy. But here the tone slides into melodrama:

> Elle oublie un mari qui veut cesser de l'être,
> Qui ne veut plus la voir qu'en implacable maître;
> Et, changeant à regret son amour en horreur,
> Elle abandonne tout à sa juste fureur.
> Elle-même leur dresse une embûche au passage,
> Se mêle dans les coups, porte partout sa rage,
> En pousse jusqu'au bout les furieux effets.
> Que vous dirai-je enfin? les Parthes sont défaits;
> Le roi meurt, et, dit-on, par la main de la reine.

It is not the violent happenings that make this melodramatic; it is the lack of moral sensitivity. Cleopatre's ill-treatment by her husband is presented not as an explanation, but as a justification, of her acts. The horrors are glossed over – 'changeant *à regret . . . juste* fureur . . . le roi meurt, et, *dit-on*, par la main de la reine'. Laonice, who is clearly meant as a sympathetic character, shows no horror at the queen's actions (and in the next scene cheerfully defends her against Rodogune's suspicions). Corneille is passing very lightly over the moral problems posed by Cléopâtre's behaviour, and the fact that Laonice is not troubled by them indicates that we must not look too deeply either.

The other main element in Act I is the presentation of the love of the two princes for Rodogune. We shall come back later to the way in which it is presented. Its significance for the plot is clear enough: two brothers who are firm friends are set between two loved women who hate each other.

Act II brings the first twist. Cléopâtre promises the throne to whichever of her sons will kill Rodogune. This scene has been called melodramatic and unlikely. These are hardly valid criticisms: many great plays have scenes as startling and as ill-prepared. (Think of the first scene of *King Lear*.) The real criticism is surely that Corneille is here using a striking situation for its own sake, and evades the larger issues it might raise. Consider this speech by Cléopâtre:

> Nicanor votre père, et mon premier époux . . .
> Mais pourquoi lui donner encor des noms si doux,
> Puisque, l'ayant cru mort, il sembla ne revivre
> Que pour s'en dépouiller afin de nous poursuivre?
> Passons; je ne me puis souvenir sans trembler
> Du coup dont j'empêchai qu'il nous pût accabler:
> Je ne sais s'il est digne ou d'horreur ou d'estime,
> S'il plut aux dieux ou non, s'il fut justice ou crime.

This is potentially tragic, and here rises towards tragedy. But Corneille sheers away:

> Mais, soit crime ou justice, il est certain, mes fils,
> Que mon amour pour vous fit tout ce que je fis.

This is untrue, and we know it. Cléopâtre is not trying to justify herself to herself, or to retain her sons' love. She is simply trying to deceive them, for political reasons, and using the devices of political rhetoric: euphemism ('le *malheur* d'un père'), pathos ('Ma vie est presque usée'), the appeal to Heaven ('Daigne du juste ciel la bonté souveraine'), and finally the invitation to complete double-think:

> Rodogune, mes fils, le tua par ma main.

The brothers are only too eager to preserve this polite veil over the unpleasant facts:

> Ce sont fatalités dont l'âme embarrassée
> A plus qu'elle ne veut se voit souvent forcée.
> Sur les noires couleurs d'un si triste tableau
> Il faut passer l'éponge, ou tirer le rideau.

Left alone together, the brothers decide to ask Rodogune to choose between them, and undertake to abide by her decision. This precipitates a neat reversal in Act III: she offers herself to whichever of them will kill the queen. After this ultimatum she abruptly leaves the stage.

Voltaire and others have taken exception to this. The complaint is that she would 'naturally' have told the brothers the reason for her desperate manoeuvre, which is that she knows of Cléopâtre's ultimatum. Many playwrights, however, have neglected this sort of naturalness in order to express more forcibly some part of their meaning. The real charge against Corneille concerns not his means but his ends: he is evading the implications of his subject – a presentation of which at this point would raise some important moral issues – and giving us instead the pleasure of suspense.

The brothers now have another scene together. This has interesting stylistic features which I will discuss later. From the point of view of the plot, all that happens is that Antiochus decides to plead with both women to relent. Séleucus sees this is hopeless. His words are interesting, not because of what they signify but because of what they do not:

> Il vous faudra parer leurs haines mutuelles,
> Sauvez l'une de l'autre; et peut-être leurs coups,
> Vous trouvant au milieu, ne perceront que vous.

In the event, Séleucus will die in this way, and Antiochus will survive to marry Rodogune. In a tragedy, this might be a stroke of tragic irony. Here, it passes without much importance as a reminder of the exciting dangers engendered by the plot.

Act IV opens with Antiochus and Rodogune. If we consider the implications of this scene, in which the adoring son of a murderous queen shows his love for her equally murderous enemy, we might expect some profound emotional cross-currents. What we get is nothing more than a rather insipid love-scene, written in a curious mixture of styles. Antiochus, overjoyed at his success with Rodogune, approaches his mother. At this point, a happy ending seems possible. Cléopâtre, finding that Antiochus will not give up Rodogune, tells him he is the elder and agrees to his marriage. Both Antiochus and Laonice now assume that all is well. But Cléopâtre is dissembling. She tries in vain to goad Séleucus to help her against his brother and kill Rodogune. Finding him immovable, she resolves to kill the three of them.

In the space of Act IV, a good deal has happened: enough to make a very exciting act, but too much to leave space for developing the meaning of the events.

This is even more evident in the fifth act. Cléopâtre has killed Séleucus, and when Antiochus and Rodogune enter in state she offers them a poisoned cup. But Timagène bursts in: he has found the dying Séleucus, who uttered a warning capable of referring either to the queen or

Rodogune. Antiochus hesitates: Cléopâtre and Rodogune each appeal to him. He decides to ignore what has happened and continue with the ceremony. But, as he raises the cup, Rodogune stops him: it has come from the queen. Cléopâtre, in a last desperate throw, takes the first drink herself. Before Antiochus can drink, the poison takes effect. She is led off to die, leaving Antiochus to mourn her and marry Rodogune.

There is no doubt that this is effective. Nevertheless, when we discussed Corneille's inconclusive endings, we might have included this one. How can Antiochus, after the deaths of his mother and brother, settle down with a wife who helped to cause their deaths, who that very day had demanded he should kill his mother, and whom a hundred lines before the end of the play he was ready to believe would murder him? These, if taken seriously, are real issues. But there is no sign that Corneille wants us to take them seriously. Just as, earlier, he avoided the deeper implications of his subject-matter, so in Act V he draws our attention away from such points and concentrates on the exciting passage of the poisoned cup from hand to hand. Indeed, he is careful through the mouth of Oronte, to emphasise that the ending leaves no moral problems:

> Dans les justes rigeurs d'un sort si déplorable,
> Seigneur, le juste ciel vous est bien favorable . . .
> Et, par un digne effet de ses faveurs puissantes,
> Le coupable est punie, et vos mains innocentes.

Rodogune is an impressive play, and the powerful plot is one source of its impressiveness. I shall discuss later what the other sources are: for the moment, it is enough to note that the moral or metaphysical significance expressed through the plot is not one of them.

2

On the whole, critics have found the characterisation in *Rodogune* inhuman, but at least one of them has praised the play's humanity and psychological realism.[2] Both these viewpoints seem to me tenable, because of the great range of techniques Corneille uses.

We will not linger over the characters of the brothers, though their rôles do contain some subtle psychological touches. Having chosen to rely principally on exciting situations and to avoid dwelling on their deeper implications, there is little Corneille can do to make them interesting. I have already remarked that Antiochus's scene with Rodogune (IV.i) is potentially profound, but that Corneille has to divert our attention from the deeper issues. Throughout the play one or other of the brothers has to react to a fundamental change in the emotional situation, and on each occasion this places Corneille in a difficulty. In discussing the verse, I shall try to show what he does to cover it up. But, despite his skill, the brothers remain feeble as characters.

Corneille's treatment of Rodogune is more interesting, and shows much psychological subtlely – though not, in my view, so as to make her a rounded character. The complexities rather reflect the mixture of techniques employed.

There is no doubt that we are meant to regard her as sympathetic, though the plot demands atrocious actions from her. This, of course, is not an insoluble problem. In a poetic play, the underlying theme may well demand that a character should commit a crime and yet remain sympathetic. If the underlying meaning being communicated is the centre of interest, we do not attribute praise or blame to the character personally in the same way as we would in real life. Hamlet, for instance, whose treatment of Ophelia, Polonius, Rosencrantz and Guildernstern, Osric and even Gertrude and Claudius would strike us as odious in real life, remains a focus of our sympathies. Many attempts have been made to interpret Hamlet as a naturalistic character, with varying results. It is a matter of opinion whether any of them are convincing, or whether the exercise is in any case misconceived. What certainly seems true is that, in a play like *Hamlet*, the overall experience communicated is more important than whether or not the characterisation is consistent in any realistic sense. There is, however, a different solution to the problem, which is basically naturalistic: the motives and compulsions of the character are so thoroughly explored that we feel our kinship and our normal condemnation of such acts is modified. This is the method of, say, *Rosmersholm*. In this case, any inconsistency in the characterisation is serious, because it cuts across the basis of the method.

In presenting Rodogune, Corneille attempts to make use of both solutions. His basic method is the poetic one. Rodogune is sympathetic because we are told she is: both princes praise her, and Laonice treats her with great respect. This approach comes out clearly in the last scene. Rodogune is now the happy princess marrying her prince, and we are supposed to forget her earlier behaviour. Then the plot requires Antiochus to wonder whether she has murdered his brother. She defends herself with energy and a perfect command of logical argument. Her speech is prefaced with the remark:

> Je me défendrai mal: l'innocence étonnée
> Ne peut s'imaginer qu'elle soit soupçonnée.

Obviously, we are not intended to take this as hypocrisy, or as a dishonest attempt to attract sympathy, as we might in a real person. The device is frequent in poetic drama: Rodogune is a helpless innocent because she says so with such clarity and force, even if this clarity and force make her sound like a practised lawyer. Nevertheless, a few lines later, the other method is used. Rodogune prevents Antiochus from drinking the poisoned cup: 'Ah! gardez-vous de l'une et l'autre main!' Here we believe her love for Antiochus because she is willing to disrupt the ceremony and put herself on a level with Cléopâtre rather than endanger his life. The method is naturalistic: we infer her motives from her words and actions, as we do with a real person.

The question is, how far does Corneille rely on this second method? It is not easy to say. There are several passages where Rodogune apostrophises Nicanor and declares her love for him. Nadal[3] suggests that they should be interpreted as an indication of her psychology: she loved the father, and her love is now transferred to the son who resembles him. Corneille was certainly capable of this psychological subtlety, and in his later plays showed his mastery of the naturalistic presentation of character. But here it is not easy to be sure whether he is using the method. An equally plausible explanation is that he introduces these passages because Rodogune's desire to avenge Nicanor adds some heroic stiffening to an otherwise insipid love-interest, and because they also help to gloss over the awkwardness of having Rodogune declare her love for her lover's son. The same doubt remains even if we take a simpler example. In Act I, Scene v, Rodogune firmly announces the supremacy of her reason:

> Quelque époux que le ciel veuille me destiner,
> C'est à lui pleinement que je veux me donner.
> De celui que je crains si je suis le partage,
> Je saurai l'accepter avec même visage;
> L'hymen me le rendra précieux à son tour,
> Et le devoir fera ce qu'aurait fait l'amour.

Seven lines later, her attitude has changed:

> Garde-toi de nommer mon vainqueur:
> Ma rougeur trahirait les secrets de mon coeur.

Should we take this as a piece of psychological byplay, as a demonstration that the young and lovable Rodogune, who is so naïvely sure of her self-control, loses it immediately? Perhaps not: perhaps Corneille is merely preparing us to accept Rodogune, in rapid succession, as both a vengeful fury and a loving princess, according to the demands of the plot. But the psychological interpretation remains possible, in this case as in the other.

But Corneille cannot afford to use the naturalistic method wholeheartedly, because he wants to avoid the detailed probing into the emotional background which it demands. It therefore cannot help him effectively to palliate Rodogune's actions or explain away her inconsistencies, which remain an embarrassment. He tries to do this by a method used by both poetic and naturalistic dramatists to cover awkward junctions – the appeal to generally-accepted truths. Rodogune is always enunciating general maxims to justify her actions:

> La haine entre les grands se calme rarement;
> La paix souvent n'y sert que d'un amusement . . .
> Mais une grande offense est de cette nature,
> Que toujours son auteur impute à l'offensé
> Un vif ressentiment dont il le croit blessé . . .
> Tel est pour moi la reine.

We are not to deduce from this that she is a hard political female: the author is putting into her mouth a generalisation which he hopes we will accept as an explanation of her conduct because we accept that the generalisation is true. This tactic is especially useful when an 'unnatural' attitude can be made plausible by appealing to conventional opinion. We know in Act I that Rodogune loves one of the brothers, but in Act III, for the purposes of the plot, she has to promise to marry whichever of them will kill Cléopâtre. She first insists that her love is subordinate to duty:

> Du secret révélé j'en prendrai le pouvoir,
> Et mon amour pour naître attendra mon devoir.

then goes on to make her proposition:

> J'aime les fils du roi, je hais ceux de la reine . . .
> Il faut prendre parti, mon choix suivra le vôtre:
> Je respecte autant l'un que je déteste l'autre.
> Mais ce que j'aime en vous du sang de ce grand roi,
> S'il n'est digne de lui, n'est pas digne de moi.

There is no need either to complain that Rodogune is inhuman or to grow subtle about the Cornelian conception of love. Corneille somehow has to join together two opposed attitudes (Rodogune's love for Antiochus and her desire to use the brothers for her own ends). An appeal to contemporary conventions of 'amour-estime' is a useful cement. This device is common in Corneille, and especially in the plays of this middle period. In *Héraclius* (III.i), when Pulchérie's lover tells her he cannot marry her because he believes (falsely) that he is her brother, she replies:

> Ce grand coup m'a surprise, et ne m'a point troublée;
> Mon âme l'a reçu sans en être accablée;
> Et comme tous mes feux n'avaient rien que de saint,
> L'honneur les alluma, le devoir les éteint.

Here again, it is beside the point to complain that Pulchérie is inhuman, or a Cornelian superwoman. The plot requires that she shall love Martian, then be ready to renounce him, then (discovering he is not after all her brother) marry him. Corneille tries to make this acceptable by appealing to the seventeenth-century idea that love can arise from a sense of duty. A modern playwright trying to make such a sequence plausible might appeal to the notions of some modern psychology. Naturally, this might seem to us more natural. But in neither case is the current opinion which the playwright invokes of central importance: it is merely a part of the device.

In spite of Corneille's subtlety of technique, few can find Rodogune very interesting as a character. But Cléopâtre we do find interesting, and she is presented quite differently. There is no indecisiveness about the treatment of her: she is a powerful embodiment of evil dynamism, and clearly Corneille felt in sympathy with her. By this we need not assume that he approved of her; he is presenting her, not as a real woman, but as a poetic figure, a symbol almost. With her, there is no need to look for subtleties of character or to make inferences from the surface of the verse: she is known immediately and at all times for what she is, by us if not by the other characters. Moreover, we hardly feel that she is unnatural: we are carried along by the conviction of her rhetoric, and the question of naturalness does not arise. This is a further sign of the hollowness of the moral pattern of the play. Ethically, the brothers and Rodogune are 'good', and Cléopâtre is 'bad'. Aesthetically, things are different. The brothers are feeble creations, and Rodogune is a patchwork of incompatible elements (some of which, if taken naturalistically, make her as bad as Cléopâtre). It is Cléopâtre who is undoubtedly the most vital and attractive character. And here I think we have a pointer to the vigour and complexity of the play. Corneille is not relying solely on the naturalistic mode. In the character of Cléopâtre, the poetic mode is used alongside it, and in a particularly bold and direct manner.

This brings us to what in *Cinna* was the form and body of the play: the verse. No-one could find the verse in *Rodogune* as indubitably the substance of the play as in *Cinna*. But a study of it can tell us much about Corneille's strategy.

3

Three things about the verse of *Rogodune* are striking: it is predominantly rhetorical, not to say declamatory; it shows a great variety of tone; and it is often very bad. No-one is likely to dispute the first of these qualities, but we may quote some evidence of the other two.

First, variety. Alongside the clangorous rhetoric, we may distinguish two other tones. One is prosaic:

> Ah! mon frère, l'amour n'est guère véhément
> Pour des fils élevés dans un banissement.
>
> (II.iv)
>
> L'avis de Laonice est sans doute une adresse:
> Feignant de vous servir, elle sert sa maîtresse.
>
> (III.ii)

This is serviceable, but no more. It would do equally well in comedy, and would lose nothing in prose.

The other tone is more suited to the idyll: languorous, precious, often lyrical in a hot-house way:

> Allons, allons l'étreindre [our friendship] au pied de leurs autels
> Par des liens sacrés et des noeuds immortels.
>
> (I.iii)
>
> Les plus doux de mes voeux enfin sont exaucés.
> Tu viens de vaincre, amour, mais ce n'est pas assez.
>
> (IV.ii)
>
> Heureux Antiochus! Heureuse Rodogune!
>
> (IV.iii)

Corneille rarely refers to natural scenery in the plays of his middle period, but there is a famous piece of scenic poetry in V.iv:

> Je l'ai trouvé, Seigneur, au bout de cette allée
> Où la clarté du ciel semble toujours voilée.
> Sur un lit de gazon, de faiblesse étendu,
> Il semblait déplorer ce qu'il avait perdu;
> Son âme à ce penser paraissait attachée;
> Sa tête sur un bras languissamment penchée,
> Immobile et rêveur, en malheureux amant.

This simpering pastoralism comes strangely at the climax of one of Corneille's most savage plays.

Even more surprising is the badness of some of the verse. *Rodogune* has choicer examples of simple and compound nonsense than *Tite et Bérénice*:

> Croyant son mari mort, elle épousa son frère.

(I.i)

> La mort d'Antiochus me laissait sans armée,
> Et d'une troupe en hâte à me suivre animée
> Beaucoup dans ma vengeance ayant fini leurs jours,
> M'exposaient à son frère, et faible et sans secours.

(II.ii)

> Ce beau feu vous aveugle autant comme il vous brûle;
> Et, tâchant d'avancer, son effort vous recule.

(III.iv)

We even have quite extended flights of nonsense:

> Recevez donc ce coeur en nous deux reparti;
> Ce coeur, qu'un saint amour rangea sous votre empire,
> Ce coeur, pour qui le vôtre à tous moments soupire,
> Ce coeur, en vous aimant indignement percé,
> Reprend pour vous aimer le sang qu'il a versé;
> Il le reprend en nous, il revit, il vous aime,
> Et montre, en vous aimant, qu'il est encor le même.

(IV.i)

Assumptions about Corneille losing his grip will not do: in *Rodogune* he is obviously in full vigour. But he was not only a great but also a very skilful and sophisticated dramatist, and if he wrote like this there is a reason for it. This does not necessarily mean, of course, that the bad verse is good, but it does oblige us to explain why he chose to write in this way. Let us start by examining some of the scenes between the brothers which we left on one side before.

Act I is not a very successful act. We may well flinch when Timagène asks to be informed about the troubles in Syria, and Laonice embarks on her long, confused and ill-written narrative. Then come two scenes, the first with Antiochus and the second with him and Séleucus, and then in Scene iv the torture begins again. The substance of these two framing scenes is purely narrative, because the complicated plot demands it, but what of the scenes they frame?

In the first of them (I.ii), Antiochus expresses his love for Rodogune. In I.iii, he and Séleucus discover that they both love her, but they agree not to let this divide them. In a sense, therefore, these scenes are also pure exposition, but they tell us little in proportion to their length (total 140 lines, about 8% of the play). Nor can they be said to reveal character: the attitudes of the princes are purely conventional, and from a naturalistic standpoint barely credible. What, then, do these scenes do? An early exchange by the brothers about Rodogune gives the clue:

> Quoi! l'estimez-vous tant?
>   – Quoi! l'estimez-vous moins?
> Elle vaut bien un trône, il faut que je le die.
> – Elle vaut à mes yeux tout ce qu'en a l'Asie.
> – Vous l'aimez donc, mon frère?
>   – Et vous l'aimez aussi.

The characteristics are parallelism and stylisation (to the verge of comedy). Corneille may not have intended the comedy, but his general purpose is clear: he is setting off the dreary narrative with a stylised passage verging on lyricism. And lyricism is what he gives us next:

> L'amour, l'amour doit vaincre, et la triste amitié
> Ne doit être à tous deux qu'un objet de pitié.
> Un grand coeur cède un trône, et le cède avec gloire:
> Cet effort de vertu couronne sa mémoire;
> Mais lorsqu'un digne objet a pu nous enflammer,
> Qui le cède est un lâche et ne sait pas aimer.

This could be the occasion for much discussion of Corneille's conception of love. But here the purpose seems plain. Corneille is entertaining us with displays of verbal skill, and being a competent poet can easily turn out a little piece of love-poetry which will make a contrast with the endless narratives. As a deep study of sexual passion or the characters of the brothers is not part of his purpose, he has little material to work with, and has to make do with contemporary clichés, but he manages to make a pleasant effect with them. Then Séleucus is given an elaborate speech of 32 lines. Antiochus has suggested they should wait and see what happens. 'But no,' says Séleucus, 'We must do more than that', and we have a long recital of the woes of Thebes and Troy, caused in one case by brothers each desiring the throne and in the other by two men loving one woman. This is very interesting for what it is not. In a tragedy, these references to Thebes and Troy might be profoundly significant. Here, we are clearly not to take them too seriously: the speech is too neat, the parallelisms too pat, the bundle is too neatly tied up at the end:

> Ainsi ce qui jadis perdit Thèbes et Troie
> Dans nos coeurs mieux unis ne versera que joie;

> Ainsi notre amitié, triomphante à son tour,
> Vaincra la jalousie en cédant à l'amour.

'Ainsi' – the word shows clearly that Thebes and Troy are merely ornamental examples. The speech is what we have called a Senecan speech: that is, it stands by itself as a speech to be admired for its own sake. When Corneille rounds off the scene with the lyrical tag we have already quoted ('Allons, allons l'étreindre au pied de leurs autels') our impression is confirmed. The scenes are surrounded by deserts of narrative. In the scenes themselves, development of moral or psychological implications is taboo, because such development would split the play apart. Corneille therefore has to fill them with something else, which if possible must give a much-needed relief. This something else is a firework display of pretty verses.

The other scene in which the brothers appear is III.v. Here the situation is agonising. Rodogune has just left them with her demand that one of them should kill their mother. In operatic terms, we might expect an ensemble (or, rather, duet) of perplexity. This is very much what we get. The brothers embark upon antiphonal chanting in the most elaborately 'galante' vein ('amour si parfaite', 'rigueur', 'blasphème', 'révolte'), including the extraordinary conceit:

> Elle fuit, mais en Parthe, en nous perçant le coeur

and the hardly less astonishing:

> Comme j'aime beaucoup, j'espère encore un peu.
> L'espoir ne peut s'éteindre où brûle tant de feu,
> Et son reste confus me rend quelques lumières
> Pour juger mieux que vous de ces âmes si fières.

Here Corneille is doing what he did in the scene between the brothers in Act I: as he cannot explore the deeper implications, he entertains us with verbal embroidery. Unfortunately, he follows contemporary fashion so closely that we find what he provides unsatisfying. But this is not the whole of the scene. The longer speeches of Séleucus are in a much plainer style – as if Corneille were here characterising him through the quality of the verse – something which we are used to nowadays, but which we hardly find in, say, Montchrestien. What is most revealing, however, is the speech of Antiochus (ll. 1063 – 80) which, having been couched in a confused but cliché-ridden style, ends with the couplet:

> Mon frère, pardonnez à des discours sans suite,
> Qui font trop voir le trouble où mon âme est réduite.

It is one of the glories of poetic drama that it can render articulate what is inarticulate and convey confusion with lucidity. In *Cinna*, for instance, the complex issues presented through the portrayal of Auguste are expressed with perfect clarity through the verse, even when Auguste is presented as hesitating between conflicting impulses. But in this speech by Antiochus the method is quite different: we believe that Antiochus is confused because his speech is confused. We are approaching the method by which a character is presented as behaving as he would in real life, and by which we are expected to judge him accordingly: this is, we are approaching naturalism. The limitation of naturalism is that it does not allow the precise and powerful communication made possible by the resources of poetry. The great naturalists have tried to circumvent this limitation. Corneille, in this case, is doing the reverse: he is making Antiochus inarticulate because at this point there is so little to be communicated.

These reflections also enable us to understand several strange features of the play. Among them is the love-scene between Antiochus and Rodogune (IV.i). I have already said that this could, in a different play, have been made tragic, but that here it is not. The reason is that refusal to explore deep implications which marks the whole of *Rodogune*. To make up for (or cover up) this refusal, Corneille uses the same tactics as in the scenes between the brothers. On the one hand, he indulges in various kinds of display: verbal embroidery (as in the passage about Nicanor's heart quoted on p. 109 above); conventional *galanterie* ('aucun de nous ne serait téméraire | Jusqu'à s'imaginer qu'il eût l'heur de vous plaire'); and conventional heroics (Antiochus's offer to kill himself, which is hardly more than a gesture). On the other hand, he takes refuge in inarticulacy: 'Mon amour . . . Mais, adieu; mon esprit se confond.'

It is clear by now that these two techniques are frequently used in *Rodogune*. It is no accident that some of the 'business' lines ('Va, je reconnaîtrai ce service en son lieu') could equally well, at this stage of Corneille's development, appear as climactic lines: colourless themselves, they take their colour from the environment. In *Rodogune*, Corneille has already travelled far along the naturalistic road. At the same time, he is reviving a technique already archaic in 1630 – that of a drama in which the individual speeches exist in their own right as separate poems. Having emptied his subject-matter of much of its meaning, he puts in these compensating decorations, which appeal (or once appealed) by their intrinsic beauty, and distract our attention from the surrounding voids. We can now see why Séleucus's death is announced with a burst of pastoral poetry: the beauty of the verse attracts attention away from it ostensible subject-matter, and so conceals its potentially tragic significance.

Although Corneille was to adopt a very different technique in his later plays, we can already see at work in *Rodogune* the factors that contribute to the badness of some of the later verse: the plot demands that things be said which go awkwardly into neo-classical verse; there are attempts to supply interest by verses which are attractive in their own right (which means that, as underlying substance is lacking, they rely too much on a seventeenth-century *préciosité* that no longer appeals); and the verse is sometimes deliberately inferior for naturalistic reasons (the confusion or hollowness of the verse reflects the confusion or insincerity of the speaker). As in the later plays, the intermittent badness of the verse is due to Corneille's chosen approach, not to ineptitude.

The view we are coming to, then, is that in *Rodogune* Corneille has abandoned the attempt to achieve tragic substance and relies instead on elaborating the separate elements of plot and character. This method has affinities with naturalism; and the naturalistic approach enables him to evade deep issues by allowing his characters to plead inarticulacy. But is this view enough? It does not explain why we feel *Rodogune* is such a powerful play; and it does not do so because it takes no account of Cléopâtre.

Whatever the variations in tone and technique in the rest of the play, the rôle of Cléopâtre is presented in a manner which is both consistent and different from that of the rest of the play. Her first entrance gives the clue. She comes onto the stage alone (though it would have been easy to bring her on with other characters) and speaks a long soliloquy. The style is revealing. Throughout the play there is a lavish use of apostrophe, perhaps as a means of providing the illusion of a moral universe behind the play (though it is such a moral order which is lacking). Cléopâtre's speeches are more than usually full of it. In this first soliloquy she invokes, with many appositional phrases, 'Serments fallacieux', 'salutaire contrainte', 'haine dissimulée', and 'imprudente rivale'. In her second soliloquy (IV.v), she apostrophises the absent Rodogune and 'nature'. In her last (V.i), she addresses the ghost of Séleucus, the poison, the 'ridicule retour d'une sotte vertu', Antiochus, and the throne. There is no attempt to shade her character naturalistically: she is presented rhetorically, almost abstractly, but with a frightening energy. Her introduction is completed in her scene with Laonice (II.ii), and here again the method is quite unnaturalistic. She presents herself openly as a machiavellian intriguer:

> Apprends, ma confidente, apprends à me connaître . . .
> . . . Connais-moi tout entière.

and upbraids Laonice for her failure to realise it:

> N'apprendras-tu jamais, âme basse et grossière,
> A voir par d'autres yeux que les yeux du vulgaire?

If we took this naturalistically, it would be ridiculous: Cléopâtre would be a naive bungler to reveal herself so openly, and Laonice would revolt at this treatment. But Corneille is not presenting a real human being: he is presenting a poetic force as directly and powerfully as he can.

Cléopâtre's later dialogue scenes are marked by two features. The first is a conscious manipulation of her victims (and we know throughout that she is misleading them). The other is a frequent use of irony. Sometimes the irony lies simply in the fact that she says something which she and the audience understand in a sinister sense, but which her interlocutor does not. She assures Antiochus:

> ce soir, destiné pour la cérémonie,
> Fera voir pleinement si ma haine est finie.
>
> (IV.iii)

He thinks she is reconciled to his marriage; she intends to murder him and his bride.

But her rôle contains more complex ironies. When confessing the murder of her husband and leading up to a demand that her sons should murder Rodogune (II.iii) she boldly adopts a pose of maternal felicity and relieved innocence:

> O fils vraiment mes fils! O mère trop heureuse!
> Le sort de votre père enfin est éclairci:
> Il était innocent, et je puis l'être aussi . . .

In IV.vi, she goads Séleucus to rise against his brother. He demurs, and she rounds on him:

> Comme reine, à mon choix, je fais justice ou grâce,
> Et je m'étonne fort d'où vous vient cette audace,
> D'où vient qu'un fils, vers moi noirci de trahison,
> Ose de mes faveurs me demander raison.

Here we have cynicism indeed, but there is a fine bravado about it. We feel that Cléopâtre not only has the wit to gull the unsuspecting but also the spirit to reverse morality and taunt them with breaking the laws she herself has flouted. Throughout, we know what Cléopâtre is up to, and we are invited to enjoy with her her deceit and relish her ironies. This impression is confirmed by the characteristic tone of her verse. It lacks the depth and complexity of Chimène's or Pauline's, but by its sweep and energy it carries us along. Although her actions are detestable, there is no doubt that Corneille admired her and invites us to admire her. She has sometimes been compared with Lady Macbeth. The comparison is hardly relevant, as Cléopâtre shows no sign of remorse. If there is a Shakespearean figure who is characterised in the same way, it is Richard III in the first half of Shakespeare's play. But essentially the method is not Shakespeare's: it is Marlowe's and Jonson's. The real cousins of Cléopâtre are, in the heroic vein, Tamburlaine, Sejanus and Catiline. But Cléopâtre's skill and delight in tickling her victims and overturning the moral order may recall other figures, from a type of sardonic, sombre, even tragic, farce: Marlowe's Barabas, Jonson's Volpone. The presentation of Cléopâtre is what gives *Rodogune* a large part of its peculiar vitality. The method and results of presenting her in this way are those of the Senecan type of poetic drama discussed in chapter 6.

4

Rodogune is not Corneille's masterpiece: it is too incoherent and lacking in substance. But we cannot maintain that in the plays of this middle period he is reproducing his earlier successes in a coarsened form. In each of his plays he is struggling to find fresh solutions to the problems that beset him. We have argued that the central aesthetic problem is this: how to reconcile his aspirations to a poetic form of drama with his tendency towards naturalism. The prescriptions of neo-classical criticism (which no doubt were themselves influenced by more general factors in the cultural climate) tended also in the naturalistic direction, and ultimately towards reducing poetry to the recording of observed fact. The alternative to this realistic approach was for poetry to sink to the level of mere decoration – a path which was to lead Thomas Corneille to such successes as *Timocrate*, and which later was to tempt Racine. In *Cinna*, Corneille had found a solution by keeping to the poetic method, but at a surprising price: he had come close to adopting optimistic, anthropocentric attitudes not only opposed to Counter-Reformation orthodoxy but also incompatible with the absoluteness of tragedy. Corneille, personally devout and immersed in moralistic views of tragedy, cannot have rested content with a form based on *Cinna*. In *Polyeucte* he tries a compromise solution, and nearly succeeds, but there are signs of strain beneath the careful surface.

In *Rodogune* he makes yet another attempt to create a new form which will satisfy the requirements of a critical age, yet retain a poetic seriousness. He does this by fragmenting his forces and advancing on different fronts and in different directions. On one front, he develops the excitements of plot with a tightness and vigour quite new to drama. On another, he reverts to a technique of writing speeches to be enjoyed as pieces of verse on their own. On another, he makes an approach towards a more naturalistic method of presenting character (partly as a means of using the inarticulacy this allows to conceal awkward joins in his structure). Finally, abandoning the attempt to give even a superficial naturalistic gloss to his central character, he concentrates, in the figure of Cléopâtre, on a quite unmoral celebration of energy which we are invited to admire without regard to its aims. To present her he adopts a poetic technique which was archaic in his day, but which gives his play a daemonic quality impossible in strict naturalism.

We can now see why *Rodogune* stands so far above *Pompée* and *Héraclius*. In the first of these, Corneille attempted to solve his dilemma by concentrating almost wholly on heroic rhetoric and precious love-poetry. In the second, he was to rely almost entirely on ingenuity of plot. But *Rodogune* combines both these strategies. The terms in which Corneille praises it in his *Examen* are revealing: he calls it an 'heureux assemblage'. The play is an audacious attempt to build a new form out of disparate elements. We may now think that the ingredients were too various, and that in such an attempt victory was impossible; but we can also see how Corneille was tempted to think he had won it.

5

Corneille was to vary his strategy continually in the other plays beside *Héraclius* in the group which followed *Rodogune*, but on the whole with decidedly inferior results. Several of the plays are characterised by a curious confusion of tone. *Don Sanche*, for instance, slides uneasily between simple heroics, irony, and bathos; the action is thin, and does not seem to be fed from any deep experience. In *Théodore*, perhaps more obviously than in any other of Corneille's plays, there is no underlying theme and no consistency of attitude. This becomes embarrassingly clear when Théodore offers to commit suicide:

> Ma loi me le défend, mais mon Dieu me l'inspire;
> Il parle, et j'obéis à son secret empire;
> Et contre l'ordre exprès de son commandement,
> Je sens que c'est de lui que vient ce mouvement.

(III.iii)

Finally, in *Pertharite,* we find the same hollowness and mixture of moods. Its most famous feature is Rodelinde's proposition in Act III ('I am bound to hate you, but find it difficult; if you give me a reason to hate you by killing my son, I will marry you'). Perhaps its most successful passage, however, is in Act V, Scene ii, when Grimoald tells Éduige of his troubles. The tone is quite domestic. In effect, he says, 'Put yourself in my place' ('Madame, cependent mettez-vous en ma place'), and goes on to explain, very reasonably, that whatever he does he is in a mess.

There is something puzzling about Corneille's career at this period. The plays are brilliant, but unsatisfactory – uneven in value, and worse that those that preceded them and some that were to follow. They seem to refer to contemporary events, but not in any simple or direct way. Corneille supported the unpopular Court party against the notables, but critics have often supposed (wrongly, in my view, though the public of the time agreed with them) that *Nicomède* presented Condé in a favourable light. Corneille was more active than ever in the theatre, but was already turning to religious poetry, and seems to have hoped for a political career.[4]

His abandonment of the theatre after *Pertharite* has attracted less speculation than that of Racine after *Phèdre,* but his motivation is obscure. He can hardly have been discouraged by a long run of failures: *Héraclius, Andromède* and *Nicomède* had all been great successes, and *Don Sanche* was at least moderately successful. Nor need we take at face value his declaration that he is getting too old: there is irony in his statement that he is getting too old *to be still in fashion,* and he goes on to say he may change his mind. If his reason for giving up was old age, it was unlikely to be weakened by the passage of time. A more probable answer would lie in discouragement at aesthetic failure to find a form that would balance poetry and naturalism. Since *Polyeucte* he had sought furiously for a new form (six tragedies of the most diverse kind, one *pièce à machines,* one *comédie heroïque,* and two comedies, all in eight years). *Pertharite*'s failure showed him that he had failed to find it. He retired, discouraged, to think over the problem.

This explanation at least helps make sense of his pattern of production during his retirement. Until 1656 he devoted himself to religious poetry – one obvious way of reconciling poetry with truth and morality. After 1656, when his mind turned again to the theatre, the problem required a less facile solution. The years from 1656 to 1660 are the years of the *Examens* and *Discours.*

8

'SERTORIUS'

I

The most convincing sign of the high quality of Corneille's later plays is that each has a distinct world of its own. *Oedipe* is a strange world in which fantasy, myth and chivalric romance jostle; it has a glittering, Cocteauesque quality. *Othon* is a world of cold politics played out with naked steel and naked reason: its verse is sharp and clear. *Agésilas* is a gentler world where love is veiled in sentiment of coquetry and political treason is unmasked and forgiven; it is almost the world of *As You Like It*. *Attila* is a world of dark and dangerous barbarism, geographically and morally outside the civilised world. *Tite et Bérénice* takes place in a palace of civilised decorum, where escape is possible and the light of reason shines. *Pulchérie* echoes *Agésilas*, but the political note is deeper and love is saddened by failure. *Suréna* is a world of menace and shadows: a suffocating world where the victims struggle in the dark.

Two plays have been left out of this list: *Sophonisbe*, which lacks internal life; and *Sertorius*. *Sertorius* was in its day, and long after, considered one of Corneille's masterpieces. Even the eighteenth- and nineteenth-century detractors of the later plays agreed that it stood out from the others.

Acts I and II set out the complicated situation. Sertorius is maintaining in Spain a republican regime in defiance of the dictator Sylla, who has sent Pompée against him. Among the republicans who have fled to him is Aristie, Pompée's former wife. Sertorius's lieutenant Perpenna is planning to kill him, partly from ambition, partly because he wishes to marry the Spanish Queen Viriate, who is contemplating a political marriage to Sertorius. Sertorius loves her, but hesitates to marry her: he is ashamed to be in love at his age, and fears to antagonise his Roman supporters. He promises to persuade her to marry Perpenna, and proposes himself to marry Aristie, who is in correspondence with the anti-Syllan party in Rome. She still loves Pompée, whom she claims to want to win back for political reasons. When Sertorius offers Viriate Perpenna as a husband, she refuses indignantly, and Perpenna's discontent is increased.

Act III is the high point of the play. Pompée comes to negotiate with Sertorius, and they launch into passionate discussion. The verse exhibits that energy peculiar to Corneille at his best. Sertorius attacks:

> Est-ce être tout Romain qu'être chef d'une guerre
> Qui veut tenir aux fers les maîtres de la terre? . . .
> Ils étaient plus que rois, ils sont moindres qu'esclaves;
> Et la gloire qui suit vos plus nobles travaux
> Ne fait qu'approfondir l'abîme de leurs maux;
> Leur misère est le fruit de votre illustre peine;
> Et vous pensez avoir l'âme toute romaine!

Pompée takes up the argument, and the scene surges forward with claim and counter-claim. The great verses spring out:

> Il est doux de revoir les murs de la patrie.

> Je n'appelle plus Rome un enclos de murailles
> Que ses proscriptions comblent de funérailles.

> Rome n'est plus dans Rome, elle est toute où je suis.

But the political discussion is fruitless, and Sertorius turns to the subject of Aristie. She enters, and Sertorius leaves her alone with Pompée. The scene that follows contrasts sharply with the other, and is full of tenderness and beauty:

> Quoi qu'on m'a fait d'outrage, il ne m'en souvient plus.
> Plus de nouvel hymen, plus de Sertorius;
> Je suis au grand Pompée; et puisqu'il m'aime encore,
> Puisqu'il me rend son coeur, de nouveau je l'adore:
> Plus de Sertorius. Mais, Seigneur, répondez;
> Faites parler ce coeur qu'enfin vous me rendez.
> Plus de Sertorius. Hélas! quoi je die,
> Vous ne me dites point, Seigneur: 'Plus d'Emilie.'

Pompée begs her to be faithful to him, but she proudly refuses.

Act IV brings crisis nearer. Sertorius realises he cannot stifle his love for Viriate, but is reluctant to drive Perpenna to revolt. Viriate refuses to delay, and reveals that her strategy is very different from that of Sertorius:

> Et que m'importe à moi si Rome souffre ou non? . . .
> Affranchissons le Tage, et laissons faire au Tibre . . .
> Quant au grand Perpenna, s'il est si redoutable,
> Remettez-moi le soin de le rendre traitable . . .
> Pour moi, d'un grand Romain, je veux faire un grand roi.

Perpenna comes in with his confidant. Sertorius has to explain that Perpenna cannot marry Viriate. He tries to justify this by political arguments. Perpenna at first recognises Sertorius's dilemma and renounces Viriate, but his confidant again goads him to murder Sertorius. In Act V, Aristie learns that Sylla has abdicated and Emilie has died; she can therefore marry Pompée again. But Perpenna has already murdered Sertorius, and comes to demand the hand of Viriate. She and Aristie defy him, and Viriate denounces him with burning irony. Perpenna hesitates, and is conscious of his crimes.

Then Pompée arrives. His troops have easily overpowered the confused partisans of Sertorius and Perpenna. Perpenna tries to pretend that he has saved Aristie from marrying Sertorius, and that he is now delivering Viriate into his hands:

> Je fais plus: je vous livre une fière ennemie,
> Avec tout son orgueil et sa Lusitanie.

To ingratiate himself further, he hands over correspondence between Aristie and the anti-Syllan faction in Rome. Pompée burns the letters without reading them ('Si vous m'aviez connu, vous l'auriez su prévoir') and sends Perpenna to his death. He takes back Aristie, and offers Viriate an honourable peace. The play ends with his tribute to Sertorius.

This review gives some idea of the play's beauties, and why it was so long regarded as a masterpiece. But it has long since dropped from the repertoire, and from its first production has been fiercely criticised. The criticisms levelled against it, if true, are very damaging. First, the construction is inept. The subject is the death of Sertorius, but this subject, broached in the first scene, soon drops out of sight. The rivalry between Aristie and Viriate, and the question of who shall marry whom, take up the rest of Act I and all of Act II. Act III, though the summit of the play, is almost entirely irrelevant: the discussion between Pompée and Sertorius is 'une belle conversation dont il ne résulte rien' (Voltaire) or a 'joute oratoire qui n'aboutit à rien' (Lemaître); the scene between Pompée and Aristie has no bearing on the fate of Sertorius. Only in Act IV does the action come back to the true subject; but the first part of Act V is again taken up with the conflict of interests between Aristie and Viriate and then with the developments in Rome which will enable Aristie to remarry Pompée. When Sertorius's death is announced, it comes as an anti-climax, and is speedily followed by Pompée's triumphal entry to punish Perpenna, reclaim Aristie, and offer peace to Viriate. Sertorius's death and funeral then form the subject of a brief final speech. This diffuseness of structure is compounded by a second disconcerting feature: although the subject-matter is mainly political, there is a great deal of incongruous love-intrigue. Worse, this love-interest is frigidly handled: as the characters remark, their love is frequently 'un pur effet de noble politique'. This links up with a third fault: the characters are bundles of rigid and frequently contradictory attitudes. Sertorius himself complains that his characters of an aged warrior and a sighing lover do not go well together. Perpenna fluctuates between being an honest soldier tormented by ambition and jealousy, an insipid gallant, and a double-dyed villain. It is largely because he fluctuates so much that we are surprised when he finally does kill Sertorius.

When such radical charges are brought against a work that makes a powerful impression, it is worth asking whether they miss the point. Let us therefore look again at *Sertorius* with these criticisms in mind and see how far they are relevant.

We start with Act III, Scene i, the famous confrontation of Sertorius and Pompée. It is the finest scene in the play, but usually it has been thought irrelevant. Let us assume, for the moment, that when Corneille included a scene of 250 lines, containing some of his finest poetry, he did so because he thought it was relevant. What is the scene mainly about? The answer is clear enough: politics. Before dismissing it as a frigid debate, we might reflect on Corneille's attitude to politics. Politics were important to him, personally and as a citizen. He had demonstrated in *Cinna* his awareness of the value of a strong monarchy, and there is no reason to think his flattery of Louis XIV insincere. Yet he had seen the misery of the peasants, the insurrections in Normandy in 1640, and their much more terrible suppression. His famous prologue to *La Toison d'Or* shows that he was aware that even the successful wars of a legitimate monarch brought misery to the people.

It is a commonplace that in his plays Corneille often presents characters who can be paralleled among the great nobles who took part in the Frondes. What is striking is the way in which these factious nobles resembled the last defenders of the Roman republic. The nobles who opposed royal absolutism had no connection with any ideal of popular democracy: they stood for the separate interests of the feudal (often impoverished) nobility against the distasteful supremacy of the king, with his bourgeois ministers. Both the aristocrats and their allies among the *Parlementaires* were looking back to a mediaeval conception of a monarchy in which the king was merely the greatest of the aristocracy and respected the rights of his lords and the ancient privileges of the communes and their magistrates. For much of the reigns of Louis XIII and Louis XIV we may believe that the bulk of the middle classes (including Corneille) and the *bas peuple* (insofar as they had political views) favoured the peace and quiet of absolutism against the power of the nobles, which often stood for no more than licence to pillage their subordinates. Even in the later part of Louis XIV's reign, the nobles who criticised his absolutism (Fénelon, Saint Simon and the circle of the duc de Bourgogne) thought solely in terms of limiting the royal power in the interests of the higher nobility. Similarly, in republican Rome the defenders of 'Liberty' and 'the Republic' were largely those privileged aristocrats to whom republican offices brought power and the opportunity of wealth. It was the Caesarian party which exploited popular feeling, and Octavian and his bourgeois ministers who established the principate. Both parties treated republican forms cavalierly – Brutus hardly less so than Octavian; both parties contained honest men struggling to uphold what seemed the better cause among the turmoil of civil war. There is ample evidence in Corneille's work that he understood the paradox that the defenders of liberty and the *concordia ordinum* (so similar to the mediaeval ideas of hierarchy and respect for established privilege asserted by the Frondeurs) were factious and selfish as well as idealistic, and that their ideals, though noble, were old-fashioned and often a cover for baser motives. There is nothing naive or sentimental about his presentation of politics – least of all in *Sertorius*.

The key text is Pompée's pronouncement in III.i:

> Lorsque deux factions divisent un empire,
> Chacun suit au hasard la meilleure ou la pire,
> Suivant l'occasion ou la nécessité
> Qui l'emporte vers l'un ou vers l'autre côté.
> Le plus juste parti, difficile à connaître,
> Nous laisse en liberté de nous choisir un maître.

The world in which we find ourselves is divided; it is difficult, perhaps impossible, to see which side is right; what decides our allegiance is chance, opportunity, or necessity; but a wise man can be detached enough to choose, instead of following blindly. This is hardly a world of great causes or lofty idealism. Pompée will concede only the validity of the limited moral laws of an honourable man: first, to be loyal to one's chosen leader–

> Mais quand ce choix est fait, on ne s'en dédit plus.

– second, to behave 'en généreux':

> L'inimitié qui règne entre nos deux partis
> N'y rend pas de l'honneur tous les droits amortis.

Comme le vrai mérite a ses prérogatives,
Qui prennent le dessus des haines les plus vives,
L'estime et le respect sont de justes tributs
Qu'aux plus fiers ennemis arrachent les vertus.

On his side, Sertorius shows in his discussions with Viriate that he
has no illusions about the nature of power:

en gouvernant le mieux on fait des mécontents

(II.ii)

and the compromises needed to maintain it:

Mais porter dès l'abord les choses à l'extrême,
Madame, et sans besoin faire des mécontents!
Soyons heureux plus tard pour l'être plus longtemps.
Une victoire ou deux jointes à quelque adresse . . .

(IV.ii)

It is against this chaotic and decidely un-ideal background that the
debate between Sertorius and Pompée is fought out. The scene starts
with elaborate compliments from each to the other on their military
skill. These serve two purposes: they show that in this division of factions the only moralities still in force are the social morality of politeness
and the personal morality of the 'homme généreux'; and they convey
forcibly that the real power of both men rests openly on their personal
ability to win battles. This last point is also used to bring out the continuity and impersonality of these military skills, independent of their
practitioners, and by implication independent of any ideals in whose
cause they are employed:

Mes exemples un jour ayant fait place aux vôtres,
Ce que je vous apprends, vous l'apprendrez à d'autres;
Et ceux qu'aura ma mort saisis de mon emploi
S'instruiront contre vous, comme vous contre moi.

Then Sertorius attacks Pompée for supporting Sylla. Pompée in reply
draws a distinction between the cause a man serves and what he feels is
right:

Mais vous jugez, Seigneur, de l'âme par le bras;
Et souvent l'un paraît ce que l'autre n'est pas.

He then enunciates the doctrine of how people choose sides in a civil
war ('Lorsque deux factions divisent un empire'); and he claims that in
following Sylla he is making sure that when Sylla dies his power will
fall into good Republican hands. Sertorius strips away this sophistry. He

also draws a distinction between the surface and the real motive, but claims that Pompée's real motive is to gain power for himself:

> Mais si je m'en rapporte aux esprits soupçonneux,
> Vous aidez aux Romains à faire essai d'un maître,
> Sous ce flatteur espoir qu'un jour vous pourrez l'être.

Pompée takes him up on this sharply:

> Permettez qu'à mon tour je parle avec franchise;
> Votre exemple à la fois m'instruit et m'autorise:
> Je juge, comme vous, sur la foi de mes yeux,
> Et laisse le dedans à pénétrer aux Dieux.
> Ne vit-on pas ici sous les ordres d'un homme?
> N'y commandez-vous pas comme Sylla dans Rome? . . .
> Les titres différents ne font rien à la chose;
> Vous imposez des lois ainsi qu'il en impose;
> Et s'il est périlleux de s'en faire haïr,
> Il ne serait pas sûr de vous désobéir.

From this to the end of the discussion, the battle is fierce. Sertorius, in lines I discussed in chapter 6, seeks to demonstrate that his faction is the real Rome; he even offers to surrender his command to Pompée if Pompée will join him. Pompée takes the more cynical line that Rome is in Rome, and that Sertorius's senate is 'un amas de bannis'. He rejects Sertorius's offer as a gesture of no practical effect:

> De pareils lieutenants n'ont de chefs qu'en idée:
> Leur nom retient pour eux l'autorité cédée;
> Ils n'en quittent que l'ombre . . .

The political debate ends with a striking passage which points the theme of deception and self-deception, of appearance and reality. Pompée urges Sertorius to surrender, as Sylla will then surrender his dictatorship. Sertorius refuses: 'Je ne m'éblouis point de cette illusion. | Je connais le tyran'. But in fact Sylla does give up the dictatorship, and so makes possible the happy ending of the play. Sertorius is deceiving himself, and prolonging the war without good reason: it is Pompée who in the end will make the peace.

The debate is a thorough demonstration of the hollowness of Sertorius's position, and of the equivocal nature of Pompée's. How should magnates behave in a civil war? Ideals are noble, but they have flaws (and in any event it is difficult to know which ideals are best). In the last resort, luck (how often Sylla the Fortunate is invoked!), skill and intelligent self-interest are the only qualities in which a man can put his trust; and even so, the interests of those he must take as friends and allies are so diverse that success is unlikely. Far from being irrelevant, this clash of ideas and values is at the centre of *Sertorius*. The scene is central in other senses than the literal one. First, it indicates without ambiguity the non-tragic nature of *Sertorius*. One element must appear in any definition of tragedy: the sense that there is somehow an unknown but absolute order which informs the action. *Sertorius*, however serious, is above all mundane. There is no hint that the world is controlled by ultimate values, by divine powers (the references to the gods are entirely conventional), or by any impersonal numinous conception such as fate; luck, skill, politeness and personal honour are the only values. Secondly, the scene shows that the method of this part of the play is poetic: Corneille is not debating abstract ideas or showing what Roman generals talked about. He is enunciating and developing thematic elements important in the pattern of the play, and is doing this primarily through the verse. The scene is not a magnificent irrelevance: it builds up and varies a theme which runs through the play and at one level constitutes its meaning.

This theme is strongly announced in I.i, by Aufide to Perpenna:

> Avez-vous oublié cette grande maxime,
> Que la guerre civile est le règne du crime?

The two of them then bring in the motif that is to be taken up and developed by Sertorius and Pompée in Act III. Aufide plays Pompée:

> Ah! s'il faut obéir, ne faisons plus la guerre;
> Prenons le même joug qu'a pris toute la terre.
> Pourquoi tant de périls? pourquoi tant de combats?
> Si nous voulons servir, Sylla nous tend les bras.
> C'est mal vivre en Romain que prendre loi d'un homme;
> Mais, tyran pour tyran, il vaut mieux vivre a Rome.

In reply, Perpenna takes up the stance of Sertorius:

> Vois mieux ce que tu dis quand tu parles ainsi.
> Du moins la liberté respire encore ici:
> De notre république à Rome anéantie,
> On y voit refleurir la plus noble partie.

What is more, Sertorius owes his command largely to luck – 'Ce bonheur imprévu qui partout l'accompagne'. This balanced statement by the two villains of the themes taken up by the two heroes cannot be fortuitous. Corneille is setting the dilemma clearly before us: there is no right or wrong in civil war; if this is so, Aufide is to Pompée as Perpenna is to Sertorius; there is no distinction between the good man and the bad; and we are not far from the world of La Rochefoucauld (the civil warrior) where 'La fortune et l'humeur gouvernent le monde.' Aufide is made to point the moral with unambiguous brutality:

> L'occasion nous rit dans un si grand dessein;
> Mais tel bras n'est à nous que jusques à demain:
> Si vous rompez le coup, prévenez les indices;
> Perdez Sertorius ou perdez vos complices.
> Craignez ce qu'il faut craindre: il en est parmi nous
> Qui pourraient bien avoir même remords que vous.

The theme of the mixture of idealism, self-interest and sheer opportunism in politics is taken up again and again. Sertorius politely pretends (both to Perpenna and to Viriate) that Perpenna's support is invaluable. In fact, Perpenna's men betrayed him by joining Sertorius, and he was obliged to tag along with them. What is more, Sertorius is now nervous of offending Perpenna, and equally anxious to placate Viriate:

> Je crains donc de l'aigrir si j'épouse Aristie.

> (I.ii)

The whole presentation of Sertorius emphasises the instability of his position and his desperate need to gather support where he can.

Sertorius is not the whole of the play, however. Corneille has flanked him by Pompée and Perpenna, each of whom presents a variation on the same theme. Both incline to opportunism rather than idealism, but Pompée is more realistic and consistent, Perpenna more vacillating and prone to rushes of goodwill. But Pompée is lucky and Perpenna is not – an interesting sidelight on the moral universe of the play. Further to prevent us from taking Sertorius as the single focus of the play, Corneille has put into it two powerful women characters, Viriate and Aristie. They are both supporters whom Sertorius needs, and yet their interests are clearly opposed to each others', and they are both pursuing their own ends. In the case of Aristie, the fact is hardly disguised: she wants to get Pompée back and to revenge herself on Sylla, and at the end she is quite happy to regain Pompée and forget about politics. The case of Viriate is more complicated. In the first two-thirds of the play she appears as Sertorius's main ally, to whom he is properly grateful. But in Act IV she suddenly reveals what has been only hinted before: she cares nothing for Rome and the republic, and her sole aim is to consolidate her kingdom, which the republic (the 'liberty' for which Sertorius is fighting) will enslave. To achieve her aim, she deliberately aims to discredit Sertorius in the eyes of his countrymen.

In Act V, Scene i, Corneille underlines this element in his theme by making Viriate expose more clearly than ever that she has been making use of Sertorius, and that she is fiercely hostile to Rome:

> J'ai fait venir exprès Sertorius d'Afrique
> Pour sauver mes Etats d'un pouvoir tyrannique . . .
> Mes sujets valent bien que j'aime à leur donner
> Des monarques d'un sang qui sache gouverner,
> Qui sachent faire tête à vos tyrans du monde,
> Et rendre notre Espagne en lauriers si féconde
> Qu'on voie un jour le Pô redouter ses efforts,
> Et le Tibre lui-même en trembler pour ses bords.

The inclusion of these women, then, serves several purposes in the development of the political theme: it demonstrates once again how self-interest comes first; it emphasises the division of aims behind an apparently united front; and it reinforces the motif, which recurs throughout the play, of deception and misunderstanding.

So far we have looked only at the political side of the play. What of the love-interest, to which many critics have taken exception? Once again, let us start from Act III, and from that other central scene which has been called peripheral, the love-scene between Pompée and Aristie. We will defer for a moment consideration of the style and the presentation of the characters, and note only two features. One is that we are clearly invited to regard the love of Pompée and Aristie as beautiful and moving, quite apart from any relevance it has to the political theme. The second point is the way in which Corneille links this love-interest to his political theme. The obstacles to the reunion of Pompée and Aristie are primarily political; and, just as Sertorius is forced to dissemble and prevaricate for political reasons, so does Pompée here. Pompée's position, like that of Sertorius, is false on both the political and the sentimental levels; and this parallelism helps to bind together the two scenes of Act III, despite the difference of their style and subject-matter. The scene between Pompée and Aristie is convincing and touching, but Corneille does not hesitate to emphasise (through the mouth of Aristie) the brutal cynicism which lies behind the action. 'Go on,' says Aristie in effect, 'Don't mind me: you have so many important things to do elsewhere.' And then:

> Surtout ce privilège acquis aux grandes âmes,
> De changer à leur gré de maris et de femmes,
> Mérite qu'on l'étale aux bouts de l'univers,
> Pour en donner l'exemple à cent climats divers.

These two features characterise the love-intrigues of the play. If we put aside for the moment our assumptions about neo-classical frigidity, we may agree that the presentation of love in *Sertorius* is natural, even touching. Perpenna in the first scene confesses his love for Viriate and his jealousy of Sertorius. The verse takes on momentarily a softer tone and colouring:

> Mais elle-même, hélas! de ce grand nom charmée,
> S'attache au bruit heureux que fait sa renommée.

The same happens in the next scene, when the love of Aristie and Pompée is mentioned: amid the hard political rhetoric the verse suddenly softens:

> Cela peut être encore; ils s'aimaient chèrement.

Sertorius's own confession of love is touching:

> J'aime ailleurs. A mon age il sied si mal d'aimer,
> Que je le cache même à qui m'a su charmer;
> Mais tel que je puis être, on m'aime, ou, pour mieux dire,
> La reine Viriate à mon hymen aspire.

The abruptness, the quick agreement that his love is incongruous, the pauses and self-correction of the third line, the rapid transition from the love he hopes for to the more reasonable political motive, all convey the conflict of Sertorius's emotions. We can certainly speak here of his emotions: Corneille is using the naturalistic technique of presenting a character as though he were a real person from whose words we infer his motivation. From this angle, even the loves of Sertorius and Perpenna appear sympathetic. Sertorius knows it is ridiculous for him to love, and his attempts either to conceal it or defiantly to proclaim it have a pathos trembling on the edge of absurdity which we would be quick to admire in a modern play. In IV.ii. we have the perfect tragicomedy of the bear in love. Viriate is the coquette:

> Vous m'en parlez enfin comme si vous m'aimiez!

Sertorius falls immediately into behaving like an intense adolescent, and then, pulling himself together, relates his sense of shame and his inner struggles:

> Souffrez, après ce mot, que je meure à vos pieds.
> J'y veux bien immoler tout mon bonheur au vôtre;
> Mais je ne vous puis voir entre les bras d'un autre . . .
> J'ai cru honteux d'aimer quand on n'est plus aimable:
> J'ai voulu m'en défendre à voir mes cheveux gris,
> Et me suis répondu longtemps de vos mépris;

> Mais j'ai vu dans votre âme ensuite une autre idée,
> Sur qui mon espérance aussitôt s'est fondée . . .
> Mais je n'ai point douté qu'il ne fût d'un grand coeur
> De tout sacrifier pour le commun bonheur.
> L'amour de Perpenna s'est joint à ces pensées;
> Vous avez vu le reste, et mes raisons forcées.
> Je m'étais figurè que de tels déplaisirs
> Pourraient ne me coûter que deux ou trois soupirs . . .
> Mais près d'un coup fatal, je sens par mes ennuis
> Que je me promettais bien plus que je ne puis.
> Je me rends donc, Madame; ordonnez de ma vie:
> Encor tout de nouveau je vous la sacrifie.
> Aimez-vous Perpenna?

To get the full effect, all we have to do is to apply to the character the same standards as we do in real life – that is, to adopt a naturalistic attitude. Of course, the method has its dangers. We may find it unnerving, when Viriate asks Perpenna if he will help her, and he replies:

> Si je le veux? J'y cours,
> Madame, et meurs déjà d'y consacrer mes jours.
> Mais pourri-je espérer que ce faible service
> Attirera sur moi quelque regard propice . . .?

(II.iv)

But this is a penalty of naturalism. To appear natural, it is often necessary to appear natural in the fashion of the day; and fashions have a way of becoming outmoded. We should attribute this rush of preciosity, not to Corneille's bad taste, but to the naturalistic method.

Given that the love-element in *Sertorius* is different in subject-matter and method from the main, political element, how far is Corneille able to harmonise them? He does so in three ways. First, he makes no attempt to sentimentalise, but brings out strongly the realistic, even cynical, background which is common to both of them. We have already quoted Aristie on divorce. Viriate is no less forthright:

> L'hymen où je prétends ne peut trouver d'amorces
> Au milieu d'une ville ou règnent les divorces.

(IV.ii)

Nor is there any attempt to gloss over the physical absurdity of Sertorius's love. On the contrary, it is emphasised by the use of a harshly realistic turn of phrase:

> Il est assez nouveau qu'un homme de son âge
> Ait des charmes si forts pour un jeune courage,

> Et que d'un front ridé les replis jaunissants
> Trouvent l'heureux secret de captiver les sens.

(II.i)

Secondly, Corneille appeals directly for sympathy for those who contend with problems of love as well as politics:

> Que c'est un sort cruel d'aimer par politique!
> Et que ses intérêts sont d'étranges malheurs,
> S'ils font donner la main quand le coeur est ailleurs!

This is a bold manoeuvre: Corneille is presenting the political issues by a basically poetic technique, in which the overall pattern – expressed principally in words – is more important than the 'characters' of his figures, and at the same time inviting us to sympathise with his figures naturalistically.

Whether this frank appeal to a double standard succeeds is a matter of opinion: I think it does. But it is made more acceptable by the third and most important part of Corneille's strategy. A prominent motif of the political part of the play is division, and especially self-division and the deceits which it leads to – the way in which a character has to hide his aims in the compromises of political life, and in which (as when Sertorius refuses to believe Sylla will abdicate) the politician is deceived by his own astuteness. The same motif is echoed in the love-intrigues: Sertorius, Viriate and Aristie forward and conceal their real motives under assumed ones, just as in the political part of the play. One link is the recurring use of 'divorce' in the sense of both 'dissension' and 'separation of spouses'. More important is the emphasis on deception, with its accompaniment of assumed frankness. In the scene between Pompée and Sertorius, the theme recurs frequently:

> Seigneur, faites qu'on se retire,
> Afin qu'en liberté je puisse vous les dire.
>
> ce franc aveu sied bien aux grands courages.
>
> Mais, Seigneur, étant seuls, je parle avec franchise.
>
> Permettez qu'à mon tour je parle avec franchise.

Much of this is ironical or deceitful; but when Aristie is mentioned, Pompée bursts out:

> Hélas! ce mot me tue, et je le dis sans feinte.

But the love-scene between Pompée and Aristie is equally played against a background of irony and hidden purposes. The motif of frankness *versus* deceit comes out again and again in the love-passages of the play. In Act I, Scene i, Perpenna decides to tell Sertorius of his love for Viriate:

> Mais je veux sur ce point lui découvrir mon âme.

In fact, he takes refuge in political arguments, until Sertorius unmasks his deceit:

> Vous-même, Perpenna, pourquoi tant déguiser?
> Je vois ce qu'on m'a dit: vous aimez Viriate;
> Et votre amour caché dans vos raisons éclate.

Finally, in Act V, Aristie and Viriate decide that only complete honesty over their political and amorous plans can save the situation:

> Mais vous pourrez me perdre, et moi vous affaiblir,
> Si le coeur mieux ouvert ne met d'intelligence
> Votre établissement avecque ma vengeance.
>
> Viriate à son tour vous doit même franchise,
> Madame; et d'ailleurs même on vous en a trop dit,
> Pour vous dissimuler ce que j'ai dans l'esprit.

This parallelism of themes helps to bind the dissimilar elements together. Indeed, Corneille boldly yokes them together in IV.iii. at a crucial moment of the play, just before Perpenna decides to murder Sertorius. Sertorius has been speaking to Viriate on Perpenna's behalf; Perpenna has been escorting Pompée on his way on behalf of Sertorius. Sertorius says he has got nowhere, though he has Perpenna's interests at heart; Perpenna agrees that he needs Sertorius's support. But they are at cross-purposes: Sertorius is referring to his discussion with Pompée, Perpenna to Sertorius's discussion with Viriate:

> Je parle de Sylla, vous le devez connaître.
> – Et je parlais des feux que la Reine a fait naître.

This has been attacked as unworthy of tragedy. But Corneille is not writing tragedy. At this point he is joining together two contrasting elements in his play, and he does so by placing them on the same plane by a *quid pro quo* which stresses the motif of misunderstanding and cross-purposes that is common to them both.

So far, we have discussed the separate political and love elements in the play; the predominantly poetic method used to present the one and the relatively naturalistic method used to present the other; and the means by which Corneille strives to harmonise the two elements. Before we can try and form any general conclusion about the play, however, another important question arises: how does Corneille manage to operate with two different methods in the same play? To answer this, we may first look at the characters, and then again at some of the verse.

It would be easy to disregard inconsistencies in the characterisation on the grounds that Corneille is more interested in the total dramatic pattern than in the representation of individuals. In the main, this is true of Sertorius and Perpenna: their attitudes are manipulated in order to express the political pattern of the play, and only intermittently (in the love passages) are we invited to consider them sympathetically as human beings. The presentation of Pompée is more complex. On the political level, he is undoubtedly an important element in the poetic pattern. He expresses, on the one hand, the cynicism of civil war, where it is every man for himself, and the just cause is 'difficile à connaître'. On the other hand, he is 'généreux', and there is more than a hint that enlightened self-interest, combined with the virtues of a 'grand courage', represent the best values possible in such a world. This combination of brute force and honourable behaviour comes out in his words at the very end of the play:

> Vous, Madame, agréez pour notre grand héros
> Que ses mânes vengés goûtent un plein repos.
> Allons donner votre ordre à des pompes funèbres,
> A l'égal de son nom illustres et célèbres,
> Et dresser un tombeau, témoin de son malheur,
> Qui le soit de sa gloire et de notre douleur.

This is the ceremonious salute of an honourable man to his defeated opponent. There is no hint of any ultimate moral order: the best that can happen to Sertorius is that he should be avenged and commemorated; his death is glossed over as his 'malheur' (a last reference to the pervading theme of luck). There seems no reason to suppose that the 'votre' is a printer's error: Pompée is in command, but gracefully acts as though Viriate were: a neat fusion of power and politeness.

Pompée, however, belongs more completely than Sertorius to both the political and sentimental sides of the play: it is he who appears in Act III in both the central scenes. His attitude in the second scene is revealing. He is presented sympathetically, as a human being, not as a poetic figure. The two opposites, his love for Aristie and his self-interest, are presented clearly, without any mixture. The two values are held, as it were, in suspense. We may infer that it is precisely this ability to hold the conflict sharply in focus without striking attitudes or rushing to heroic extremes which is presented by Corneille as admirable. At the end of the play, Pompeé does strike attitudes, but only when the situation has changed, and the showy gesture is also the most sensible.

I have avoided till now discussion of Aristie and Viriate. Critics who have attacked the presentation of the men have praised that of the women. The fact in itself is interesting, but not less so than Corneille's technique of presenting them. Aristie is first referred to (by Sertorius in Act I) as wishing to revenge herself on Pompée by taking 'un plus illustre époux'. She herself professes this, but she soon finds plenty of political reasons for trying to win back Pompée instead. Her speeches are full of ringing Cornelian lines:

> Si je réduis Pompée à chasser Emilie,
> Peut-il, Sylla régnant, regarder l'Italie?
> Ira-t-il se livrer à son juste courroux?
> Non, non; si je le gagne, il faut qu'il vienne à vous . . .
> Vous aurez des amis par ce nouveau divorce;
> Vous aurez du tyran la principale force,
> Son armée, ou du moins ses plus braves soldats,
> Qui de leur général voudront suivre les pas;
> Vous marcherez vers Rome à communes enseignes.
>
> (I.iii)

Clearly, we are not meant to take this too seriously: we see that her real aim is to remarry Pompée. In other words, we are to take notice not of what she says but what we infer she means. In her scene with Pompée in Act III she denounces his perfidy; but the moment he reminds her that he is her husband, she relents:

> Ah! si ce nom vous plaît, je suis encore à vous.

When he refuses to remarry her immediately, she again turns on him, despite her love. The scene is moving, and the psychology subtle. The method and effect aimed at are naturalistic.

This is nothing new in Corneille's work, but in parts of *Sertorius* the naturalistic method is applied with a thoroughness which is new – notably in the presentation of Viriate. We can best demonstrate this by trying to answer a simple question: does Viriate love Sertorius? On the surface, the answer is 'No'. She tells Sertorius to his face:

> Je sais vous obéir,
> Mais je ne sais que c'est d'aimer ni de haïr;
> Et la part que tantôt vous aviez dans mon âme
> Fut un don de ma gloire, et non pas de ma flamme.
>
> (IV.ii)

Her avowed motive for wanting Sertorius as her husband is that she needs his support politically:

> Ce ne sont pas les sens que mon amour consulte . . .
> Et son feu, que j'attache aux soins de ma grandeur,
> Dédaigne tout mélange avec leur folle ardeur.
>
> (II.i)

Despite some support from Corneille's own comments, however, there are reasons for not taking these statements as the whole truth.[1] The other characters assume that Viriate does in fact love Sertorius:

> Mais à parler sans fard, votre amour me surprend.
>
> (*Thamire*, II.i)
>
> Vous le voyez, Seigneur, comme on vous joue.
> Tout son coeur est ailleurs.
>
> (*Aufide*, II.v)

Viriate herself acts as though she loves him, and this comes out in the tone of her references to him:

> ce héros si cher . . .
> Sertorius, lui seul digne de Viriate,
> Mérite que pour lui tout mon amour éclate . . .
> J'aime en lui ces cheveux tout couverts de lauriers,
> Ce front qui fait trembler les plus braves guerriers,
> Ce bras qui semble avoir la victoire en partage . . .
>
> (II.i)

In the context, which includes the naturalistic presentation of Aristie, there is little doubt that we may assume that Viriate is in love with Sertorius. If so, many passages take on an added effectiveness. When Sertorius asks if he can see into her inmost heart, she replies:

> Il est si peu fermé, que chacun y peut lire,
> Seigneur, peut-être plus que je ne puis vous dire:
> Pour voir ce que s'y passe, il ne faut que des yeux.
>
> (II.ii)

This is frigid if we take it to mean, 'My (political) motives are obvious; I have explained them often enough.' But if it means, 'It is only too obvious that I love you', its mixture of naivety, coquetry and modesty is charming. The whole character takes on a vivid life. Viriate is young, with the idealism and grandiloquence of youth. Although she loves (as young women often do) a successful man much older than herself, she is anxious to conceal it behind fine phrases; but she is angry if he takes them too seriously. We can therefore, if we wish, take her fine Cornelian speeches as hollow. If we wish – for one of the pleasures and pitfalls of naturalism is that the literary record is a guide to the truth but is not the whole truth: there is a gap between the text and the character which must be filled by interpretation, by the reader for himself or by the actor for the audience. There is scope to play Viriate as a cold virago, a charming coquette, or anything in between. Many effective interpretations are possible: the interpretation chosen will alter the play, but Corneille has so contrived things that no reasonable interpretation can upset its balance. We may admire the skill with which he has combined this control of the overall meaning of the play with the scope for interpretative variation.

Despite its mixture of the poetic and naturalistic modes, *Sertorius* is written in very successful verse. Corneille has no difficulty in compassing a forthright, almost Cinna-esque, style for the political parts of the play. It is the more naturalistic parts that show his technique at its most interesting: he adopts what I described in chapter 6 as 'heightened speech' and the 'senecan' type of speech, and uses them to splendid effect. I take two examples, both from the scene between Pompée and Aristie in Act III. The first is Aristie's lyrically patterned speech, part of which we have already quoted:

> Sortez de mon esprit, ressentiments jaloux;
> Noirs enfants du dépit, ennemis de ma gloire,
> Tristes ressentiments, je ne veux plus vous croire . . .
> Rentrez dans mon esprit, jaloux ressentiments,
> Fiers enfants de l'honneur, nobles emportements,
> C'est vous que je veux croire; et Pompée infidèle
> Ne saurait plus souffrir que ma haine chancelle:
> Il l'affermit pour moi. Venez, Sertorius.

This is *par excellence* a speech that draws attention to itself, a virtuoso piece. The elaboration serves two purposes: it is beautiful in itself and it enables a poetic set-piece to be manufactured when there is no underlying poetic pattern of which it can form a part. The difficulty of writing a naturalistic scene in a mainly poetic play is thus overcome.

The second example again shows the use of repetition. Pompée says, 'If you love me'–

> Plaignez-vous, haïssez, mais ne vous donnez pas.

Then, a few lines later, 'Don't marry anyone else'–

> Plaignez-vous, haïssez, mais ne vous donnez pas.

Again, the repetition has two purposes: it gives a poetic allure to sentiments that could equally well be expressed by prose; and, more subtly, it recalls the repetition used in the preceding scene between Pompée and Sertorius, where it was used to articulate the poetic structure. There, Sertorius and Pompée had caught up and reechoed each others' phrases about 'l'âme toute romaine' and 'franchise', so pointing up the simultaneous celebration and undercutting of heroism that are so important to the poetic theme of the play. Here, the reechoing by Pompée is for a less serious purpose, and perhaps appears sentimental; but it makes its local effect, and gives the two modes of the play a superficial similarity of style which helps to unify them.

No-one has ever denied that there are many things to praise in *Sertorius*. The criticisms have been that it is loosely articulated and contains too many things that do not go well together. On the whole, critics have tended to call it a failure. In my view, this judgment is wrong, and is made possible by two misconceptions. The first is the failure to recognise, behind Corneille's formidably poetic front, the degree of naturalism in his approach. The second is the mistaken idea that Corneille was wrong in his celebrated assertion (in his *Premier Discours*) that a love-story by itself cannot sustain a tragedy, which requires 'quelque grand intérêt d'Etat, ou quelque passion plus noble et plus mâle que l'amour'.[2]

Before we condemn this, let us reflect that here Corneille means by *tragédie* a serious play in verse of a specially elevated kind. Secondly, the passage was presumably written after the failure of *Pertharite* and certainly before 1660 – a period during which, if the general drift of our argument is right, he was meditating on the problems of a serious play in verse which was basically naturalistic in method. Now, if his plays are not tragic, and if his later ones are basically naturalistic, what would it mean if love were their dominant or only theme? By now, we have had plenty of plays whose claim to interest is that they display with sympathy and psychological insight all the nuances of love in naturalistically-presented characters. The results are sometimes pleasing, but in the long run insipid. Think of Donnay's *Les Amants* (so famous in its day), or *The Voice of the Turtle*, or any of a hundred successful plays. It may be heresy to say so, but Corneille is right: in a naturalistic play, love by itself cannot hope to hold our interest for long. A characteristic of the naturalists of the late nineteenth and early twentieth centuries is their interest in treating broad social and political issues (a more subtle version of Corneille's 'intérêt d'Etat'), and in their plays as a whole love 'se contente du second rang'.[3] For a play of the type to which Corneille was tending, personal love-stories are not a strong enough support.

We can now return to the formidable criticisms of *Sertorius* quoted earlier, and see how they miss the point. In *Sertorius*, Corneille has abandoned the attempt to write poetic tragedy in the strict sense. Instead, he gives us something which suits his characteristic gifts and methods much better: a serious play in verse which includes among its elements a serious political theme (handled in a predominantly poetic manner); a good deal of incidental observation of character; and an eloquent and charming (though subordinate) presentation of love at variance with political interests. All these are held together in the framework of a plot which gives plenty of striking situations, and expressed in verse which can move from poetry to naturalism without incongruity. We can now see why at first glance the structure appears so ramshackle. A more vigorous plot would have been out of place, because it would have been false to the variety of the subject-matter and tones of the play: indeed, if executed with full rigour, it would have crushed all the other elements beneath it, like the plot in *Héraclius*. What we have is a carefully-balanced structure which holds all the elements together in a pleasing and expressive pattern.

We can see how this works in Act V. It begins with a scene between Viriate and Aristie which at first sight is dramatically useless. They formally recapitulate their divided aims; Viriate explains how, far from Sertorius using her, she has used him; both take up the idea that frankness, instead of clever manoeuvring, may point a way out of their problems. This scene does not advance the plot, but it carries forward a theme important in both the political element and the love element in the play. Then Aristie learns that Emile is dead and that Sylla has abdicated, so that Pompée can now marry her. This may not bear on the murder of Sertorius, but it adds its ironic commentary on the political theme: Sylla's abdication has more effect on the political situation than all the battles and manoeuvring of Sertorius's faction. Whether Sertorius lives or dies is now irrelevant as far as the liberty of Rome is concerned. In fact, when Thamire comes to announce his murder, it does seem irrelevant. If Corneille had made more of it he would have been giving it a false emphasis. It is not the central subject of the play, even though Sertorius is a central element in the political pattern. Corneille therefore prepares and announces it so as to minimise any heroic or tragic significance and immediately passes on to the confrontation of Perpenna with Aristie and Viriate. This and the following scenes with Pompée not only provide a series of effective climaxes: they also express the ironical twists of fortune, and the nice balance of heroism and opportunism, which are central to the meaning of the play.

We may perhaps clarify our impression of *Sertorius* by comparing it with *Rodogune*. I argued that *Rodogune* was a bold, but only partially successful, attempt to synthesise a new form which would combine the virtues of poetic drama with a more diffused, naturalistic approach. We may feel that it failed for three reasons: Corneille was still anxious to achieve the intensity and grandeur of tragedy, and this led him to a violent straining after effect; he was still groping for a naturalistic form for parts of the play, and these parts are clumsily-handled and ill-matched with the more violent parts of it; and finally, in his search for a unifying source of interest to replace the missing central meaning, he elaborates his plot with such thoroughness that it comes to dominate the whole play. *Rodogune* was the product of a period of desperate experiment, followed by discouragement and seven years' silence. When Corneille returns to the theatre, he has meditated long on the problem, and has devised a new approach. *Oedipe* is a thorough demonstration of it. First, he abandons the attempt at tragic intensity.[4] Secondly, he develops a wider range of interesting elements – misunderstandings, mistaken identities, political interests, an added love-story, philosophical speeches, oracles, miracles and realism – a confection of rich ingredients skilfully combined. In *Sertorius* he advances further: he is able to treat his subject more seriously than in *Oedipe*, and to make greater use of the resources of poetry while at the same time avoiding the faults of *Rodogune*. There is no attempt at the emotional rigour of tragedy, and the lowered temperature allows a better mingling of poetry and naturalism; plot is reduced to a state in which it can set off and articulate the elements of the play in a meaningful way without drawing all the attention to itself. In addition, Corneille has broadened the basis of his play: *Sertorius* contains a richer and more balanced appreciation of both love and politics than *Rodogune*. Richness, balance, poetry, irony, sentiment, psychological nuance, seriousness without tragedy, skilled theatre-craft which does not swell into melodrama: *Sertorius* is much the better play. In my view, it is one of Corneille's best: perhaps the best of all except *Cinna*. It is outstanding even among the very fine group of the later plays.

2

I have tried to show that in Corneille's work, as in neo-classicism as a whole, the trend towards naturalism in the arts and the expression of a narrowly literal ideal of truth was already far advanced. I have argued that one part of Corneille's importance is that he felt the force of this trend and prefigured – often in very bold terms – the changes in dramatic forms to which it was to lead. In doing so, he came to abandon the old concept of a poetic form which expressed a meaning which could not be expressed in discursive terms. In its place, he adopted a more fragmented form in which more and more areas of life are brought together in one work, as though extension could compensate for lack of depth. Hence the extraordinary range of tone in his later plays – the serious and the comic, high dignity and *galanterie*, heroics and cynicism – which sometimes seems so disconcerting.

But this is only part of the picture. He also strove to evolve a form which could live in the new climate and yet have the strength and subtlety of the old poetic form. In *Agésilas*, he reached boldly for a less obtrusive and more prosaic literary form. But an important part of his achievement is that in experimenting with the new, naturalistic, form, he retained and exploited the literary resources of the old. The poetry in these plays is not so deeply rooted as in a purely poetic form of drama, though he does occasionally still use something of the old poetic technique to emphasise recurring themes. More usually, the poetry serves three purposes: it raises the base-line of the convention to a level more articulate than prose; it often serves as a local attraction in itself; and it provides a binding medium with which the playwright can combine his diverse materials into a unity. Corneille, in his special position between the two methods, is able to reanimate the flagging poetic form with new, naturalistic, sources of interest, and at the same time to use poetic resources to prevent naturalism from disintegrating entirely the aesthetic form.

How, then, should we judge the plays from *Oedipe* to *Pulchérie*? (I will leave *Suréna* for separate consideration.) All criticism is at bottom subjective: in my view this group is on the whole much superior to the plays from *Pompée* to *Pertharite*, which are on the whole much cruder in conception and execution; further, I think it contains one masterpiece (*Sertorius*) and at least two near-misses (*Othon* and *Attila*). Nevertheless, a critic can at least try and give reasons for his judgments. It would be pointless to judge these later plays as though they were rigorous poetic tragedies – or indeed tragedies at all. The balance between poetry and naturalism varies from play to play (for instance, in *Attila* it tilts towards poetry, in *Tite et Bérénice* towards naturalism), but both elements are always present. We should, therefore, apply two sets of criteria. The first set would hardly be relevant to strict poetic drama, but is very relevant to the naturalistic: the range and importance of the aspects of life which they bring together, and the liveliness and conviction with which each element is realised. If we would only read these plays without being hypnotised by an ideal of French classical tragedy, (or, better still, if we could see them in modern productions), we should find that most of them succeed marvellously by these criteria. Our second set of criteria is relevant to the peculiar problems of a drama that mixes the poetic and naturalistic modes: negatively, the degree to which the various elements are kept within the poetic form without disintegrating it; positively, the degree to which the play-wright succeeds in using the resources of verse to build the elements into a structure which can contain and reconcile them. The task is obviously delicate, and it is here that we must have the most reservations about Corneille's success. But not always: *Sertorius* succeeds by both sets of criteria.

'SURÉNA'

I

Steiner has been tempted to call *Suréna* Corneille's masterpiece. What-ever value we assign it, it stands apart from the other plays. Its charac-ters are few, its plot simple, love predominates over politics, it exhales a languorous pessimism. There are not qualities we call Cornelian, and we might suspect the influence of Racine: *Suréna* was, after all, written later than most of Racine's plays. Nevertheless, the general impression left by *Suréna* is not at all Racinian. We are on firmer ground if we look at *Suréna* by itself and ask ourselves two questions: what is Corneille trying to express? and are the means of expression appro-priate?

The key to *Suréna* is its language. Corneille's verse is usually forth-right: we expect simply rhythms, sonorous abstract words, clear anti-theses, straightforward heroics, irony or invective. The verse of *Suréna* is consistently unlike this. Its vocabulary is in general that of neo-classical tragedy, but some of the words it uses with relatively unusual frequency for Corneille: 'mystère', 'secret', 'soupçon'; 'craindre', 'deviner', 'murmurer', 'taire'.[1] The constructions are also charac-teristic: the conditional, negative, subjunctive, pluperfect; 's'il', 'il n'y a que', 'ce n'est que', 'trop de'. The rhythms are unusual in Corneille: sometimes elegiac, often hesitant or broken, as if uncertain of their direction. The verse has a fluidity, a suggestiveness, unique in Corneille, yet quite without the luminous directness that accompanies these qualities in Racine.

I will take a short passage from Act III, Scene ii. Orode, King of Parthia, owes his throne to Suréna, and wonders how to reward him. At the same time, Orode not only is anxious at having such a powerful subject, but also suspects that Suréna hopes to marry Eurydice, a princess who for political reasons must marry Pacorus, Orode's son and heir. Orode decides that the only solutions are to kill Suréna or to offer him his daughter Mandane in marriage. If Suréna accepts Mandane, he obviously does not love Eurydice, and the marriage will both reward him and bind him more closely to Orode. If Suréna refuses Mandane, it will be clear that he loves Eurydice, and is thus a danger to Orode. When Suréna comes in, Orode addresses him thus:

Suréna, vos services
(Qui l'aurait osé croire?) ont pour moi des supplices;
J'en ai honte, et ne puis assez me consoler
De ne voir aucun don qui les puisse égaler.
Suppléez au défaut d'une reconnaissance
Dont vos propres exploits m'ont mis en impuissance;
Et s'il en est un prix dont vous fassiez état,
Donnez-moi les moyens d'être un peu moins ingrat.

What are we to make of this? The verse is indirect, even slow. Is this clumsiness and fatigue, an inability to force the words and sense into a clear form? Apparently not. There is undoubted skill in the way in which the lines express Orode's convoluted thought by the careful placing of the clause in parentheses and the complicated manipulation of negatives and subjunctives. The lines express exactly the deviousness behind the king's attitude: he cannot make up his mind whether to kill or reward Suréna, and is quite unsure of Suréna's real attitude. Two qualities in the lines are notable. The first is ambiguity. It is notoriously difficult, in a sentence that contains several negatives, to be certain whether the sentence means what it seems to mean or the exact opposite. Corneille makes full use of this. After Orode's first sentence, we may well wonder whether the king is expressing gratitude or hostility: Corneille not only presents Orode as not knowing, but also leaves the audience and Suréna in doubt about the king's intentions. The use of language, then, reflects and expresses by literary means the immediate dramatic situation.

The second feature is paradox. Orode is king, Suréna is a subject, but Orode approaches Suréna with deference ('J'en ai honte, et ne puis . . .', 'Suppléez au défaut'). Suréna has served the king well and returned him to power; but these 'services' are 'supplices', these 'exploits' 'm'ont mis en impuissance'. The king wishes to reward Suréna, but cannot see a gift that is sufficient: he therefore asks Suréna to give him the means with which to give (though this is just what Suréna has done in restoring the king to his throne, and this is why Orode wishes to reward him). This paradoxical quality, reinforced by the ambiguity, gives the lines a resonance which is audible at many levels: it expresses the immediate situation; it points to a paradoxical quality in the play as a whole; and it evokes suggestions of a mysterious significance beyond the immediate prose sense of the lines or the immediate (rather banal) situation. Nor does the ambiguity end here. The situation is on the face of it political: it could easily be accommodated in *Nicomède*. But the treatment points to something quite different. There are definite, if muted, sexual undertones. 'Ingrat', in seventeenth-century French tragedy, is the regular word for a loved one who does not return or appreciate the love bestowed on him. 'Services', 'supplices', 'reconnaissance' are words which, though ordinary in themselves, are often found with specialised meanings in the conventional language of *galanterie*. 'Consoler' and 'impuissance' have obvious sexual connotations. This undertone is relevant, not just to the immediate situation, but to the whole pattern of the play. Nor is the relevance just a vague fitting-in with the general mood. Some of the words ('supplice', 'impuissance', 'ingrat') have a very precise significance in the pattern. To examine what the pattern is, we shall review briefly some of the main features of the play.

First, plot. As has often been remarked, the plot is extremely simple. Orode has decided that Pacorus, who has loved and is loved by Suréna's sister Palmis, shall marry Eurydice for political reasons. Eurydice loves Suréna, and is manifestly reluctant to marry Pacorus. Orode and Pacorus realise that this is because she loves Suréna. Orode therefore has Suréna murdered. Eurydice dies (whether of grief or by suicide is not clear from the text, but, as we shall see, the significance in either case is the same). The plot material is as slight as in *Bérénice*. But Corneille handles it in a way which is very unlike Racine's.

In Act I, Eurydice tells Ormène, her confidante, that she must marry Pacorus, though she loves Suréna. She is jealous of Mandane, whom she thinks Suréna is likely to marry. Several points call for comment. Although Eurydice dwells lyrically on her love for Suréna, she never questions that she will in fact marry Pacorus; her grief springs hardly more from her impending marriage than from her jealousy of Mandane; this premonition that Mandane is intended to marry Suréna is so far quite unconfirmed; and Ormène says plainly that Eurydice's grief has a self-inflating quality:

> Votre douleur, Madame, est trop ingénieuse.

Palmis appears, and Eurydice confesses her love for Suréna. Palmis in turn confesses her love for Pacorus. Suréna comes in, and he and Eurydice express their love for each other. Again, the precise manner in which these banal exchanges are treated is illuminating. Eurydice does not exactly reveal her secret: it is communicated to Palmis without actually being put into words:

> Savez-vous mon secret?
>   – Je sais celui d'un frère.
> – Vous savez donc le mien.

Nor do Suréna and Eurydice exactly express their love, still less propose to do anything about it. Eurydice is mainly concerned that Suréna shall not marry Mandane, though she is quite willing for him to marry someone else; and when Suréna is about to react to this strange requirement, she cannot even let him finish:

> N'achevez point: l'air dont vous commencez
> Pourrait à mon chagrin ne plaire pas assez . . .
> Mais adieu; je m'égare.

Act I, then, is characterised by simplicity only if we think of the plot-material. The emotional content and the verse are characterised by over-refinement and inconclusiveness.

The same goes for Act II. Pacorus asks Suréna whether Eurydice loves someone else. Suréna evades the question. Pacorus asks Eurydice. She agrees that she loves someone else, but refuses to say whom. Pacorus asks Palmis to tell him, and she refuses. In Act III, Orode tries to find out whether Suréna is the mysterious lover; Suréna evades him and Palmis rebuffs him. By the beginning of Act IV, Orode has presumably made up his mind, as he has the palace gates closed and guarded. Palmis also seems to assume that the secret is out, as she begs Eurydice to marry Pacorus immediately and so divert suspicion from Suréna. Pacorus himself is now convinced that Suréna is his unknown rival, though no-one has told him so. Suréna still refuses to commit himself. By the beginning of Act V, everyone assumes that Orode will now kill Suréna, though still nothing definite has been revealed about any of the characters' intentions. At the same time, it seems to be assumed that Eurydice could save Suréna by marrying Pacorus, or by allowing Suréna to marry Mandane. Nevertheless, we feel that Suréna is doomed. Sure enough, he is killed – no doubt by order of Orode, but the assassin is not named:

> A peine du palais il sortait dans la rue,
> Qu'une flèche a parti d'une main *inconnue*;
> Deux autres l'ont suivie; et j'ai vu ce vainqueur,
> *Comme si* toute trois l'avaient atteint au coeur,
> Dans un ruisseau de sang tomber mort sur la place.

Eurydice dies (presumably through suicide): that is, she says she is dying and according to the usual convention is carried off-stage, but no doubt we are meant to assume that she dies. We may certainly say that the plot of *Suréna* is simple, but the effect it makes is not: Corneille elaborately surrounds even the simplest action with ambiguities: it is not so much that nothing happens as that the action advances in spite of the fact that nothing happens.

Let us now look at the characters. The central oppositions are clear enough: Orode suspects Suréna of loving Eurydice; Eurydice loves Suréna but is required to marry Pacorus. Having said this, immediate doubts arise. What is Orode's attitude, and what are his reasons for it? He appears at first as, above all, anxious:

> Qu'un tel calme, Sillace, a droit d'inquiéter
> Un roi qui lui doit tant qu'il ne peut s'acquitter!
>
> (III.i)

Suréna is too great for a subject, and Orode fears him – yet his fear (like Eurydice's jealousy) is 'trop ingénieuse'. There is no sign that Suréna is disloyal: what worries Orode is 'un tel calme' – that is, that there is no apparent cause for worrying. Orode tyrannically draws the conclusion that he must either marry Suréna to Mandane or kill him. Then, immediately, he revolts against the thought:

> Son trépas . . . Ce mot seul me fait pâlir d'effroi;
> Ne m'en parlez jamais: que tout l'Etat périsse . . .
> Avant que je défère à ces raisons d'Etat
> Qui nommeraient justice un si lâche attentat!

When he meets Suréna, he wavers between gratitude and threats. Suréna refuses to marry Mandane, and Orode veers. He explains frankly that Suréna is dangerous to him:

> Vous êtes mon sujet, mais un sujet si grand,
> Que rien n'est malaisé quand son bras l'entreprend.
> Vous possédez sous moi deux provinces entières,
> De peuples si hardis, de nations si fières,
> Que sur tant de vassaux je n'ai d'autorité
> Qu'autant que votre zèle a de fidélité.
> Ils vous ont jusqu'ici suivi comme fidèle;
> Et, quand vous le voudrez, ils vous suivront rebelle . . .
> Et s'il faut qu'avec vous tout à fait je m'explique,
> Je ne vous saurais croire assez en mon pouvoir,
> Si les noeuds de l'hymen n'enchaînent le devoir.

Frank speaking, for once in the play. But is it? Orode is presented here as a man ruled by political realism, but he is not quite like this in most of the play. In this very scene he is shown on the one hand firmly announcing that Pacorus must marry Eurydice ('La paix de l'Arménie à ce prix est jurée'), and then plaintively asking Suréna to confirm that the decision is right and that he cannot now break off the marriage:

> Mais, Suréna, le puis-je après la foi donnée? . . .
> Que dira la princesse, et que fera son père?

Is Orode a cynical statesman, caressing his victims to disarm their resistance, or is he, as this passage suggests, a much put-upon man doing his best in difficult circumstances? The answer is that he is both, and these two attitudes are held in suspense throughout the play. When in Act V he makes his last appearance, his attitude is still ambiguous. On the one hand, he is preparing to murder Suréna; on the other, he seems sincerely anxious to find a solution:

> Empêchez-la [the murder], Madame, en vous donnant à nous;
> Ou faites qu'à Mandane il s'offre pour époux.
> Cet ordre exécuté, mon âme satisfaite
> Pour ce héros si cher ne veut plus de retraite.

Nor are Orode's actions and motives just obscure; Corneille presents them as obscure by choice:

> Ne me l'avouez point; en cette conjoncture,
> Le soupçon m'est plus doux que la vérité sûre;
> L'obscurité m'en plaît, et j'aime à n'écouter
> Que ce qui laisse encor liberté d'en douter.
>
> (V.i)

To the very last, Orode's motives and actions are left ambiguous. Suréna is killed – and by Orode's orders, though we are never told so explicitly. He is killed for disobeying the king – but we are told so in the most oblique way possible, by what a confidante thought she heard an (unknown) person say:

> Et je pense avoir même entendu quelque voix
> Nous crier qu'on apprît à dédaigner les rois.

In Orode's character, then, we have ambiguities in plenty: we are as far as possible from the clear-cut marionettes which nineteenth-century critics alleged populated Corneille's later plays. But the point is certainly not that Orode is presented 'in the round' (as the phrase goes) as a man who must also act as a king. The vacillation is part of the design of the play, not a part of a naturalistic character-study.

If this is true of Orode, it is doubly true of Eurydice and Suréna. Undoubtedly they love each other, but their actions are curiously oblique. Will Eurydice marry Pacorus? Of course:

> Epousez-moi, Seigneur, et laissez-moi me taire . . .
> Je ferais ce que font les cœurs obéissants . . .
> Ce que je fais enfin.
>
> (II.ii)

But she will not marry him yet:

> Il (Pacorus) se verrait, Seigneur, dès ce soir mon époux,
> S'il n'eût point voulu voir dans mon coeur plus que vous . . .
> Pour peine il attendra l'effort de mon devoir . . .
> Le devoir vient à bout de l'amour le plus ferme.
>
> (V.i)

She is willing that Suréna should marry anyone else but Mandane; she is willing that he should save himself by marrying Mandane, providing he does not ask her permission:

> Qu'il s'y donne, Madame, et ne m'en dise rien.
>
> (IV.ii)

She repeatedly (and justly) vows to kill herself if Suréna is killed, yet she refuses on the following grounds to save him by telling him to marry Mandane:

> Savez-vous qu'à Mandane envoyer ce que j'aime,
> C'est de ma propre main m'assassiner moi-même?
>
> (V.iv)

Eurydice loves Suréna, yet she will not save him (as Palmis tells her in V.iv, 'Il court à son trépas, et vous en serez cause'). In obeying her 'devoir' she agrees to give him up, but by refusing to give him up she kills him. The paradox is carried down from the broad design to the details. In Act I, Scene ii, she tells Palmis that Suréna can hardly love her, because he avoids her:

> Mais dites-moi, Madame, est-il bien vrai qu'il m'aime?
> Dites; et s'il est vrai, pourquoi fuit-il mes yeux?

Four lines later, when he has come in, she says to him:

> Je vous ai fait prier de ne me plus revoir,
> Seigneur: votre présence étonne mon devoir.

In a different play, this might be psychological subtlety ('Ah! je ne croyais pas qu'il fût si près d'ici'). Here, it is so only incidentally: it is a local manifestation of an all-pervading paradox. This comes out most clearly in the presentation of the hero. Suréna is a hero in all senses: brave, virile, a warrior. But here he appears in a passive rôle. He takes the true heroic stand:

> J'ai vécu pour ma gloire autant qu'il fallait vivre,
> Et laisse un grand exemple à qui pourra me suivre.
>
> (IV.iv)

The threats and hints of Pacorus do not move him:

> Je fais plus, je prévois ce que j'en dois attendre;
> Je l'attends sans frayeur; et quel qu'en soit le cours,
> J'aurai soin de ma gloire; ordonnez de mes jours.
>
> (IV.iv)

Nevertheless, he is adept at evading the issue (Orode complains of this: Suréna m'a surprise, et je n'aurais pas dit | Qu'avec tant de valeur il eût eu tant d'esprit), and he is capable of equivocation, even lies, when Pacorus asks him if Eurydice had any suitors:

> Durant tout mon séjour rien n'y blessait ma vue;
> Je n'y rencontrais point de visite assidue,
> Point de devoirs suspects, ni d'entretiens si doux
> Que, si j'avais aimé, j'en dusse être jaloux.
>
> (II.i)

Again, this ambiguity is not to be taken as a personal trait showing his lack of heroic qualities: Suréna is a hero, because we are told so in verse that is unmistakably serious. He is not a king:

> Mais il sait rétablir les rois dans leurs Etats.
> Des Parthes le mieux fait d'esprit et de visage,
> Le plus puissant en biens, le plus grand en courage,
> Le plus noble.
>
> (I.i)
>
> Il n'est rien d'impossible à la valeur d'un homme
> Qui rétablit son maître et triomphe de Rome.
>
> (III.ii)

The point of the contrast is that it is paradoxical. The paradox is sustained to the end. In the last two acts, it becomes suffocatingly certain that Suréna will die. The gates of the palace are shut, and we can only wait for the murder. In Act V, Scene iii, it is quite obvious that Orode has decided to kill him, and that there is no escape from the palace save through death. But Suréna does not see this:

> Non, non, c'est d'un bon oeil qu'Orode me regarde;
> Vous le voyez, ma soeur, je n'ai pas même un garde.

Corneille is not trying to manipulate alternatives of hope and fear so as to generate suspense. Nor is he indulging in psychological byplay about the obtuseness of heroes. Even as Suréna speaks, we know that escape is hopeless. What we have is the supreme paradox, the trapped animal who cries, 'Je suis libre'.

Suréna leaves the palace, and even this detail has its significance in the close tissue of the play. Corneille usually avoids mentioning the rooms in which the actions of his plays take place, lest we should accuse him of infringing the unity of place. In his third *Discours*, he introduces the concept of a *lieu théâtral* in which it is assumed that characters can tell their secrets as they would in their own apartments. As he points out, this is no more than an arbitrary convention. Nevertheless, the *lieu théâtral* in principle represents a place where the characters could, in real life, reasonably carry out their business, as the strict critics of the time demanded. Usually we can make out which concrete place it represents at any one time. A clear example is *Tite et Bérénice*. Act I takes place in Domitie's apartment: she voices her secret thoughts there, and Domitian comes to visit her. Act II is in Tite's audience chamber: Domitan, Domitie and Bérénice all come to him there. Tite expressly sends Bérénice to her apartment, and Domitie resolves to visit her there. Act III, then, is set in Bérénice's apartment, and the others come to visit her. In these three acts, we have three different rooms in the palace, and the reasons for the characters' comings and goings between them are plainly accounted for, as in any naturalistic play. They could be represented by three different sets, and the fact that they were all represented by one *palais à volonté* is purely a concession to the exigencies of stage-setting and the demands of the critics for exact unity of place. In Acts IV and V, however, Corneille cannot manage so neatly: the complications of the plot demand too much coming and going. He therefore takes refuge in vagueness. But this vagueness is due to embarrassment about the unity of place: we feel he would set his scenes in a definite room if he could.

There is nothing of this feeling in *Suréna*. The action takes place in an ideal space: a palace with gates that can be closed and with a street outside, but with no precise geography. Here the lovers meet, here the king consults his counsellor, here the king comes to visit Eurydice, but the place is impossible to define realistically. It is at once an open space to which all can come, a prison from which there is no escape, and an enclosure which anyone leaves at his peril: when Suréna leaves, he dies. It is not a series of physical rooms: it is a *lieu vague*; a place where dreams cross.

We can now perhaps look back at some of the features of the verse. It is full of the seventeenth-century jargon of love – 'feux', 'flammes', 'soupirs'. What is extraordinary is how Corneille gives life and vigour to these banalities. Pacorus says he cannot marry Eurydice if she loves someone else:

Que sera-ce, grands dieux! si toute ma tendresse
Rencontre un souvenir plus cher à ma princesse,
Si le coeur pris ailleurs ne s'en arrache pas,
Si pour un autre objet il soupire en mes bras!

(II.i)

The first two lines are insipid enough, but with the last two the dead metaphors revive. 'Arrache', with its cruel tearing sound; its association with 'coeur' (a key word in the play); the way in which the abstract 'objet' takes on a new significance by association with the physical reality of a woman 'sighing' (another word that comes in again and again) actually in the arms of her husband; these catch up the dull jargon into the more intense life of poetry.

We may find a controlling purpose in the apparent clumsiness of some of the verse. Ormène reports to Eurydice:

Oui, votre intelligence à demi découverte
Met votre Suréna sur le bord de sa perte.
Je l'ai su de Sillace; et j'ai lieu de douter
Qu'il n'ait, s'il faut tout dire, ordre de l'arrêter.

(IV.i)

Even in this fragment the themes of the play appear: 'à demi décou-vert' (the secret throughout is revealed without being revealed – nothing is unambiguously stated); 'votre Suréna . . . sa perte' (Eurydice is causing the death of her lover); 'j'ai lieu de douter | Qu'il n'ait . . . ordre de l'arrêter' (the characteristic doubt again); 's'il faut tout dire' (the reluctance to speak directly which characterises the play and allows the action to proceed without proceeding); and the placing of the last phrase, where the sentence is checked, like a current running back on itself (the theme of paradox that runs through the play). And what follows this speech is significant. After the ambiguities and the check to the forward movement, we have a decisive lunge forward: 'On n'oserait, Ormène; on n'oserait.' This juxtaposition of contraries is also characteristic of the play, and even here the paradoxical form is maintained: the verb 'to dare' appears in the negative and the conditional.

It should now be clear that Corneille is following a consistent method. The consistency with which indirectness and paradox are expressed at every level – the plot, the setting, the characters, the language; the avoidance of any temptation to set up peripheral centres of interest; the lack of any neat 'meaning' that can be formulated in prose terms; above all, the completeness with which the action is controlled by and embodied in the verse: all these confirm abundantly that

Suréna is poetic in method. Why, more than thirty years after *Cinna*, should Corneille return to the poetic form? And what shall we call the result?

2

The clue can be found only if we listen carefully to the verse:

Ne me parle plus tant de joie et d'hyménée.

(I.i)

Ma flamme dans mon coeur se tenait renfermée.

(I.i)

L'amour, sous les dehors de la civilité

(I.i)

Plus je hais, plus je souffre, et souffre autant que j'aime.

(I.ii)

Mais qui cherche à mourir doit chercher ce qui tue.

(I.iii)

Il est hors d'apparence
Qu'il fasse un tel refus sans quelque préférence,
Sans quelque objet charmant, dont l'adorable choix
Ferme tout son grand coeur au pur sang de ses rois.

(III.iii)

Happiness is refused; love, though greatly desired, is held back from expression; the pleasure of love is therefore pain. In the last line quoted, we have an almost physical enactment of the central image: the heart, the seat of life and passion, is closed against the blood, as though the symbol of life itself refused to live (which is what Eurydice and Suréna both do). Moreover, this refusal is the result of a conscious effort. This comes up strongly in the passage quoted on p. 146, where Orode refuses to learn the secret he desires to learn. Its fullest development is in the lovers' scene at the end of Act I. Suréna will die of grief, but Eurydice (symbolic name!) adjures him:

Vivez, Siegneur, vivez, afin que je languisse,
Qu'à vos feux ma langueur rende langtemps justice.
Le trépas à vos yeux me semblerait trop doux,
Et je n'ai pas encore assez souffert pour vous.
Je veux qu'un noir chagrin à pas lents me consume,
Qu'il me fasse à longs traits goûter son amertume;
Je veux, sans que la mort ose me secourir,
Toujours aimer, toujours souffrir, toujours mourir.

It is this deliberate holding-back which forbids escape:

> Où dois-je recourir,
> O ciel! s'il faut toujours aimer, souffrir, mourir!

The sexual imagery is obvious enough, and is carried forward to the end. Suréna dies, and immediately Eurydice dies:

> Non, je ne pleure point, Madame, mais je meurs.

Whether she swoons or kills herself, the erotic parallel is plain. The tension is discharged, and in Palmis's last words the normal pattern of Cornelian energy reasserts itself. There is nothing languid about the last lines of Corneille's last play:

> Suspendez ces douleurs qui pressent de mourir,
> Grands dieux! et, dans les maux où vous m'avez plongée,
> Ne souffrez point ma mort que je ne sois vengée!

Corneille is of course not merely exploiting the sexual suggestiveness of his theme. Still less is he imitating Racine: his theme is based on the image of refusal to become directly conscious of passion, which is very different from what we find in Racine. We must look for a deeper reason for his use of this imagery. The reason is that he is writing tragedy.

Tragedy demands a sense of the inevitable, of a daemonic and perhaps malevolent power beyond conscious human control. Corneille as a poet had never admitted such a power; his plays, however harsh, leave men's destinies either in the hands of men, or at least formally in the hands of a benevolent providence. In *Suréna*, perhaps because Racine had shown that such a conception was possible, he turns inwards to find this ineluctable fate. To be sure, it is not embodied in the instincts themselves – this is not Corneille's view of human nature – but in the conscious effort to control these impulses. But – and this is the distinctive feature of *Suréna* – this conscious effort has become merged with the automatisms it suppresses. Hence this curious paradox, this flowing back of the stream upon itself, which gives the play its inner tension. This is a difficult conception to render, and one which is equally far removed from optimistic metaplay and the ritual and public tragedy of the Greeks. In *Suréna*, fate is inevitable, yet private and human: it is still caught and held 'sous les dehors de la civilité'.

3

Suréna is the most difficult of Corneille's plays to judge. The best starting point is perhaps the critique by Steiner,[2] who, though he sees the high merit of the play, finally decides that it fails by a small margin to achieve greatness. His reasons are three: the verse is uneven because of the attempt to express things for which the heroic couplet is not suited ('Sometimes the complex motion – the attempt to maintain a free impulse beneath a rigid surface – produces in the verse a curious sag or concavity'); there is a softness about the play which is elegiac rather than dramatic ('Corneille's purpose . . . I take it, was the creation of a kind of dramatic elegy – a drama of lament rather than of conflict'); and the action is too weak ('Perhaps the action is too slight to sustain the elaboration and the complexity of the poetic means').

The overall judgment is hard to fault, and the adverse criticisms obviously have substance. Nevertheless, if the reading suggested in this chapter is correct, we might formulate them rather differently. *Suréna* is a poetic play, and the poetry is of a high order. The occasional weaknesses of the verse – by which Steiner perhaps means the awkwardness of such passages as Ormène's speech quoted on p. 150 – are not weaknesses of expression at all: they result from the thoroughness with which the overall design of the play is made to inform every detail. Nor is it quite fair to complain of the elegiac softness of the plot: the indirectness and ambiguity spring from the rigour with which the form of every element is dictated by the central meaning of the play. In my view it is also slightly misleading to speak of the action as being too slight to sustain the elaboration and complexity of the poetic means: in *Suréna*, to a quite remarkable extent, the poetic means *are* the drama. Rather than saying that the action will not sustain the poetry, we might say that the action and the verse, each in their own mode, are the exact expression of the meaning of the play. It is not as though indirectness and slowness of action in themselves make a play undramatic. There are many works of the highest quality which in their several ways are more tenuous, more obscure, more lacking in plot, than *Suréna*: *Prometheus Bound*, *The Trojan Women*, *En Attendant Godot*, *Long Day's Journey into Night*, *The Caretaker*, *La Guerre Civile*. In each of these, we feel that the apparent lack of action is appropriate, because the simple structure of incidents is exactly what is needed to express the underlying theme; in each of them, we feel the action is dramatic, because the underlying theme is dramatic. Where we might legitimately find *Suréna* lacking is in the dramatic quality of its central idea. The tragic quality of the play depends very much on the concept that in complicity with our unconscious desires we may consciously seek our own destruction. This may strike us as true, and profound. But on the stage, it will nearly always seem that a conscious drive can be reversed, and if the drive is not reversed the destructiveness appears merely wilful. It is for this reason, if at all, that the play seems to lack essential strength.

I have said 'if at all' and 'seems to lack'. We have no opportunity to see the play's effect in the theatre. In the absence of this vital evidence, we cannot reach a firm conclusion about *Suréna*. It lacks the sweep and energy of *Sertorius*, just as *Sertorius* lacks the purity and concentration of *Suréna*. In Corneille's work, only *Cinna* combines formal perfection and strength. It is a matter of choice whether we place energy before purity of form. In our more wideawake moments we must prefer *Sertorius*. But *Suréna* will always be loved by those who value formal perfection.

10

CORNEILLE – SOME CONCLUSIONS

This study of Corneille's work has been concerned only with one particular aspect. Nevertheless, it has perhaps enabled us to form views about some of the problems of Cornelian criticism. How far was Corneille at home in neo-classicism? Are any of his plays truly tragic? How shall we regard the astonishing range of his experiments? What are we to make of the wide variations of tone within many of his plays? Is it true, as used to be thought, that only a handful of his plays are good, and the later ones miserable failures? If modern critics are right to stress that the later plays are of high quality, what should we admire in them and why are they so different from the earlier ones?

In trying to answer the first question, I have emphasised a basic confusion in neo-classicism which few of its exponents faced squarely. The trend towards naturalism is strong, but the older, vatic idea of poetry is still powerful, and provides elaborate literary forms and patterns. This conflict is shown sharply in the work of Corneille. As a poet, he was no doubt inclined to assert the primacy of poetry; but, as a highly intelligent and thoughtful poet, he realised the validity of the trend towards naturalism. The paradoxes of his career make sense if we analyse his work in terms of the tug between these opposing forces, which he often has difficulty in bringing into balance.

He did not at first accept the rules, but later did so because he felt the need to defend and rationalise the continued writing of serious poetry. But his rules are not necessarily those of Chapelain and d'Aubignac. Where rules help poetry to avoid the strictures of rationalistic critics, he accepts or even adds to them. But other rules – including some fundamental ones – he rejects or ignores, because they take no account of the difficulties and advantages of naturalism. A naturalist playwright must have freedom to exploit incidental sources of interest. He cannot afford to abide by the strict separation of genres, which presupposes a degree of selection from experience which fits in well with the purposes of poetry, but not those of naturalism. Nor can he afford to exclude far-fetched incidents and stick to conventional morality: to do so will often condemn him to dullness. Corneille therefore insists on his right to use extraordinary incidents, evades the demand that he should preach morality, and in his later plays mixes comic and serious elements.

Corneille hardly ever attempts pure tragedy. In the earlier group of serious plays, from *Médée* to *Polyeucte*, there is a largely unresolved tension between the old poetic form and the new naturalistic one. There is also a tendency which is at odds both with tragedy and with the usual naturalistic type of play: much of the vitality of these early plays comes from the tension between the limits of the moral universe in each and the liberating realisation that these can be expanded by human effort and human discipline. This extraordinary moral dynamism, evident mainly in the works of his early maturity, is one element in the characteristically 'Cornelian' quality, and one reason for the mistaken view that his best work is concentrated in this small group of plays. This energising element is something new in French serious drama, and in most of the plays is developed in uneasy partnership with peripheral sources of interest. In *Cinna* alone does the pattern of the play realise perfectly the impelling idea. We have no name for the type of play which *Cinna* represents, but it is certainly not tragedy. Corneille's only tragedy proper is *Suréna*. This was written after Racine had revived the genre, and marks a return to the poetic mode. In the plays of his middle period (from *Pompée* to *Pertharite*) Corneille relies on the excitements of plot and rhetoric, or begins to experiment with new blends of emotional effects: the question of tragedy hardly arises. In the plays after *Pertharite*, political discussion and sentimental comedy predominate.

The struggle between poetry and naturalism also explains Corneille's variety. After *Polyeucte*, having abandoned the attempt to realise an underlying poetic pattern, he seeks constantly for new sources of interest. Hence the surprising range of experiments in his middle period – comedies, a *comédie heroïque*, plays of intrigue, machine plays; plays set in Egypt, Paris, Lyons, Syria, Byzantium, Greece, Spain, Asia Minor and Lombardy. Despite this apparent variety, few critics have felt the presence of real variety in the plays of this period. In my view, this is because Corneille has largely abandoned poetic form without finding a new form which will accommodate a more naturalistic vision. The superficial variety is an attempt to compensate for this underlying failure. We can see this if we compare them with the later plays. The later plays lack the melodramatic drive of the middle plays, but far surpass them in subtlety and human interest.

The contrast is clear if we examine the characterisation in them. It used to be said that Corneille's characters are inhuman. We can now see that he creates human characters when he wants to, and that whether he wants to depends on the type of play he is writing. In the poetic plays, naturalistic portraiture is rarely needed: *Cinna* and *Suréna* are full of human interest, and the characters are predominantly elements in the total design. In the more naturalistic plays, the matter is more complicated. Few will deny that in his comedies, or in *Le Cid* or *Polyeucte*, Corneille displays a gift for creating characters. But the same is true of his later plays, in which in many ways he displays greater subtlety than ever. The charge of inhumanity applies only to the middle plays, where Corneille puts the main emphasis on exciting plot and rhetorical adornment. Where these interests are paramount, subtle characterisation gets in the way, and its absence is hardly noticed. We may take as extreme examples *Héraclius* and *Pulchérie*. In the first, the characters are rudimentary, and all the efforts of the author and spectators have to be devoted to the plot. In the second, the characters are subtle and realistic, but the plot lacks urgency and interest. In character-drawing, as in everything else, we cannot judge what Corneille has done until we understand what he is trying to do.

Although he remains in some senses limited, recent critics have certainly been right to emphasise his variety within these limits. He is not the poet of heroism alone. His work ranges over a wide field of human experience, embracing comedy more frequently than tragedy. This variety is a manifestation of a sophisticated and inventive intellect. Underlying it is a constant grappling with new techniques, new attitudes to his art, new interpretations of human experience. I have tried to demonstrate some of the techniques he used, some of his responses to the aesthetic problems confronting him. His range is combined with a special type of complexity. It is not the complexity (found in many great poets, including Racine) by which a weight of experience of which we are usually only half-conscious is brought to bear on a superficially simple idea or situation: it is the more conscious complexity which results from unexpected combinations of moods and techniques, combinations which often aim at a new type of effect. *Cinna* is not a desiccated tragedy, *Nicomède* is not a heroic play with comic passages, *Tite et Bérénice* is not a tragedy that topples into bathos, *Suréna* is not a heroic play that has run out of energy: each is the result of a new attempt to realise a particular effect.

It is here that I hope the perspective adopted in this book shows its value. In examining each play, I have tried to think in terms both of the problems of literary technique with which Corneille was struggling and of the attitudes to playwriting which lie behind them. We may surmise that behind these attitudes were some more general cultural factors. These attitudes were not peculiar to Corneille. We find them, in one form or another, in critics such as Chapelain. We shall find them again, at different times, in Boileau and Racine.

11

RACINE – CAREER AND BACKGROUND

I

Racine's career seems at first glance full of contradictions. Orphaned at an early age, he was brought up in strict Jansenist circles, largely at Port-Royal itself. In his late teens he began to break away from this background, and after a period of hesitation embarked on a career as a playwright. After a modest debut with *La Thébaïde* (1664), he attained celebrity with *Alexandre* (1665), and from then until *Phèdre* (1677) his career was an almost unbroken series of triumphs. During this period he was also making his way at Court. In 1677, he left the relatively disreputable profession of playwright for the honourable calling of Historiographer Royal. He composed *Esther* (1689) and *Athalie* (1691) for Madame de Maintenon, but neither was performed on the public stage in his lifetime. In his last years his piety grew more austere and less indulgent to the theatre, but he continued to oversee editions of his plays.

There remains a sense of mystery about Racine that we do not feel about Corneille. He seems to balance uneasily between disparate worlds. In his relation with each of them, there is a curious mixture of intimacy and withdrawal, of prickliness and perfect docility. This is especially obvious in his relations with Port-Royal, but it is hardly less evident in his relationship with the public theatre, which he embraced and then rejected. It is even apparent in his relations with the Court. In his later years he was high in favour, yet he re-established a connection with that Jansenism which was so hateful to the king. As Pommier has remarked, he would have been seriously compromised if he had been alive in 1703, when the seizure of Quesnel's private papers revealed the nature of his sympathies.[1]

The apparent contradictions in Racine's life link with a contradiction which I shall try to demonstrate in his literary techniques. I shall argue that, like Corneille's, his art shows a hesitation between the poetic and naturalistic modes, though in his case the resolution of the conflict is different, and in some ways unexpected in the context. I shall argue, in fact, that in many ways Racine's literary procedures run counter to neo-classic orthodoxy. This contradicts the view frequently expressed that Racine is the perfect neo-classicist, the most docile exponent of the rules. Nevertheless, the argument may look less paradoxical if we recall two well-known pieces of evidence. First, if we look at his prefaces, we find him constantly defending himself against the contention that he has offended against the rules. Secondly, there is a point which many scholars have stressed. Racine's tragedies were an exception in their theatrical context: even in the hey-day of the French theatre, the taste of the public ran to complexity, romantic plays and spectacle.

In what follows I shall concentrate on analysis of Racine's plays, in an endeavour to isolate their formal principles. But first I shall look briefly at some aspects of the criticism and theatre of his time, to show the context against which his plays can be measured.

2

The idea that there was a 'school of 1660' which was tutored by Boileau in a new and pure classical doctrine has long been discredited. Nevertheless, some account of the relationship of Racine to Boileau and Boileau's ideas is relevant to understanding Racine's development.

In his early works, Boileau shows little sign of any settled literary doctrine. As an anti-establishment satirist who attacked literary targets very much at random, he was sarcastic about the poets paid to flatter the government, including 'un Racine, un Ménage'. His attitude to Racine's work seems to have been ambiguous or unfriendly until at least 1672, when Madame de Sévigné reports his strictures on *Bajazet*. The friendship between Racine and Boileau seems to date from about 1673. It becomes closer with the dispute over *Phèdre*, closer still when they are partners as Historiographers Royal, with Racine as the wealthy and influential courtier smoothing the way for the less adroit Boileau. There is little room in all this for the idea that Boileau influenced or helped Racine in his evolution as a poet until his theatrical career was almost over.

In his works after 1670, however, Boileau does begin to develop a critical position, although even then it is perhaps a mistake to think of him as setting out a formal system. His main aim in *L'Art Poétique* seems to have been to express stylishly for sophisticated audiences current critical ideas, and at the same time to satirise outmoded authors. His expression of neo-classical doctrines adds little to what had been said by Chapelain, who in turn relied heavily on earlier Italian critics.

What is perhaps significant, however, is the direction in which Boileau continues the neo-classical tradition. It is difficult to decide how far his pronouncements in *L'Art Poétique* are to be taken at face value, rather than as statements designed to achieve a particular type of poetic effect. Nevertheless, it is striking how firmly he insists on the virtually complete subordination of poetry to morality, and specifically to religion. This is most obvious in his discussion of the epic in Chant III. This discussion shows some falling away from his usual acumen, but it seems to reveal with especial clarity one of his deepest preoccupations. The epic must not use Christian machinery, because Christianity is true and poetry is lies:

> De la foi d'un chrétien les mystères terribles
> D'ornements égayés ne sont point susceptibles.
> L'Evangile à l'esprit n'offre de tous côtés
> Que pénitence à faire, et tourments mérités,
> Et de vos fictions le mélange coupable
> Même à ses vérités donne l'air de la fable.

> (Ch. III, ll. 199–204)

Although merely 'fictions', poetry is harmless, even useful, provided it respects religion and keeps to a rigidly Christian morality. The only way in which it can become serious is to teach useful truths:

> Auteurs, prêtez l'oreille à mes instructions.
> Voulez-vous faire aimer vos riches fictions?
> Qu'en savantes leçons votre muse fertile
> Partout joigne au plaisant le solide et l'utile.
> Un lecteur sage fuit un vain amusement
> Et veut mettre à profit son divertissement.

> (*Ibid.*, Ch. IV, ll. 85–90)

The sentiment is Horatian, but Boileau's attitude is more rigid than Horace's. Despite Boileau's wish to avoid pedantry, it has a harsh didacticism which goes beyond Chapelain, whose criticism is more tolerant than his nineteenth-century reputation suggested. In Boileau the basic attitudes behind neo-classicism have hardened, and poetry is more clearly than before regarded as a secondary activity.

This has, I think, some relevance to Racine's literary development. There is nothing in Boileau's career or his relationship with Racine to suggest that in the 1660s Racine shared the views enunciated in *L'Art Poétique* in 1674. In the 1670s the two poets drew closer together (perhaps for reasons which were doctrinal as much as literary), and in the years after 1677 there is little sign of disagreement between them on literary questions. What their careers do suggest, in my view, is that the dogmatic and naturalistic trend in neo-classical criticism continued to gather strength during the century, and that from the 1670s onwards it was increasingly accepted by both of them.

However interesting an examination of a poet's relationship to contemporary critical ideas may be, it is unlikely to be as revealing as a comparison with his less gifted contemporaries in his own sphere. Thomas Corneille forms a convenient point of reference. His writing life overlapped at both ends Racine's career as a dramatist, and he seems to have followed and reflected the taste of his times very exactly. He started with romanesque comedy and tragi-comedy, and later turned towards opera. At the height of his career, however, he produced two tragedies – *Ariane* (1672) and *Le Comte d'Essex* (1678) – of considerable merit, which have often been regarded as influenced by Racine's success. *Ariane* will be discussed in connection with *Phèdre*. Here, we will consider briefly *Le Comte d'Essex*.

The play is certainly not negligible. It is not a mere concoction of fashionable ingredients: it is slightly unconventional in taking a subject from English history and it violates the unity of place (Act IV takes place in Essex's prison). The plot is simple, but provides interesting situations. The character of Henriette is touching, and the figure of Elisabeth hesitating between love, jealousy, pride, shame and political necessity is strikingly dramatic and has a prickly pathos. There is a touch of genuine tragedy in her dilemma, which her nature and position impose on her against her wishes. The verse rarely rises to great heights, but it is mainly simple and adequate to the demands of the play. It can compass pathos:

> Douceur trop peu goûtée, et pour jamais finie!
> J'en faisais vanité; le ciel m'en a puni.

and at least one vigorous *maxime*:

> Le crime fait la honte, et non pas l'échafaud.

In spite of these virtues, why is *Le Comte d'Essex* so null in comparison with a play by Racine? True, there are some weaknesses in the mechanism. Essex's rôle is passive and his character not strongly delineated, the perfidy of Cécile is strongly emphasised but never developed in any depth, there is a certain monotony in the way in which Essex and Elisabeth reiterate their attitudes without developing them, and so on. But many plays we regard as masterpieces have faults which are superficially as serious.

We may get nearer the reason if we examine the verse. Although on the surface very similar in form and diction to that of Corneille and

Racine, it lacks resonance and subtlety. More important, it seems to lack substance. Many of the lines are perceptive and skilful, but we may feel that they are not striking enough to stand by themselves without support from the pattern of the play. This is a difficult point to define precisely, but we can perhaps see its significance if we look closely at one of the most effective passages in the play. In Act II, Scene v, Elisabeth tries to persuade Essex to ask for mercy. He refuses to admit that he has committed treason, and she replies as follows:

> Et n'as-tu pas, perfide, armant la populace,
> Essayé, mais en vain, de te mettre en ma place?
> Mon palais investi ne te convainc-t-il pas
> Du plus grand, du plus noir de tous les attentats?
> Mais, dis-moi, car enfin le courroux qui m'anime
> Ne peut faire céder ma tendresse à ton crime;
> Et si par sa noirceur je tâche à t'étonner,
> Je ne te la fais voir que pour te pardonner:
> Pourquoi vouloir ma perte? et qu'avait fait la reine
> Qui dût à sa ruine intéresser ta haine?
> Peut-être ai-je pour toi montré quelque rigueur,
> Lorsque j'ai mis obstacle au penchant de ton coeur.
> Suffolk t'avait charmé; mais si tu peux te plaindre
> Qu'apprenant cet amour j'ai tâché de l'éteindre,
> Songe à quel prix, ingrat, et par combien d'honneurs
> Mon estime a sur toi répandu mes faveurs.
> C'est peu dire qu'estime, et tu l'as pu connaître:
> Un sentiment plus fort de mon coeur fut le maître.
> Tant de princes, de rois, de héros méprisés,
> Pour qui, cruel, pour qui les ai-je refusés?
> Leur hymen eût, sans doute, acquis à mon empire
> Ce comble de puissance où l'on sait que j'aspire:
> Mais, quoi qu'il m'assurât, ce qui m'ôtait à toi
> Ne pouvait rien avoir de sensible pour moi.
> Ton coeur, dont je tenais la conquête si chère,
> Etait l'unique bien capable de me plaire;
> Et si l'orgueil du trône eût pu me le souffrir,
> Je t'eusse offert ma main afin de l'acquérir.
> Espère, et tâche à vaincre un scrupule de gloire,
> Qui, combattant mes voeux, s'oppose à ta victoire:
> Mérite par tes soins que mon coeur adouci
> Consente à n'en plus croire un importun souci:
> Fais qu'à ma passion je m'abandonne entière;
> Que cette Elisabeth si hautaine, si fière,
> Elle à qui l'univers ne saurait reprocher

Qu'on ait vu son orgueil jamais se relâcher,
Cesse enfin, pour te mettre où son amour t'appelle,
De croire qu'un sujet ne soit pas digne d'elle.
Quelquefois à céder ma fierté se résout;
Que sait-tu si le temps n'en viendra pas à bout?
Que sais-tu . . .

This is worth quoting at length, as an example of what a minor writer could do within the conventions of seventeenth-century French tragedy. The shifts of mood from proud irony to pathos, back to pride and finally to unwilling humility; the tension behind the lines as Elisabeth struggles with her incompatible feelings; the changes in rhythm to match the mood: these give light and shade to the speech. The speech is certainly dramatic, but the dramatic quality does not spring mainly from the language. It comes firstly from the imagined character behind the language, and secondly from the experience which the actress is able to project, on the basis of the character she has imagined. If we imagine the play in production, the sequence is that the actress reading the play creates a character of Elisabeth and then projects it, making use of the words provided by the author. For this purpose, it would not matter greatly if the words were rather different: it would not matter greatly if they were in prose instead of verse. Lessing hit the critical nail on the head:

Neither the earl nor the queen is delineated by the poet with such force that their parts cannot be strengthened by the actors. Essex does not speak so proudly but that the actor can show greater pride in every posture, every look, every situation. Indeed it is essential to pride that it expresses itself more by outward bearing than by words. Essex's words are often modest, and he lets us see rather than hear, that it is a proud modesty.[2]

This is why *Le Comte d'Essex* is so unmemorable, in spite of its merits. There is no central substance in the play which is controlled and expressed by the verse. There is, in fact, no substance at all which plot, characters and verse together exist to embody; such substance as the play has is embodied separately in the plot as plot and the characters as characters, and in the basis these give for the actors' skill. Nor is this the end of the matter. There is a type of play in which the basic method is naturalistic but the verse is used as one of the separate elements which is elaborated as an attraction in its own right. In *Le Comte d'Essex* the verse is not elaborated in this way, and must not be, for the reason Lessing implies: the method is deliberately to keep expressiveness out of the verse and leave it to the actors. Nor, for the same reason, does the verse perform the minimal function of raising the baseline of the convention within which the characters are articulate. When matters have come to this, the advantages of using verse are lost. Worse, the disadvantages begin to weigh heavily. Much of the effectiveness of such a play must come from the plot, and it is difficult to make clear, within the tightly circumscribed conventions of French tragic verse, everything that needs to be said for the conduct of an exciting plot. The result is the vagueness and confusion we find in the details of the plot in this play, as in many of the plays of Voltaire. In *Le Comte d'Essex*, the verse has no particular function: it has simply become a hindrance. We would not easily say this of Racine.

12

RACINE – THE BEGINNINGS

I

The first play of Racine's of which we hear is *Amasie*. All we know of it is the title. Presumably it was in verse. Possibly the hero was a character from *Le Grand Cyrus*.[1] It was written in 1660 and submitted to the Marais, who first praised it, then rejected it. In 1661, Racine tried again, with *Les Amours d'Ovide*. This presumably dealt with Julia the daughter of Augustus and the banishment of Ovid. Racine sought and accepted the advice of the actress Mlle de Beauchâteau in the composition of his play, which was nevertheless rejected by the Hôtel de Bourgogne. After this we hear nothing of any dramatic projects until on 4 July 1662 Racine writes to Le Vasseur from Uzès that he is melancholy and preoccupied and wishes he could get down to work on a play. We know the title of one other lost play: *Théagène et Chariclée*. It presumably dates from the end of 1662 or the beginning of 1663.

Finally, we come to *La Thébaïde*. We know from Racine's correspondence with Le Vasseur that the play was written in the last part of 1663. Tradition has it that Racine embarked on it at the request of Molière, who wanted to rival the Hôtel de Bourgogne's production of Boyer's *La Thébaïde*, and that Molière drew up the scenario and helped in writing the verses. This tradition rests on the late and unreliable evidence of Grimarest, Boileau and La Grange-Chancel; the evidence of Racine's own letters is ambiguous. Modern scholars are not agreed on whether the tradition is true. Adam defends it.[2] Picard stresses its extreme improbability.[3]

From the facts we can be sure of, two things are clear. Racine is determined from the age of twenty to make his way in the theatre, and to do so is willing to adapt himself to the requirements of the actors. The combination of a determination to arrive and a willingness to conform to the demands of his environment does much to explain puzzling features in his later life. If we can deduce anything from the more uncertain parts of the evidence, it is rather surprising – especially if we think that Racine was disposed by his Jansenist background and his knowledge of Greek towards the rigours of Greek tragedy. His first plays all sound like romantic tragi-comedies. Nor is it obvious that his taste was evolving towards tragedy: we know nothing about *Amasie*, but we can be reasonably certain that *Les Amours d'Ovide* was not tragic, and certain that *Théagène et Chariclée* was not. If it is true that he turned to tragedy only at the request of Molière, he was very fortunate. Whether it is true or not, we can hardly believe that *La Thébaïde* was written under Molière's detailed supervision. Edwards has pointed out the importance of the play for an understanding of Racine's later work.[4] It has too many premonitions of the later Racine, too many themes which lie near the centre of his poetic universe, to have been dictated by another.

2

In 1664, Racine had already moved into the smart literary world of the capital and written poems for courtly occasions. His first produced play might easily have been an adroit exercise in the latest fashionable taste. *La Thébaïde* is not: its most surprising feature is its archaism.

To begin with, it is a *tragédie*. We think all too easily of Racine as coming to an established form and perfecting it. Nothing could be more misleading. As we have seen, Corneille himself was hardly successful as a writer of tragedy in the narrower sense, and a large number of his plays were not even labelled tragedies. When Racine began to write, even tragedy in the wider sense was out of fashion. Schérer has shown that the number of plays designated as tragedies produced during the decade 1650–9 shows a steep drop in absolute terms compared with the previous decade, and a much steeper decline than the number of new comedies over the same period.[5] On the other hand, the number of pastoral plays increased over the two decades. Lancaster put the point succinctly: 'In 1664–1672, when Racine was establishing his reputation, he was, so far as can be determined, the only new author whose tragedies were being acted at Paris.'[6]

Not only is *La Thébaïde* a *tragédie*, but it has a subject taken from Greek legend – a rarity in the early 1660s. The last play with a subject from Greek legend which figures in Schérer's list is Corneille's *pièce à machines* – *La Toison d'Or* (1660); the last tragedy based on a Greek legend had been Corneille's *Oedipe* (1659).

La Thébaïde also contains one technical feature which by 1665 was clearly archaic. It has three soliloquies, which had been out of fashion for some years, and one of these (V.i) takes the form of *stances*, which had had their heyday in the 1630s and were generally abandoned about 1660. In *La Thébaïde* they make almost their last appearance.

Whether encouraged by Molière or not, Racine clearly was not afraid to attempt an unfashionable form, using unfashionable materials and methods. What did he make of them?

The quality of *La Thébaïde* as a stage play is hard to judge, but it is undeniably maladroit. Racine manages to make his plot intelligible and to keep it moving: unlike Rotrou, he takes only so much of the legend as he can reduce to unity, and he delays his big scene – the confrontation Etéocle and Polynice – until Act IV. But the action moves by fits and starts, and he seems not to have a clear idea of what drives it. The theme of fatality is insisted on, but on the simple plot-level the whole imbroglio is engineered by Créon. In V.iii, Antigone tells him so in set terms:

> N'imputez qu'à vous seul la mort du roi mon frère,
> Et n'en accusez point la céleste colère,
> A ce combat fatal vous seul l'avez conduit.[7]

In several key scenes the dialogue moves awkwardly from subject to subject, as if Racine could bring forward only one thing at a time. In I.v, there is a disjointed discussion between Créon and Jocaste, mainly on political matters. After some 60 lines of this, Antigone (who has been on the stage for 243 lines, but has not spoken for the last 234) joins in the discussion, and we learn that Créon and Hémon are both in love with her. Créon goes out, and the conversation turns back to politics, without any sign from Jocaste that she is aware of the love-tangle. Again, the first part of Act III is taken up with the suicide of Créon's son Ménécée, who has hoped to appease the gods. Jocaste praises Ménécée and curses Créon. Etéocle and Créon come in (III.iv), and Jocaste proceeds to discuss with Etéocle the implications of the suicide. It is not till 43 lines after his entrance that Créon speaks, and until then neither Jocaste nor Etécole have taken any notice of him. The most striking example of this awkwardness is the treatment of Jocaste's death. She always wishing to die, but does not do so until the interval between Acts IV and V. We are then told of her death in one banal line in a lyrical soliloquy:

> A quoi te résous-tu, Princesse infortunée?
> Ta mère vient de mourir dans tes bras.

Edwards suggests that this recurrent awkwardness is a deliberate attempt to express the lack of connection ('désaccord') which is the play's theme. I am inclined to think it is mainly due to Racine's lack of skill, as it occurs at points where it seems to have no thematic function. Nevertheless, it is strange that Racine, with his prodigious theatrical flair and his close involvement with theatre people, had not yet mastered the technique of keeping in play all the characters he brings on stage at one time. This does suggest that his attention is turned to expressing an underlying theme rather than to superficial neatness of form. If there is clumsiness, it is in a significant direction.

As is to be expected, parts of *La Thébaïde* are very second-hand. The villainies of Créon and his political discussion with Jocaste and Attale seem like Cornelian pastiche, though not always bad:

> L'intérêt de l'état est de n'avoir qu'un roi,
> Qui d'un ordre constant gouvernant ses provinces
> Accoutume à ses lois et le peuple et les princes.
> Ce règne interrompu de deux rois différents,
> En lui donnant deux rois, lui donne deux tyrans.
> Vous les verriez toujours, l'un à l'autre contraire,
> Détruire aveuglément ce qu'aurait fait un frère,
> L'un sur l'autre toujours former quelque attentat,
> Et changer tous les ans la face de l'état.
> Ce terme limité que l'on veut leur prescrire
> Accroît leur violence en bornant leur empire;
> Tous deux feront gémir les peuples tour à tour.

But the general weakness of the verse is revealing, because it shows the progress Racine was to make later. Sometimes it is insipid in a precious way that now seems especially unbearable. Hémon addresses Antigone thus:

> Permettez que mon coeur en voyant vos beaux yeux
> De l'état de son sort interroge ses dieux . . .
> Souffrent-ils sans courroux mon ardente amitié,
> Et du mal qu'ils ont fait ont-ils quelque pitié? . . .
> Ah! d'un si bel objet quand une âme est blessée,
> Quand un coeur jusqu'à vous élève sa pensée,
> Qu'il est doux d'adorer tant de divins appas!

Much worse is the inert regularity of the verse that forms the staple of the play:

> Mais pour vous ce malheur est un moindre supplice
> Que si la mort vous eût enlevé Polynice;
> Ce prince était l'objet qui faisait tous vos soins;
> Les intérêts du roi vous touchaient beaucoup moins.

In spite of these faults, *La Thébaïde* is not negligible: it bears evident traces of the true Racine. The most striking of these is the tragic note introduced by the theme of fatality. It has been said that this indicates the influence of Jansenism. But the tragic fate of *La Thébaïde* is some-thing more radical. The note is first struck by Jocaste:

> O toi, qui que tu sois, qui rends le jour au monde,
> Que ne l'as-tu laissé dans une nuit profonde?
> A de si noirs forfaits, prêtes-tu tes rayons,
> Et peux-tu sans horreur voir ce que nous voyons?
> Mais ces monstres, hélas! ne t'épouvantent guères,
> Le seul sang de Laïus les a rendus vulgaires;
> Tu peux voir sans frayeur les crimes de mes fils,
> Apres ceux que le père et la mère ont commis:
> Tu ne t'étonnes pas si mes fils sont perfides,
> S'ils sont tous deux méchants, et s'ils sont parricides:
> Tu sais qu'ils sont sortis d'un sang incestueux,
> Et tu t'étonnerais s'ils étaient vertueux.

Like Phèdre, she realises that innocence is no defence. The gods who caused her crime will punish it:

> Et toutefois, ô dieux, un crime involontaire
> Devait-il attirer toute votre colère?
> Le connaissais-je, hélas! ce fils infortuné,
> Lorsque dedans mes bras vous l'avez amené?
> C'est vous dont la rigueur m'ouvrit ce précipice.
> Voilà de ces grands dieux la suprême justice:
> Jusques au bord du crime ils conduisent nos pas;
> Ils nous le font commettre, et ne l'excusent pas.
> Prennent-ils donc plaisir à faire des coupables . . .?

We are far from the providential God of Christianity. Jocaste knows that any hopeful turn of events is illusory:

> Connaissez mieux du ciel la vengeance fatale.
> Toujours à ma douleur il met quelque intervalle,
> Mais, hélas! quand sa main semble me secourir,
> C'est alors qu'il s'apprête à me faire périr.

These statements are not well harmonised with the structure of the play (we have already noted the uncertainty whether the catastrophe is brought about by inexorable fate or the manoeuvres of Créon), but there are signs that Racine was already striving for means of accom-modating them in the mechanisms demanded by neo-classical drama-turgy. The archaic use of *stances* and soliloquy points to a concern less with forwarding the plot than with lyricism and the poetic develop-ment of a theme. This impression is heightened by Racine's handling of his fourth act. This is the climax of the play, and he has contrived to delay until this point the fatal interview of the two brothers. It would have been easy to present the interview as capable of ending well or ill. This would have been in accord with the orthodox theory that suspense be maintained as long as possible. Racine does something quite different. Etécole explains himself clearly to Créon before Polynice enters:

> Nous verrons ce qu'il veut, mais je répondrais bien
> Que par cette entrevue on n'avancera rien.

The result is settled in advance. The interest is concentrated on why this is so:

> Je sais que Polynice est d'une humeur altière,
> Je sais bien que sa haine est encor tout entière;
> Je ne crois pas qu'on puisse en arrêter le cours,
> Et pour moi je sens bien que je le hais toujours.

Créon reminds him that Polynice may be willing to make the concessions needed to appease this hatred. Etécole knows better: he is possessed by a hatred deeper than reason:

> Je ne sais si mon coeur s'apaisera jamais.
> Ce n'est pas son orgueil, c'est lui seul que je hais.
> Nous avons l'un et l'autre une haine obstinée;
> Elle n'est pas, Créon, l'ouvrage d'une année.
> Elle est née avec nous, et sa noire fureur
> Aussitôt que la vie entra dans notre coeur.
> Nous étions ennemis dès la plus tendre enfance . . .
> On dirait que le ciel, par un arrêt funeste,
> Voulut de nos parents venger ainsi l'inceste,
> Et que dans notre sang il voulut mettre au jour
> Tout ce qu'a de plus noir et la haine et l'amour;
> Et maintenant, Créon, que j'attends sa venue,
> Ne crois pas que pour lui ma haine diminue;
> Plus il approche, et plus il allume ses feux,
> Et sans doute il faudra qu'il éclate à ses yeux.
> J'aurais même regret qu'il me quittât l'empire.
> Il faut, il faut qu'il fuie, et non qu'il se retire;
> Je ne veux point, Créon, le haïr à moitié,
> Et je crains son courroux moins que son amitié.
> Je veux pour donner cours à mon ardente haine
> Que sa fureur au moins autorise la mienne.

It is no wonder that Racine returned again and again to this speech over more than thirty years to polish and adorn it. Something happens in it which we will meet again in Racine. All rational motives are swept aside. A passion wells up that is more primitive and terrible than any rational motive – a love that is at the same time a lust for destruction – and the character enters into a state of possession in which the dark gods of the mind have mastery. The means are literary. The verse no longer marches in neat squadrons: the rigid prosody is overborne by the force of possession:

> Et maintenant/ Créon/ que j'attends sa venue,
> Ne crois *pas*/ que pour *lui*/ ma *haine* diminue . . .
> Il *faut*/ il *faut*/ qu'il *fuie*/ et *non* qu'il se retire . . .
> Je *veux*/ pour donner cours à mon *ardente haine*
> Que sa fureur au moins *autorise* la mienne.

'Autorise' – the stress falls on this revealing word. The action only appears to proceed on rational assumptions; in reality, it proceeds by its own logic, for which the logic of fact merely supplies pretexts. The interview proceeds to its fated end. The arguments which should lead to reconciliation only nourish hatred. Jocaste vainly points out that Polynice's cruelty discredits him. He answers her:

> Ah! si je suis cruel on me force de l'être,
> Et de mes actions je ne suis pas le maître;
> Si je suis violent c'est que je suis contraint . . .
> Mon coeur, jaloux du sort de ces grands malheureux,
> Veut s'élever, Madame, et tomber avec eux.

All argument is useless ('Madame, il n'est plus rien qui les puisse arrêter'), and the brothers rush out to die.

There are a few glimpses of the later Racine in other places (notably in the rôle of Antigone). But the main Racinian element in *La Thébaïde* is this sense of an inexplicable fate connected with uncontrollable passion.

Without wishing to place too much emphasis on them, we can say that *La Thébaïde* shows two features which are important for Racine's development. It does not rely solely on the peripheral interests of plot, characters and verse for its interest, but attempts (in part, at least) to express a central poetic concept, even by unfashionable means. Secondly, this theme is tragic. We need not attribute this to Racine's Jansenist upbringing – Jansenists, like all Christians, believed in a providential God – or to his knowledge of the Greek tragic poets – the Greek authors he studied in childhood were Homer, Plato, Plutarch and the saints and novelists of the decadence, and he did not turn seriously to the great tragedians until the late 1660s – but we should mark how clearly it distinguishes him from his contemporaries. Corneille, in *Oedipe*, had firmly stated the orthodox line on fate and free-will. The fate that appears in *La Thébaïde* is something mysterious and over-powering. It puts the gauche *La Thébaïde* in a quite different category from the competent emptiness of *Le Comte d'Essex*.

3

Alexandre is Racine's worst play, and made his reputation. It is therefore worth a little attention: the not-so-good plays which are greatly successful show what an age thinks it wants, which is not always what the masterpieces provide.

Here we have Racine's first success, written when he was twenty-four or twenty-five – very early in his career, yet only a year or two before his first undoubted masterpiece. Let us look at it, therefore, as though we knew nothing of his later glory. On the evidence of this work, how is the young poet trying to find his true path? What paths, on the evidence of this play, could he have taken which were not those he eventually chose? Above all, why is it that *Alexandre*, for all its merits, is now a play merely read by scholars, whereas *Andromaque,* written so soon afterwards and outwardly in many ways so similar, has kept its unwithering freshness?

No doubt *Alexandre* was 'influenced by Quinault', as the saying goes, but let us look at its Cornelian qualities. The great Cornelian success of recent years had been *Sertorius*, and there are distinct echoes of it in *Alexandre*. Pompée ends *Sertorius* thus:

> Allons donner votre ordre à des pompes funèbres,
> A l'égal de son nom illustres et célèbres,
> Et dresser un tombeau, témoin de son malheur,
> Qui le soit de sa gloire et de notre douleur.

Racine's play closes like this:

> Oui, Madame, pleurons un ami si fidèle;
> Faisons en soupirant éclater notre zèle,
> Et qu'un tombeau superbe instruise l'avenir
> Et de votre douleur et de mon souvenir.

In Corneille's play, Sertorius sends Perpenna to plead his love to Viriate, who does not love him. She receives him thus:

> Vous m'aimez, Perpenna; Sertorius le dit;
> Je crois sur sa parole, et lui dois tout crédit.
> Je sais donc votre amour; mais tirez-moi de peine:
> Par où prétendez-vous mériter une reine?

A quel titre lui plaire, et par quel charme un jour
Obliger sa couronne à payer votre amour?

Perpenna replies:

Par de sincères voeux, par d'assidus services,
Par de profonds respects, par d'humbles sacrifices . . .
Quoi que vous m'ordonniez, tout me sera facile.

In Racine's play, Alexandre sends Taxile to plead his love to Axiane, who does not love him. She receives him thus:

Approche, puissant roi,
Grand monarque de l'Inde, on parle ici de toi,
On veut en ta faveur combattre ma colère;
On dit que tes désirs n'aspirent qu'à me plaire,
Que mes rigueurs ne font qu'affermir ton amour.
On fait plus, et l'on veut que je t'aime à mon tour.
Mais sais-tu l'entreprise où s'engage ta flamme?
Sais-tu par quels secrets on peut toucher mon âme?
Es-tu prêt . . .

Taxile replies:

Ah! Madame, éprouvez seulement
Ce que peut sur mon coeur un espoir si charmant.
Que faut-il faire?

At the end of the play, Alexandre's clemency recalls that of Auguste:

Votre fierté, Porus, ne se peut abaisser:
Jusqu'au dernier soupir vous m'osez menacer.
En effet, ma victoire en doit être alarmée . . .
Je ne laisserai pas ma victoire imparfaite.
Vous l'avez souhaité, vous ne vous plaindrez pas.
Régnez toujours, Porus: je vous rends vos états.
Avec mon amitié recevez Axiane;
A des liens si doux tous deux je vous condamne.

There is the same insistence on the enemy's stubbornness, followed by not only pardon but superadded benefits. But here we touch on the weakness of *Alexandre*. The clemency of Auguste has behind it the pressure of a whole world of thought and feeling, a world which the play has built up and made alive. The clemency of Alexandre has no such fullness of experience behind it. There has been no struggle. From the beginning, as at the end, Alexandre, is perfect:

Allez, Ephestion. Que l'on cherche Porus;
Qu'on épargne sa vie, et le sang des vaincus.

His clemency is an impressive gesture, but no more than a gesture. We can now perhaps see the cause of both the weakness and the strength of *Alexandre*. Liberated from any necessity to express a central meaning, it is free to display those qualities the public wants. Some of these things seem insipid now, though very much to seventeenth-century taste:

De ses retranchements il découvre les vôtres:
Mais, après tant d'exploits, ce timide vainqueur
Craint qu'il ne soit encor bien loin de votre coeur . . .

Il faut vaincre, et j'y cours, bien moins pour éviter
Le titre de captif, que pour le mériter.

But there is much we can still relish. There are some successful heroics, and lines and passages with a Cornelian vigour and realism:

Quelle étrange valeur, qui, ne cherchant qu'à nuire,
Embrase tout, sitôt qu'elle commence à luire;
Qui n'a que son orgueil pour règle et pour raison;
Qui veut que l'univers ne soit qu'une prison,
Et que, maître absolu de tous tant que nous sommes,
Ses esclaves en nombre égalent tous les hommes!

Adieu; tu me connais. Aime-moi, si tu veux.

There are also lines of exquisite tenderness:

Hélas! nous l'admirions sans en être jaloux.
Contents de nos états, et charmés l'un de l'autre,
Nous attendions un sort plus heureux que le vôtre.

The verse is elegant and skilful, but lightweight. The play has no deep inner meaning: its rôle is to reflect in a flattering way the world that exists outside it. Hence the flimsy elegance of the plot, characters and verse. Hence the complete abandonment of tragedy.

Nevertheless, the play has its place in Racine's development. The verse is more accomplished than in most of *La Thébaïde,* partly because of its liberation from content. More important, there are traces of a characteristic of the later Racine: the subordination and sometimes dislocation of the machinery of the formal plot in the interests of a quasi-lyrical expression of emotion. An example is IV.i, where Axiane laments the defeat and supposed death of Porus. It is interesting for several reasons. It is irrelevant to anything that might normally be called plot. It takes the form of a long soliloquy (which was then definitely archaic). The emotion is not so much stated as sung: the verse takes on a lyrical life of its own which seems to accompany rather than express the banal content of the speech, and so gives its banality a strange resonance. The speech starts in the measured rhythms of rational discourse:

> N'entendrons-nous jamais que des cris de victoire
> Qui de mes ennemis me reprochent la gloire?
> Et ne pourrai-je au moins, en de si grands malheurs,
> M'entretenir moi seule avecque mes douleurs?
> D'un odieux amant sans cesse poursuivie,
> On prétend malgré moi m'attacher à la vie.

But then, something happens. The verse leaves the ground:

> On m'observe, on me suit. Mais, Porus, ne crois pas
> Qu'on me puisse empêcher de courir sur tes pas.

The rest of the speech wavers uneasily between the staid forms of rational discourse (with its logical framework and antithetical verse-forms) and a quite different structure, more musical than conceptual, in which the rhythm, rather than logical relationships, dictates where the main accents shall fall:

> Combien de fois, tes yeux forçant ma résistance,
> Mon coeur s'est-il vu prêt de rompre le silence!
> Combien de fois, sensible à tes ardents desirs,
> M'est-il en ta présence échappé des soupirs!

This is normal enough, but in the next few lines the verse again starts to lift:

> Mais je voulais encor douter de ta victoire;
> J'expliquais mes soupirs en faveur de la gloire:
> Je croyais n'aimer qu'elle. Ah! pardonne, grand roi,
> Je sens bien aujourd'hui que je n'aimais que toi.
> J'avoûrai que la gloire eut sur moi quelque empire:
> Je te l'ai dit cent fois; mais je devais te dire
> Que toi seul en effet m'engageas sous ses lois.
> J'appris à la connaître en voyant tes exploits.

but then, suddenly, the afflatus subsides:

> Et de quelque beau feu qu'elle m'eût enflammée

only to revive, equally suddenly, in the last line of this movement:

> En un autre que toi je l'aurais moins aimée.

The effect of this double structure here is clumsy, but it is one which Racine was to exploit later with more success.

The most Racinian feature of *Alexandre* is the lyricism of Axiane's soliloquy. But the most interesting thing about the play is the way in which it is uncharacteristic of Racine. This gives ground for thought about which qualities are Racinian. It is usually said that the qualities characteristic of Racine – those by which his plays differ from other men's, and in particular from Corneille's – are simplicity, neat construction, and concentration on love. *Alexandre* is simple enough. Alexandre's invasion of India is opposed by Porus and Axiane; Taxile joins them only because he loves Axiane. Taxile's sister, Cléofile, loves Alexandre and persuades her brother to abandon Porus. Porus kills Taxile, but is defeated. Alexandre pardons him. This minimal plot is cleverly spread out over five acts to provide a neat series of interesting and varied situations. In spite of war and politics, love carries all before it: Taxile loves Axiane, Axiane loves Porus, Porus loves Axiane, Alexandre loves Cléofile, Cléofile loves Alexandre. If the critical clichés were right, *Alexandre* would be Racine's most typical play. In fact, it is his least typical: the text has a quite different feel from that of any of his other tragedies. The reason, of course, is that Racine's characteristic qualities are not a matter of external features. *Alexandre* is untypical of him because of its emptiness. It lacks any central meaning, just as *Le Comte d'Essex* does. In it we see the decorative but trivial art into which neo-classicism was declining. It is clearly in a different category from *Andromaque*.

APPROACHES TO TRAGEDY

I

One of the contentions of this book is that Corneille, in general, is not a writer of tragedy in the strict sense. Another contention is that Racine is. If so, there is an evident discontinuity between his works and those of his predecessors and contemporaries. *Andromaque* and *Britannicus* are the first two of his plays which are undeniably great, and as, even on the most severe judgment, they aspire to tragedy, they may show how Racine approached his task.

How does *Andromaque* differ from *Alexandre*? We will not start with the obvious features – the incomparably more subtle characterisation, the superior deftness of plot, the extraordinary firmness and subtlety of the dialogue. It is true that Racine has been gaining experience as a man and as a playwright. We may rate his emotional development as more important than his increase in technical skill. There is a sense in which Racine evolves, whereas Corneille experiments. But this evolution, and the results of it, cannot draw their characteristic qualities solely from the increase in his emotional and professional experience. What made *Andromaque* possible is an evolution in Racine's literary attitudes which enables him to organise his experience and skill into a form very different from what his contemporaries understood by tragedy. Let us look first, then, for some underlying difference, some inner strength, which makes the external differences possible.

It is easiest to start with what *Andromaque* is not. Vinaver quotes Janet's description of the subject of *Andromaque* as a sort of square-dance:

On pourrait presque donner à ce quadrille la forme d'une proposition arith-métique et dire: Hermione et Pyrrhus sont les deux moyens dont Oreste et Andromaque sont les deux extrêmes . . . Quel est maintenant le jeu du drame? Il est tout entier dans le va-et-vient de ces deux moyens termes, tantôt se rapprochant, tantot s'éloignant des deux extrêmes. Tantôt, en effet, Pyrrhus désespéré se détourne d'Andromaque et revient à Hermione, qui alors se dépêche d'abandonner Oreste, et ainsi les deux extrêmes restent seuls, Andro-maque dans sa joie, Oreste dans sa fureur. Tantôt, au contraire, l'espoir ramène Pyrrhus vers Andromaque, et Hermione, à son tour désespérée et ulcérée, se retourne vers Oreste, pleine de mépris et de rancune d'abord, puis de rage et de vengeance.[1]

Here, we might think, is one secret of the play. As has been said, in competent hands such a plot could hardly fail. Nevertheless, Racine's handling of it appears strange if we compare it with Janet's description – a description which, though inaccurate, perhaps represents the mechanical perfection we think ought to be there. It is obviously difficult to locate a moment when Andromaque 'reste dans sa joie'. It is also, on reflection, difficult to find one particular moment when Oreste remains isolated 'dans sa fureur'. (I shall return to this point.) It is not even certain that Pyrrhus is ever 'led back' to Andromaque by 'hope'. To see the use Racine makes of his ingenious plot, we will look at two key scenes: II.ii and IV.v.

The first of these is Oreste's initial interview with Hermione. Racine has clearly indicated the background. Oreste, hearing that Pyrrhus does not want Hermione, hopes to persuade her to love him. He has said this plainly in I.i:

> Heureux si je pouvais, dans l'ardeur qui me presse,
> Au lieu d'Astyanax, lui ravir ma princesse . . .
> J'aime: je viens chercher Hermione en ces lieux,
> · La fléchir, l'enlever, ou mourir à ses yeux.

Pylade hints that Hermione is favourably disposed:

> Quelquefois elle appelle Oreste à son secours.

Hermione herself loves Pyrrhus and is indifferent to Oreste, but it is obviously in her interest to use him as best she can – to make Pyrrhus jealous, or to avenge her, or simply to take her back home. We can, therefore, see quite clearly what form this scene should take in the scheme of the play: Oreste pleads with her to love him; she makes use of him to further her own ends; a decision is reached that Oreste will do something which will forward the plot. Perversely, the scene does none of these things. True, it starts off as though it might. Hermione receives Oreste with affected coquetry, and he replies with a recital of his love and her cruelty. But then it goes off on a different track. Hermione, in spite of her desire to cajole Oreste, shows quite plainly that she loves Pyrrhus. Oreste knows this:

> Déjà même je crois entendre la réponse
> Qu'en secret contre moi votre haine prononce.

Hermione protests, and he insists:

> Ouvrez vos yeux: songez qu'Oreste est devant vous.

The scene now develops in a very topsy-turvy way. Hermione insists that she loves Oreste, and he tries to persuade her she does not:

> Le coeur est pour Pyrrhus, et les voeux pour Oreste . . .
> Vous me voulez aimer, et je ne puis vous plaire . . .

Hermione becomes exasperated:

> Qu'on fasse de l'Epire un second Ilion.
> Allez. Après cela direz-vous que je l'aime?

Oreste is reduced to urging her to realise that she loves Pyrrhus:

> Et vous le haïssez? Avouez-le, Madame,
> L'amour n'est pas un feu qu'on renferme en une âme:
> Tout nous trahit, la voix, le silence, les yeux;
> Et les feux mal couverts n'en éclatent que mieux.

In a neatly-plotted play, we might expect each important scene to lead to a decision which furthers the plot. This is one of the axioms of neo-classical dramaturgy.[2] But the decision reached at the end of this scene is disappointing. Hermione decides that Oreste shall tell Pyrrhus he must give up Astyanax or forfeit the friendship of the Greeks. In the monologue which follows, Oreste confirms he will do this. The decision is disappointing because he has already done just this in Act I. Moreover, the decision, such as it is, is made nugatory in the next scene, when Pyrrhus announces (before Oreste can open his mouth) that he has decided to give up Astyanax and marry Hermione. Not only has Racine written his scene in the reverse way to what we might expect; he has made no use of it to further his plot. The decision in which it results has already been put into effect, and is in any case already overtaken by events.

Act II is not perhaps the place for paroxysms of plot, so let us go to IV.v, which is certainly one of the tensest scenes in the play. Pyrrhus has definitely abandoned Hermione, who has ordered Oreste to murder him. Then Pyrrhus unexpectedly comes to see Hermione. Again, the dramatic purpose of the scene – or, rather, what the purpose might be in other hands – is quite clear. Will Hermione succeed in winning back Pyrrhus? If not, will she decide to have him murdered after all, or will he succeed in placating her? Will she succeed in concealing her plans, or will he sense his danger and take precautions? Unfortunately, Racine misses his chances of introducing exciting twists and turns in the plot. Pyrrhus starts by saying flatly that he is going to marry Andromaque:

> Je ne viens point, armé d'un indigne artifice,
> D'un voile d'équité couvrir mon injustice:
> Il suffit que mon coeur me condamne tout bas;
> Et je soutiendrais mal ce que je ne crois pas.
> J'épouse une Troyenne.

Pyrrhus, then, is hardly trying to placate Hermione, She, for her part, makes no attempt to win him back, but overwhelms him with irony:

> Vous vous abandonniez au crime en criminel . . .
> Tout cela part d'un coeur toujours maître de soi,
> D'un héros qui n'est point esclave de sa foi . . .
> Que peut-on refuser à ces généreux coups?

Pyrrhus is not listening, anyway. His thoughts are with Andromaque, and he replies with careless politeness:

> Rien ne vous engageait à m'aimer en effet.

Hermione can then indeed appeal to him to love her, or at least to save himself:

> Pour la dernière fois je vous parle peut-être:
> Différez-le d'un jour; demain vous serez maître.

But she is talking to herself. She knows this, without a word from him:

> Vous ne répondez point? Perfide, je le voi,
> Tu comptes les moments que tu perds avec moi!
> Ton coeur, impatient de revoir ta Troyenne,
> Ne souffre qu'à regret qu'un autre t'entretienne.

and she can burst out into threats:

> Porte aux pieds des autels ce coeur qui m'abandonne;
> Va, cours; mais crains encor d'y trouver Hermione.

If this were really a drama in which the plot were pushed along solely by the psychological reactions of the characters, the characters would have to react upon each other. In this scene, Pyrrhus and Hermione never make contact. At the end of it, the plot is where it was at the beginning: Hermione still intends to murder Pyrrhus, and he is still oblivious of the danger. A detail is revealing. Racine makes a concession to conventional playwriting in the introduction to the scene, when he has Hermione send Cléone to stop Oreste from doing anything without consulting her. The implication is that the scene with Pyrrhus may affect the action. We never hear whether Oreste does consult Hermione again, or what their attitudes would have been if he had: at the beginning of Act V Hermione seems to have no idea of what Oreste is doing or intending to do. We never learn what came of the little plot-manoeuvre sketched at the end of IV.iv; and by Act V Racine (and the audience) have forgotten it.

It is difficult, then, to maintain that the force of *Andromaque* comes from the cunning manipulation of its plot. There is a skilful arrangement of incidents, certainly, but – in a way that is difficult to define – they seem to accompany the action rather than form its essence.

We are brought to a similar conclusion if we examine the plot from another angle, that of the psychological shifts within the characters which allegedly provide the motive-power. Bailly, for example, says:

c'est à la peinture de cet amour que Racine réduit le sujet de sa pièce, par une simplification et un souci d'enchaînement logique qui fondent chez nous un système dramatique nouveau. Dans *l'Andromaque* d'Euripide, la jalousie d'Hermione et la mort de Pyrrhus formaient presque deux actions distinctes. Racine les lie l'une à l'autre, en faisant de cette jalousie la cause de cette mort; et l'une et l'autre, il les soumet aux décisions d'Andromaque, qui, moteur unique et souverain de l'action tragique, la suspend à ses hesitations, et en commande toutes le peripéties.[3]

This presumably means that, in any given situation, the attitude of A causes B to take up another attitude, which then reacts on the attitude of A or C, and so on. It is remarkably difficult to find examples of this in *Andromaque*. Let us take Andromaque herself, whose decisions Bailly says are the sole and sovereign motive-power of the play. In Act I she makes no decisions. In the face of Pyrrhus's threats and blandishments she remains steadfast: she will neither be unfaithful to Hector nor marry Pyrrhus to save Astyanax. In Act II she does not appear, though presumably her continued refusal to make any concession decides Pyrrhus to surrender Astyanax and marry Hermione. We can perhaps say that this refusal to change her attitude is a decision, and that this decision is what pushes Pyrrhus into his new attitude. It might be more exact to say, however, that Andromaque's passivity throws Pyrrhus back on the conflict of his own emotions, so that the decision, if any, is left to him. Andromaque has not acted on Pyrrhus: by refusing to do so she has left him to act on himself.

In Act III, she does decide to do something: she appeals to Hermione. This has no effect on the plot, as Hermione naturally refuses to help. In an agonising scene (III.vi), Andromaque does consider appealing to Pyrrhus to save her son. But her actual appeal (ll. 927–46) is addressed more to herself and to Hector than to Pyrrhus. She can hardly be said to have taken a direct decision to enlist the help of Pyrrhus, and it is he who poses the dilemma:

> Je vous le dis: il faut ou périr ou régner . . .
> Songez-y: je vous laisse; et je viendrai vous prendre
> Pour vous mener au temple où ce fils doit m'attendre;
> Et là vous me verrez, soumis ou furieux,
> Vous couronner, Madame, ou le perdre à vox yeux.

The only decision-making by Andromaque is portrayed in the last scene of Act III and first of Act IV. III.viii shows her refusal to take any decision at all. When she reappears after the interval she has indeed taken one, and it affects the whole course of the action. But the quality of the decision is worth examining. It has the same strange lack of rapport with the factual situation that we find in other areas of the plot. Although Andromaque decides to marry Pyrrhus, and so sets the catastrophe in motion, she has not changed her attitude. Her decision is an 'innocent stratagem'. The marriage will be no marriage. Her thoughts are still on Hector and her son:

> Quoi donc? as-tu pensé qu'Andromaque infidèle
> Pût trahir un époux qui croit revivre en elle? . . .
> Mais son fils périssait: il l'a fallu défendre . . .
> Si tu vivais pour moi, vis pour le fils d'Hector . . .
> Fais connaître à mon fils les héros de sa race . . .
> Il est du sang d'Hector, mais il en est le reste;
> Et pour ce reste enfin j'ai moi-même, en un jour,
> Sacrifié mon sang, ma haine et mon amour.

So Andromaque passes out of the play.[4] The action has progressed, and partly through her, but she herself has not changed. Nothing could be less true than to say that any deep psychological development has dictated her decision. Driven into a corner, she does not change her basic attitude: she resorts to a ruse.

Although Andromaque gives her name to the play, her part is shorter than those of the other principals. The longest is that of Oreste, who has nearly twice as many lines as Andromaque, and whose part in the plot is apparently more active. But this appearance is deceptive. In Act I, he sets the plot in motion by putting to Pyrrhus the Greek demands (though these are external to his main purpose, which is to win Hermione). We have already seen how in Act II, far from urging Hermione to love him, he tries to persuade her she does not, and how the decision (such as it is) to which their scene leads is immediately shown to be irrelevant. It is presumably in Acts II and III that Oreste 'reste seul dans sa fureur'. In fact, he is in this condition throughout the play. Never does he delude himself that Hermione loves him or that he can be happy. In Act III, he decides to carry off Hermione, but this comes to nothing. In Act IV, Hermione orders him to kill Pyrrhus. Pyrrhus is killed in Act V, but not finally at Oreste's instigation. He has planned the assassination, but we learn in Act V, Scene ii, that he is still undecided about it. In the event, his Greek followers kill Pyrrhus, and for political motives, not on behalf of Hermione. Oreste comes back to apologise. He admits that the Greeks have 'trahi votre vengeance' and that he himself has not laid a finger on Pyrrhus ('je n'ai pu trouver de place pour frapper'). But he sees Hermione's growing fury, and tries to excuse himself by claiming that 'c'est moi dont l'ardeur leur a servi d'exemple; Je les ai pour vous seule entraînés dans le temple'. This is untrue, as Racine has taken care to tell us. It seems from ll. 1499–500 that Oreste's followers are in the temple before he gets there, and they are certainly there dispersed and not under his leadership; and ll. 1514–20 show that they act without a signal from him. The dénouement is not brought about by the reactions of the main characters, 'psychological' or otherwise: in *Andromaque*, as in *Nicomède*, the knot is untied by the external agency of 'le peuple' – in this case Oreste's followers (who spontaneously attack Pyrrhus) and Pyrrhus's subjects (who rally to the side of Andromaque). In fact, if we look carefully at the rôle of Oreste, what impresses us is that it is static – as static as the rôle of Andromaque.

The reason is, of course, that Racine is not really writing the sort of play in which a well-made plot is pushed forward to an exciting conclusion by the interactions of the characters. This is clear if we look at the verse, and especially in the first scene, where Racine is careful to set out the basis of his play. The main speech is that by Oreste from l. 37 to l. 104. The opening dialogue, however, has plenty of clues if we listen:

> Ma *fortune* va prendre une face nouvelle;
> Et déjà son *courroux semble* s'être adouci . . .
> Qui l'eût dit, qu'un rivage à mes yeux si *funeste* . . .
> J'en rends grâces au ciel, qui, *m'arrêtant sans cesse,*
> *Semblait* m'avoir fermé le chemin de la Grèce,
> Depuis le jour *fatal* que la *fureur* des eaux . . .
> Je craignais que le ciel, par un *cruel secours,*
> Ne vous offrît *la mort que vous cherchiez* toujours . . .
> Hélas! *qui peut savoir le destin* qui m'amène? . . .
> Par quel *charme*, oubliant tant de tourments soufferts . . .
> Vous me *trompiez,* Seigneur.

These themes – overshadowing fates, hostile but impersonal gods, uncertainty, self-deception and enchantment – are developed in the main speech:

> Je me *trompais* moi-même.
> Ami, n'accable point un malheureux qui t'aime . . .
> Tu vis mon dés espoir . . .
> *Je fis croire et je crus* ma victoire certaine;
> Je pris tous mes transports pour des transports de haine . . .
> Voila comme *je crus étouffer* ma tendresse.
> En ce *calme trompeur* j'arrivai dans la Grèce;
> Et je trouvai d'abord ses princes rassemblés,
> Qu'un péril assez grand *semblait* avoir *troublés.*
> J'y courus. Je *pensai* que la guerre et la gloire
> De soins plus importants rempliraient ma mémoire . . .
> Mais admire avec moi le sort, dont la poursuite
> Me fait courir alors au piège que j'évite . . .
> Toute la Grèce *éclate* en murmures *confus* . . .
> Andromaque *trompa* l'ingénieux Ulysse . . .
> Ménélas, *sans le croire,* en *paraît* affligé . . .
> Parmi les déplaisirs où son âme se noie,
> Il s'élève en la mienne une *secrète* joie.
> Je triomphe; et pourtant *je me flatte* d'abord
> Que la seule vengeance excite ce *transport.*

These themes lead up to a comprehensive statement of his purpose from which Oreste never budges:

> Puisqu'après tant d'efforts ma résistance est vaine,
> Je me livre en aveugle au destin qui m'entraîne;
> J'aime; je viens chercher Hermione en ces lieux,
> La fléchir, l'enlever, ou mourir à ses yeux.

We now see why the rôle of Oreste must be static: 'Je me livre en aveugle au destin qui m'entraîne' (or, as in the first version, 'au transport qui m'entraîne'). He is possessed by a passion which is also his fate. He cannot act, he cannot even deceive himself into thinking that action would do any good. All he can do is to conduct his actions on a plane where he knows they are irrelevant. This realisation bursts out most bitterly when he takes his fruitless decision to carry off Hermione:

> Mon innocence enfin commence à me peser.
> Je ne sais de tout temps quelle injuste puissance
> Laisse le crime en paix et poursuit l'innocence.
> De quelque part sur moi que je tourne les yeux,
> Je ne vois que malheurs qui condamnent les dieux.

Méritons leur courroux, justifions leur haine,
Et que le fruit du crime en précède la peine.

The climax of his rôle comes at its end, when he attains to a sort of apotheosis, a realisation of his status as victim. This comes in one of the most terrifying lines in Racine:

Grâce aux dieux! Mon malheur passe mon espérance!

and then develops into a sort of serenity before the final delirium:

Oui, je te loue, ô ciel, de ta persévérance.
Appliqué sans relâche au soin de me punir,
Au comble des douleurs tu m'as fait parvenir.
Ta haine a pris plaisir à former ma misère;
J'étais né pour servir d'exemple à ta colère,
Pour être du malheur un modèle accompli.
Hé bien! je meurs content, et mon sort est rempli.

Superficially, this is bitterly ironical. But here Racine's poetry expresses in concentrated form a complex of emotions. In the first line, 'Grâce aux dieux!' not only plays bitterly on the usual meaning 'Praise be!') but also takes up the other meaning ('Thanks to the gods' — i.e., the gods have caused this). Yet there is another and deeper layer of meaning. To a Christian audience, 'Grâce' could not but recall the grace of God, which in Christian theology saves man, but here is the means of Oreste's misery. Oreste takes on the status of divine victim of the gods: 'soin' and 'former' continue the suggestion of loving care. Then, in l. 1620, the two contrasting moods ('I am persecuted by malignant gods' and 'I am the sacred victim') are again forcibly presented: Oreste 'dies happy' and his fate is fulfilled. This is the tragic realisation which we find in Oedipus at the grove of Colonus or Heracles when he learns the cause of his death. It is the realisation of Seneca's Hercules, in a play which Racine certainly knew: 'Habet, peractum est, fata se nostra explicant.' The substance is tragic. The method, in contrast to that of *Alexandre*, is poetic. Oreste is not so much a character as a poetic image. The same is true of Andromaque. We do not think of her as doing something. We think of her as a mood, a complex of intensely human emotions, an image composed of tenderness, serenity and grief, just touched with a barely perceptible irony and coquetry, all expressed in lines of magical simplicity:

On craint qu'il n'essuyât les larmes de sa mère.

Ma flamme par Hector fut jadis allumée;
Avec lui dans la tombe elle s'est enfermée.

Sans espoir de pardon m'avez-vous condamnée?

Conventionally, the seventeenth-century alexandrine is endstopped and has a caesura after the sixth syllable. Racine accepts this convention, but makes use of it: he strikes from it all the effects that a departure from a rigid norm can achieve. *Andromaque* is full of energetic lines with a strong caesura earlier than the sixth syllable, and sometimes even after the first:

> Vous l'abhorriez; enfin, vous ne m'en parliez plus.
>
> J'y courus. Je pensai que la guerre et la gloire . . .
>
> Il l'aime: mais enfin cette veuve inhumaine . . .
>
> Fuyons . . . Mais si l'ingrat rentrait dans son devoir!
>
> Je l'épouse. Il semblait qu'un spectacle si doux . . .
>
> Je t'entends. Mais excuse un reste de tendresse . . .
>
> Dissimulez: calmez ce transport inquiet.
>
> Allez: en cet état soyez sûr de son coeur.
>
> Et l'ingrat? jusqu'au bout il a poussé l'outrage?
>
> Quoi? toujours l'instrument et l'objet de sa rage . . .

This willingness to depart from the norm opens the way to an extraordinary flexibility:

> Je vous cherchais, Seigneur. Un peu de violence
> M'a fait de vos raisons combattre la puissance,
> Je l'avoue; et, depuis que je vous ai quitté,
> J'en ai senti la force et connu l'équité.
> Hélas!
>   – Ne me suis point, si ton coeur en alarmes
> Prévoit qu'il ne pourra commander à tes larmes.
> On vient. Cache tes pleurs, Céphise, et souviens-toi
> Que le sort d'Andromaque est commis à ta foi.
> C'est Hermione. Allons, fuyons sa violence.

From these simple resources Racine can suddenly conjure a lyricism which leaps out all the more strongly from the rigid frame:

> Prévenez-les.
>   – Non, non. J'y consens avec joie:
> Qu'ils cherchent dans l'Epire une seconde Troie.
>
> Songe aux cris des vainqueurs, songe aux cris des mourants,
> Dans la flamme étouffés, sous le fer expirants.

It is this poetic method, and the subtlety and strength of verse-technique which make it possible, that make *Andromaque* different from

Alexandre: the poetic life accompanies and overrides the superficial action. The immense superiority of Racine over his contemporaries is a superiority in verbal expressiveness: dexterity in handling plot, psychological subtlety, have little to do with it. Racine knew this, and said so: 'La différence entre Pradon et moi, c'est que moi je sais écrire.' It is in *Andromaque* that this superiority first becomes apparent. Yet this is not the whole story. Obviously, a poetic drama is not just a play containing beautiful poetry. The poet must find a dramatic method which produces the essential theatrical experience, but one in which his poetry provides the substance, not the decoration. In *Andromaque* Racine has not yet solved this problem. The most obvious indication is the separation between the poetic life and the plot: the poetic images of Andromaque and Oreste are, as it were, free-floating parallel to the action, hardly moving it or being moved by it.

There is a second indication which shows the difference between Racine's dramaturgy and that of his contemporaries. I have tried to show how the emotional – or, better, the poetic – life of the play overshadows the formal intrigue which, in contemporary theory and practice, was the centre of attention. I have also argued that the seventeenth-century reduction of the idea of a play from that of a complete showing-forth of a poetic idea to that of a good plot plus good characters plus good verse, each having no significance in itself, is essentially a part of that trend we call naturalism. *Andromaque* shows clear signs of this trend, and this is what long enabled critics to see Racine as a more refined continuation of Corneille. It is not simply that here and there Racine makes a gesture towards normal conventions of dramatic suspense (as when Hermione sends Cléone to Oreste in IV.iv). Both Pyrrhus and Hermione are presented partly naturalistically. They are often shown as saying things which we infer are the opposite of what they mean. This is a very typical method of naturalism, and the method by which Hermione's attempts to deceive herself are represented:

> Mais c'en est trop, Cléone, et quel que soit Pyrrhus,
> Hermione est sensible, Oreste a des vertus.
> Il sait aimer du moins, et même sans qu'on l'aime . . .
> Ah! je ne croyais pas qu'il fût si près d'ici.

With Pyrrhus the method is the same:

> Je vois ce qui la flatte:
> Sa beauté la rassure; et, malgre mon courroux,
> L'orgueilleuse m'attend encore à ses genoux.

Je la verrais au mien, Phoenix, d'un oeil tranquille.
Elle est veuve d'Hector, et je suis fils d'Achille;
Trop de haine sépare Andromaque et Pyrrhus.
– Commencez donc, Seigneur, à ne m'en parler plus.

Naturalism slides easily towards comedy, as in many of Corneille's later plays. At least one scene in *Andromaque* (II.v) is frankly comic, and most of the scenes in which Hermione appears could seem so if they were written at a slightly lower temperature ('Qui vous l'a dit, Seigneur, qu'il me méprise?'; 'Rien ne vous engageait à m'aimer en effet'; even 'Qui te l'a dit?'). Naturalism's characteristic resources are the copying of contemporary jargon and (when strong emotion is required) moral indignation laced with sarcasm. *Andromaque* falls more often than Racine's later plays into preciosity; Hermione's denunciation of Pyrrhus at the end of Act IV recalls the ironical tirades of Corneille's plays after *Polyeucte*.

I have also pointed out that a typical requirement of any doctrine which subordinates art to external definitions of truth is that it should inculcate morality. This demand is especially strong in seventeenth-century classical theory, which was influenced by both theological and representational criteria of external truth: it results in the doctrine of 'poetic justice'. In *La Thébaïde* Racine flouted this law, and portrayed the gods as punishing the innocent. The same conception appears in *Andromaque*, and is one of the signs of its greatness. As Butler has pointed out,[5] however, *Andromaque* shows signs of compromise. It is just possible to take the death of Pyrrhus, the madness of Oreste and the preservation of Andromaque as the results of poetic justice, and a seventeenth-century audience was probably quicker so to take them than we are. With this moral neatness, neo-classicism (like other art-forms which veer towards naturalism) tends to demand neatness of form. One of the distinguishing marks of Racine is that he, like Euripides in his tragedies, follows the inner logic of his theme rather than any external criterion of form. In *Andromaque* he at first hesitated to dismiss his title-character two-thirds of the way through the play. He therefore brought her on stage again in Act V, even though there was nothing for her to do. Worse, he found that he could hardly avoid making her mention Pyrrhus's death, and that this detracted from the poetic purity of her rôle, focused as it is on Hector and her son. The lines he gave her therefore balanced uneasily between tributes to Pyrrhus and assertions of her continuing devotion to Hector and Astyanax. In 1673, he realised his error and let Andromaque vanish after IV.i. To judge the originality of Racine, we may compare his treatment of these two points with that of Ambrose Philips when he came to translate *Andromaque* for Augustan England. Philips corrected Racine in accordance with the recognised principles of neo-classicism. In *The Distrest Mother* he spreads Andromaque's rôle more evenly over the play by confining her scene with her confidante at the beginning of Act IV to an announcement of her decision to marry Pyrrhus, and by adding a new scene between Andromaque and her confidante at the end of Act IV in which she explains her 'innocent stratagem'. He also brings in at the end of Act V first Phoenix to point out the wickedness of Oreste's crime and then Andromaque to express her satisfaction and set out the moral:

> Though plung'd in ills, and exercis'd in care,
> Yet never let the noble mind despair:
> When prest by dangers and beset with foes,
> The gods their timely succour interpose;
> And when our virtue sinks, o'erwhelmed with grief,
> By unforeseen expedients brings relief.

It is very difficult to see Racine as the docile exponent of neo-classical ideals.

In *Andromaque*, for almost the first time in the history of French classical tragedy, we have a work which stands to be judged as tragic. In 1667, after *Cinna* and *Sertorius*, this is Racine's real originality. The reasons for feeling that the play touches tragedy are many: the recognition of the tragic emotion, as distinct from plot, as the centre of the play; the rejection of 'poetic justice'; the recognition of numinous but irrational forces in human life; above all, the ability to sink shafts of poetry into the subterranean springs of feeling. *Andromaque* is undoubtedly a work of compelling power, as a poem and a stage play. If we have any doubts at all, they would centre on two points: the relatively schematic treatment of fate as an element in the rôle of Oreste, and Racine's hesitation between a tragic (Andromaque/Oreste/unmoral) and intrigue (Pyrrhus/Hermione/poetic justice) type of play. The two difficulties are connected: they mark areas in which Racine's tragic vision and poetic method clashed with the rational, naturalistic forms of drama codified by the critics and adopted by Corneille. Racine was to spend his dramatic career tackling these difficulties, now from one angle, now from another. In *Andromaque* his success is almost complete, but the antinomy between intrigue and emotion is over-ridden rather than solved. In *Britannicus* he was to try a different approach.

2

Vinaver first illuminated the dilemma of Racine as a poet who attempted to clothe a poetic and tragic vision in the approved forms of neo-classic drama, with their emphasis on intrigue and the arousing of suspense.[6] From the point of view of the development of Racinian tragedy, the most significant part of *Britannicus* is the 122 lines (in the final text) which follow the report of Britannicus's death. These are the part of the play which Racine defends most hotly in his first preface. Their importance is that they are the area in which the conflict between the intrigue and the emotional pattern of the play comes into the open. In *Andromaque*, Racine had allowed his tragic theme and formal intrigue to develop in parallel, but with a strange lack of connection. In *Britannicus*, he writes four-and-a-half acts almost wholly at the level plot–characters–effective verse, and then in these last 122 lines allows his poetic theme to reveal itself. Vinaver concludes that this coda cannot raise the work to the level of tragedy. Precisely because the body of the play is kept at the 'intrigue' level, that part of it can be developed with perfect coherence; but when the tragic theme is made manifest it cannot attach itself to what has gone before, and remains disembodied.

There is no doubt that Vinaver has seized accurately the nature of the first four-and-a-half acts. The verse in which they are written gives the clue. The lines are firm, energetic, eloquent. Yet the style of much of the play remains not quite satisfying. It expresses what the characters think and feel, but does not contribute to any overall pattern of experience in the play. The demands of Agrippine, for example, could hardly be put more pointedly or concisely:

> De mes accusateurs qu'on punisse l'audace,
> Que de Britannicus on calme le courroux,
> Que Junie à son choix puisse prendre un époux,
> Qu'ils soient libres tous deux, et que Pallas demeure,
> Que vous me permettiez de vous voir à toute heure.

– but what is this but resonant prose given extra force by rhyme? The verse can nimbly and economically indicate the psychological situation, as when Narcisse and Junie quickly change their tactics when they see they are irritating Néron:

> Craignez-vous . . . Mais, Seigneur, vous ne la craignez pas.
> C'est votre frère. Hélas! c'est un amant jaloux!

yet the real source of power in these lines is the emotion in Néron which we infer from his behaviour as he hears them, not from any poetic current which flows through them.

In one feature of *Britannicus* I can show arithmetically that Racine was going against his usual practice and adopting that of his contemporaries. Seventeenth-century critics disapproved of soliloquies. Corneille abandoned them in his later plays, and Racine's contemporaries rarely used them. Racine was unorthodox in refusing to dispense with them. The figures are revealing:

Play	Number of soliloquies	Total lines in soliloquies
La Thébaïde	3	60
Alexandre	2	56
Andromaque	3	69
Britannicus	2	13
Bérénice	4	98
Bajazet	3	95
Mithridate	3	81
Iphigénie	4	33
Phèdre	5	55

The picture would be even clearer if I added the soliloquies deleted from *Bérénice* and *Phèdre*. Even so, the last column brings out sharply the special position of *Britannicus*.

In most of *Britannicus*, then, Racine is writing a play that conforms to neo-classical doctrine. It may be that he was trying to rival Corneille, but that hardly affects the issue. Corneille's plays and critical ideas, however refractory on points of detail, were in principle fully in accord with the doctrine. The point is that Racine was, for once, trying to follow the approved pattern. It is with this in mind that we should read the famous first preface. He had conscientiously embraced an alien aesthetic, only to find that the result was a failure. What had gone wrong? He had certainly worked hard ('Quelque soin que j'aie pris pour travailler cette tragédie'). He had taken some pains about factual accuracy (no other preface of Racine gives such a list of references: he defends the accuracy of his picture point by point). He has even leaned over on the side of morality ('je n'ai pas ouï dire qu'il nous fût defendu de rectifier les moeurs d'un personnage'). Despite all this, the critics are not satisfied, and his bitterness wells over in the celebrated exaltation of simplicity in tragedy and denunciation of the dramatic system of Corneille. This passage is often quoted, but we should be careful how we apply it. Critics sometimes say the plot of *Britannicus* is simple, but why? In what way is the plot of *Rodogune*, with its clear-cut dilemmas, more complicated than that of *Britannicus*, with its continual comings and goings, plots and counterplots, between Néron, Agrippine, Britannicus and Narcisse, with the off-stage supporters whom they invoke – Pallas, Locuste, 'les chefs de la noblesse'? *Britannicus* is not poor in that 'quantité d'incidents' and those 'jeux de théâtre' of which the preface complains. We have at least two scenes (II.vi and III.viii) where Racine, against his usual practice, goes to quite Scribean pains to contrive and lead up to strong situations. We have (within twenty-four hours) the abduction of Junie, the exile of Pallas, the arrest and release of Britannicus and Agrippine, the revocation of Pallas's exile, the procuring of poison from Locuste, the banquet and the death of Britannicus, the entry of Junie into the Vestal Virgins, and the death of Narcisse by the intervention of the mob. By contrast, in *Rodogune* the situation works itself out entirely between the main characters, without any need for them to canvass external support, or for any external force to assist the dénouement. The second half of Racine's preface is a defence of his dramatic aesthetic, but not of *Britannicus*. We might paraphrase it thus: 'To please you, I have abandoned my own ideas and tried to write a play your way; I have done my best (far better than your hero Corneille), but you still don't like it; so here's what I think of your dramatic system; and I am going back to work on my own, which is founded on quite different principles.' Racine is showing his disgust at the failure of *Britannicus*, in which he had gone as far as his taste allowed to compromise with the Cornelian form of drama, and in revulsion from it is expressing the ideals he was to follow in writing *Bérénice*.

We can now return to the questions posed by Vinaver's discussion of those last 122 lines of the play. The test of whether *Britannicus* is tragic is whether the play as a whole has the emotional effect of tragedy. This comes down to two questions: is the underlying theme tragic? and, if so, is it adequately expressed in the play?

If we are seeking tragedy, Racine tells us where to look. In the first preface, where he is anxious to show that he had followed the most approved critical principles, he defends his choice of Britannicus as hero. In the second preface, dating from the time he was writing *Phèdre*, he has come to see more clearly how he approaches tragedy: 'ma tragédie n'est pas moins la disgrâce d'Agrippine que la mort de Britannicus'. Agrippine is of central importance: 'C'est elle que je me suis surtout efforcé de bien exprimer.'

In the first scene of his play, as is his custom, Racine sets out his dramatic themes, and it is in Agrippine's statement of the situation that we hear the first note of tragedy:

> L'impatient Néron cesse de se contraindre . . .
> Il commence, il est vrai, par où finit Auguste;
> Mais crains que, l'avenir détruisant le passé,
> Il ne finisse ainsi qu'Auguste a commencé.
> Il se déguise en vain.

This is not a foreboding that Néron will govern badly ('Que m'importe, après tout, que Néron, plus fidèle | D'une longue vertu laisse un jour le modèle?'). Agrippine grimly accepts (that is, Racine presents her as accepting) her own crimes, and even the future crimes of Néron:

> J'ai fait ce que j'ai pu: vous régnez, c'est assez.
> Avec ma liberté, que vous m'avez ravie,
> Si vous le souhaitez, prenez encor ma vie,
> Pourvu que par ma mort tout le peuple irrité
> Ne vous ravisse pas ce qui m'a tant coûté.

But the verse also transmits a deeper, more insidious undertone. The people may be 'irrité', as Néron has been, and so may 'ravish' the throne (as he has 'ravished' Agrippine's freedom and wishes to ravish Junie). What powers the action is not a rational distaste for bad government but something altogether more terrifying and inaccessible to reason: the sense that there is in Néron an unassuageable daemon which must reveal itself sooner or later:

> Enfin, Burrhus, Néron découvre son génie.
> Cette férocité que tu croyais fléchir
> De tes faibles liens est prêt à s'affranchir.

This motif is associated with a special quality in Néron's verse: a peculiar, refined perversity which sets it off from the forthrightness of the rest. The key words are 'irrite', 'caresse', 'flatte', 'las', 'charmants', 'pleurs'. The rhythms are suave and insidious:

> J'aimais jusqu'à ses pleurs que je faisais couler
>
> Et c'est cette vertu, si nouvelle à la cour,
> Dont la persévérance irrite mon amour.
>
> Je me fais de sa peine une image charmante.
>
> Prince, continuez des transports si charmants.

For almost the first time in Racine, we have a potent alliance between his poetry and the deep and tangled roots of our emotional life. We tend to think of an interest in these areas of mental life as modern, but of course the seventeenth century was as aware of their effects as we are, and some thinkers had come very close to our modern view of them.

If we agree that the greatest poetry draws its strength from these roots, we have here in *Britannicus* signs of that characteristic of Racine's art that was to power his greatest work.

The struggle between Agrippine and Néron is between two daemonic powers ('Mon génie étonné tremble devant le sien'). Here and there Racine develops the parallelism between them: it seems likely, for instance, that the melodramatic idea of having Néron watch Junie and Britannicus from behind a curtain is meant to echo the reference to Agrippine watching the senate from behind a curtain ('J'étais de ce grand corps l'âme toute-puissante'). At this level, there can be no solution in political or moral terms. The frail condition of peace is that Néron shall contain himself. The catastrophe is unleashed when he realises the intoxicating truth that he desires evil, and has the power to accomplish it. To achieve his desire, he does not have to act. All he need do is let go: 'Ainsi Néron commence à ne se plus forcer.'

Once he does let go, the movement is irreversible. Burrhus has already put this to Néron:

> Vous n'avez qu'à marcher de vertus en vertus.
> Mais si de vos flatteurs vous suivez la maxime,
> Il vous faudra, Seigneur, courir de crime en crime.

This is the theme which comes out clearly into the open in those last 122 lines of the play, in the terrible vista of self-torturing and self-perpetuating evil which Agrippine evokes in her denunciation of Néron:

> Poursuis. Tu n'as pas fait ce pas pour reculer . . .
> Tes remords te suivront comme autant de furies;
> Tu croiras les calmer par d'autres barbaries;
> Ta fureur, *s'irritant soi-même* dans son cours,
> D'un sang toujours nouveau marquera tous les jours.

In its emotional power, its daemonic quality which is beyond the rationalising morality of neo-classical criticism, this theme is surely tragic enough.

Our doubts must centre on the second question: how far this theme is adequately expressed in the play. On the one side, the telling point is Racine's: in the theatre, the ending strikes with immediate force. We can also point to the thematic links with the first four-and-a-half acts, and show how Racine's poetry (as in the instances we have quoted) is intermittently preparing for the full showing-forth of his theme. But, on the other side, it is difficult to disagree with Vinaver's point that the bulk of the play is so much in the mode of the closely-written *pièce bien faite* that the change to a direct, almost depersonalised, expression of the tragic theme is disconcertingly abrupt and insufficiently integrated with the rest. There is a hesitancy about Racine's approach here which is compounded by his hesitation over the emotional effect he is trying to achieve. The major impression left by the ending is the tragic vision evoked by Agrippine. But it is also possible to read the ending (especially the account of the death of Narcisse and Néron's reaction to Junie's escape) as an example of poetic justic. This element provokes an emotion quite different from the other. It is in accord with the providential morality of neo-classical criticism, based originally on Counter-Reformation precept; but when we have said that, we have said that it does not evoke the tragic emotion.

Whatever our final judgment on these points, it is clear that *Britannicus* shows two trends which are important for Racine's development as a tragic poet. The first is a growing, but as yet not fully successful, determination to fuse the tragic emotional pattern completely with the formal intrigue required by neo-classical theory. The second trend is far less orthodox, and implies some sacrifice of neo-classical neatness. It is towards a poetry which draws on very deep, irrational forces in the mind – a poetry which was to make possible the full bodying forth of that tragic compulsion set out schematically in the rôle of Oreste and fitfully evident in *Britannicus*. It was to be some years before the promise of this second tendency was realised. The fulfilment of the first was to be achieved in *Bérénice*.

'BÉRÉNICE'

I

Opinions about *Bérénice* have been more various than about any other play by Racine. Is it a feeble interlude in his development, or is it his most perfect achievement? Is it the most Racinian of his plays, in that love is virtually the whole subject, or the most Cornelian, in the sense that duty triumphs? Is its simplicity the logical culmination of trends in neo-classical, and especially Racinian, drama, or is it an experiment running counter to orthodox theory and practice? Is its tone tragic, or merely sentimental? Is Titus impelled by his duty to Rome, or to his own self-respect, or by some impulse to destroy his own happiness? Does Bérénice leave because she recognises that he must follow his vocation as Roman and emperor, or because she feels that this is the only way to avert his suicide?

The play begins as, on the deep, narrow stage of the Hôtel de Bourgogne, two actors make their way slowly through the groups of fashionable spectators to the front and begin to declaim. One is obviously a potentate; he wears Roman costume, with a vaguely Eastern crown and accessories. The other, also vaguely Eastern, is his confidant. Their opening duologue has two unusual features. First, it is largely given up to describing precisely where the action takes place:

> Souvent ce cabinet superbe et solitaire
> Des secrets de Titus est le dépositaire . . .
> De son appartement cette porte est prochaine,
> Et cette autre conduit dans celui de la Reine.

Secondly, the duologue is very short. We learn that Bérénice expects to marry Titus, and that Antiochus once loved her. The confidant withdraws. No other characters enter, and Antiochus begins a soliloquy. At this date, soliloquies are rare, and frowned on by the critics; an expository soliloquy is by now unheard of. Moreover, Antiochus is not part of the familiar historical story, so that Racine has left himself free to put into the soliloquy what he likes. Although we cannot be dogmatic about seventeenth-century acting, it is likely that actors regarded soliloquies as special 'numbers', to be performed with great virtuosity and in a more chanted style than was used for dialogue. If so, this would further mark out Antiochus's soliloquy as of special importance. We may therefore listen to it with care, as the first major statement of what the play is about.

The speech is lyrical, but orderly. It starts from an immutable *donnée*: 'Hé bien, Antiochus, es-tu toujours *le même*?', and turns it to and fro. The conclusion is that the *donnée* is indeed immutable: Antiochus loves Bérénice, he knows that she does not love him, and he still (as before the soliloquy) intends to see her. In this speech four themes are sounded. The first, which we find again and again in Racine, is that of paradox: 'Pourrai-je, sans trembler, lui dire: "Je vous aime"? | Mais quoi! déjà je tremble, et mon coeur agité | Craint autant ce moment que je l'ai souhaité'; 'Il l'épouse. Ai-je donc attendu ce moment | Pour me venir encor déclarer son amant?' Paradox is both a sign and precipitant of tension. Poets and thought-reformers know that paradox bewilders the waking surface of the mind and enables them to work on the depths.

Secondly, we have the dilemma of the lover who deserves love, yet receives no reward, yet loves on unselfishly:

> Belle Reine, et pourquoi vous offenseriez-vous?
> Viens-je vous demander que vous quittiez l'Empire?
> Que vous m'aimiez?

If we know the story of Titus and Bérénice in advance, as Racine surely assumed, this has a double pathos.

The speech introduces two other themes that lie near the heart of the play: that of camouflage or deceit (including self-deception):

> D'un voile d'amitié j'ai couvert mon amour . . .
> Retirons-nous, sortons; et sans nous découvrir,
> Allons loin de ses yeux l'oublier, ou mourir.

– and that of the need to let go, to speak out, to be rid of an intolerable burden:

> Hé quoi? souffrir toujours un tourment qu'elle ignore? . . .
> Quoi qu'il en soit, parlons: c'est assez nous contraindre.

After this overture, Arsace returns, and there begins what seems a banal exchange between master and confidant. But the pattern of the scene is significant. It enacts a refusal by Antiochus to speak out: the theme is that truth does not get through. This is partly a device to heighten the dramatic interest, but the insistence that all is not yet told reinforces the theme of truth hidden or not yet to be revealed. If we listen to the verse, this theme is emphasised by the first words of Arsace:

> Seigneur, j'ai vu la Reine;
> Mais, *pour me faire voir, je n'ai percé qu'à peine*
> Les flots toujours nouveaux d'un peuple adorateur
> Qu'attire sur ses pas sa prochaine grandeur . . .
> Et, *si j'en crois,* Seigneur, l'entretien de la cour,
> *Peut-être* avant la nuit l'heureuse Bérénice
> Change le nom de reine au nom d'impératrice.

Never mind that this is only a speech by a confidant: it expresses clearly the notion of truth 'piercing through' in spite of flattery (including self-flattery?); and it again hints at the doubtful status of what is known at present.

Two other notes are sounded. One is that of self-destruction ('Quel caprice vous rend ennemi de vous -même?'). The other is that of war, with its association of fame with suffering and death:

> Un prince qui jadis, témoin de vos combats,
> Vous vit chercher *la gloire et la mort* sur ses pas . . .
> Il se souvient du jour *illustre et douloureux*

The war is, of course, the Jewish war, in which Bérénice helped Titus against her own people. We should note how Racine uses it. It is introduced partly to raise our opinion of Antiochus, but mainly to amplify a theme: the image of the siege again suggests resistance to something coming from outside, and also the painful combination of struggle and achievement. In 'la rebelle Judée', the verse delicately insinuates that Bérénice represents the element that resists. What we do not get is any suggestion that Bérénice has betrayed her God or her people by helping Titus. This is not because the conventions of French classical drama prevented a dramatist from presenting such conflicts. Corneille's Bérénice boasts of her services to Tite, to which Domitie scathingly replies:

> Tite y peut ajouter que je n'ai point la gloire
> D'avoir sur ma patrie étendu sa victoire,
> De l'avoir saccagée et détruite à l'envi,
> Et renversé l'autel du dieu que j'ai servi.

Corneille's Bérénice interprets her disgrace as a punishment for her treachery:

> Sans lui [Tite], sans l'espérance à mon amour offerte,
> J'aurais servi Solyme, ou péri dans sa perte;
> Et quand Rome s'efforce à m'arracher son coeur,
> Elle sert le courroux d'un dieu juste vengeur.

Far from conforming to classical decorum, Racine is flouting its naturalistic insistence that reference should be made to the emotions which the 'real' Bérénice would 'really' have felt. He even went so far as to make Bérénice swear by the gods in the original text, but in response to his critics later revised these passages. The deliberate avoidance of what his original audiences might have expected may warn us that Racine is not simply trying to present a psychological study of a woman in difficult circumstances. In particular, he carefully avoids using the Jewish war in the way Corneille does, to stress the political background. As we shall see, he takes great pains to be ambiguous about how far political necessity forces Titus to give up Bérénice.

At last Bérénice comes in. Antiochus confesses his love. She is angry with him, and he leaves. The elegance and psychological exactness of this scene are justly famous, but we may also listen for the themes sounded in the verse:

> Enfin *je me dérobe* à la joie importune
> De tant d'amis nouveaux que me fait la fortune;
> Je fuis de leurs respects l'inutile longueur,
> Pour *chercher* un ami *qui me parle du coeur.*
> *Il ne faut point mentir*: ma juste impatience
> Vous accusait déjà de quelque negligence.

Again there is this emphasis on concealment, evasion, and truth nevertheless breaking through, and this is the persistent undertone of the scene:

> Ce long deuil que Titus imposait à sa cour
> Avait même *en secret* suspendu son amour.
>
> Et même en ce moment, *sans qu'il m'en ait parlé* . . .
>
> Seigneur, de ce départ quel est donc *le mystère?*
>
> Je vois que votre coeur m'applaudit *en secret.*
>
> Un *voile* d'amitié vous *trompa* l'en et l'autre.

But Antiochus also announces another development, which is ultimately to displace this theme:

> Le ciel sembla promettre une fin à ma peine.
> Vous pleurâtes ma mort, hélas! trop peu certaine.
> Inutiles périls! Quelle était mon erreur!
> La valeur de Titus surpassait ma fureur.
> Il faut qu'à sa vertu mon estime réponde.

Truth, in fact, will out, if a man will make the effort to acknowledge it.

Antiochus's verse also develops another motif already sounded in his soliloquy and which is to form one part of the play's emotional pattern: the theme of immutability:

> Et je viens donc vous dire un éternel adieu.
>
> Mon coeur faisait serment de vous aimer sans cesse.

Antiochus's rôle, like that of Oreste, is to realise constantly that nothing can change, and his verse echoes that of Oreste:

> Mais enfin succombant à ma mélancolie,
> Mon désespoir tourna mes pas vers l'Italie.
>
> Mon sort est accompli. Votre gloire s'apprête.

His realisation recalls that of Oreste before Hermione:

> Que vous dirai-je enfin: Je fuis des yeux distraits,
> Qui me voyant toujours, ne me voyaient jamais.

Such parallels emphasise how just below the surface of what some have seen as a *tragédie à l'eau de rose* there is the bottomless despair of Oreste.

The scene between Bérénice and Phénice after Antiochus has gone is famous for its style. For the moment, however, let us simply attend to what it says. Why does Bérénice say:

> Cette prompte retraite
> Me laisse, *je l'avoue*, une douleur *secrète*.

In naturalistic terms, this could only mean either that Bérénice really loves Antiochus (which is nonsense) or that she is obliged to conceal her pity for him (which hardly seems more reasonable, as she is now alone with her confidante). But if we listen to it as part of the poetic pattern, it makes very good sense: it expresses once more the theme of concealment/revelation.

The scene also contains statements about the political situation:

> Titus n'a point encore expliqué sa pensée.
> Rome vous voit, Madame, avec des yeux jaloux;
> La rigueur de ses lois m'épouvante pour vous:
> L'hymen chez les Romains n'admet qu'une Romaine;
> Rome hait tous les rois, et Bérénice est reine.

Bérénice replies:

> Le temps n'est plus, Phénice, où je pouvais trembler.
> Titus m'aime, il peut tout, il n'a plus qu'à parler.

The original audience would surely have taken this, as we do, as pathetically ironic. It does not follow, however, that they would take it to mean that Phénice, being emotionally less involved, sees the truth, and that Bérénice deludes herself because she wants to. The best indication of how much weight to attach to a given statement is the tone and quality of the verse in which it is expressed. Phénice's lines are clear and emphatic, but prosaic; they contrast with the lyrical élan of Bérénice's reply. Moreover, Bérénice's opinion is borne out by Antiochus, whose emotional situation disposes him to believe the reverse:

> après m'être longtemps flatté que mon rival
> Trouverait à ses voeux quelque obstacle fatal,
> Aujourd'hui qu'il peut tout . . .

When in a seventeenth-century tragedy we are told something in beautiful and lyrical verse by a virtuous king and queen, and told the opposite in prosaic verse by a confidante, we are meant to believe the king and queen. Racine is here following the usual practice of making the confidante give the mundane, irrelevant, interpretation apparent to a vulgar mind, and the principal actors give the real, significant, interpretation which they perceive in their capacity of superior beings.[1] In other words, we are to understand at this point that Titus could marry Bérénice if he wished, in spite of public opinion. This real situation is affirmed by the speech which closes the act. Titus is all-powerful: the real obstacle which is to come between him and Bérénice is the fact that he does indeed deserve his glory.

In Act II, we have the scene between Titus and Paulin in which the political situation is set out. Paulin expounds Rome's hatred for all Queens, but he recognises that Titus can override this ('Vous pouvez tout') and does not defend the Romans' attitude ('Soit raison, soit caprice'). There is no mistaking, however, that this Roman feeling is a fact ('Rome, par une loi qui ne se peut changer') and that it can be overruled only with danger, and by an emperor determined to outdo all tyrants. The tenor of Paulin's statement is not that Titus cannot overrule Rome's attitude. The point is that if Titus did exert his power in this way he would be a tyrant worse than Caesar, Antony, Caligula and Nero, who had at least respected this law, and that he would therefore be demeaning himself by marrying Bérénice. We are certainly not to take seriously Paulin's statement that the senate will beg Titus not to marry Bérénice: the senate does come (ll. 1241–4), and with a 'grand peuple', but only to express its sycophancy. The structure of the scene is significant. Paulin does not persuade Titus to give up Bérénice.

Titus's decision is already made. Racine makes no attempt here – and hardly any in the rest of the play – to depict Titus as swaying between alternative courses of action. Titus's attitude does not change: it simply becomes clearer. This is borne out by the verse, which continues to sound the motif of secrecy giving way to a revelation of the truth:

> les secrets de son coeur et du mien
> Sont de tout l'univers devenus l'entretien.
>
> J'ai fait plus. Je n'ai rien de secret à tes yeux.
>
> De mon aimable erreur je fus désabusé.

To emphasise this, Racine makes Titus use words very similar to those of Arsace to Antiochus (ll. 52–3), and Bérénice to Antiochus (ll. 135–9):

> J'ai voulu que des coeurs vous fussiez l'interprète;
> Qu'au travers des flatteurs votre sincérité
> Fît toujours jusqu'à moi passer la vérité.

Truth pierces through the delusions. The difference here is that Titus has arranged this deliberately, whereas Bérénice, more passive, is 'importuned' by her flatterers.

The situation, then, is that Titus could if he wished marry Bérénice, but only at the price of becoming a tyrant. This is what he fears, and all the more because he knows that (like Néron) all he has to do to be a tyrant is to let go:

> Ma jeunesse, nourrie à la cour de Néron,
> S'égarait, cher Paulin, par l'exemple abusée,
> Et suivait du plaisir la pente trop aisée.

We might take Titus at this point as a Cornelian hero, but something is lacking. There is no sense of triumph, no energy liberated by the resolution of a conflict:

> Je connais mon devoir, c'est à moi de le suivre:
> Je n'examine point si j'y pourrai survivre.

Contemporaries were shocked by Titus's behaviour: brutal in his decision to send Bérénice away in spite of his promises to her, he is too soft to do his duty with a proper sense of exhilaration. Even less heroic is his behaviour in Scene iv, when he fails to tell Bérénice the truth and runs away. The pattern of this scene is again an enactment of the theme of truth that does not get through. Bérénice's lines are full of the key words of the first half of the play:

Ne vous offensez pas, si mon zèle indiscret
De votre solitude interrompt le *secret* . . .
. . . je sais que cet ami *sincère*
Du *secret* de nos cœurs connaît tout le *mystère* . . .
Dans vos *secrets* discours étais-je intéressée?

Coupled with this theme is one that we may admire, but which scandalised seventeenth-century ideas of self-respect:

Depuis quand croyez-vous que ma grandeur me touche?
Un soupir, un regard, un mot de votre bouche,
Voilà l'ambition d'un coeur comme le mien.

Racine is deliberately leading us from the plane of politics to the plane of emotion. Bérénice could say to Titus what Antiochus said in l. 39: 'Viens-je vous demander que vous quittiez l'Empire?' Worse, in Scene v Racine emphasises something he could have passed over, and which shows Titus even more sadly lacking by contemporary notions of decency:

Il craint peut-être, il craint d'épouser une reine.
Hélais! s'il était vrai . . . Mais non, il a cent fois
Rassuré mon amour contre leurs dures lois;
Cent fois.

Titus has given his word, and we know he will not keep it.

There are often scenes in poetic drama which apparently do not advance the plot or reveal character but which are important to the meaning of the play. Act III, Scene i, is important for the plot, because Titus orders Antiochus to tell Bérénice the truth; but most of it is taken up by another announcement by Titus that he is going to leave Bérénice, and his explanation of his reasons. Why does Racine spend a hundred lines going over this ground again? The answer is clear if we attend to the structure of the scene. In the first movement (ll. 667–84) the verse recapitulates a number of themes relevant to Titus and Bérénice as much as to Titus and Antiochus: Titus wants an explanation of Antiochus's 'fuite', and is anxious to know 'Que diront avec moi la cour, Rome, l'Empire?' He recalls that for Antiochus, as for Bérénice, 'Mon coeur vous fut ouvert tant qu'à vécu mon père: | C'était le seul présent que je pouvais vous faire.' He points out that he can now repay Antiochus (as in ll. 441–4 he pointed out that he can now repay Bérénice), and he asserts that he is not preoccupied with his 'grandeur'. This interweaving of Titus/Bérénice, Titus/Antiochus motifs would be puzzling, or perhaps merely insipid, if this were a naturalistic play in which Antiochus, Bérénice and Titus were separate, individualised characters. But Racine is playing a double game: *Bérénice* makes sense at this level, but it is also a poetic play, and the essential action is expressed in the poetry. At this poetic level, Antiochus, Bérénice and Titus are not characters at all: they are elements in a pattern of themes, and it is the pattern which is important.

After a few exchanges, the verse passes on to a middle movement. Titus points out that he owes much of his 'gloire' to Antiochus (as in ll. 502–22 he said he owed his 'gloire' to Bérénice). Bérénice is also under an obligation to Antiochus ('à vos soins redevable') and the result of this network of obligations is that Antiochus must, against his will and hers ('invitus invitam') tell Bérénice the truth. Antiochus recoils, and Titus then has a long speech (ll. 719–70) in which he again states the position. There is no attempt to defend Rome's prejudice ('Rome, contre les rois de tout temps soulevée, | Dédaigne une beauté dans la pourpre élevée . . . Et Rome avec plaisir recevrait de ma main | La moins digne beauté qu'elle cache en son sein') and Titus repeats the allegation ('Demain elle entendra ce peuple furieux | Me venir demander son départ à ses yeux') which the rest of the play does nothing to confirm. The speech turns on a crucial line:

> Epargnez à mon coeur cet éclaircissement.

It is this 'éclaircissement' which is the action of the play, and which the second half is to consummate. The speech then gathers to its final statement: Titus can do anything, and the senate will acquiesce ('Je sais que le Sénat, tout plein de votre nom, | D'une commune voix confirmera ce don') but he will not marry Bérénice:

> Adieu: ne quittez point ma princesse, ma reine.

The word 'reine' has a horrible ambiguity.

Titus stands fixed in the truth. So does Antiochus:

> Hélas! de ce grand changement
> Il ne me reviendra que le nouveau tourment
> D'apprendre par ses pleurs à quel point elle l'aime.

Bérénice does not: she learns the truth but rejects it:

> Hélas! pour me tromper je fais ce que je puis.

This is the turning-point. Here Bérénice's suffering truly begins. Her soliloquy in Act IV, Scene i, is different in style from her earlier utterances: breathless, distracted, as if physically painful:

> Je m'agite, je cours, languissante, abattue;
> La force m'abandonne, et le repos me tue.

She complains, in words that Phèdre will echo, of her 'vains orne-ments'. We may think that the same deep movements in Racine's mind which were to give birth to *Phèdre* are at work here, or that he is remembering their common source in *Hippolytus*, ll. 198–202. In either case, there is no doubting the emotional violence.

In Titus's long soliloquy the themes we have already met are again expressed and reinforced. He takes up the words of Antiochus's soliloquy in Act I ('Hé bien, Antiochus, es-tu toujours le même' – 'Hé bien, Titus, que viens-tu faire?'; 'Quel fruit me reviendra d'un aveu téméraire?' – 'Ou viens-tu, téméraire?') – but this time the theme of concealment (Antiochus's 'D'un voile d'amitié j'ai couvert mon amour') is replaced by that of knowledge of the truth ('Titus, ouvre les yeux'). More clearly than ever, the decision is represented as the work of Titus ('Qui l'ordonne? Moi-même') and not of any direct political pressure:

> Car enfin Rome a-t-elle expliqué ses souhaits?
> L'entendons-nous crier autour de ce palais?
> Vois-je l'état penchant au bord du précipice?
> Ne le puis-je sauver que par ce sacrifice?
> Tout se tait: et moi seul, trop prompt à me troubler,
> J'avance des malheurs que je puis reculer.

Underlying this is the motif of self-destruction already sounded by Arsace when he reproaches Antiochus: 'Quoi! ne vous plairez-vous qu'à vous gêner sans cesse?'[2]. But Titus will not do the honourable thing by seventeenth-century standards: unlike Tite, he will not offer to renounce the empire.

Racine has delayed until now the first articulate confrontation of Titus and Bérénice. Titus's first speech to her is clear:

> *Forcez* votre amour à se taire;
> Et d'un oeil que la gloire et la raison *éclaire*,
> *Contemplez* mon devoir dans toute sa *rigueur*.

This 'rigueur' is brutal, not admirable, and Racine does not pretend otherwise. He emphasises that Titus owes much of his glory to Bérénice ('Rappelez bien plutôt ce coeur, qui tant de fois | M'a fait de mon devoir reconnaître la voix'); that he knew the position when he promised to marry Bérénice ('Ignoriez-vous vos lois, | Quand je vous l'avouai pour la première fois? . . . Tout l'empire a vingt fois conspiré contre nous. | Il était temps encor: que ne me quittiez-vous?'); and that he is able to marry Bérénice if he wants to ('Lorsque Rome se tait' – we cannot pretend that on this point Bérénice deceives herself and ignores the truth: Racine gives her words which echo those of Titus in l. 1005). Titus does not contest these charges – only the charge that he does not love her. Racine, when he revised this scene for the edition of 1676, stressed still further the 'barbarie' of Titus by adding the following awkward lines on Roman heroes:

> L'un, jaloux de sa foi, va chez les ennemis
> Chercher avec la mort la peine toute prête;
> D'un fils victorieux l'autre proscrit la tête;
> L'autre, avec des yeux secs et presque indifférents,
> Voit mourir ses deux fils, par son ordre expirants.

'Jaloux de sa foi' bites with cruel irony.

What is emphasised is that these heroes imposed these duties on themselves, not that they were forced by outside pressures. The weight of the scene falls on Titus's line: 'Et c'est moi seul aussi qui pouvais me détruire.' Against this, Bérénice can only express her love. The harsh background makes her famous lines more heart-rending:

> Pour jamais! Ah! Seigneur, songez-vous en vous-même
> Combien ce mot cruel est affreux quand on aime?
> Dans un mois, dans un an, comment souffrirons-nous,
> Seigneur, que tant de mers me séparent de vous?
> Que le jour recommence et que le jour finisse
> Sans que jamais Titus puisse voir Bérénice,
> Sans que de tout le jour je puisse voir Titus!

The end of the act brings together the most important themes of the play. Titus is in control of the situation and Bérénice is helpless ('n'avez-vous pas | Ordonné dès tantôt qu'on observe ses pas?'). Titus's fear is that he will become a tyrant ('Néron, tant détesté, | N'a point à cet excès poussé sa cruauté'). The Roman senate and people send a delegation to him (ll. 1241–4) – not, as it turns out, to beg him to send Bérénice away, but to fawn on him (ll. 1270–2). The last words of the act (in the 1671 edition) were an expression of Antiochus's desire to hide himself; in the final text, they are an affirmation by Titus that he will make the truth clear. Racine hesitated on which aspect of his theme he wanted to emphasise at this crucial moment, but in either case the theme is that of concealment/revelation. Two other themes are noteworthy. One – the connection between love and death – I shall discuss later. The other – the paradox by which both Titus and Antiochus seek the end of their own hopes – was originally sounded by Antiochus in the final speech of the act. The theme is important, and it is perhaps a pity that in dropping the speech Racine left it unexpressed at this crucial point. But after some hesitation he was surely right to end the act unambiguously with his principal hero and a statement of the theme that is to dominate the fifth act: the unanswerable unveiling of the truth.

Act V begins ambiguously. The Roman delegation has fêted Titus, but he returns to Bérénice. Antiochus again insists on the motif of immutable conflict:

> Tous mes moments ne sont qu'un éternel passage
> De la crainte à l'espoir, de l'espoir à la rage.

Bérénice is suffering the last paroxysms of her refusal to face the truth: 'Non, je n'écoute rien.' She thinks the senate has persuaded Titus to renounce her. His answer is plain: 'Non, je n'ai rien promis.' (We may note in passing his scorn for the Roman people: 'une foule insensée'.) Racine makes as clear as he can that the senate and people have continued to adore Titus, without any indication from him that he intends to send Bérénice away. The 'engagements' which bind him are imposed by Titus himself, not by outside pressure. And now Titus, not content with breaking his promise to Bérénice, commits another ungentlemanly act by snatching a letter from her ('Vous m'avez arraché ce que je viens d'écrire'). Bérénice intends to kill herself. This brings on the final crisis. Bérénice sits down – the action symbolises paralysis by conflicting emotions, as with Phèdre and Athalie – and Titus begins a long and stately speech. The beginning sets the tone: 'Madame, il faut vous faire un aveu *véritable*.' The speech then proceeds, with the unshakable authority of facts understood, accepted, and clearly articulated, without any evasions or excuses:

> Rome de votre sort est encore incertaine . . .
> Ne vous attendez point que las de tant d'alarmes,
> Par un heureux hymen je tarisse vos larmes . . .
> Je dois vous épouser encor moins que jamais.
> Oui, Madame; et je dois moins encore vous dire
> Que je suis prêt pour vous d'abandonner l'Empire . . .
> Vil spectacle aux humains des faiblesses d'amour.

There is nothing sentimental here. Titus could marry Bérénice, but will not: it is in his own judgment that he sees 'L'Empire incompatible avec votre hyménée.' Now we come to a movement which has been much attacked: Titus threatens to kill himself. This shocked critics at the time. Butler (p. 234) cites the Abbé de Villars: 'J'avais pourtant eu quelque espérance que le caractère de Titus serait héroïque . . . mais quand je vis que tout cela n'aboutissait qu'à se tuer par maxime d'amour, je connus bien que ce n'est pas un héros romain que le poète veut représenter.' It should also shock those critics who make play with Racine's political insight. Here we have an emperor threatening to kill himself, and not a word is said about the succession; Domitian is not mentioned in the play.

If Racine is cavalier in his treatment of politics, he treats other matters at great length. Throughout the play, he spends much time associating unhappy love with death:

> Allons loin de ses yeux l'oublier, ou mourir.
>
> Je n'examine point si j'y pourrai survivre.
>
> Titus m'aime. Titus ne veut point que je meure.
>
> Que sais-je? j'espérais de mourir à vos yeux.
>
> Vous verrez que Titus n'a pu, sans expirer . . .
>
> Je vous crois digne, ingrat, de m'arracher la vie.
>
> Si devant que mourir la triste Bérénice
> Vous veut de son trépas laisser quelque vengeur.
>
> Paulin, je suis perdu, je n'y pourrai survivre.
> La Reine veut mourir.

The whole play is heavy with death. This, not any concern with the historical background, still less with any thought of evoking a conflict between Bérénice and Titus or between Bérénice and her people's heritage, is the main reason for the references to the Jewish war:

> Il se souvient du jour illustre et douloureux
> Qui decida du sort d'un long siège douteux . . .
> Vous seul, Seigneur, vous seul, une échelle à la main,
> Vous portâtes la mort jusque sur leurs murailles.
> Ce jour presque éclaira vos propres funérailles:
> Titus vous embrassa mourant entre mes bras,
> Et tout le camp vainqueur pleura votre trépas.
>
> Enfin, apres un siège aussi cruel que lent,
> Il dompta les mutins, reste pâle et sanglant
> Des flammes, de la faim, des fureurs intestines,
> Et laissa leurs remparts cachés sous leurs ruines.

There is no need to be surprised (and it comes over with beautiful inevitability in performance) when Titus threatens to kill himself. The action of the play consists in large part of bringing into the open what has been 'veiled' and 'secret'. The play is not to end in death, and therefore even here the death motif is not enunciated with the relentless clarity of the others. What is important, however, is that the motifs of love, death and necessity are inextricably connected. The verse makes this clear by recalling the Roman heroes who have committed suicide – and by recalling those earlier lines in which Titus appealed to Roman examples as a reason for sending Bérénice away: 'trop de malheurs ont lassé leur constance' (l. 1411); 'Rome a de mes pareils exercé la constance' (l. 1159). Titus is not compelled by any external force. It is the internalised 'Rome' which makes him abandon Bérénice, and which also makes him love her to the death, just as it is Bérénice who has made him achieve the 'gloire' which prevents him from marrying her.

We have now reached the point where Racine starts his last scene: Titus has not changed his mind about suicide; Bérénice has not yet admitted he still loves her; but the hidden threat of suicide on both sides has been brought into the open. Then Antiochus comes in, and reveals the one truth which is still unknown to Titus: that he, Antiochus, also loves Bérénice. This precipitates Bérénice's decision: she leaves. How exactly does this avowal bring about the dénouement? No doubt we can finesse about Racine's feeling for psychology, but just how Antiochus's avowal brings about the resolution of the pattern of the play remains a mystery unless we listen to the key words of this last scene:

> Soyez ici *témoin* de toute ma faiblesse . . .
> . . . *Je crois tout: je vous connais* tous deux . . .
> Mais *connaissez* vous-même un prince malheureux . . .
> . . . Il est temps que je vous *éclaircisse* . . .
> . . . Vous aimez, on vous aime;
> Vous vous êtes rendu: *je n'en ai point douté.*
> Pour la dernière fois, *je me suis consulté.*

The dominant theme is knowledge, truth that can no longer be mistaken. The remedy that threatens is death:

> Il faut d'autres efforts pour rompre tant de noeuds:
> Ce ne'est qu'en expirant que je puis les détruire;
> J'y cours.

But the whole meaning to which the play gathers is that the truth is the truth, and that the knowledge of it cannot be evaded. This is the theme of Bérénice's last speech:

> Mon coeur vous est *connu* . . .
> La grandeur des Romains, la pourpre des Césars,
> N'a point, *vous le savez,* attiré mes regards . . .
> *Je connais mon erreur,* et vous m'aimez toujours . . .
> *Je crois,* depuis cinq ans jusqu'à ce dernier jour,
> Vous avoir assuré d'un *véritable* amour . . .
> . . . Titus m'aime, il me quitte.

In the first half of the play, the verse emphasised the themes of concealment, evasion, secrecy; here the emphasis is on the revelation and acknowledgment of the truth. This is not the realisation by three individuals of something unpleasant. It is poetic 'realisation' – a making real in concrete terms – expressed through the pattern of the play, in which the three characters are elements. The end is a true epiphany: Racine makes Bérénice distance it, and emphasises its supra-personal character, by 'a gesture as of showing':

> . . . Servons tous trois d'exemple à l'univers
> De l'amour la plus tendre et la plus malheureuse
> Dont il puisse garder l'histoire douloureuse.

'Douloureuse': there is no Cornelian joy in a conflict surmounted, no surge of liberated energy; only the painful recognition of inevitability. The pattern is complete, and the play ends.

2

If this interpretation is of any value, I can dispose quickly, at the superficial level, of some of the questions with which I began. *Bérénice* is not Cornelian: it is not comic, and depends for its effect neither on the energetic overcoming of conflict nor on the excitements of strong plotting. It is also something of a sport among French tragedies. The literal observance of the unities is unusual – a *gageure*[3] – and the conduct of Titus, let alone Bérénice, is undignified by seventeenth-century standards. *Bérénice* is not a work in which Racine is conforming to the expectations of his public.

Answers at this level, however, are obviously of little use. We may as well ask the blunt question: what makes *Bérénice* valuable?

Not, certainly, its merit as a historical play or a political study. As we have seen, Racine is quite casual about the historical and political background. In this, *Bérénice* contrasts with *Tite et Bérénice*, which is much taken up with the problem of the succession and the Jewish problem, and even mentions the eruption of Vesuvius. Racine omits the political issues (just as he manipulates the alleged protests or apparent acquiescence of the senate and people) because he is interested in something different.

But the conventional view is that Racine is the poet not of politics but of the human heart, and especially of love. Critics of all eras, and not least of the later nineteenth century, have praised Racine the psychologist. Even Archer, the strict supporter of Ibsenite naturalism, conceded this: Racine is 'characteristically a psychologist'.[4] It is daunting, however, to discover that also among the psychologists are Galsworthy, Pinero and Granville Barker.[5] We can judge what Archer means from his praise of individual plays or scenes: for instance, Donnay's *La Douloureuse*, where in 'the terrible peripety in the love of Philippe and Hélène' the author 'lets his lovers unpack their hearts with words until they are exhausted, broken, dazed with misery, and have nothing more to say'.[6] We need not deny that Racine is a subtle psychologist, but this can hardly be his whole secret if it puts him on a level with Donnay and Pinero. And if psychological subtlety and tender portrayal of love are what we want, we can find them in other places than *Bérénice*. The scenes between Domitie and Bérénice in *Tite et Bérénice* show no lack of insight into human motives, and this passage between Bérénice and Tite seems as touching as anything in Racine's play:

> Pouvez-vous jusque-là me bannir de votre âme?
> Le pouvez-vous, Seigneur?
>   – Le croyez-vous, Madame?
> – Hélas! que j'ai de peur de vous dire que non!
> J'ai voulu vous haïr dès que j'ai su ce don:
> Mais à de tels courroux, l'âme en vain se confie;
> A peine je vous vois que je vous justifie.
> Vous me manquez de foi, vous me donnez, chassez.
> Que de crimes! Un mot les a tous effacés.

No doubt Racine is more gracefully and consistently successful on both counts, but this hardly explains why *Bérénice* is a masterpiece and *Tite et Bérénice* is a delightful but minor play. *Bérénice* is superior because it is different in kind.

In discussing verse in drama I have already pointed out that apparently simple verse – as in the famous dialogue between Bérénice and Phénice – may still exemplify the poetic method. We can take the point a little further by studying the last speech of that scene. It is an act of adoration of Titus: we see him through the eyes of Bérénice:

> De cette nuit, Phénice, as-tu vu la splendeur?
> Cette foule de rois, ces consuls, ce sénat,
> Qui tous de mon amant empruntaient leur éclat . . .
> Parle: peut-on le voir sans penser, comme moi,
> Qu'en quelque obscurité que le sort l'eût fait naître,
> Le monde, en le voyant, eût reconnu son maître?

This has been seen as a compliment to Louis XIV, and does in fact take up a phrase from the description of him in the *Portraits Divers* dedicated to Mademoiselle. Nevertheless, let us note Racine's method. The literature of the age abounds in flattering allusions to the king. Corneille has one in *Tite et Bérénice*. Another example is in *Attila*, where Octar praises Mérovée's peacemaking, sieges, conquests and pleasures, and then proceeds as follows:

> Ce que j'en ai vu passe un homme tel que moi:
> Mais je ne puis, Seigneur, m'empêcher de vous dire
> Combien son jeune prince est digne qu'on l'admire.
> Il montre un coeur si haut sous un front délicat,
> Que dans son premier lustre il est déjà soldat.
> Le corps attend les ans, mais l'âme est toute prête,
> D'un gros de cavaliers il se met à la tête,
> Et, l'épée a la main, anime l'escadron
> Qu'enorgueillit l'honneur de marcher sous son nom.

In these and similar passages we can have no doubt of the reference. Corneille takes a series of contemporary facts (Louis concludes a successful peace, but Europe still fears his ambition; he reviews his troops at Conflans on 8 February 1666 and has the little dauphin lead a regiment). Corneille then puts them in general terms and applies them to someone heroic in his plays. We may say without exaggeration that for the purposes of these passages Tite and Mérovée are Louis XIV. Racine's method is different. His eye is not on any contemporary incidents. He starts from the love of Titus and Bérénice and the part they play in his poetic design. From them and from details chosen from the Roman background he builds his evocation of Titus as the ideal monarch – a rôle which he and his audience felt Louis was playing in seventeenth-century Europe. But Racine is not describing Louis: Titus is set among the eagles at his father's pyre, and the flames and the night not only raise the splendour of the image but also play their part in the pattern of the play. The point of connection between Louis and Titus is not any reference to a contemporary event: it is the awareness by the audience of a monarchical ideal which both Louis and Titus embody. In Corneille's play, we miss much if we do not grasp the allusions to Louis. In Racine's play we miss nothing if we ignore the existence of Louis as a person (though we lose much if we cannot imagine ourselves responding to such an ideal of kingship). What we must not miss in Racine's speech is its significance for the meaning of the play. In our reading of the text we emphasised that this speech brings before us the reality of Titus's power. We also noted how the first half of the play abounds in references to secrets, dissembling, veiling or holding back of the truth. This theme is heard as an undertone throughout this speech: 'cette nuit', with its suggestion of secrecy and hidden thoughts; 'cette foule . . . Qui tous de mon amant *empruntaient* leur éclat'; 'tous les coeurs *en secret* l'assuraient de leur foi'; 'en quelque *obscurité* . . .'; 'des transports *retenus* si longtemps'. The speech works at many levels: as a panegyric on a contemporary theme; as a natural expression of the 'real' feelings of Bérénice; and, on the poetic level, as a statement of the major themes of the play. This points to the difference between *Tite et Bérénice* and *Bérénice: Bérénice* is a poetic play which expresses a theme. Weinberg has pointed out that the spectators' feelings are attached to the total situation rather than to the separate characters, and he links Racine's method with that of the Renaissance dramatists.[7] The theme of *Bérénice* cannot be expressed in any other terms than the play itself – though we might express it approximately as the inevitability of the lovers' parting, as a paradigm of the way in which some emotions by their nature prevent their own fulfilment.

The play is organised to express an underlying meaning of this kind; but the striking fact is that it can be read as a naturalistic play as well. In my study of *La Thébaïde, Andromaque* and *Britannicus*, my view has been that in his plays up to *Bérénice* Racine is struggling to reconcile his poetic (and tragic and daemonic) intentions with the naturalistic (rationalised and tightly-plotted) form of neo-classic drama. In *Bérénice*, by transmuting the daemonic element into the rationally acceptable form of a love-story, and by stripping down his intrigue to the simplest possible series of incidents, he manages to merge the incompatibles. Here is the explanation of the simplicity of *Bérénice*, to which Racine attached such importance. The play functions perfectly at both the poetic and naturalistic levels: the plot is entirely *vraisemblable*, and is un-obtrusive enough to be moulded exactly to fit the poetic pattern. *Bérénice* is the culmination of the first stage of Racine's career. In it he achieved the supreme triumph of a poet in an age of naturalism: to write a poetic play that fits the naturalistic form so perfectly that to all but the most captious it appears naturalistic.

But is *Bérénice* tragic? In his preface, Racine makes clear he thought so. We should perhaps ask another question: why do we associate tragedy with death? Obviously, death is not tragic simply because of the pain or grief it causes. But one reason why we regard it as charac-teristic of tragedy is that it has just that quality of inevitability com-bined with unexpectedness that we find in the tragic catastrophe. Each of us knows his death is certain, just as the death of everyone around us is certain, but no-one knows the time or manner of it. Death is known to all, yet unfamiliar. Death has another characteristic of tragedy: it gives meaning. It is only when death has ended a life that we can see (or invent) the shape: the ups and downs and what the final achievement has been. When this illumination comes to a man while still alive, we feel something of the tragic awe. When a man knows how and when he must die – by incurable illness or by execution – we feel that from then on he is an awesome, even sacral, being. The feelings aroused by such a situation are surely at the basis of the work of art we call tragic; and the feelings are called forth by the fact that someone has been faced with the realisation that he must undergo an inevitable fate which is linked to the experience of all of us, but which normally we can avoid facing.

If this is true, I think we have described what makes *Bérénice* tragic. The play is an epiphany, a showing-forth, of a truth which is painful but must be known, and which is potentially at least an element in our own experience. Titus loves Bérénice, Bérénice loves Titus, Antiochus loves Bérénice. Their separation is agonising because their love is profound and each realises the feelings of the others: none of them can find any reason which will palliate or disguise their pain. Titus cannot say that Rome has forced him: 'Rome se tait', and it is the Rome in himself that compels him. Bérénice cannot pretend that Titus does not love her, or that he doubts her love for him, or that he has been forced to send her away: it is his integrity and his glory, which she herself has helped to create, which compel him. Antiochus cannot cease to love, yet cannot hope to be loved. Suicide or violence would be futile – attempts to break out of the circle, when the tragedy is that the circle is known to be unbreakable. Racine achieves this effect without implying any dynamisms beyond those operating in normal life. In *Bérénice*, if anywhere, we have the perfectly rational tragedy.

This brings us to a point of fundamental importance. Racine, at least when he wrote *Bérénice*, had an attitude to the human condition very different from the received wisdom of his time. Butler describes the seventeenth-century view of man as partaking of two worlds: the 'animal' (instinctual) and the 'superior' (spiritual). Against this he sets a view irreconcilable with it, which is Racine's:

Chez Racine, les impulsions de l'homme, passions et devoirs, désirs et sacrifices naissent dans les mêmes régions de son être; ni les uns ni les autres ne sont d'une nature essentiellement différente ou privilégiée.[8]

It is in this profound sense of the interconnection of all aspects of human thought and emotion, this refusal to invoke metaphysical discontinuities, which gives Racine's art its overwhelming humanity.

THE DRAMATIC ART OF RACINE

I

After 1670, Racine was the reigning monarch of the stage. *Bajazet* was acclaimed not just as a success but as an improvement on his earlier plays. *Mithridate* triumphed, and was Louis XIV's favourite tragedy. Then came *Iphigénie* – Racine's greatest success, with the Court, the Town, and the critics. Until the end of the eighteenth century and beyond, it was regarded as one of his greatest plays – perhaps his greatest. I will consider for a moment these three plays by Racine at the height of his success, and try to discover from them some of the characteristics of his mastery.

Traditionally, the great strength of Racine is his portrayal of women in love. *Bajazet* may stand as an example. We may instance Act II, Scene i, with its powerful and subtle drawing of Roxane's conflicting emotions. She swings from formal elegance to a direct proposal of marriage. When Bajazet prevaricates, she first reasons with him, and then becomes indignant, though for a moment her rage is so suppressed by her effort to remain calm that it comes through only as irony. Then her brutality and rage break through, and she threatens him with death. At this, she recoils, and pleads with him with tenderness and urgency – only to rebound into threatening violence at his coldness. The dramatic power is obvious. The verse expresses every nuance of feeling, every shift in the situation. The tension builds up, the twists and the resolution are unexpected yet logical. This is one example among many, and a relatively simple one, but it justifies Racine's reputation for psychological subtlety combined with dramatic urgency.

Mithridate has the same qualities. It also shows more clearly than *Bajazet* another quality for which Racine is famous: the sweetness and elegance of his verse, especially in scenes of pathos or sentiment (as in the rôle of Monime). More relevantly for our present purpose, it also shows qualities which are often undervalued in Racine, and which we more readily associate with Corneille: a poetry of energy, heroism and politics. If we admire the discussion of Auguste with Cinna and Maxime, it is hard to withhold our approval from Mithridate's discussion with his sons. The scene lacks nothing in firmness and energy of expression, and shows a grasp of political realities: if Mithridate overrates the

Italians' respect for blue blood ('If they followed Spartacus, how they will fight for a king!') we can say that this shows Racine's awareness of the psychology of a half-oriental monarch. In *Mithridate* he skilfully brings together a romantic plot and an historical background and makes them set each other off: the pathetic dilemma of the old king gains in intensity when seen as part of the situation of a man who has long made headway against the power of Rome, and in defeat plans an audacious counterstroke.

At this stage Racine seems to have reached the point where he can do what he likes with his medium. In *Iphigénie*, more than in any of his other plays, an interesting plot leads smoothly from dramatic situation to dramatic situation. As in *Bajazet*, suspense is aroused to a high degree, but here we never feel that the machinery is arbitrary. There are four, even six, interesting and well-drawn characters, subtly contrasted, each drawing our sympathy or admiration in various degrees, but none of them appearing either too evil or too good to be interesting. Their reactions are subtly observed and expressed. Each character is satisfying as an individual creation, and together they form a beautifully balanced group. But the great glory of *Iphigénie* is its verse. For the rôle of Iphigénie herself, Racine has found a perfect harmony and simplicity, but the range of tone is wide. Against Iphigénie's tenderness we can set the deeper note of Clytemnestre's rage. Nor is there lacking that strange sexual undertone that creeps into Racine's verse and gives it just a hint of perversity:

> Dans les cruelles mains par qui je fus ravie
> Je demeurai longtemps sans lumière et sans vie.
> Enfin mes tristes yeux cherchèrent la clarté;
> Et me voyant presser d'un bras ensanglanté,
> Je frémissais, Doris, et d'un vainqueur sauvage
> Craignais de rencontrer l'effroyable visage . . .
> Je le vis: son aspect n'avait rien de farouche;
> Je sentis le reproche expirer dans ma bouche.
> Je sentis contre moi mon coeur se déclarer.

Most beautiful of all – and it is on the significance I give to these that my estimate of the play must largely rest – are the lines that cluster round the rôle of Agamemnon, especially in the first scene of Act I:

> Heureux qui, satisfait de son humble fortune,
> Libre du joug superbe où je suis attaché,
> Vit dans l'état obscur où les Dieux l'ont caché!
>
> Nous partions; et déjà par mille cris de joie
> Nous menacions de loin les rivages de Troie.

> Un prodige étonnant fit taire ce transport:
> Le vent qui nous flattait nous laissa dans le port.
> Il fallut s'arrêter, et la rame inutile
> Fatigua vainement une mer immobile.

In *Bajazet*, *Mithridate* and *Iphigénie*, we seem to have all the dramatic virtues. Yet have we? These three plays are such that it is difficult to trace any weakness in them, yet do we find them really compelling? This question is so important for an understanding of Racine that we must look at them again.

Bajazet is sometimes considered the weakest of the three. From its first appearance, critics have fastened on the *grande tuerie* at the end, which has been thought insufficiently prepared. In realistic terms, however, the deaths seem well prepared. It is likely enough that those who plot treason at the court of an Eastern despot will get killed, and virtually certain if they mix love and politics – much more probable and inevitable, for instance, than that those who drive chariots will be killed because sea-monsters frighten the horses. To try and get at the reasons for dissatisfaction with the dénouement, let us examine the verse.

The plainness of much of it is famous (Madame, j'ai reçu des lettres de l'armée'). Frequently it has also a prosaic, disenchanted realism:

> Roxane en sa fureur peut raisonner ainsi.
> Mais moi, qui vois plus loin, qui, par un long usage,
> Des maximes du trône ai fait l'apprentissage,
> Qui d'emplois en emplois vieilli sous trois sultans,
> Ai vu de mes pareils les malheurs éclatants,
> Je sais, sans me flatter, que de sa seule audace
> Un homme tel que moi doit attendre sa grâce.

The style of Act V is especially revealing. In the earlier acts, there is time to drape the bare facts in poetic conventions; but by the last act the pace is too hot ('Les moments sont trop chers pour les perdre en paroles'). Racine can here draw great dramatic effect from the simplest phrases: 'Retirez-vous'; 'Que faut-il faire?'; 'Sortez'; 'Qu'est-ce?'; 'Quoi! lui?' But the force comes from the context of events, not from the verse: the banal phrases are energised by the happenings around them, not by any poetic current which they themselves generate. Where the verse is less abrupt, it often has difficulty in accommodating the events it has to present, and on occasion its awkwardness recalls that of some of the verse in Corneille's later plays:

> Je puis le retenir. Mais s'il sort, il est mort.
> Vient-il?

> – Oui, sur mes pas un esclave l'amène;
> Et loin de soupçonner sa disgrâce prochaine,
> Il m'a paru, Madame, avec empressement,
> Sortir, pour vous chercher, de son appartement.

Even the emotional statements have a bluntness that pretends to no literary grace:

> Mais je m'étonne enfin que pour reconnaissance,
> Pour prix de tant d'amour, de tant de confiance,
> Vous ayez si longtemps par des détours si bas
> Feint un amour pour moi que vous ne sentiez pas.
> – Qui? moi, Madame?
>   – Oui, toi.

Bajazet's death can be announced with the most banal fierceness:

>   Bajazet est sans vie.
> L'ignoriez-vous?

Clearly, *Bajazet* is not poetic in method. The separate virtues of plot, character, and even verse are great, but the play has no pretensions to tragedy. It is because the tragic spirit is lacking that the final deaths, however probable and necessary, appear arbitrary.

If the verse of *Bajazet* is coarse in texture, that of *Mithridate* has an elegance which doubtless helped to make it Louis XIV's favourite tragedy. But since the seventeenth century it has never been regarded as one of Racine's greatest plays, whereas *Iphigénie* has. Boileau's tribute in *Epître VII* is well-known, and critics have reasonably seen the ideal of tragedy set forth in Chant III of *L'Art Poétique* as related to *Iphigénie*. Later neo-classic critics endorsed this estimate of the play. Voltaire's views are well known ('J'avoue que je regarde *Iphigénie* comme le chef-d'oeuvre de la scène') and in *L'Ingénu* he holds it up as a touchstone of true taste, apparently because of its power to play on the audience's emotions.

These judgments and the continued success of *Iphigénie* on the stage are certainly not without justification. Yet, despite all its virtues, would we really place *Iphigénie* on the same level as *Phèdre* and *Athalie*? Despite Voltaire, we clearly would not. To ask a more difficult question: do we prefer *Iphigénie* to *Andromaque*, whose standing is more equivocal? Again, the answer is clear: despite the slight awkwardness of *Andromaque* when compared with the ripeness and perfection of *Iphigénie*, in the last analysis the later play is less impressive than the earlier. Why, then, is *Iphigénie* inferior, when its evident merits are so great?

In an attempt to answer this, I look first at the one element in *Iphigénie* which has been adversely criticised: the handling of the mythological *donnée*. Obviously, this presented great difficulty to a seventeenth-century poet, committed at the same time to *le vraisemblable* and *les bienséances*. How could refined members of seventeenth-century French society be at ease with the concept of gods who would hold up the winds until a princess was sacrificed? Such ideas were unacceptable, not necessarily because the temper of the age was sceptical (though sceptical currents of thought were certainly influential in certain quarters), but because at the level of secular society they were uncouth, and at the level of orthodox religious thought they were either untrue or simply evil. Caught between these two conflicting but powerful devaluations of myth, poets were recommended to regard the individual myths as ornament – at best expressing allegorically some truth of conventional wisdom, at worst merely decorative. This is Boileau's position, and is implicit in neo-classical theory, with its pronounced tendency towards naturalism. Racine, with his earnest desire to recapture the seriousness of ancient tragedy, had little room for manoeuvre: it was unthinkable that he should treat the myth as a fairy-tale with a few allegorical trimmings – this was the operatic solution, which, in his preface he by implication repudiates. Alternatively, he could hardly adopt a whole-heartedly rationalistic interpretation, in which the whole affair was a fraud devised by wicked priests: the time was fortunately not ripe for such a solution to be popular, and Racine must surely have perceived that its crudity quite removed it from the sphere of tragedy. Faced with this dilemma, he equivocates.

The legend of Iphigenia inevitably raises one terrible question: why did the gods demand the sacrifice? Racine evades it: he accepts the demand, and the assumption that after the sacrifice the winds will blow again, as Aristotelian 'improbabilities before the drama'. The advantage of this is that he can avoid all the moral and theological difficulties the question raises. The disadvantage is that he had to direct the audience's attention away from a natural source of interest in his play, and must therefore provide sufficiently attractive alternatives. His solution, at the beginning of the play, is to focus the interest on Agamemnon. The evocative lines in the first scene mark a powerful attempt to direct us to this alternative theme: that of a proud king seeing himself as the victim of the gods because of his position, and following, though reluctantly, his destiny. Vinaver has persuasively maintained that the poetic centre of the play is to be found in this direction. Basing himself solidly on what are undoubtedly the most impressive clusters of verse in the text,

he draws the conclusion that through the agency of these 'vers pres-
tigieux' Racine assimilates his courtly drama to the more significant
realm of myth:

> A tout moment, dans chacune des scènes où figure Agamemnon, le mythe
> tragique côtoie et explique le drame humain, et dans la crainte même d'y faire
> apparaître les dieux, on sent un respect qui, peu à peu, grandit, se nuançant de
> terreur. Malgré son pretendu souci de l'"ordinaire', Racine n'avait jamais poussé
> aussi loin le culte du surnaturel, ni sa poésie accompli miracle plus rare.[1]

Yet we may doubt whether this is so. The theme is certainly present
in Act I, but the ruse of the letter, and then Iphigénie's arrival, point to
other and more superficial sources of interest: the surprise and suspense
engendered by the plot. In Act II, Racine's hesitations between the
myth and the plot are resolved: he introduces 'l'heureux personnage
d'Eriphile, sans laquelle je n'aurais jamais esé entreprendre cette tragédie'.
The scene between Eriphile and Doris includes those subtly sensual lines
we have quoted, and which point to a deeper source of Racine's
strength. But there can be little doubt that the matters of interest he is
more concerned to offer us here are psychology (the nuances of
Eriphile's emotions) and suspense (the mystery of Eriphile's origins and
fate). From now on, the play runs securely on the 'intrigue' level. We
may have a scene of pathos when Iphigénie greets Agamemnon (II.ii),
a scene of jealousy between Iphigénie and Eriphile, and so on. It is
difficult to believe that Racine is focussing on any of them. He is certainly not focussing on the rôle of Agamemnon. Act IV magisterially
plays all the variations on Agamemnon's situation, but the interest is in
the feelings of the characters and the twists and turns of the plot.

Finally, Act V raises in the most acute form questions which Racine
has tried to evade: the significance of the sacrifice itself, and hence the
rôle of the gods in the action. Before looking at his treatment of the
sacrifice and its attendant miracles, we may glance at his handling of
the gods – bearing in mind that he had to keep in play, yet avoid com-
mitting himself too completely to, two different conceptions of them:
the gods as real *numinosa* (which was incredible to his audience's Christian or sceptical beliefs – 'quelle apparence de dénouer ma tragédie par le
secours d'une déesse . . . qui pouvait bien trouver quelque créance du
temps d'Euripide, mais qui serait trop absurde et trop incroyable parmi
nous?') and the gods as dignified ornaments (which was acceptable to
his audience, but denatured his subject).

If we look at the text, the extent of his equivocation is obvious. 'Dieu'
or its plural occurs no less than eighteen times in the act, but the mixture

of tones in which it is used betrays Racine's uncertainty. Some references appear to invoke real *numinosa*:

> il faut des Dieux apaiser la colère . . .
> Leurs ordres éternels se sont trop déclarés.

But others are merely sentimental:

> Dieux plus doux, vous n'avez demandé que ma vie . . .
> vivez, digne race des Dieux.

Others again are no more than expletives:

> Dieux! Achille?
>
> Mais, Dieux! ne vois-je pas Ulysse?

When Iphigénie goes off to the sacrifice, there remains the prospect of tragedy: we believe she is to be killed, and there is perhaps still time for Racine to invest her death with significance. Clytemnestre denounces Agamemnon in impressive verse. Then thunder sounds, and she attributes it to the gods. Arcas also credits them with interrupting the sacrifice – 'N'en doutez point, Madame, un Dieu combat pour vous' – but this interpretation is rather devalued by the line which follows: '*Achille* en ce moment exauce vos prières.' The struggle is between Achille and a demagogic priest: 'Achille est à l'autel, Calchas est éperdu.' Then Ulysse comes to relate the dénouement. Iphigénie is safe, and it is the work of the gods: but 'the gods' are little more than a figure of speech. The narration is a careful balancing act. Achille's purely secular intervention 'partageait les Dieux'. Calchas then reveals the secret of Eriphile's parentage. Racine makes him attribute this to 'Le Dieu qui maintenant vous parle par ma voix', but is careful to add that Calchas had purely human means of knowing, and to hint that he may merely be expressing his malice towards Eriphile:

> Je vis moi-même alors ce fruit de leurs amours.
> D'un sinistre avenir je menaçai ses jours.

Eriphile kills herself, but not out of deference to the sacredness of Calchas's words:

> Le sang de ces héros dont *tu me fais* descendre
> Sans tes *profanes* mains saura bien se répandre.

So Iphigénie is not *the* Iphigénie; the subject of the play is not the sacrifice of Agamemnon's daughter; and the central character is Eriphile. Now we come to the miracles. Racine starts with the more credible parts (the weather could break and the winds blow), and boldly associates them with another miracle: 'La flamme du bûcher d'elle-même s'allume.' This detail is not in Euripides: Racine is surely trying to make his miracle more credible by appealing to his Christian audience's recollection of the pyre on Mount Carmel at which Elijah confounded the priests of Baal. But immediately he equivocates again:

> Le *soldat* étonné *dit* que dans une nue
> Jusque sur le bûcher Diane est descendue,
> Et *croit* que s'élevant au travers de ses feux,
> Elle portait au ciel notre encens et nos voeux.

The final couplet of the play keeps the balance: Clytemnestre attribute the happy ending to the gods and to Achille.

It is clear enough, from this brief survey of the text, that Racine is careful not to commit himself on the central issue of his play. He is not using the elements of his play to express any coherent pattern of experience: he is exploiting them for what interest they will yield in their own right. Barthes puts his finger on the play's weakness:

Iphigénie est une 'grande comédie dramatique', où le Sang n'est plus un lien tribal, mais seulement familial, une simple continuité de bénéfices et d'affections. La conséquence critique est que l'on ne peut plus réduire les rôles entre eux, tenter d'atteindre le noyau singulier de la configuration; il faut les prendre les uns après les autres, définir ce que socialement, et non plus mythiquement, chacun d'eux réprésente.[2]

The method, of course, has certain advantages. Hence the brilliance of the play, the perfectly articulated plot, the range and subtlety of the verse and characterisation: there is no central meaning to make things difficult, and Racine can display his virtuosity. Indeed, to make his play interesting at all, he must decorate it as brilliantly as he can.

If we now go back over the scenes in these middle plays which we singled out as showing Racine's mastery of his medium, we can see what they lack. In Act II, Scene i of *Bajazet*, the portrayal of Roxane's emotions and the control of dramatic tension are masterly, but they are the only two elements of interest in the scene. There is no larger significance to them, as there is in a scene like IV.v of *Bérénice*, where an equally acutely observed scene at the same time functions as part of the expression of a complex poetic theme. As with *Bajazet*, so with *Mithridate*. Its excellences are many, but what is the subject? We can only describe it in terms of the characters and plot: we cannot divine from the play any central theme, any reinterpretation of human experience. Why is the scene in which Mithridate explains his plans to his sons so inferior to Act II,

Scene i of *Cinna*? Not because of any obvious weakness in Racine's verse, nor because Corneille shows a firmer grasp of political realities. It is certainly not because of any superiority in Corneille's character-drawing: in his scene he plays havoc with the characters of Cinna and Maxime. The reason for the difference in quality is that the scene in *Cinna* means something. It is part of a pattern which involves us in a particular interpretation of experience. In *Mithridate*, the political scene is just a political scene: another scene we can enjoy in a play which is full of them. *Mithridate* is close to some plays of Corneille's middle period, in method if not in content. Like so many of Corneille's plays after *Cinna*, it could very easily slide into domestic comedy: it is not for nothing that one of the most famous scenes recalls a situation in *L'Avare*. Again like Corneille's more naturalistic plays, *Mithridate* is full of that other symptom of naturalism, a complacent indulgence in contemporary jargon. Hardly anything in Corneille, even in *Oedipe,* can match the reaction of Xipharès when Monime says she has betrayed him:

> Quoi! Madame, c'est vous, c'est l'amour qui m'expose?
> Mon malheur est parti d'une si belle cause?
> Trop d'amour a trahi nos secrets amoureux?
> Et vous vous excusez de m'avoir fait heureux?

We may believe that *Mithridate* pleased contemporary taste.

This brings us back to the question of the reputation of these plays. It has often been remarked that all Racine's plays, except his first two, have retained their place on the stage. The situation with Corneille is very different: plays such as *Pompée* and *Rodogune* have steadily lost their reputations. But let us look more closely at the fortunes of *Bajazet*, *Mithridate* and *Iphigénie*. The reputations of masterpieces, or at least the reasons for which they are admired, often fluctuate: their power to arouse violent reactions and to provoke different interpretations is a sign of their greatness. The fate of *Bajazet*, *Mithridate* and *Iphigénie* is more depressing. Their evident merits have always been admired, but after their rapturous reception by contemporaries their reputations have suffered a slow but uninterrupted decline. The naturalist is committed to investing in the representation of contemporary behaviour: he may get quick returns, but the stock is ephemeral. *Bajazet*, *Mithridate* and *Iphigénie* suffer from just this weakness.

It follows from our argument that these three plays are not among Racine's best. Racine's mastery in them – of plot, character and verse – is of course as great as anyone has ever said it is. The difficulty is that this mastery is present to a higher degree in them than in his acknowledged masterpieces; and if we accept that excellence of plot, character and verse are the criteria of the value of a play we can hardly avoid calling *Iphigénie* Racine's masterpiece, as Voltaire was logical and honest enough to do. If we are not prepared to do this, it follows that the reason for the superiority of some of Racine's other plays is more basic. I have maintained, in my studies of *Andromaque, Britannicus* and *Bérénice*, that the reason for this superiority is that in them Racine makes use, with increasing sureness, of the poetic as distinct from the naturalistic method. This brings us face to face with another question: what type of theme does Racine use this poetic method to express? *Cinna* is poetic, but none of Racine's plays resembles it in tone or content. I have argued, and will argue, that Racine's best plays are tragic. Our central problem is this: on what basis was Racine able to found his tragedy?

2

The best starting-point is perhaps to look again at the most obvious strength of Racine, which has figured in every critical evaluation of his work from the appearance of *Andromaque* onwards. It has always been said that his special strength is in the portrayal of love. Whatever reservations we may make on his method of expression, Turnell is undoubtedly right to stress the importance of the erotic instinct in Racine.[3] But I think we should emphasise that in Racine this erotic element is more all-embracing than that of a romantic love-story. We certainly do not attribute his power to the elegance with which he portrays his young lovers. The insipidity of Britannicus, Bajazet or Xipharès makes this one of the weakest features of his plays. By 'love' we really mean the elemental passion which he portrays: passions which may be profoundly sensual, as in Phèdre, but which are also often touched with sadistic and masochistic impulses, as in Néron or Titus, and may be more a lust for power than any other lust, as in Agrippine. Racine's contemporaries were very understandably shocked by the subversiveness of his plays. The way in which he wrote about love leaves no doubt of the daemonic force behind it.

It is no part of my purpose to discuss the scientific status of any psychological theory. Nevertheless, when modern critics discuss Racine, they are often drawn to speak of him in terms of modern depth psychology. This tendency seems to me a sound one, if only because it highlights some aspects of Racine which are difficult to account for in any other terms. If we discuss here the idea of the unconscious, our concern is with it as an idea, a concept which is related to those obscure feelings we try to express when struggling to describe the power of great poetry. A passage from Jung, though rationally indefensible, perhaps conveys the emotional fascination which is relevant in this context, and which is not confined to the ramifications of Freudian sexuality:

Though consciousness is intensive and concentrated, it is transitory and is trained upon the immediate present and the immediate field of attention . . . But matters stand very differently with the unconscious. It is not concentrated and intensive, but shades off into obscurity; it is highly extensive and can juxtapose the most heterogeneous elements in the most paradoxical way. More than this, it contains, besides an indeterminable number of subliminal perceptions, the accumulated deposits from the lives of our ancestors, who by their very existence have contributed to the differentiation of the species. If it were possible to personify the unconscious, we might think of it as a collective human being combining the characteristics of both sexes, transcending youth and age, birth and death, and, from having at its command a human experience of one or two million years, practically immortal. If such a being existed, it would be exalted above all temporal change; the present would mean neither more nor less to it than any year in the hundredth millenium before Christ; it would be a dreamer of age-old dreams and, owing to its limitless experience, an incomparable prognosticator. It would have lived countless times over again the life of the individual, the family, the tribe and the nation, and it would possess a living sense of the rhythm of growth, flowering and decay.[4]

This idea of the unconscious brings, among other things, the possibility of understanding that feeling of simultaneous likeness and unlikeness of ourselves to men of earlier ages which the art of the past so often evokes. It is reasonable to suppose that, just as the physical structure of our species is relatively constant, so are the basic processes of our mental functioning. Unconscious mental processes, unlike those of the conscious mind, are extremely longlasting and resistant to change. Naturalistic art tries to gain seriousness by incorporating accurate observation of contemporary manners and pieces of contemporary theory. Manners change, and theories change rapidly; the basic patterns of the mind change very slowly, if at all. We may expect, then, that the enduring qualities in a work of art are those which, to use our mythologem, are closest to the unconscious.

As the passage from Jung powerfully conveys, the forces of the unconscious, being so much stronger than our conscious desires and so difficult to influence, appear as overwhelming numinous powers. At the same time – again, taking the theories of the depth psychologists as our mythologem – these impulses are not abstractions, but parts of our

lives whose effects we experience constantly. These impulses are connected with intimate and emotion-laden experiences: our attitudes to
our bodies and their functions, our love-objects and the objects of our
hate. An artist who touches on these impulses can awaken in us an
intensity of emotion, a sensuous immediacy, more compelling than any
representation of outward behaviour or any abstract theory. More
important, he himself can be seized by them; and while he is in touch
with them he cannot be demoralised by the feeling that his art is only a
secondary and superficial activity: they are too compelling for that. In
short, he is unlikely to suffer demoralisation in the face of the devalua-
tion of poetry implied in neo-classical or naturalistic critical theory.

Before I close this line of argument, I shall dwell for a moment on the
particular relevance of the unconscious for tragedy. Tragedy is felt to be
of special seriousness and importance. It demands a sense of absoluteness – any cure for tragic suffering is unthinkable. It cannot exist when
there is a sense that there is a known and predictable moral framework.
It is paradoxical: it requires a sense of inevitability and yet of freedom.
It must include the sense of numinous powers outside the reach of men's
wills, yet at the same time is man-created and humanistic. It involves
violent and sensual passions. It demands, in fact, qualities which we will
never find in the surface nuances of social behaviour or in intellectually
formulated theory, but which we may experience in the effects of
unconscious mental processes.

We can now return to Racine. My argument so far can be summarised
as follows. The experiences to which the concept of the unconscious
refers give poets a claim to seriousness in their work which enables
them to evade the secondary rôles imposed on poetry by critical doctrines of the type of neo-classicism and naturalism; and these experiences
are especially relevant to tragedy. My argument will now be that
Racine based himself on a similar appeal to the unconscious to evade
the naturalistic critical demands powerful in his environment, and that
this opened his way to tragedy.

I believe that this assertion is supported by the evidence of his plays,
but it may seem less odd if we link it with two other lines of thought.
The first is the generally accepted view that he has affinities with the
Greek tragic poets. I will come back to this in my next chapter. To anti-
cipate, I think we must agree with Lapp that Racine's special affinity is
with Euripides,[5] and that it shows itself not by any means in sympathy
with Euripidean technique ('The Greek writer's structure could only
have seemed erratic to the Frenchman. And compared to the highly
inventive Euripides, who added to or changed the established stories at

will, Racine was extremely cautious, requiring a precedent for almost every innovation') but in a common attitude to the deep, irrational forces of the mind and their relation to the civilised, conscious order ('The lack of any specific divine cause for the tragedies of Racine's Jocaste, his Agamemnon, his Phèdre, is thus essentially Euripidean . . . for Racine as well as the Greek dramatist the natural life force is equated with the divine'). The affinity, in fact, is in a common attitude to 'the gods'. 'The gods', in Greek thought, are not theological abstractions: 'They are not merely dramatic fictions, but they personify the forces of necessity to which man must yield'.[6] As such, they are often equivalent to powerful psychological impulses: 'A "god" is the personification of any more than human power in nature, or any force within the heart of man which is also greater than the individual because it is shared by all individuals'.[7] As such, they come close to the modern concept of the unconscious, and to the seventeenth-century concept of *le coeur*.

This brings us to our second line of thought. There is one very significant tradition of thought in seventeenth-century France which was concerned to analyse as precisely as possible the irrational compulsions that determine human behaviour. La Rochefoucauld is sometimes presented as an author of cynical wisecracks. If we examine the *Maximes* at all carefully, we find they embody a more sombre attitude than this judgement implies:

> La durée de nos passions ne dépend pas plus de nous que la durée de notre vie. (5)

> Nous n'avons pas assez de force pour suivre toute notre raison. (43)

> Qui vit sans folie n'est pas si sage qu'il croit. (209)

> Il y a plus de défauts dans l'humeur que dans l'esprit. (290)

> Il s'en faut bien que nous ne connaissions toutes nos volontés. (295)

> On ne souhaite jamais ardemment ce qu'on ne souhaite que par raison. (469)

La Rochefoucauld's theme is one from which Euripides and Freud would not have dissented: 'L'esprit est toujours la dupe du coeur' (102).

As Bénichou pointed out,[8] La Rochefoucauld's work rests on the concept of unconscious mental processes. What is striking is that he sees them as truly unconscious, not merely at the margin of consciousness. The similarity of his attitude and subject-matter to those of more recent psychologists is notable, particularly in some of the material he cancelled.[9] The original opening 'Maxime' reads like a passage from *The Book of the It* or a Freudian paper on the instincts.[10] Maxime XXXIII of the original edition describes the mechanism of projection.[11] Maxime XLIV in the definitive edition insists on the biological basis of psychology. The suppressed No XII of the *Réflexions Diverses* propounds a psycho-somatic theory of disease.[12] The *Maximes* show a concern with the most bizarre aspects of human behaviour: La Rochefoucauld seems to have been especially fascinated by the incident of the lackey who danced on the scaffold before being broken on the wheel.

Adam links the *Maximes* with the work of Saint-Réal,[13] who for a while was the mentor of Racine.[14] Saint-Réal was drawn to 'l'étude du coeur humain', which soon led him to see 'que la bizarrerie ou la folie sont le plus souvent les causes des actions les plus éclatantes, que la malignité est le plus fréquent motif de nos sentiments, que surtout chez les femmes et chez les enfants il y a plaisir à faire le mal et à voir souffrir'.[15] Adam adds a note:

Saint-Réal n'est pas seul à s'intéresser à ces régions obscures de la vie des senti-ments. Dans une de ses *Lettres*, Méré cite un mari qui 'plaisait plus à certains hommes qu'un homme ne doit souhaiter', et ce mari ne pouvait trouver son plaisir avec sa femme, qui était très belle, qu'en l'imaginant dans les bras d'un autre . . . Il posait devant son sécrétaire, sur un ami inconnu, ces étranges questions: 'Pourquoi voit-il une putaine si laide, lui qui a une si belle femme? Comment peut-il aimer les garçons?'

We need not think that in emphasising Racine's irrationalism we are merely projecting back into the seventeenth century our twentieth-century views: the student of Euripides, the contemporary of La Roche-foucauld and the friend of Saint-Réal had ample opportunity to arrive at such views for himself.

There is a strong negative argument for the hypothesis: how else can we account for the strength of Racine? As I have tried to show, we can hardly explain his compelling force if we regard him only as con-tinuing and perfecting Corneille. Precision of plotting, subtlety and force of characterisation, sweetness and strength of verse: all these are present to a high degree in *Mithridate*, and to the point of perfection in *Iphi-génie*. But neither of these plays can take us by the throat as some others can. They are much superior to *Le Comte d'Essex*, but they are not obviously different in kind. We may feel that Thomas Corneille, if only he had possessed a little more skill and sensitivity, might have risen to *Mithridate*. *Phèdre* is of a different order entirely. It is this differentness of Racine that the critic has to explain.

We can approach the question from another angle. There is one special strength of Racine which marks him out from his minor contemporaries, of which he himself was conscious, and which is obviously a major source of his power: his poetry. Poetry, far more than prose, is equipped to embody intuitions from below the level of consciousness. As Brereton has remarked, Racine's verse 'retains the slight haze always necessary to poetry'.[16] Poetry is based directly on experience: it can afford to draw only a little material at second-hand, from the findings of external disciplines. It characteristically has a range of meanings that cannot be formulated in prose – simultaneous views, as it were, of many sides of an experience. It is this richness which produces the haze. This does not mean that poetry is less clear than prose; on the contrary, it can say with immediate clarity and force what prose cannot say at all. This is true to an especially high degree of poetic drama: the whole complex of means of expression – plot, character, situation and the rest, which are elements in the poetic substance – is removed further still from conceptual discourse than that of a non-dramatic poem, which consists of words alone. If the only elements called into play are the non-verbal ones, the work will lack the conceptual clarity which words, uniquely, combine with emotional resonance derived from the whole range of human experience. If this combination of verbal and non-verbal means is essential to the statement made by the work (and not merely sugaring of a prose pill) the meaning expressed must therefore be inexpressible by normal prose statements. Such inexpressibility is characteristic precisely of those experiences which are closest to the unconscious mental processes. It is possible for a very great artist to match the elements which express the meaning inexpressible by prose so exactly with a rational surface that the irrational part of the total statement can be missed by the insensitive. I have argued that this almost perfect matching occurs in *Bérénice*. More commonly, in responding to a work of art we feel the daemonic impulsion, and are aware that it could not be accommodated in prose terms. In all the most powerful of Racine's plays we feel this compelling presence of a meaning that is more than the plot or the characters and cannot be reduced to any prose message. We may also note in Racine's verse surface features that fit awkwardly into the conventions of rational discourse: ambiguities, unexpected collocations, recurring images and patterns, and, above all, paradox. Neoclassical poets are fond of antithesis, but in Racine the antitheses – especially in *Phèdre* and *Athalie* – are sharpened to the point of paradox.

This brings us to a further problem. We have argued that the basic tradition of neo-classicism was naturalistic, and that in the age of Louis XIV it was evolving ever towards greater reasonableness, greater formal elegance, and away from any inconvenient attempt to express a central substance. Set in this tradition we have Racine, a profound poet, struggling to express his sense of passion and violence in human experience. This poetic impulse put him in touch with those unconscious forces whose strength and immediacy gave him a firm base from which to resist the secondary rôle assigned to the arts by naturalism. At the same time, the critical code of elegant decencies forbade expression of these uncouth impulses; and Racine himself certainly subscribed to the code. What might we expect would be his technique in such a situation?

It may help us to look at two analogies: Freud's theory of dream-formation and Eliot's tactics in writing his plays. Freud came to the conclusion that the conflict between unconscious forces and the moral and other tendencies resisting their expression is temporarily resolved (still below the level of consciousness) in a compromise: the repugnant unconscious material is disguised behind a façade which is acceptable to the repressing tendencies, but which is found, on analysis, to express the unacceptable content behind it. This façade is as far as possible given a reasonable, coherent form by a process of 'secondary revision' which takes account of the standards of rationality of the conscious mind. In a perfect dream, the façade might appear perfectly rational. In practice, there are always some incongruities which betray the fact that the dream conceals something more elemental.

Eliot's tactics, though quite conscious, involve a somewhat similar process. They are set out most starkly in a letter to Pound:

IF you can keep the bloody audience's attention engaged, then you can perform any monkey tricks you like when they ain't looking, and it's what you do behind the audience's back so to speak that makes your play IMMORTAL for a while.

If the audience gets its strip tease it will swallow the poetry.[17]

We can see this technique in, for instance, *The Cocktail Party*. In this case, the 'monkey tricks' are the Christian meaning which Eliot wishes to convey, and which he thinks his audience will reject as alien; the 'strip tease' is the popular West End light comedy. The problem is then to convey the meaning in this form: the Christian idea of martyrdom must be expressed through drawing-room comedy. Here again, but this time by design, a few elements which cannot be assimilated to the humdrum surface direct our attention to the meaning underneath: the Guardians pour libations. This approach is not characteristic of all poetic drama, and is unlikely to succeed if applied in cold blood. In Eliot's case it fails. This is not necessarily because the method is at fault. It seems more likely that if it fails in this case, this is because the meaning to be expressed is not a poetic meaning inexpressible in other terms than those of the play itself, but a preconceived doctrine which he wishes to insinuate in a sugared form.

These two examples are offered as models of Racine's method, which may be stated as follows. He takes a story or situation, not simply because it offers striking characters or an exciting plot, but because he feels that it can help him to embody the meaning he is struggling to express. His task, as a poet, is to bring out and articulate with the greatest possible clarity this hidden meaning. But the literary conventions of his day forbid a crude expression of some elements of this hidden meaning: what these conventions (which he shared) do demand are a clear plot, interesting characters and elegant verse, all conforming to orthodox morality and common sense (except insofar as poetry may have licence to tell agreeable lies, providing they are not to be taken seriously.) His problem is then to find a naturalistic surface which will satisfy his critics (and himself) and at the same time serve as a façade which will harmonise with his underlying meaning. In Racine, this façade (the 'strip tease') is always beautifully constructed. To the careless eye, the effect of the play seems to be due to the perfection of the façade. But this is not so, as two pieces of evidence show: first, the plays with the most perfect façades (*Mithridate* and *Iphigénie*) are not the most powerful; and second, in some of the most powerful of his plays (*Andromaque, Britannicus, Phèdre* and *Athalie*) there are evident discontinuities between the façade and the meaning behind it. I have already discussed the curious lack of connection between the 'intrigue' and 'emotion' levels of *Andromaque* and the change of method in the last 122 lines of *Britannicus*. In the next two chapters I shall note the discontinuities in *Phèdre* and *Athalie*.

This view of Racine explains much in his prefaces. He defends laboriously the historical accuracy and 'vraisemblance' of every detail of his plays – that is, of their façades. But two things arouse him to fury: when the critics are not satisfied with his façade, in spite of all his trouble with it (see the first preface to *Britannicus*); and when they suggest that he has broken the 'rules' in general – that is, that although he may have meticulously observed the individual rules of the unities, the *liaison des scènes*, and so on, he has departed from the basis of neo-classical dramaturgy. The second accusation hurts because it is true. Racine's defence is the only possible one: he appeals to the powerful effect his plays make on the spectators who are not concerned with the rules. There is a fundamental discrepancy between the two imperatives of neo-classical art: 'to please' and 'to follow the rules'. In Racine the two imperatives correspond to the two levels of his plays: 'to please', he relied on the powerful appeal of the latent content to our passions; but 'to follow the rules' it is necessary to produce a façade pleasing to the rational mind. We find in his art, in fact, an ambivalence which we find also in his attitude to Jansenism and to his life at Court: an anxiety to please, shadowed by an inner defiance.

I have travelled around a good deal in an effort to illuminate Racine's tragic method. My purpose, however, has been to set off and make understandable the nature of his achievement, not to subordinate it to yet another schematic explanation. We are still left with the paradox of Racine, the perfect neo-classicist and poet of anarchic passion. In the last analysis, perhaps we can only say it was his temperament, or his genius – in either case, an insoluble mystery – which led him to intrude the archaic bull into the Dresden china shop. But even genius must have some path along which to travel, some associative link to connect his intuitions with an accepted form which can help him express them. This link lay to hand in another element in the neo-classical tradition: the use of antique subject-matter. Tradition approved the use of either ancient history or mythology. Racine, far more than Corneille or his own contemporaries (except when they were being operatic) chose myth. The great myths of Greece live because they are intimately connected with the most emotion-laden and frequent experiences of human beings. If we want to explain the differentness of Racine, we must reaffirm what has been said by many others: Racine alone, in the words of Vinaver,[18] 'entrera dans le domaine du mythe avec la volonté d'en respecter les données éssentielles et d'émouvoir le spectateur par les choses mêmes "qui avaient mis autrefois en larmes le plus savant peuple de la Grèce".' We may doubt whether this is true of *Iphigénie*. There is no doubt that it is true of *Phèdre*.

3

My view, then, is that the basis of Racine's art was his concern to express those irrational and even infantile passions that are fed from the unconscious, but that he masked them as far as possible behind a perfect neo-classical façade. I will now look at this hypothesis in the light of the evidence about his method of working. This evidence is of two kinds: anecdotes, and what we can deduce from the work itself – especially his revisions of his plays.

Racine was an extremely painstaking craftsman, and revised his plays in both minor details and more important points, both after they were first performed and after they were printed. Seventeenth-century critical theory stressed the value of craftsmanship, and Racine was sensitive enough to criticism to attempt to remove what seemed to himself or others were blemishes on his work. But on my view, his main aesthetic problem was to provide a façade of approved design for the profoundly unconventional content of his plays. It follows that the problem was most acute when the latent content was most at odds with the current literary conventions, and that in these plays the need to polish and adjust the façade was most pressing. If we look at the secular plays from *Andromaque* to *Phèdre*, this assumption is amply borne out. *Iphigénie* was hardly altered, and *Bajazet* and *Mithridate* were retouched only on matters of detail. But in the greatest plays, *Andromaque, Britannicus, Bérénice* and *Phèdre* – those where the effort to reconcile the poetic content with the neo-classical form had to be most strenuous – whole scenes are cut or recast entirely.[19]

Our other piece of evidence from the works themselves is the plan of Act I of *Iphigénie en Tauride*. Unfortunately, lack of information makes it hard to interpret. As I shall argue, it was presumably drafted about the time Racine was pondering *Iphigénie* – that is, in what in my view was his period of relative naturalism. It relates only to the first act – the part of a play which is largely concerned with conveying factual exposition, and for which it was perhaps most necessary to plan logically, whatever the poet's approach. The real difficulty, however, is that we do not have the finished act to compare it with. The plan is often adduced as evidence that Racine wrote his plays first in prose and then turned them into verse. It certainly confirms what we already knew from Racine's statement about his project for *Les Amours d'Ovide*, that he planned his plays carefully in advance. But it does not prove that his method of working was logical and pedestrian as might appear. The finished work may well come out rather different from what the author had in mind at the outset. In anything that requires real skill and imagination the work is done largely below the level of consciousness, and what emerges is not what the conscious mind itself would have written. The act of trying to write a plan in advance may not produce a plan of what eventually is produced, but it may well serve at least three other functions: to assist the inner (preconscious) process of crystallisation; to alert the conscious mind to what is coming so as to make it more receptive; and to ensure that the conscious mind feeds into the preconscious process those rational elements which are needed in the making of the final product.

We now come to the anecdotal evidence, none of it very well authenticated. Louis Racine's story of Racine reciting speeches in *Mithridate* with such frantic abandon in the Tuileries garden that the workmen

thought him about to commit suicide goes some way towards counter-
acting the view of a prosaic Racine plodding from outline plan to
prose version to verse, but in itself is trivial. Of more interest is Louis
Racine's famous statement about his father: 'quand il entreprenait une
tragédie, il disposait chaque acte en prose. Quand il avait ainsi lié toutes
les scenès entre elles, il disait: "Ma tragédie est faite", comptant le reste
pour rien.' The facts may be right, but there is nothing in them to make
us revise our hypothesis. The correct view is surely that of Vinaver:

> Cette légende, si tant est qu'elle soit digne de foi, n'évoque plus à nos yeux
> l'image d'un dramaturge subordonnant tous ses efforts à la mécanique du drame,
> mais bien celle d'un poète confiant de pouvoir découvrir, au delà des diffi-
> cultés de composition, 'assez d'abondance et de force' pour y faire germer le
> mystère tragique. Non qu'un tel poète puisse dédaigner les nécessités matérielles
> du plan, ses 'malices' comme les appellera Flaubert. Mais il les exécute calme-
> ment, comme si elles n'engagaient point l'idée organique, le dessein profond de
> l'oeuvre.[20]

4

This is the natural point to consider Racine's projects for *Alceste* and
Iphigénie en Tauride. It is almost certainly wrong to assume that he was
still considering them after *Phèdre*. 1677 is occupied first by the dispute
over *Phèdre*, then by the events leading up to his marriage on 1 June and
his nomination as Historiographer Royal in September, which was
made official in October. What evidence there is suggests strongly that
the projects for both plays belong to 1673–6. Racine is said to have intended to follow each of his plays since *Andromaque* with an *Alceste*, and
the preface to *Iphigénie* shows him much occupied with the subject.
The plan of Act I of *Iphigénie en Tauride* is undated, but there is a
plausible tradition (based on the interested statement of Le Clerc) that
Racine hesitated between the two Iphigenia stories before writing his
Iphigénie.

These impressions are confirmed by a study of the pattern of the
plays. *Bérénice* marks the climax of a definite stage in his evolution. The
next three plays bear signs at the same time of repetitiveness and a conscious desire to find new paths. After *Mithridate* there is a pause in his
creative rhythm. From *Andromaque* to *Mithridate*, plays appeared at
almost regular yearly intervals. The gap between *Mithridate* and *Iphigénie* is nineteen months, and between *Iphigénie* and *Phèdre* twenty-
eight. These four years bear the marks of a period of experiment, in
which projects might be carried to an advanced stage and then dropped:

Racine is at the same time moving towards an aesthetic, a social and a psychological turning-point.

The choice of subjects is interesting. We have discussed the difficulty in *Iphigénie* over Racine's treatment of the supernatural, which is one aspect of a fundamental difficulty in his plays. On the one hand, he is drawn to the violent and significant world of myth, which his poetic approach fitted him to express; on the other, the literary and social conventions of his day inclined him to less strenuous forms, in which poetry was reduced to decoration of a basically naturalistic frame. In *Iphigénie*, he faced two problems: how to reconcile civilised elegance with the barbaric motif of human sacrifice, and how to handle the essential premise that the gods will make the winds blow in exchange for the sacrifice. In an *Iphigénie en Tauride* the second problem does not exist, and the first faced him in a very attenuated form. Iphigénie is a priestess; she is in a remote and barbarous country; she does not know the identity of the victim; and the sacrifice does not in fact take place. The subject offers nothing that cannot be reconciled with naturalism, and the mythological element is easily reduced to mere decoration. *Iphigénie en Tauride* might well have been charming, full of striking situations and delicate verse. We may be sorry not to have it. Equally, we may be glad that Racine did not fall into the temptation of entering on this easy but unrewarding path.

With *Alceste*, evasion would have been more difficult. A husband who lets his wife die in his place, a wife who is literally brought back from the dead: these demanded clear-cut aesthetic decisions. Racine would have had either to accept frankly the barbaric and supernatural elements or to reduce the story to a level that literal-minded critics would accept. It is doubtful whether even Racine could have made the first alternative acceptable to his contemporaries. To achieve the second, he would have had either to use a diluted form of the story acceptable in naturalistic terms, or to treat the subject on the level of mere fairy-tale (as in his view Quinault and Lully had done). To a poet with high classical ideals of tragic seriousness, either course would have been repugnant. It has been conjectured that Racine wrote his *Alceste* and destroyed it. If so, his judgment was doubtless correct. It would be fascinating to know which of the impossible alternatives he chose, or whether he refused to make a choice, striving (and failing) by the use of all his skill on the surface to hide the incompatibles beneath. Even his admirers may suspect he did the latter. In *Phèdre* he chose a better way.

'PHÈDRE'

I

Phèdre is Racine's masterpiece, and the most developed example of his tragic method. To understand it we must abandon those critical assumptions which make it so hard to distinguish from *Bajazet*, *Mithridate* and *Iphigénie*. Criticism based on these assumptions have been levelled at it from its first production: that the rôles of Thésée, Hippolyte and Aricie are ineffective; that the Hippolyte/Aricie scenes are insipid and incongruous; that the plot-machinery is arbitrary and not well-integrated with the characters; that the 'récit de Théramène' is unnatural and too ornate; above all, that the rôle of Phèdre is so tremendous that all the other elements seem feeble or tiresome.

Against this, we can emphasise the 'well-made' aspect of the play. Barrault has emphasised that *Phèdre* is a 'tragédie à huit personnages',[1] and has demonstrated its symmetry in terms of plot, character and its pattern of lyrical moments. In Act I, Hippolyte, and then Phèdre, confess their love to their confidants. In Act II, Hippolyte, and then Phèdre, confess their love to those they love. In Act III, Hippolyte and Phèdre 'optent tous deux pour leur passion'.[2] The symmetry of the last two acts is as real, though less obvious: Hippolyte and Phèdre both confess their loves to Thésée, and both die. The lyrical structure is as carefully balanced. Barrault analyses how the *récitatifs* at the high points of the play balance and complement each other. For example, the lines in which Hippolyte swears to marry Aricie (ll. 1392–1406) are a lyrical celebration of their spiritual marriage, and form a pendant to the *oraison funèbre* of the 'récit de Théramène'.

This may show that Racine intended the play to be evenly balanced. It does not prove that he succeeded. To prove this we must find a viewpoint from which the symmetry can be not merely described but felt by actors and audience. A hint of a solution can be found if we attend to a common reply to the criticisms: that the rôle of Phèdre suffices to sustain the play, and that it can do so because it is a masterly psychological study.

We need not doubt that there is profound psychological insight in the play. What we may doubt is whether it is embodied in the rôle of Phèdre in quite the way implied. We may clarify the point by asking a few questions. How old is Phèdre? We must decide for ourselves: the text gives no help.[3] Phèdre meets Thésée when she is sixteen, has two children by the time she is nineteen, and is twenty-one when she dies. This timetable is quite compatible with seventeenth-century tragedy.[4] She is therefore an experienced woman, but still young and attractive – young enough to be a more suitable mate for Hippolyte than for Thésée, who is old enough to be her father. Alternatively, she is a woman in her late forties, her passions reinforced and deranged by the menopause. This also adds point – but a different one – to her situation: it is incongruous, as well as incestuous, that the ageing 'veuve de Thésée ose aimer Hippolyte'. When so much seems to hang on a point on which Racine gives us no certain information, it is clear we are seeking to understand his effects in the wrong way.

Next, what are we to make of Phèdre's feelings for her children? She refers to them often, but Racine presents her affection for them very inconsistently: her concern that they shall inherit the throne motivates her to see Hippolyte before she dies, but her affection does not influence her decision to die, either in Act I or Act V; nor, indeed, does she mention them in her farewell speech to Thésée. The reason is surely that her feeling for her children is irrelevant, and is brought in only when dramatic convenience requires.

This points the contrast between 'psychological insight' in the naturalistic sense (as we find it explained, for instance, in Strindberg's preface to *Miss Julie*) and the quality which we find in *Phèdre*. The naturalist's aim is to explore and express the psychological forces at work on a character conceived as a real human being. He must allow for (and account for) the effect of every element in the character's situation. He can hardly ignore such matters as a woman's age and her attitude to her children. Obviously, Phèdre is not a character in this sense at all. We might suspect this from the preface, which is even more tendentious than most. When Racine defends the character of Phèdre as 'ce que j'ai peut-être mis de plus raisonnable sur le théâtre' (and in this context 'raisonnable' means something very like 'naturalistic') we may surmise that contemporary criticisms that Phèdre showed too much love and too much effrontery had hit him on a very sensitive spot. And contemporaries also made points that later critics with a naturalistic bias should logically make: that Thésée is too rash and credulous, and should have demanded proof from Oenone instead of acting like a character in a tragedy, and that Aricie is the only really well-drawn character. It is true, if we read or see the play, that Aricie, and even Panope, can easily be construed as character-studies. But it is also true (and this comes out very powerfully in performance) that Thésée, despite his extremely improbable behaviour, makes a strikingly impressive tragic figure. Critical assumptions which produce such topsy-turvy results must be wrong. We will try and ask more pertinent questions than Phèdre's age, or what are her feelings for her children, or what rules of evidence Thésée should have followed. Why do 'fuir' and its derivatives appear 38 times, whereas in *Andromaque* (where the plot gives at least as much scope) they appear only 6 times, and in *Iphigénie* (which is longer and in which the heroine's attempted flight is an important part of the plot) no more than 19 times? Why do 'chercher' and 'cacher' also appear so frequently? What use does Racine make of his insipid or pompous neo-classical phrases:

> J'ai couru les deux mers que sépare Corinthe.
>
> De son fatal hymen je cultivais les fruits.
>
> Hercule à désarmer coûtait moins qu'Hippolyte;
> Et vaincu plus souvent, et plus tôt surmonté,
> Préparait moins de gloire aux yeux qui l'ont dompté.
>
> Portant partout le trait dont je suis déchiré.
>
> Je l'adore, et mon âme, à vos ordres rebelle,
> Ne peut ni soupirer ni brûler que pour elle.

In other words, we must concentrate on the words of the text, examining not only the meaning of the words but also the method by which Racine uses his poetic medium to unite different levels in the play. We shall thus pursue the triple contention that Racine is a poetic dramatist; that the basis of his tragedy is a pre-logical intuition of what we should call, in our language, deeply unconscious mental processes; and that the problem which preoccupied him was how to express these eminently uncivilised intuitions through an elegant and relatively naturalistic form. We need therefore to shuttle continuously between an examination of the emotional background of *Phèdre*, the rational structure, and the poetic means by which the two are united.

2

First, let us look briefly at some classical sources. Knight has shown the extent and limits of Racine's hellenism. His Greek scholarship and feeling for Greek literature were exceptional for the seventeenth century, but his plays were further removed from those of the Greeks than he liked in the latter part of his career to pretend. *La Thébaïde* is closer in structure and content to Rotrou (and Seneca) than to Euripides, whom at that stage Racine had probably not read.[5] *Andromaque* bears no resemblance in structure or feeling to Euripides's play on the subject: Racine gives his source as Virgil. The mid-career plays are Roman or Turkish. Much has been made of the Greekness of Monime, but *Mithridate*, with its sentimental and political intrigues, is far removed from fifth-century B.C. tragedy. *Iphigénie* borrows largely from Euripides. But it is the Euripides of 'West-end half tragedy' (Kitto), and *Iphigénie* is just that. Racine's preface dwells on the romantic and sentimental aspects of the play. He is happy to find another Iphigénie who enables him to save his virtuous princess, and so repeat the lachrymose success of Euripides. He uses his knowledge of Greek to decorate his play with ornaments not generally available, and sneers at Perrault, who read *Alcestis* in a Latin translation.

A similarly superficial attitude marks his annotations of the Greek tragic poets. Commonly he is picking out striking thoughts and turns of phrase – a frequent seventeenth-century procedure, but not one that has much to do with a profound understanding of tragedy. The most interesting notes are those which contain his critical remarks, especially on the dramatic machinery: 'Le Pédagogue explique le lieu de la scène, le temps, et le sujet même';[6] 'bel artifice d'instruire le spectateur sans éclaircir l'acteur';[7] 'elle rend raison pourquoi elle est venue sur la scène'.[8] Most of these comments are fairly adverse, especially on Euripides: 'Tout ceci n'est point de l'action';[9] 'la raison n'a pas besoin de longs discours';[10] 'cela devrait être préparé avec bien plus d'éclat';[11] 'Cela est bien brusque';[12] 'repentir trop prompt';[13] 'Cela est bien tiré par les cheveux'.[14] Clearly, Racine is criticising the Greeks from the point of view of the naturalistic well-made play. Is the plot clearly developed, are the *coups-de-théâtre* well prepared, are the reasons given for the characters' exits and entrances adequate, is the psychology convincing, are the long speeches natural? Such an approach is hardly likely to reveal the secret sources of tragedy. Critics have generally exaggerated the importance of the resemblances between Racine and the Greeks at the superficial level of verbal borrowings and subject-matter, and have underemphasised the deeper resemblance, which is an affinity in basic attitudes. It is at this deeper level that we must agree with Knight that, although Racine's closeness to the Greeks is a legend, 'La légende est très près d'être la vérité'.[15]

By contrast, there has often been a tendency to underemphasise the resemblances at both the superficial and the deeper levels between Racine and Seneca. Racine himself seems reluctant to admit them, perhaps because admiration for Seneca was considered bad taste. In the prefaces to *Andromaque* he acknowledges Seneca's influence only indirectly, yet the relationship between his play and Seneca's *Troades* is evident. Andromache's dilemma of having to betray either her son or her dead husband (*Troades*, ll. 642–62) prefigures Andromaque's. In both plays, great poetic and dramatic importance is given to the tomb of Hector. Ulysses's speech in *Troades* (ll. 529–51) explaining that Astyanax must die parallels Oreste's speech on the same subject in *Andromaque* (ll. 151–72); Agamemnon's refusal to sacrifice Polyxena (*Troades*, ll. 279–87) parallels Pyrrhus's refusal to give up Astyanax (*Andromaque*, ll. 197–220). There are numerous verbal parallels: compare *Troades* ll. 281–7 with *Andromaque* ll. 209–20, and *Troades* ll. 478–81 with *Andromaque* ll. 197–204.

In *Phèdre* we can compare directly the influence of Euripides and Seneca. Even if we assume that Racine is basing himself on Euripides's *Hippolytus* and Seneca's *Phaedra*, it is evident that he draws more from the Latin dramatist than the Greek. As Lapp remarks,[16] Racine completely misunderstands *Hippolytus* when he takes the Greek Phaedra as an Aristotelian heroine. *Phèdre* contains many verbal borrowings from Euripides, but leans more heavily on Seneca. Its structure resembles that of the Latin play more closely than that of the Greek: the scenes of Phèdre's avowals to Hippolyte and Thésée are based on Seneca, and the former scene, which is one of the high points of Racine's play, owes a great deal to him.

But the matter becomes clearer still if we look beyond *Hippolytus* and *Phaedra*. In a poetic play, thematic structure is more important than structure of incidents, and there are striking thematic resemblances between *Phèdre* and the Senecan (perhaps spurious) *Hercules Oetaeus*. *Phèdre* differs from both *Hippolytus* and *Phaedra* in many important ways, and when it does so it often resembles *Hercules Oetaeus*. Racine gives an important place to the love of Hippolyte for Aricie, and Phèdre's furious jealousy. There is no hint of this in *Hippolytus* or *Phaedra*; but in *Hercules Oetaeus* Dejanira is consumed by sexual passion for her husband, and is driven to the act that causes his death by frantic jealousy of Iole, who eventually marries Hyllus. Euripides's Phaedra, like Racine's, has a horror of her passion, but she is much more the passive and virtuous victim than Phèdre: she lacks the combination of extreme complicity with and extreme revulsion from her passion which is so important in Racine's play. Seneca's Phaedra, unlike Racine's, is brazen in her love. But his Dejanira, like Phèdre, is physically shaken with horror at her own passion. 'A wandering tremor steals through my shivering limbs, my hair stands up in horror,' says Dejanira.[17] Phèdre echoes her: 'Chaque mot sur mon front fait dresser mes cheveux.' Phèdre despairs at the thought that in Hades she will be judged by her father. Dejanira appeals to her father-in-law Jupiter to punish her,[18] and sees the underworld open before her.[19] In *Phèdre*, a recurrent motif is that of 'monstres', and of Thésée as a second Hercules who purges the earth of monsters. This theme does not appear in *Hippolytus*, and hardly in *Phaedra* (Hercules and his labours are mentioned briefly in the first chorus). It recurs constantly in *Hercules Oetaeus*.[20] In Euripides, Phaedra and Hippolytus never meet. When Seneca's Phaedra confesses her love, Hippolytus threatens to kill her, and she says this would be the fulfilment of her prayer: she will die by his hand with her honour saved. But the comparable moment in *Phèdre* recalls a moment in *Hercules Oetaeus*. Phèdre, having confessed her love to Hippolyte, begs him to kill her, and to be worthy of his father in slaying the monster before him. Dejanira, having confessed to Hyllus the crime against his father to which love has driven her ('scelus est amoris'), implores him in these words: 'Why do you turn away your face? This deed [of killing me] would be goodness . . . Son of Alcides, are you afraid? Will you not do as you are commanded and crush evil creatures, following the example of your father?'.[21]

The point is not, of course, that *Hercules Oetaeus* is the source of *Phèdre*. A masterpiece has no source in this simple sense. But we may reasonably assume that Racine found in Seneca's play themes and phrases which helped to germinate the seeds of *Phèdre*. But the evident links with *Hercules Oetaeus* may at least serve as a reminder that *Phèdre* is more than a thrilling dramatisation of the story of Phaedra and Hippolytus. The play expresses a central meaning. The 'story' is part of the means by which Racine is able to express it.

3

Less than five years before the first production of *Phèdre*, the loves of Thésée, Phèdre and Ariane had been staged with great success in Thomas Corneille's *Ariane*. There are many similarities of phrase and situation between the two plays. I will compare them briefly, not to show that Racine was imitating or improving on Thomas Corneille, but to bring out the difference of his approach.

The plot of *Ariane* is simple. Thésée and Ariane, fleeing from Crete, take refuge at the Court of Oenarus, king of Naxos; Oenarus falls in love with Ariane, who rejects him; Phèdre and Thésée, who are already in love, elope together, leaving Ariane in despair. Pirithoüs, as Thésée's confidant, plays a considerable part in the action.

The touching portrayal of Ariane's grief is the play's main strength, but her role is not all pathos: her rage when she learns of Thésée's infidelity recalls Hermione or Roxane:

> Pour venger votre amour que prétendez-vous faire?
> – L'aller trouver, la voir, et de ma propre main
> Lui mettre, lui plonger un poignard dans le sein.
> Mais, pour mieux adoucir les peines que j'endure,
> Je veux porter le coup aux yeux de mon parjure,
> Et qu'en son coeur les miens pénètrent à loisir
> Ce qu'aura de mortel son affreux déplaisir.
> Tout perfide qu'il est, ma mort suivra la sienne.
>
> (IV.iii)

Thomas Corneille, like Racine, expresses the fatality of love:

> D'un aveugle penchant le charme imperceptible
> Frappe, saisit, entraîne, et rend un coeur sensible;
> Et par une secrète et nécessaire loi,
> On se livre à l'amour sans qu'on sache pourquoi.
>
> (I.i)

In *Ariane*, as in *Phèdre*, there is a sense that passion is inspired from outside, but that once we avow it we become its accomplices and are guilty:

> Mais si ce feu trop prompt n'eut rien de volontaire,
> Il dépendait de moi de parler, ou me taire.
> J'ai parlé, c'est mon crime.
>
> (III.i)

In both plays, then, we find the psychological commonplaces of seventeenth-century French tragedy. The resemblances extend also to matters of detail. Occasionally they are so close that we may suspect that phrases in *Ariane* played a part in forming certain lines in *Phèdre*. When Ariane learns that Thésée loves someone else, she cries out:

> A ma honte partout ma flamme aurait fait bruit,
> Et ma lâche rivale en cueillera le fruit!
>
> (IV.iii)

Her greatest pain is at the thought of her rival's success:

> Peut-être en ce moment aux pieds de ma rivale
> Il rit des vains projets où mon coeur se ravale.
>
> (V.v)

Nevertheless, the differences between the plays are great. Act II of *Ariane* is especially full of situations, motifs, and sometimes verbal patterns, resembling those of *Phèdre*. In Scene i, Ariane is advised by her confidante not to offend Oenarus. She replies by praising Thésée, and expresses displeasure that Phèdre does not also praise him. Here is her praise of Thésée:

> Et puis-je trop l'aimer, quand, tout brillant de gloire,
> Mille fameux exploits l'offrent à ma mémoire?
> De cent monstres par lui l'univers dégagé
> Se voit d'un mauvais sang heureusement purgé.
> Combien, ainsi qu'Hercule, a-t-il pris de victimes!
> Combien vengé de morts! combien puni de crimes!
> Procuste et Cercyon, la terreur des humains,
> N'ont-ils pas succombé sous ses vaillantes mains?

This resembles Hippolyte's praise of his father:

> Tu sais combien mon âme, attentive à ta voix,
> S'échauffait aux récits de ses nobles exploits,
> Quand tu me dépeignais ce héros intrépide
> Consolant les mortels de l'absence d'Alcide,
> Les monstres étouffés et les brigands punis,
> Procuste, Cercyon, et Scirron, et Sinnis,
> Et les os dispersés du géant d'Epidaure,
> Et la Crète fumant du sang du Minotaure.

But the effect of the two passages is different, and the difference is clearly in poetic quality. In Thomas Corneille the passage is banal. Ariane is describing her lover's exploits, and the poet tries to work up a little magnificence by exaggeration ('mille fameux exploits') and decorative classical allusions. Hippolyte's references have a quite different resonance. Ariane's merely embroider a static statement of her love: Hippolyte's show the tension between his active ideal and his timid horror of love, and as he speaks these lines he is trying to hide the second under the cover of the first. The allusions in the passage from Racine are also significant for the world of the play: *Phèdre* is played against a background of mythological monsters and dark powers who destroy human beings even when ostensibly their friends, and whose power continues, even though a hero spends his life slaying them. *Ariane*, on the other hand, has no supernatural background. (Schlegel complained that the rocks of Naxos were smoothed down into a modern drawing-room.) Moreover, the references in *Phèdre* have a bitter significance for the actions of the play. Phèdre's passion is monstrous; Thésée has committed crimes

which ally him to the monsters he has killed; Thésée sees Hippolyte as
a monster comparable to those of which he has purged the earth;
Hippolyte dies when a monster rises from the sea. The superiority of
Racine's lines stems from the multiple significance he makes them convey.
In contrast, Thomas Corneille is merely trying to lend elegance to a
flat statement. We have here the contrast between a poetic drama in
which poetry does the dramatic work, and a naturalistic drama in which
it is fancy dress. We may say that Racine wrote poetic plays because he
was a good poet. It might be better to say that his dramatic poetry is
good because it serves a dramatic purpose.

Method cannot be divorced from content, and the content of the
scene from *Ariane* is banal. As written, it has pathos, but it could so easily
seem different. The basic situation of *Ariane* – faithless lover, trusting
mistress, knowing maid, intriguing flirt, honest but rejected lover –
could easily come from a Restoration comedy, and so could the more
emotional scenes. *The Relapse*, for instance, accommodates scenes of
sentiment, and *Ariane* is at its best when it stays within this modest
range. The comparison is worth making, not to disparage *Ariane*, but
to emphasise two points. First, despite political and religious differences
(and differences in the progress of science) there is a basic similarity in
the literary attitudes current in Louis XIV's France and Restoration
England, which helps to explain resemblances between the two theatrical forms. Secondly, *Ariane* could be transposed into a Restoration
comedy without being utterly destroyed: it would be a transposition,
not a burlesque. This would certainly not be possible with *Phèdre*.

Our next point of comparison between the two plays is Act II,
Scene iv of *Ariane*, between Ariane and Thésée. He has decided not to
marry her, but she as yet has no inkling of this. She suggests that
Pirithoüs should marry Phèdre. Thésée cannot bring himself to tell her
the truth. The scene, then, is one of intending, but failing, to reveal a
painful secret. There is a parallel in Act IV of *Phèdre*, when Phèdre
comes to confess to Thésée and so save Hippolyte. Phèdre's verse
expresses her inner tension, but is firm and controlled. Racine admits one
interrupted sentence ('Neptune vous la doit! Quoi? vos voeux irrités
. . .'), but the sense is clear, and from that point the verse is as articulate as ever. The poetic effort goes into expressing the meaning. Thomas
Corneille's method is different:

> Mais, Madame, le roi . . . Vous savez qu'il vous aime.
> S'il faut . . .
>   – Je vous entends: le roi trop combattu
> Peut laisser à l'amour séduire sa vertu.

Cet inquiet souci ne saurait me déplaire;
Et, pour le dissiper, je sais ce qu'il faut faire.
– C'en est trop . . . Mon coeur . . . Dieux!
                          – Que ce trouble m'est doux!
Ce qu'il vous fait sentir, je me le dis pour vous.
Je me dis . . .
              – Plût aux dieux! vous sauriez la contrainte . . .
– Encore un coup, perdez cette jalouse crainte:
J'en connais le remède; et, si l'on m'ose aimer,
Vous n'aurez pas longtemps à vous en alarmer.
–Minos peut vous poursuivre, et si de sa vengeance . . .
– Et n'ai-je pas en vous une sûre défense?
– Elle est sûre, il est vrai; mais . . .
                          – Achevez.
                                  – J'attends . . .
– Ce désordre me gêne, et dure trop longtemps.
Expliquez-vous enfin.
              – Je le veux, et ne l'ose.

Superficially, this resembles ll. 621–4 of *Bérénice*, when Titus fails to tell Bérénice she must leave. But in the Racinian passage only one line (l. 623) is incoherent. The words that Titus does get out ('Rome . . . l'Empire') are key words, and the moment of incoherence is only a moment: in the play as a whole the emotion is precisely articulated. In *Ariane*, the passage is much longer, and the incoherence is truly incoherent. It shows clearly the technique to which we have long been used in drama: incoherence in place of expressiveness; incoherence justified as natural in the circumstances; and the assumption by the dramatist that the audience can construct its own meaning out of what it infers the characters are thinking. This method is basic to *Ariane*. The last words which Thésée speaks in the play are symptomatic. Phèdre agrees to flee with him. He replies: 'En vain . . .' Phèdre breaks in with a brisk: 'Le temps se perd quand nous en consultons.' We never know what Thésée was going to say. From that 'En vain . . .' it would be difficult to guess.

Just how far this method is basic to *Ariane* appears near the end of Act II, when Ariane (who does not know that Phèdre is her rival) first laments to Phèdre Thésée's unfaithfulness. Her first line on learning she has a rival is again echoed in *Phèdre*:

Ah! ma soeur, savez-vous ce qu'on me vient d'apprendre?

After telling Phèdre the news, she begins the first of those speeches of grief and despair on which most of the play's effect depends. Or, rather, Thomas Corneille tries to write such a speech, but by the fifth line has got no further than flatness:

> Et personne jamais n'a tant aimé que moi.

This obviously will not do, so he tries a tactic that has since made its way in the world:

> Se peut-il qu'un héros d'une vertu sublime
> Souille ainsi . . . Quelquefois le remords suit le crime.
> Si le sien lui faisait sentir ces durs combats . . .
> Ma soeur, au nom des dieux, ne m'abandonnez pas.

Here we have inarticulacy as a substitute for poetry. The inference is that Ariane would have said more, were not her heart too full for rhetoric. How natural – but now different from Racine. At the end of Act IV of *Phèdre*, we may allow that Phèdre is as full of strong and conflicting emotions as Ariane, but Racine does not take refuge in inarticulacy: his poetry becomes more evocative, more densely packed with meaning – more articulate, not less. This is the method of the poetic dramatist, but not of Thomas Corneille.

As a final example of how he achieves his not inconsiderable effects, we may take the last part of Act II, Scene vi, of *Ariane*. Ariane sends Phèdre to plead with Thésée on her behalf. If you were in love, she says,

> Vous trouveriez bien mieux le chemin de son coeur;
> Vous auriez plus d'adresse à lui faire l'image
> De mes confus transports de douleur et de rage:
> Tous les traits en seraient plus vivement tracés.
> N'importe; essayez tout: parlez, priez, pressez.
> Au défaut de l'amour, puisqu'il n'a pu vous plaire,
> Votre amitié pour moi fera ce qu'il faut faire.
> Allez, ma soeur; courez empêcher mon trépas.

The parallel is with Act III, Scene i of *Phèdre*, where Phèdre sends Oenone to plead with Hippolyte. Obviously, the superiority of Racine is a superiority of poetry. (We may also compare the use Thomas Corneille makes of 'le chemin de mon coeur' with the use Racine makes of it in another passage.) But, again, this superiority goes with the importance of the words in the pattern of *Phèdre* – an importance which we shall discuss later. In *Ariane*, the focus of interest is not the words but the situation. Ariane is asking Phèdre to plead for her, and Phèdre is her rival. Thomas Corneille underlines this twice in twelve lines. Great artistry in words is unnecessary for the effect here: all they need do is to convey information and the general emotional tone and to point to the drama inherent in the situation.

I have pursued *Ariane* far enough for the conclusion to be clear. Not only is the play naturalistic in method (and to an extent which shows how far the commonplace devices of naturalistic drama had become the staple of French tragedy), but the content is perforce scaled down to suit naturalistic resources: none of the happenings or emotions involved in the action calls for a stronger or more precise means of expression than inarticulate or low-pressure verse. The verse can be feeble because it has so little to do.

In all this, *Ariane* is the antithesis of *Phèdre*. We can sharpen the contrast still further by pointing to another feature of *Ariane*, irony:

> Certes, l'avis est rare! et si j'ose vous croire,
> Un noble changement me va combler de gloire!
>
> (II.v)
>
> Un héros tel que vous, à qui la gloire est chère,
> Quoiqu'il fasse, ne fait que ce qu'il voit à faire;
> Et si ce qu'on me dit a quelque vérité,
> Vous cessez de m'aimer, je l'aurai mérité.
>
> (III.iv)

There is little of this irony in *Phèdre*. It makes a fleeting appearance in Act V, Scene iii, in Thésée's confrontation with Aricie, but not at any of the high points of the play. In *Phèdre*, the emotion is fully brought out in the text: that is, it is presented directly and seriously, and there is no need for this evasive irony.

I cannot now avoid taking a plunge. In some superficial ways, *Ariane* is very similar to *Phèdre*. It has the simplicity of action, the tenderness, even some of the ferocious psychological insight, to which Racine's superiority has been attributed. But *Phèdre* is not a superior *Ariane*: it is different in kind. We shall never identify or appreciate this difference if we discuss the minutiae of plot, or characterisation, or even verse – though the verse gives a clue to the difference. *Ariane* is insignificant because it signifies nothing. If we are still fascinated by *Phèdre*, it is because it means something of importance to us, and it is able to mean something of importance only because Racine's means of expression enabled him to express it. We have already indicated where in our view the source of this meaning lies: in the workings of the unconscious mind, to which the plays of Racine appeal and those of his contemporaries by and large do not.

4

Phèdre, more than any other of Racine's plays, has lent itself to Freudian interpretations. Turnell notes that 'we are more aware in "Phèdre" than in any of the other plays of the workings of the unconscious with its complexes, repressions and sense of guilt'.[22] I want here, however, to confine myself for the moment to two aspects of the play which perhaps recall more the Kleinian picture of the early mental life of children, with its preoccupation with body fluids (and especially urine and faeces) and with its terrifying inner world (Hell) of persecutory objects. This is not, of course, to imply that these psychoanalytical interpretations are 'true', and that they 'explain' *Phèdre*. This would be only a more sophisticated version of the older view that the play is a psychological study. My purpose is to draw attention to aspects of the play which are unexpected in a French classical tragedy, and which emphasise the power and strangeness of the emotional elements in it.

Phèdre is full of references to body fluids:

> Me nourrissant de fiel, de larmes abreuvée,
> Encor dans mon malheur de trop près observée,
> Je n'osais dans mes pleurs me noyer à loisir.

The exaggeration of 'dans mes pleurs me *noyer* à loisir' is not what we might expect from the impeccably tasteful Racine invented by some critics, but it is characteristic of the play, and we shall see later that it has a purpose in his design.

The commonest reference is to 'sang'. In itself, the word can be banal:

> au plus beau sang de la Grèce et des Dieux.

But two features make it significant in *Phèdre*: the extraordinary number of times it is used, and the way it is used. Racine writes, conventionally enough:

> Phèdre est d'un sang, Seigneur, vous le savez trop bien

but goes on:

> De toutes ces horreurs *plus rempli* que le mien.

In the first line, 'blood' is simply 'family'; but in the second, 'filled' gives it back its full force as a physical fluid. A few lines later, Phèdre implores Thésée, again with the greatest banality:

> Respectez votre sang, j'ose vous en prier

249

but goes on:

> Sauvez-moi de l'horreur de l'entendre crier.

Delicate critics have reproved this image. The phrasing might be
more elegant, but Racine is here not concerned with elegance. He is
emphasising the savage reality of 'blood' (not 'family'), which he does
by using the primitive Old Testament image; and by yoking it so
violently with 'horreur' he not only underlines his purpose but also
echoes with a hideous (tragic, not sarcastic) irony, Hippolyte's primness:

> Je me tais. Cependant Phèdre sort d'une mère,
> Phèdre est d'un sang, Seigneur, vous le savez trop bien,
> De toutes ces horreurs plus rempli que le mien.

Again and again Racine uses 'sang' in some banal phrase and yet
contrives to give it physical actuality. Thésée wishes to flee the 'sang-
lante image' of his son: conventional in itself, the phrase has a sickening
reality when we remember the details:

> Tout son corps n'est bientôt qu'une plaie . . .
> De son généreux *sang* la trace nous conduit;
> Les rochers en sont teints; les ronces dégouttantes
> Portent de ses cheveux les dépouilles *sanglantes*.

Thésée will not himself shed Hippolyte's blood, but his disclaimer
evokes the picture of fingers dabbling in blood:

> en mon sang ma main n'a point trempé

an image that Phèdre will use with even greater concreteness:

> Mes homicides mains, promptes à me venger,
> Dans le sang innocent brûlent de se plonger.

We now come to the directly excremental references in *Phèdre*. In
psychoanalytic terms, loose motions, flatus and urine are burning and
destructive. Excrement is '*dirty*', and a whole complex of ideas is
associated with dirtying or smearing (in the literal or metaphorical
sense), and with absolute purity or vigorous cleansing. These ideas are
strongly present in *Phèdre*, and are often phrased in such a way that the
link with urine, flatus or faeces is clear:

> la Crète *fumant* du sang du Minotaure
> Moi, que j'ose opprimer et *noircir* l'innocence!
> D'un perfide ennemi j'ai *purgé* la nature.
> Pour parvenir au but de ses *noires* amours

Reste *impur* des brigands dont j'ai *purgé* la terre
Sans que ta mort encor, honteuse à ma mémoire,
De mes nobles travaux vienne *souiller* la gloire.
De ton horrible aspect *purge* tous mes Etats.
Et toi, Neptune, et toi, si jadis mon courage
D'infâmes assassins *nettoya* ton rivage . . .
Un effroyable cri, sorti *du fond des flots*
Et du sein de la terre une voix formidable
Repond en *gémissant* à ce cri redoutable.
Cependant sur le dos de *la plaine liquide*
S'élève à *gros bouillons une montagne humide*;
L'onde approche, se brise, et vomit à nos yeux,
Parmi des *flots d'écume*, un monstre furieux . . .
La terre *s'en émeut*, l'air en est *infecté*.

The last three of these quotations link up with another motif: the insistence on the sea, and especially its waves. Oenone (a detail not from Euripides or Seneca, but from the obscure Gilbert) drowns herself. Thésée (another detail which tradition did not oblige Racine to use) is, early in the play, rumoured to have been drowned ('Les flots ont englouti cet époux infidèle'). Racine brings in this motif at the cost of some verbal oddities:

Lorsque de notre Crète il traversa les flots.

The waves of the sea are a banal symbol of passion. In the context in which Racine sets these references, they seem to me another indication of the depth of the mental forces involved, as though explosive infantile passions are breaking out.

Against these violent and guilt-obsessed motifs are set the relief of micturition:

Mes jours moins agités coulaient dans l'innocence.

or a prudish insistence on absolute purity:

Hélas, quand son épée allait chercher mon sein,
A-t-il pâli pour moi? me l'a-t-il arrachée?
Il suffit que ma main l'ait une fois touchée.
Je l'ai rendu horrible à ses yeux inhumains;
Et ce fer malheureux profanerait ses mains.

et que jamais une bouche si pure
Ne s'ouvre pour conter cette horrible aventure.

The astonishing thing is that these violent contrasts are contained by the verse; and this is the source of some of Racine's most extraordinary effects. Excrement equals burning equals flames; excrement equals dirt equals blackness. Racine crystallises all these into a phrase borrowed from La Pinelière: 'une flamme si noire'. Superficially, this is nonsense. Here, it strikes home because in this context the ideas behind 'flamme' and 'noire' are related. Racine can also contain contraries within a perfect serenity. The role of Phèdre, and almost the play, ends with this perfectly harmonious expression of opposites:

> Et la mort, à mes yeux dérobant la clarté,
> Rend au jour, qu'ils souillaient, toute sa pureté.

If excremental motifs are prominent in *Phèdre*, cannibalistic motifs are hardly less so:

> Le fer moissonna tout, et la terre humectée
> But à regret le sang des neveux d'Erechthée.

> Qu'un soin bien différent me trouble et me dévore!

> Ah! plutôt que du ciel la flamme me dévore!

> Livré par ce barbare à des monstres cruels
> Qu'il nourrissaient du sang des malheureux mortels

> A ses monstres *lui-même a servi de pâture.*

This last line is not a mere picturesque detail. It prepares (and, in retrospect, reinforces) a similar motif introduced at the death of Hippolyte:

> Traîné par les chevaux que sa main a nourris.

This bloodthirsty devouring is a key motif in the play, and links up with Racine's emphasis on physical dismemberment. We have already quoted the clinical details of what happened to Hippolyte. Phèdre's description of her sacrifices is equally insistent on the physical facts:

> De victimes moi-même à toute heure entourée,
> Je cherchais dans leurs flancs ma raison égarée.

Racine's willingness to evoke the physical facts with the utmost directness enables him to give a terrible concreteness to worn metaphors. 'Phèdre is a prey to her passions'; 'Death will not give up its prey' – these are banalities. But in a text full of blood and devouring and the heaped-up corpses of victims, these phrases take on a horrifying reality:

> C'est Vénus tout entière à sa proie attachée
> Et l'avare Achéron ne lâche point sa proie.

The importance of the underworld is touched on several times in the play, and the association of Thésée with the underworld is important to the theme. The most dreadful element in the emotional atmosphere of the play is that Hell is inside, and this breaks out with anguished intensity at a key point in the action:

> Où me cacher? Fuyons dans la nuit infernale.
> Mais que dis-je? mon père ye tient l'urne fatale;
> Le sort, dit-on, l'a mise en ses sévères mains:
> Minos juge aux enfers tous les pâles humains.
> Ah! combien frémira son ombre épouvantée,
> Lorsqu'il verra sa fille à ses yeux présentée,
> Contrainte d'avouer tant de forfaits divers
> Et des crimes, peut-être inconnus aux enfers!
> Que diras-tu, mon père, à ce spectacle horrible?
> Je crois voir de ta main tomber l'urne terrible,
> Je crois te voir, cherchant un supplice nouveau,
> Toi-même de ton sang devenir le bourreau.
> Pardonne. Un Dieu cruel a perdu ta famille:
> Reconnais sa vengeance aux fureurs de ta fille.
> Hélas! du crime affreux dont la honte me suit
> Jamais mon triste coeur n'a recueilli le fruit.
> Jusqu'au dernier soupir, de malheurs poursuivie,
> Je rends dans les tourments une pénible vie.

All the contradictory ideas and impulses are nakedly expressed. Phèdre wishes to hide, to flee, as though she could dissociate herself from her guilt. But projection merely means that the world outside appears full of pain and menace, so that there is no escape. Her father, who should love her, becomes her executioner. She disclaims responsibility, which she imputes to an external 'Dieu'. Because the evil (though projected) is internal, there is no escape except in death. Nevertheless – and here Racine boldly goes beyond the pretence that Phèdre's emotion at this point is simply remorse – the projected and disowned passions are acknowledged, and only their lack of fulfilment is deplored ('Jamais mon triste coeur n'a recueilli le fruit'). Finally, if we disregard for a moment the surface meaning and attend to what Racine is saying in the order in which he says it, we find something revealing. The underlying logic is that Phèdre in despair tries to flee, finds herself nevertheless arraigned as guilty, and then is tormented until she dies ('Je rends dans les tourments une pénible vie'). But this is at odds with the surface meaning, which is that death takes her to Hades, where her punishment begins, and from which death cannot deliver her. A common neo-classical proceeding (for example, as in Boileau's *Ode sur la Prise de Namur*) is for the poet to pretend to be disordered by enthusiasm but nevertheless to maintain a procession of logical ideas. Racine inverts the proceeding. He follows the illogical movement of the passions, but covers them with a more or less logical façade – in this case, Phèdre talks of torments and Hell and then of torments and dying, but the surface logic is that she will die first and be tormented afterwards. If we examine the speech from the standpoint of our rational waking selves, the assemblage of contradictory ideas is close to nonsense. But this never occurs to us if we respond to the lines. At the level on which Racinian tragedy is based, our minds do not follow this waking logic.

If we attend to this level in *Phèdre*, and for the moment suspend our conscious prejudices, we can throw some light on two difficulties in the play.

One is the rôle of Oenone. To a seventeenth-century audience, the fact that Oenone was *servile* doubtless explained her conduct, and allowed Racine to dismiss her so cavalierly in Acts IV and V. Although he no doubt shared this social prejudice, as well as being willing to make use of it, a modern audience is tempted to adopt another one. Oenone is activated by devotion to Phèdre. Her plight is pathetic ('Mon pays, mes enfants, pour vous j'ai tout quitté'). Her attitude to sexual deviation and the gods may seem humane and sensible:

> La faiblesse aux humains n'est que trop naturelle . . .
> Mortelle, subissez le sort d'une mortelle.
> Vous vous plaignez d'un joug imposé dès longtemps.
> Les Dieux mêmes, les Dieux, de l'Olympe habitants,
> Qui d'un bruit si terrible épouvantent les crimes,
> Ont brûlé quelquefois de feux illégitimes.

If we were to apply to the play the criteria we apply in twentieth-century life, we should find something odious in Phèdre's bland shuffling off of guilt onto Oenone: 'La détestable Oenone a conduit tout le reste.' Why is it we do not find this distasteful in the play when performed? The answer begins to become clear if we think of the close connection between Phèdre and Oenone:

> Mais quel nouveau malheur trouble sa chère Oenone?
> N'allons point plus avant. Demeurons, chère Oenone.
> Je t'avoûrai de tout; je n'espère qu'en toi.
> Va: j'attends ton retour pour disposer de moi.
> Fais ce que tu voudras, je m'abandonne à toi.
> Dans le trouble où je suis, je ne puis rien pour moi.

The answer becomes obvious when we link this with an element which we remarked in connection with Phèdre's delirium in Act IV (and which we shall see is important for the play as a whole): the violent attempts by Phèdre to split off, project and deny the passions that torment her. There is a level in *Phèdre* – an important level – at which it is pointless to try to argue about the relationships of the characters as if they were real people. At this level, Oenone is not just Phèdre's confidante – she represents the opportunistic Phèdre who is in complicity with her passion, and which the tormented Phèdre can both make use of and repudiate.

We can go further along this path, and consider a second difficulty: the rôle of Aricie. From one point of view, her rôle is a weakness: not because she is not a carefully-observed character (in some ways she is the most naturalistically portrayed) but because she appears pale beside Phèdre. This viewpoint soon leads us to place all the value of the play in the rôle of Phèdre, and regard all the rest as scaffolding. This runs contrary to our experience of the play as acted, and later on we shall try and show that it makes nonsense of the clear pattern of the play. As a preliminary, we can look for the significance of Aricie at the pre-logical level we are now examining. The clue is the famous passage in which her predatory nature is stressed:

> J'aime, je l'avoûrai, cet orgueil généreux
> Qui jamais n'a fléchi sous le joug amoureux.
> Phèdre en vain s'honorait des soupirs de Thésée:
> Pour moi, je suis plus fière, et fuis la gloire aisée
> D'arracher un hommage à mille autres offert,
> Et d'entrer dans un coeur de toutes parts ouvert.
> Mais de faire fléchir un courage inflexible,
> De porter la douleur dans une âme insensible,
> D'enchaîner un captif de ses fers étonné,
> Contre un joug qui lui plaît vainement mutiné:
> C'est là ce que je veux, c'est là ce qui m'irrite.
> Hercule à désarmer coûtait moins qu'Hippolyte,
> Et vaincu plus souvent, et plus tôt surmonté,
> Préparait moins de gloire aux yeux qui l'ont dompté.

Let us insert some of the more striking phrases in these lines among their analogues in the rest of the play. 'Qui jamais n'a fléchi sous le joug amoureux' recalls Phèdre's prayer to Venus: 'Hippolyte te fuit, et bravant ton courroux, | Jamais à tes autels n'a fléchi les genoux.' Aricie's 'Et d'entrer dans un coeur de toutes parts ouvert' and 'De porter la douleur dans une âme insensible' recall other metaphors of wounding:

Hippolyte's 'Portant partout le trait dont je suis déchiré' and Phèdre's 'Ton triomphe est parfait: tous tes traits ont porté.' Aricie's 'Préparait moins de gloire aux yeux qui l'ont dompté' recalls the second mention of Venus in the play: 'Quels courages Vénus n'a-t-elle point domptés?', and is echoed by Thésée's bitter sarcasm: 'Vos yeux ont su dompter ce rebelle courage.' This last line takes up Aricie's 'fléchir un courage inflexible' and Phèdre's 'Attaque un ennemi qui te soit plus rebelle' and 'Ce farouche ennemi qu'on ne pouvait dompter'. We may also remember the first reference to Aricie in the play:

> Hippolyte en partant fuit une autre *ennemie*:
> Je fuis, je l'avoûrai, cette jeune Aricie,
> Reste d'*un sang fatal* conjuré contre nous.

The linking of Phèdre and Aricie as enemies of Hippolyte, and the reference to Aricie's membership of a hostile family, state plainly the hostility latent in Racine's presentation of the Hippolyte/Aricie relationship. Hippolyte's real 'enemy' is a goddess; and Aricie explicitly links him with Hercules, the classical example of a hero hounded by the wrath of a goddess.

At this level of the play, Aricie is Hippolyte's enemy: Venus. This is underlined by the sinister undertones of some of the phrases in the speech we have quoted (and furnishes further examples of how Racine takes the banal conceits of gallantry and invests them with a poetically powerful meaning). To say that a mistress 'conquers' or 'tames' her lover is a commonplace, but the commonplaces take on a darker colouring when associated with the terrible Venus of the play. 'D'arracher un hommage' and 'porter la douleur' are distinctly sinister if we think of 'Vénus tout entière à sa proie attachèe'. Hippolyte calls himself (l. 557) an 'offering' to Aricie. This also is banal, until we remember the offerings by Phèdre to Venus ('De victimes moi-même à toute heure entourée'). The Venus who attaches herself to her prey is a nightmare, an incubus. There is an interesting double-entendre in Aricie's use of 'surmonté'. In the sense of 'conquered', this suggests a perverse (and destructive) dominion of the woman over the man. In the sense of 'surmounted' it suggests the reversal of the traditional 'missionary' position in sexual intercourse. This, in another context, would be amiable enough: but in the context here the implied preference for the reversed position links Aricie with the classical 'incubi' who were believed to ride men ('soumis', 'apprivoisé') in this way. In other words, Aricie is the destructive aspect of Venus. The stress on her purity is another example in the play of the splitting-off and denial of violent emotions. In a sense, Aricie kills Hippolyte (ostensibly, Phèdre's move to save him is stopped by the news that he loves Aricie), and the monster is her unacknowledged violent aspect. The 'récit de Théramène' places the two halves side by side: after the monster has caused the death of Hippolyte, 'La timide Aricie est alors arrivée', and her purpose, as Venus in her destructive aspect, is to consummate her marriage with him, which equals death:

> Elle venait, Seigneur, fuyant votre courroux,
> A la face des Dieux l'accepter pour époux.

The point is not that Aricie is 'really' Venus: it is no part of our purpose to regard *Phèdre* as a sort of crossword puzzle for solving. What is important is that *Phèdre* cannot be understood at the level of plot, character and verse: underneath all this there is a deeper, poetic level at which different laws operate. Characters and events merge and decompose and shift in the service of an otherwise inexpressible meaning. This is the level which so many critics have neglected, but which we have to attend to in trying to understand Racine. At this level, Aricie is neither a tiresome plot-device nor merely a concession to a French taste for amorous heroes and heroines: she is a significant element in the poetic pattern.

We have considered here passions and procedures which lie near the roots of poetry. But in Racine's day poetry (officially, at least) was ruled by very different processes. We shall now return to this rational world.

5

There is a lot of politics in 'Phèdre'. Thésée keeps under surveillance the heiress (Aricie) of a collateral line which has challenged his claim to the throne. When he is reported dead, there are thus three claimants to the throne: this heiress, his eldest son (Hippolyte), and his eldest son by Phèdre, his second queen (ll. 325–30). The characters take politics seriously. Hippolyte suggests partition of Thésée's dominions (ll. 505–8). Phèdre seeks an interview with him, allegedly to press her son's claims (ll. 355–61). When Thésée returns, Phèdre feels that Hippolyte's loyalty to his king will make him reveal the truth (l. 847). Hippolyte, when he has been banished, suggests to Aricie that they should join their claims and appeal for support to Athens and Sparta (ll. 1365–70). At the very end of the play, Thésée adopts Aricie as his daughter, despite her family's past intrigues.

All this can be substantiated in detail from the text, but when we think of *Phèdre* the political element hardly crosses our minds. The politics may be important for the mechanics of the plot, but they do not play an important part in the effect which the tragedy has on us.

It has often been remarked that the plot of *Phèdre* seems to depend on external happenings. At the end of Act I, news arrives of Thésée's death, and Phèdre decides not to kill herself but to approach Hippolyte. At the end of Act II, 'un héraut chargé des volontés d'Athènes' arrives to settle part of the political issue, and Théramène hears a rumour that Thésée may be alive. In Act III, just as Phèdre surrenders to her passion, Thésée reappears. It is as though Racine were constantly relying on external happenings to move his plot along.

But things are more complicated than that: the preparation and motivation of even important moves in the plot are left vague. We have already noted the doubt surrounding Phèdre's attitude to her children: the theme of 'Phèdre's children' is taken up and dropped with such nonchalance that we cannot believe Racine took it very seriously. I shall take one instance where this theme is invoked to bring about a move essential to the play: Phèdre's decision to approach Hippolyte. The motivation is apparently clear: she consents to live, and to see Hippolyte, in order to plead the claims of her son:

> J'oublie, en le voyant, ce que je viens lui dire.
> – Souvenez-vous d'un fils qui n'espère qu'en vous.

Clearly, the alleged motive is a façade: but why does Racine bother with a façade? To make Phèdre appear more sympathetic, perhaps? This can hardly be the whole story. The mention of Phèdre's children by Thésée points up the nature of her passion: having had intercourse with the father, she now wants it with his son. If Racine was looking for an innocent reason for Phèdre to meet Hippolyte, one lay ready to hand: Hippolyte, in accordance with convention, has to present himself before her for a formal leave-taking. In fact, Racine has already told us in Act I that this is what will happen:

> Ne verrez-vous point Phèdre avant que de partir,
> Seigneur?
>   – C'est mon dessein: tu peux l'en avertir.
> Voyons-la, puisqu'ainsi mon devoir me l'ordonne.

The meeting is carefully prepared, but this offering of two unrelated reasons should warn us that Racine is not concerned merely with the interaction of the characters.

The clearest example of this is in Act IV. Superficially, the chain of cause and effect is quite rational: Oenone accuses Hippolyte; Hippolyte fails to defend himself convincingly; Thésée curses him; Phèdre comes to defend him; she does not, because she hears that he loves Aricie. Here we have the arousal of suspense, the to-and-fro of dramatic forces, the 'Will Hippolyte clear himself, will Phèdre save him?' plot-line. This is the dramatic system which contemporaries expected: they correctly perceived that Racine had not used it. Subligny complained that Thésée did not make proper enquiries before accusing Hippolyte. Dryden complained that Racine had 'missed in essentials', making Hippolyte 'too nice' (scrupulous) to reveal the truth (preface to *All for Love*). This last point was taken up by nineteenth-century critics, who pointed out that Euripides had given Hippolytus a pretext for not revealing the truth (he had promised not to). Obviously, Racine could have invented some compelling reason. If he did not bother, there is a good reason for it. I shall suggest later what this reason is.

Contemporary critics might equally well have made a third criticism of the same kind. We are repeatedly assured that Neptune will infallibly grant Thésée's prayer. There can therefore be no doubt that from his appeal in l. 1073 onwards Hippolyte is irrevocably doomed. It is useless for Hippolyte to defend himself, for Phèdre to contemplate confessing, for Aricie to plead with Thésée, even for Thésée to revoke his curse. From l. 1073 to the entry of Théramène at l. 1487 the plot is only apparently concerned with whether Hippolyte will die. That is, Racine is only apparently following the neo-classical prescription for a series of scenes which accelerate or retard the dénouement. The end of Act IV of *Phèdre* is certainly the highest point of the play, but it is occupied by a pathos, a crisis of emotion, not by a tightening of suspense.

What happens in IV.v and IV.vi requires careful definition. It is certainly not a revelation of character. What can we be said to learn about anyone's character from these two scenes? We have indeed a résumé of all Phèdre's traits: her subservience to passion, her shame at this, her intolerance of a rival, her feelings of guilt and contamination, her sense that her exalted family is partly a cause and partly an aggravation of her shame, her tendency to blame Oenone for everything. But all these are quite evident from earlier parts of the play. And why does Racine top his climax by making Phèdre denounce Oenone? Is it this trait in Phèdre's character which he wants to impress upon us at the supreme moment of his play?

I leave this point until our examination of the themes of the play. For the present, I need only emphasise how the treatment of the climactic moment of the play demonstrates Racine's curious handling of his plot. It is not enough to say that the adventitious happenings in *Phèdre* show the 'return of the romanesque' (Brunetière), or that the plot is subordinated to the characters. What we have is something more interesting, which we found was so marked in *Andromaque*: the sense that the plot and the characters are somehow free-floating – running parallel to the action rather than embodying it.

There is a similar tendency in other features of the play: the morality and the mythology.

In his preface, Racine is at pains to emphasise how full his play is of moral lessons: a very school of virtue. Arnauld was indeed gullible if he believed this. A rigid rule of neo-classical criticism was that moral justice should be done, and Butler has clearly demonstrated that in failing to observe it Racine was profoundly at odds with his contemporaries.[23] In *Ariane*, Thésée is made to predict that he will suffer for abandoning Ariane and eloping with Phèdre:

> Je le crois comme vous, le ciel est juste; un jour
> Vous me verrez puni de ce perfide amour.
>
> (III. iv)

In *Phèdre*, the general effect is certainly not edifying. Théramène and Oenone unhesitatingly advise their patrons to indulge their passions, and Phèdre regrets bitterly, not just that she has loved incestuously, but that the affair has not been consummated. Nor is this merely the weakness of human nature: the gods are also presented as quite unmoral. Hippolyte thinks otherwise ('Sur l'équité des Dieux osons nous confier'), but the event does not justify his optimism. Everyone else in the play attributes moral enormities to them. Oenone reflects on their incestuous tastes (ll. 1304–6); Théramène says their anger, not Thésée's, has killed Hippolyte (l. 1569); Phèdre repeatedly attributes her passion to Venus (ll. 277–8, 813–22, 1289, 1625); Thésée realises they are inexorable; Aricie emphasises they are merciless (ll. 1435–8). A few shreds of the conventional attitude remain: Oenone remarks laconically that she has deserved Phèdre's curses (l. 1328); Aricie implies that the automatic way in which the gods execute their promises is a means of balancing the moral books (l. 1438). In short, we have another example of Racine's dual method: the universe of *Phèdre* is flagrantly unmoral, but he occasionally offers a sop to conventional morality.

Finally, there is a similar equivocation in his treatment of mythology. He congratulates himself in his preface for his success in conserving 'la vraisemblance de l'histoire, sans rien perdre des ornements de la fable, qui fournit extrêmement à la poésie'. It is not always a good sign when Racine congratulates himself ('j'ai été heureux de trouver dans les anciens cette autre Iphigénie'), and here he is papering over an awkward crack. There is no problem about using mythology as a stock of metaphors, but when mythological events form part of the action itself the dramatist must decide whether to present them as real or not. Here, as in *Iphigénie*, though for a more profound purpose, Racine is ambiguous. He adopts the rationalising explanation that Thésée visited Epirus, not Hades, but he undoubtedly makes serious use of the allusion to the underworld. His equivocation comes out clearly in a single couplet:

> Moi-même, il m'enferma dans des cavernes sombres,
> Lieux profonds, et voisins de l'empire des ombres.

In the latter part of the play, he is bolder: Hippolyte is certainly killed as a result of the appearance of a monster sent by Neptune. Once again, Racine is paying lip-service to the neo-classical conventions when he conveniently can, but is all the time pursuing a purpose which is fundamentally at odds with them.

We may see more clearly what he was doing if we compare him with an English neo-classic in whom purity of doctrine was unhindered by genius. In 1707, Edmund Smith produced his *Phaedra and Hippolytus*, in which he undertook to improve Racine in accordance with the most correct principles of neo-classicism, culled mainly from the French critics. ('There was not a tract of credit, upon that subject,' we are told, 'which he had not diligently examined, from Aristotle down to Hedelin and Bossu',[24] As a result, the play stands Racine's (and the Greek myth) on its head: Hippolytus survives his stepmother's calumny. Theseus draws attention to his own superiority to Thésée:

> Then learn from me, ye kings that rule the world:
> With equal poize let steady justice sway,
> And flagrant crimes with certain vengeance pay,
> But till the proofs are clear, the stroke delay.

and Hippolytus ends the play with a vigorous rebuttal of Racine's morality:

> The righteous gods, that innocence require,
> Protect the goodness which themselves inspire;
> Unguarded virtue human art defies,
> Th'accus'd is happy, while th'accuser dies.

Myth is confined to the rôle of ornament, and the action of the play is thoroughly rationalised. At the beginning, Theseus is away leading his army 'To meet the numerous troops of fierce Molossians'; at the end, there is no need for a monster from the sea. But Smith furnishes his play with what is lacking, or only apparently present, in *Phèdre*: a villain, who receives exemplary punishment, and a great deal of political byplay.

Perhaps enough has now been said to demonstrate the discontinuities in *Phèdre*. Three features are cardinal to orthodox neo-classical dramaturgy: plot is a rational sequence of events proceeding from cause to effect and producing suspense; an agreed code of conventional morality is observed and explicitly supported; and all the incidents conform to what is *vraisemblable*. These three features are only superficially present in *Phèdre*. Racine's purpose is not to represent or exemplify any truths conceived as external to his art, but to convey a meaning which can be conveyed only by the work of art itself. His methods are adapted to this end, though he is careful to conform as far as possible to the conventions accepted by his contemporaries. Inevitably, this sophisticated technique of operating simultaneously on the levels of inner 'meaning' and surface 'representation' leads to discontinuities – which is not to say that these discontinuities are faults. I have now looked briefly at some characteristics of both levels in *Phèdre*. It is time to try and draw the threads of the discussion together.

6

The themes in the first scene of *Phèdre* are on the one hand hiding and separation, on the other seeking and revealing:

> Le dessein en est pris: je *pars*, cher Théramène,
> Et *quitte* le séjour de l'aimable Trézène.
>
> Depuis plus de six mois *éloigné* de mon père,
> J'ignore le destin d'une tête si chère;
> J'ignore jusqu'aux lieux qui le peuvent *cacher*.
>
> Et dans quels lieux, Seigneur, l'allez-vous donc *chercher*?
>   dans quels heureux climats
> Croyex-vous *découvrir* les traces de ses pas?
>
> Qui *sait* même, qui *sait* si le Roi votre père
> Veut que de son *absence* on *sache* le *mystère*?
>
> Seigneur, m'est-il permis d'*expliquer* votre *fuite*?
>
> Peux-tu me *demander* le *désaveu* honteux?
>
> *Avouez-le*, tout change.

It is not enough to say that these expressions are used because the first scene concerns a journey and a hidden passion: Racine has chosen to start his play by bringing in a set of words and themes which he will use again and again throughout the play. We may especially note two features in his choice of words. First, he is careful to link the actual physical movements of departing and arriving with the wish to shun, or the inability to shun, an unacceptable idea or emotion:

> Et je *fuirai* ces lieux que je n'ose plus voir.
> Tout a changé de face,
> Depuis que sur ces bords les Dieux ont *envoyé*
> La fille de Minos et de Pasiphaé.
> Je *fuis*, je l'avoûrai, cette jeune Aricie.
> Heureux si j'avais pu *ravir à la mémoire*
> Cette indigne moitié d'une si belle histoire !

Secondly, Racine uses turns of phrase which evoke these motifs of hiding and separation, seeking and explaining, even when their use is rather unexpected:

> J'ai couru les deux mers que *sépare* Corinthe.
> De ses jeunes erreurs désormais *revenu*
> Une femme mourante et qui *cherche* à mourir
> Craint-on de *s'égarer* sur les traces d'Hercule?

An important point is Théramène's statement that 'le ciel' decides our fate, regardless of our wishes; but this is rather oddly expressed in terms of 'not wanting to know':

> Le ciel de nos raisons ne sait point s'informer.

The point is that one of the dominant themes expressed in the poetry of the first scene is that of strong emotion evaded. Round this centre there cluster a number of related motifs. Self-knowledge is important, concealment worse than useless:

> Je me suis applaudi quand je me suis connu.
> Tu sais comme à regret écoutant ce discours,
> Je te pressais souvent d'en abréger le cours;
> Heureux si j'avais pu ravir à la mémoire
> Cette indigne moitié d'une si belle histoire !
> Mais que sert d'affecter un superbe discours?
> Vous périssez d'un mal que vous dissimulez.

The obstacle to realisation (in both senses) is felt to be unbreakable:

> Ne souviendrait-il plus à mes sens égarés
> De l'obstacle éternel qui nous a séparés?

(and is expressed in terms of movement away and separation); but the obstacle increases the desire:

> Thésée ouvre vos yeux en les voulant fermer;
> Et sa haine, irritant une flamme rebelle,
> Prête à son ennemie une grâce nouvelle.

Holding back the unwelcome emotion is linked, conventionally enough, with holding back or taming wild animals:

> Implacable ennemi des amoureuses lois,
> Et d'un joug que Thésée a subi tant de fois?

> Avouez-le, tout change; et depuis quelques jours
> On vous voit moins souvent, orgueilleux et sauvage . . .
> Tantôt, savant dans l'art par Neptune inventé,
> Rendre docile au frein un coursier indompté.

though it is certainly significant that both Neptune and Venus are first mentioned in connection with this imagery.

More strangely, this scene announces a theme which recurs throughout the play: that it is by taming wild creatures, and on occasion monsters, that one acquires the right to love:

> Dans mes lâches soupirs d'autant plus méprisable,
> Qu'un long amas d'honneurs rend Thésée excusable,
> Qu'aucun monstres par moi domptés jusqu'aujourd'hui
> Ne m'ont acquis le droit de faillir comme lui.

There is even a hint that Thésée, by submitting to and carrying through his desires, has justified himself:

> Vénus, par votre orgueil si longtemps méprisée,
> Voudrait-elle à la fin justifier Thésée?

The focus of Hippolyte's feelings is Aricie. She has a decidedly ambivalent significance, and is linked with 'blood' and fatal enmity:

> Reste d'un sang fatal conjuré contre nous.

If we take this first scene as an exposition of the main themes of the play, rather than simply of the main facts of the story, Racine has given us the clues we need.

Oenone then enters and describes Phèdre's misery, but again the themes of hiding and separation are sounded:

> Elle meurt dans mes bras d'un mal qu'elle me cache
> . . . et sa douleur profonde
> M'ordonne toutefois d'écarter tout le monde.

In the first of these lines, the parallelism of Phèdre and Hippolyte is stressed ('Vous périssez d'un mal que vous dissimulez'). This prepares us for Scene iii, where Phèdre's avowal takes up the themes of Hippolyte's in Scene i. But here the intensity is greater, the details more terrifying, the motifs of concealment and seeking more emphatically expressed:

> Vous vouliez vous *montrer* et revoir la lumière.
>
> Vous la voyez, Madame, et prête à vous *cacher*
> Vous haïssez le jour que vous veniez *chercher*!
>
> Je meurs, pour ne point faire un *aveu* si funeste.
>
> *Oublions-les*, Madame. Et qu'à tout l'avenir
> Un silence éternel *cache* ce souvenir.
>
> Je *cherchais* dans leurs flancs ma raison *égarée*.
>
> Je l'*évitais* partout. O comble de misère!
> Mes yeux le *retrouvaient* dans les traits de son père.
>
> Ce n'est plus une ardeur dans mes veines *cachée*:
> C'est Vénus tout entière à sa proie attachée.

Again the motifs of physical approach and separation occur, but with greater vehemence:

> Voyage infortuné! Rivage malheureux,
> Fallait-il *approcher* de tes bords dangereux?
>
> Mon mal *vient de plus loin*.
>
> Par mon époux lui-même à Trézène *amenée*,
> J'ai revu l'ennemi que j'avais *éloigné*.

Phèdre's secret, like Hippolyte's, is now out, and already we have a hint that the situation is changing:

> Je t'ai tout avoué; je ne m'en repens pas.

Panope enters with news of Thésée's death, repeating at a more prosaic level the motifs of concealment and avowal:

> Je voudrais vous cacher une triste nouvelle,
> Madame; mais il faut que je vous la révèle.

Oenone now expresses her conviction that things have changed. Phèdre does not at this stage protest, and the act ends quietly.

Act II begins with Aricie. The references to 'conquering' and 'surmounting' now come thick and fast, linking Aricie with the savage Venus of Act I. Hippolyte arrives, and the themes of I.i are again taken up. His avowal is prefaced by a statement that once the secret begins to be revealed it is too late to stop the slide towards chaos:

> Je me suis engagé trop avant.
> Je vois que la raison cède à la violence.
> Puisque j'ai commencé de rompre le silence,
> Madame, il faut poursuivre.

The avowal takes up the themes of physical displacement, of domination despite desperate attempts to escape, of the destruction of a victim by the god:

> Par quel trouble me vois-je *emporté loin de moi*?
> Portant partout le trait dont je suis *déchiré*.
> Tout vous livre à l'envi le *rebelle* Hippolyte.
> D'un coeur qui s'*offre* à vous quel farouche entretien! . . .
> Mais l'*offrande* à vos yeux en doit être plus chère.

These references are again linked with Neptune:

> Je ne me souviens plus des leçons de Neptune . . .
> Et mes coursiers oisifs ont oublié ma voix.

These lines recall Hippolyte's avowal in Act I, Scene i (ll. 131–2) and point forward to his death, when his horses, frightened by Neptune's monster, 'ne connaissent plus ni le frein ni la voix' (ll. 1536). As in all of this scene, it is pointless to assert – or complain – that Racine is using contemporary jargon or neo-classical periphrases. He is using precisely those terms of contemporary language which express his theme: they come to life because even the most banal (for example, the heart that offers itself) take on a terrible concreteness in its context (in this case, of deities that are indeed worshipped with blood-sacrifices); and because each of them takes its part in the poetic pattern of the play.

The repetition of these themes in the scene between Hippolyte and Aricie is taken up with more intensity in the scene between Hippolyte and Phèdre. Phèdre's arrival is announced in the same terms which sound throughout the play:

> Elle vous *cherche*.
>   – Moi?
>   – J'*ignore* sa pensée . . .
> Cependant vous *sortez*. Et je *pars*. Et j'*ignore* . . .
> *Partez*, Prince, et suivez vos généreux desseins . . .
> Va, que pour le *départ* tout s'arme en diligence.

The phrasing of Phèdre's first speeches emphasises the same themes of physical movement and separation:

266

Le voici. Vers mon coeur tout mon sang *se retire* . . .
Je tremble que sur lui votre juste colère
Ne poursuive bientôt une odieuse mère . . .
J'ai voulu par des mers en être *séparée*.

Her avowal takes up with redoubled force all the motifs of hiding and separation, seeking and explaining, that we have found throughout the earlier scenes, but endows them with a sensuous concreteness: here 'blood', 'burning', 'waves' and 'devouring' bring in their physical associations, and the word 'monstre' sounds repeatedly (ll. 249, 701, 703).

The action reaches a peak of almost physical violence, then is interrupted: Théramène enters with news of the herald from Athens and the rumour that Thésée is still alive. The phrases that accompany his intervention are familiar:

Est-ce Phèdre qui *fuit*, ou plutôt qu'on entraîne?

Théramène, *fuyons*.

Mais moi qui l'y *cherchait*, Seigneur, je sais trop bien.

Examinons ce bruit, *remontons à sa source*.
S'il ne mérite pas d'interrompre ma *course*,
Partons.

At the beginning of Act III, all is disorder. The themes of physical motion, hiding, realisation and domination are brought to a new height:

Ah! que l'on *porte ailleurs* les honneurs qu'on m'*envoie*.

Cache-moi bien plutôt, je n'ai que trop parlé.

Dans de plus nobles soins *chercher* votre repos,
Contre un ingrat qui plaît recourir à la *fuite*.

Fuyez.
    – Je ne le puis *quitter*.
– Vous l'osâtes bannir, vous n'osez l'*éviter*.

Oenone, il peut *quitter* cet orgueil qui te blesse.

Cherchons pour l'*attaquer* quelque endroit plus sensible.

Pour le *fléchir* enfin tente tous les moyens.

The first half of the play culminates in Phèdre's prayer to Venus (ll. 813–24). In these twelve lines are brought together the phrases that link love with wounding and domination, and Venus with Aricie: the way in which the Hippolyte/Aricie and Hippolyte/Phèdre motifs each express the basic pattern is succinctly emphasised before the action starts a new phase with the reappearance of Thésée.

What does his reappearance at this point signify? We can begin to answer this question by gathering up the references to him in the play so far. He is the object desired but 'unknown' and 'hidden', and so fits closely into the themes we have noted. But he is also associated with two distinctive motifs: that of killing monsters and so acquiring the right to love; and that of the underworld. This underworld is associated with bounds that cannot be broken:

> il n'a pu sortir de ce triste séjour,
> Et repasser les bords qu'on passe sans retour.

with waves and cannibalism:

> Les flots ont englouti cet époux infidèle

and with gods who make human beings their prey:

> l'avare Achéron ne lâche point sa proie.

When Thésée is about to reappear, these themes crystallise round the dilemma of 'knowing' and yet 'hiding'. Oenone's interpretation is that Phèdre must go back to her preceding state:

> Rappelez votre vertu passée.

Phèdre states the opposite view: that there can never be any going back or hiding:

> Pense-tu que sensible à l'honneur de Thésée,
> Il [sc. Hippolyte] lui *cache* l'ardeur dont je suis embrasée? . . .
> Il se tairait en vain. Je *sais* mes perfidies . . .
> Je *connais* mes fureurs, je les rappelle toutes.

The theme of acknowledgment of what was hitherto denied is now coming to the fore, but it is still linked with a tendency to dissociate from the self this impulse to confess, and to attribute it to an external agency:

> Il me semble déjà que ces murs, que ces voûtes
> Vont prendre la parole, et prêts à m'accuser,
> Attendent mon époux pour le désabuser.

The imagery of walls and vaults so clearly suggests a physical echo that it is obvious that the source of the accusation is Phèdre herself.

Until now, approach to the loved one has meant destruction of the self, and flight has been the answer. Now, the impulse is still to flight, but the desire is to destroy the loved one:

> Je le vois comme un monstre effroyable à mes yeux.

Thésée enters, and Phèdre flees, with again the thematic references to 'approaching' and 'hiding':

> Indigne de vous plaire et de vous approcher,
> Je ne dois désormais songer qu'à me cacher.

Phèdre has expressed her solution to the dilemma posed by Thésée's return: flight, and the slaying of the 'monster'. Hippolyte now states *his* solution: flight and the slaying of monsters:

> Ne pourrai-je, en fuyant un indigne repos,
> D'un sang plus glorieux tiendre mes javelots? . . .
> Souffrez, si quelque monstre a pu vous échapper,
> Que j'apporte à vos pieds sa dépouille honorable.

The two main characters have thus, at this central point in the action, emphasised this central pair of motifs. Thésée now introduces a different motif. His long speech (ll. 953–87) is extremely important thematically. He emphasises, and deplores, the motif of 'flight':

> Que vois-je? Quelle horreur dans ces lieux répandue
> Fait fuir devant mes yeux ma famille éperdue? . . .
> Tout fuit, tout se refuse à mes embrassements.

The central part of his speech emphasises different themes. His isolation is mentioned ('Je n'avais qu'un ami'). He recognises and condemns the wrongdoing of Pirithoüs, but without repudiating him or refusing sympathy:

> Son imprudente flamme
> Du tyran de l'Epire allait ravir la femme;
> Je servais à regret ses desseins amoureux;
> Mais le sort irrité nous aveuglait tous deux . . .
> J'ai vu Pirithoüs, triste objet de mes larmes,
> Livré par ce barbare à des monstres cruels
> Qu'il nourrissait du sang des malheureux mortels.

Thésée himself has been confined to the underworld, but he has survived. Not only has he survived, but he has made the destructive force destroy itself:

> D'un perfide ennemi j'ai purgé la nature;
> A ses monstres lui-même a servi de pâture.

There is a calmness about Thésée's utterances, even in his distress and dismay; and, unlike Phèdre and Hippolyte, he reacts not by trying to conceal the facts or avoid an explanation, but by seeking an explanation:

Entrons. C'est trop garder un doute qui m'accable.
Connaissons à la fois le crime et le coupable.
Que Phèdre *explique* enfin le trouble où je la voi.

Beside this decisiveness, Hippolyte appears feeble. He is left to lament his guilt. He clings to his passion for Aricie, but lacks the directness and honesty of Thésée:

Allons, cherchons ailleurs par quelle heureuse adresse
Je pourrai de mon père émouvoir la tendresse.

Thésée's determination attains, not the truth, but falsehood. Immediately, the most violent tensions inherent in the play manifest themselves. Thésée rejects Hippolyte as violently as possible, and the rejection, as usual, is expressed as physical separation:

Fuis, traître. Ne viens point braver ici ma haine . . .
Fuis, dis-je; et sans retour précipitant tes pas,
De ton horrible aspect purge tous mes Etats . . .
Fusse-tu par delà les colonnes d'Alcide,
Je me croirais encor trop voisin d'un perfide.

This violent rejection is also associated with 'monsters', 'purging' and 'cleansing'. Hippolyte replies to it with a statement of impossible purity:

Elevé dans le sein d'une chaste heroïne,
Je n'ai point de son sang démenti l'origine . . .
On sait de mes chagrins l'inflexible rigueur.
Le jour n'est pas plus pur que le fond de mon coeur.

He does mitigate this black and white opposition to the extent of admitting his love for Aricie; but it is now too late to save him.

Then, once again, Phèdre takes up the motifs expressed at the Hippolyte level, but with a more desperate intensity. We have already remarked on the sequence of IV.iv, v and vi, the greatest passage in all Racine. Here, we can try and sum up the theme: it is the combination of the most extreme complicity with, and the most extreme repudiation of, the same complex of emotions.

The essential theme of *Phèdre* is this violent combination of involvement and rejection. This is why Hippolyte does not tell Thésée the truth – on the 'Hippolyte' level, the central fact is that the guilt can only be repudiated, cannot be allowed even to be mentioned. This is also why Act IV ends on Phèdre's violent rejection of Oenone. It is not part of the 'character' of Phèdre that she blames other people for her misfortunes. It is part of the theme 'Phèdre' that complicity is both acknowledged and repudiated with desperate violence. For this reason, we do not condemn Phèdre's action as unworthy: 'Phèdre' and 'Oenone' are both elements in the thematic pattern.

The explosive tensions within this pattern reach their greatest intensity at the end of Act IV. Act V sees the working out of the destructive forces. This is shown under four aspects: Aricie, Hippolyte, Phèdre and Thésée. The four types of resolution form a continuous series, of which the first term (Aricie) shows an affinity with the last and apparently most different (Thésée). We will take them one by one.

Aricie is the least tragic. Her attitude is that the truth should be revealed ('Eclaircissez Thésée'). She remains at the conventional level: Hippolyte must marry her before he can have her (ll. 1379–85), and she moralises about the gods granting our wishes in order to punish us (ll. 1437–8). Racine gives her a theatrically effective confrontation with Thésée (V.iii), but he must not make too much of her. One aspect of his theme demands the complete separation of absolute black and absolute white. Aricie's identification with the destroying Venus is therefore blanked off, and the stress is now laid on 'la timide Aricie'. The violence of 'Venus' is now all in the monster which kills Hippolyte. Aricie will not then even acknowledge the evil of her fate, let alone take any responsibility for it:

> Elle veut quelque temps douter de son malheur;
> Et ne connaissant plus ce héros qu'elle adore,
> Elle voit Hippolyte et le demande encore . . .
> Par un triste regard elle accuse les Dieux;
> Et froide, gémissante, et presque inanimée,
> Aux pieds de son amant elle tombe pâmée.

The resolution of the Hippolyte theme is rather different. Hippolyte also refuses to acknowledge the evil, insisting instead on complete purity:

> Tout ce que je voulais me cacher à moi-même . . .
> Oubliez, s'il se peut, que je vous ai parlé,
> Madame; et que jamais une bouche si pure
> Ne s'ouvre pour conter cette horrible aventure.

But the impulses aroused cannot be ignored or repressed. Critics have objected to the exaggeration of the 'récit de Théramène', but the exaggeration is the point. Against the impossibly pure Hippolyte comes the most violent, concrete and monstrous of monsters. It is essential that against purity Racine shall set the utmost impurity, against spirituality the most concrete animality. Hence the 'gros bouillons', the 'flots d'écume', the 'cornes menaçantes', the 'écailles jaunissantes', the 'gueule enflammée', the onomatopæic effects, the emphasis on blood, wounds and disfigurement. Not that there is any suggestion that Hippolyte deserved his death. Whatever the special pleading in the preface, Racine makes no attempt in his text to moralise the death. Hippolyte is made to rely on the gods to justify him, in order to emphasise that they do nothing of the sort; and Racine's prose declaration that Hippolyte is 'un peu coupable' is formally contradicted by his verse:

> J'ai vu des mortels périr le plus aimable,
> Et j'ose dire encor, Seigneur, le moins coupable.

In the Hippolyte theme, there is no reconciliation between the extremes: Hippolyte meets his opposite and dies after fighting it.

Phèdre represents a new element again. Her rôle in Act V is short: she confesses the truth and dies. She dies entirely: first as Oenone, her worldly self, then in her own person. Her last speech sounds a new note: the conscious taking of responsibility for her actions. Racine keeps a delicate balance. Oenone is still blamed and rejected ('La détestable Oenone a conduit tout le reste'). But there is also a new authority, a new self control:

> J'ai voulu, devant vous *exposant* mes remords,
> Par un chemin plus lent descendre chez les morts.
> J'ai pris, j'ai fait *couler* dans mes brûlantes veines
> Un poison que Médée apporta dans Athènes.

Before, the 'poison' came from outside ('Quel funeste poison/L'amour a répandu sur toute la maison!'); now, in that emphatic self-correction ('j'ai fait couler'), Phèdre takes the responsibility. Racine is able to complete her rôle with his marvellous synthesis of blackness and light:

> Et la mort, à mes yeux dérobant la clarté,
> Rend au jour, qu'ils souillaient, toute sa pureté.

Far from being a play for one character only, *Phèdre* makes use of all the characters as elements in its pattern, and not the least interesting is Thésée. He is the least naturalistic, his part the most refractory to any blurring or softening of the play in performance. As the man who has killed monsters, loved, visited the underworld, and lived, he represents the fourth and most fully conscious resolution of the pattern. The key word is 'éclaircir'. It occurs only three times in the play, each time in Act V and with reference to Thésée (ll. 1339, 1459, 1647). Thésée, who in Act IV left to beg Neptune to destroy Hippolyte, here reappears praying for the truth:

> Dieux, éclairez mon trouble, et daignez à mes yeux
> Montrer la vérité que je cherche en ces lieux.

Unlike Hippolyte, he insists on the details of the truth:

> Je veux de tout le crime être mieux éclairci.

He admits without circumlocution the position in which he has placed himself:

> J'ai peut-être trop cru des témoins peu fidèles;
> Et j'ai trop tôt vers toi levé mes mains cruelles.
> Ah! de quel désespoir mes voeux seraient suivis!

After the news of Hippolyte's death, his utterance is again clear and unshrinking:

> O mon fils! cher espoir *que je me suis ravi*!
> Inexorables Dieux, qui m'avez trop servi!
> A quels mortels regrets ma vie est réservée!

When Phèdre comes to confess, he takes refuge for a moment in denial ('Je le crois criminel, puisque vous l'accusez') but then lucidity returns with a terrible authority:

> Tout semble s'élever contre mon injustice.
> L'éclat de mon nom même augmente mon supplice.
> Moins connu des mortels, je me cacherais mieux.

It is Thésée alone who envisages reparation:

> Allons de ce cher fils embrasser ce qui reste,
> *Expier* la fureur d'un voeu que je déteste.
> Rendons-lui les honneurs qu'il a trop mérités;
> Et pour mieux *apaiser* ses mânes irrités,
> Que, malgré les complots d'une injuste famille,
> Son amante aujourd'hui me tienne lieu de fille.

Thésée's curse on his own son has brought him to this misery, but he can at least face it, admit responsibility, and try to put things right. At this realistic level, he can join hands with the conventional Aricie.

Phèdre, then, expresses with dreadful intensity the struggle between on the one hand violent and primitive passions and on the other the attempt to split them off from the self and deny them utterly. At the end, in varying degrees, the characters both have been destroyed by and have assimilated these passions. On any reading, *Phèdre* is tragic. My interpretation tries to illuminate the meaning of the play as a whole. But the meaning of *Phèdre*, by definition, is *Phèdre*, and *Phèdre* can express this meaning only because Racine has found this form. It is therefore not always adapted to embodying those peripheral elements so dear to neo-classical and naturalistic critics: plot and character. The dramatist who pursues meaning is always faced with this dilemma. I have pointed out some of the discontinuities in the surface of *Phèdre* which reveal this difficulty. I will now skim briefly through the play again to show how Racine's concern with the meaning at every point dictates the form, and what implications this has for his technique.

Act I, Scene i expresses perfectly the themes Racine puts into it, but two oddities reveal his lack of concern with formal plot and characterisation. Someone has to announce in memorable terms the themes of fate and submission to love. Théramène is given the job, unsuitable though it is for a tutor (ll. 114–26). Secondly, Racine has to indicate that Hippolyte and Phèdre are to meet. He therefore makes Hippolyte say that protocol demands it (ll. 139–42). But then, as we have seen, he forgets about it. At the end of the act, Racine wants to give an excuse for Phèdre to see Hippolyte and for Oenone to express approval of Phèdre's love without appearing quite ridiculous. He therefore brings in Panope to announce that Thésée is dead. This (like Phèdre's concern for her children) is obviously just a dramatic convenience. At the end of Act II, the arrival of the Athenian herald and the rumour of Thésée's survival come equally pat. The herald is never heard of again, but his arrival gives further opportunities for displaying the theme:

> Ah! que l'on porte ailleurs les honneurs qu'on m'envoie . . .
> Moi, régner! Moi ranger un Etat sous ma loi,
> Quand ma faible raison ne règne plus sur moi!

When Thésée appears, and Phèdre hurries out, we might reasonably expect him to hurry after her, or at least to discuss matters with Hippolyte. We might expect Hippolyte to be wary. But Racine is not interested in this probable behaviour, or even in the interplay between the characters. Hippolyte, very relevantly to the theme but with little regard for the situation, starts to talk about monsters, flight and death. Thésée, with even less regard for normal behaviour, hardly talks to Hippolyte. Indeed, he hardly refers to Phèdre's withdrawal except at the beginning and the end of his big speech. The speech is about something quite different, and is virtually a soliloquy: he baldly states 'Je n'avais qu'un ami', and proceeds to relate his adventures in Epirus. That is, he makes a major poetic statement which is vital to the play, but quite irrelevant to the plot or even the situation in which it is ostensibly set. There is a certain disconnectedness about this scene: it is as though Racine were returning to the disjointed manner of *La Thébaïde*, but this time for a clear purpose and not for any lack of skill.

In Act IV, Scene ii, Thésée again does not behave realistically. Critics have complained that he does not examine the evidence. But the point is that his search for truth leads to falsehood, and that his repudiation of Hippolyte is total and violent. To present him as scrutinising the evidence would be distracting, as well as irrelevant. Racine does not follow the neo-classical technique by which a scene starts with a problem or conflict, debates it, and ends with a decision. He follows the order of Euripides: Thésée decides at once, and curses Hippolyte; the discussion takes place afterwards, too late to affect the course of events. That is, Thésée's violent repudiation is followed by Hippolyte's profession of absolute purity, and then, too late, by Hippolyte's confession; and this is the correct order for the unfolding of the theme. Racine makes no effort at this point to justify Hippolyte's keeping of Phèdre's secret: the motif of repudiation is sufficient reason.

In Act V, Théramène makes his famous narration. The theme demands the greatest possible emphasis on physical detail in the circumstances surrounding Hippolyte's death to set against the abstract purity of Hippolyte's ideal of himself, and this is what Racine sets out to provide, with little regard for *vraisemblance* and none at all for classical restraint.

We have two curious features in the presentation of Phèdre in this last act. The first is (again) her attitude to her children. Racine describes her. (ll. 1471–9) caressing them, but in her last speech she does not even refer to their fate after her death – something she was much concerned about earlier. Why does Racine mention them at all? Not mainly to emphasise the pathos of her situation or to show us the maternal side of her character: both aims could have been achieved more powerfully by making her commend them to Thésée in her final speeches. The clue is in the verse:

> Quelquefois, pour flatter ses secrètes douleurs,
> Elle prend ses enfants et les baigne de pleurs;
> Et soudain, renonçant à l'amour maternelle,
> Sa main avec horreur les repousse loin d'elle.

'Flatter' is associated with Oenone (e.g. in the denunciation at the end of Act IV) and hence with aspects of herself which Phèdre wishes to repudiate; the 'repousse loin d'elle' also emphasises utter rejection. In these lines, Racine is expressing the conflict between violent rejection and emotional involvement which is at the heart of the play.

This is confirmed by the second strange feature. Why does Phèdre show no reaction to the news of the loved one's death? Surely any woman so obsessed with her passion would make some reference to such news? To ask the question is to answer it. Racine is not here concerned with the probable behaviour of a real woman, but with the realisation of his theme. The death of Hippolyte has already been recounted and lamented. Racine turns to another aspect. Phèdre's last speeches have another purpose: to express her destruction by passion, yet her partial acceptance and control of it. Anything else would be irrelevant, and the speech therefore strikes us as perfectly natural.

How does Racine override these contradictions between his underlying pattern and his neo-classical surface? By his use of words, the articulation of which in the theatre evokes our responses, and the analysis of which enables us to express conceptually some approximation to his theme. I have compared my thesis that there are two levels in the tragic plays of Racine with the psychoanalytic distinction between the latent and manifest content of a dream. Freud's remarks on the part which, in his theory, words play in dream formation are illuminating:

Words, since they are the nodal points of numerous ideas, may be regarded as predestined to ambiguity; and the neuroses (e.g. in framing obsessions and phobias), no less than dreams, make unashamed use of the advantages thus offered by words for purposes of condensation and disguise.[25]

It is apparent that in *Phèdre* the dramatic articulation of a large part of the theme rests precisely on the simultaneous psychological and physical meaning of a few key words: 'fuir', 'chercher', 'quitter', 'monstre'. We have already emphasised another way in which Racine exploits the essential ambiguity of language: his ability to play on the metaphorical and literal meanings of such words as 'sang', 'brûler', 'flamme'. This brings us back to a play we looked at earlier: *Médée*. We argued that *Médée* contained poetic and tragic elements which are absent from most of Corneille's later work. Almost always in Corneille, the use of contemporary jargon is a sign of naturalism, the imitation of contemporary fashion. In Racine, the constant re-concretisation of the banal metaphors presents us with the opposite process: the underlying poetic pattern is felt so powerfully throughout the play that the dead metaphors used locally within it are energised by it and play their part in the pattern. This is a characteristic of the poetic method, and we find it intermittently in *Médée*. The 'flammes' and 'poison' of love are concretised in the deadly robe which Créuse is 'burning with desire' to put on (*Médée*, l. 1146). In Phèdre, the technique is brought to perfection.

Here, Racine is able to convert even the emptiest conventions of language into powerful means of expression. Let us take one example: pompous neo-classical periphrasis. Clearly, such a line as 'La fille de Minos et de Pasiphaé' is not only mysteriously beautiful but also means more than 'Phèdre'. But the method goes further than this. Why does Théramène say

> J'ai couru les deux mers que sépare Corinthe?

For two reasons. First, 'separation' is a key motif in the play: this very phrase is echoed later:

> J'ai voulu par des mers en être séparée.

Secondly, the reference to Corinth may remind us of another myth – that of Medea – which must have been much in Racine's mind when he wrote *Phèdre*. We have already mentioned his imitations of Corneille's *Médée*. He also imitates lines from Euripides's *Medea* (ll. 1037–40 and 1471–4 of *Phèdre*). In the last scene he mentions Medea, and the references to the sun also link Phèdre with her. When he makes Théramène use this roundabout formula he is not being pompous: each element is important in the pattern of the play.

But surely this other use of periphrasis is indefensible?

> De son fatal hymen je cultivais les fruits.

It may help us to decide if we recall the other appearances of the word 'fruit':

> Quel fruit espères-tu de tant de violence?
>
> Quels fruits recevront-ils de leurs vaines amours?
>
> Hélas! du crime affreux dont la honte me suit
> Jamais mon triste coeur n'a recueilli le fruit.

The important motif is bitterness at lack of fulfilment, and the word 'fruit' enables Racine to contrive an associative bridge between these references, and to another expression of the same theme:

> J'ai perdu, dans la fleur de leur jeune saison,
> Six frères.

Racine is not being pompous, and certainly not being coy: in all these cases he is choosing the words which will help him unfold his meaning.

His use of periphrasis is one example of that amazing chameleon-like quality of his: the combination of subtlety and daring with which he turns the most banal and clumsy conventions to his purpose. In every feature – plot, character, and verse – those plays that seem on the surface so lucid reveal extraordinary profundities.

The conclusion is Butler's: 'la simplicité tant vantée de Racine n'est qu'un mythe. Le génie, l'art de Racine ne sont pas simple.'[26] The notion that Racine is merely a supremely skilful exponent of the type of drama pioneered by Corneille is nonsense. It is tenable only if we look at those plays which have least pretentions to tragedy – especially *Mithridate* and *Iphigénie*. If we look at *Andromaque* and *Phèdre*, it is apparent that the reputed virtues of perfect simplicity, clarity and technical ease hardly exist in them: these two plays are full of the strangest discontinuities and contradictions – though only if we examine them carefully.

None of this is said in disparagement. My argument is that the naturalistic forms of Cornelian drama were inimical to tragedy, but that Racine contrived to use them to express his tragic vision. His craftsmanship was indeed meticulous, but in a deeper sense than is sometimes implied. He used his enormous skill to make plays which expressed with perfect subtlety and accuracy an underlying poetic and tragic meaning. Certainly, if expression of his meaning and surface neatness could be reconciled (as in *Bérénice*), he achieved the surface neatness. But this achievement was secondary. If the underlying theme was fully expressed, his main task was complete, and if any surface discontinuities remained, no matter. What he did not do in his tragic plays was to deform his theme in order to achieve superficial elegance. Racine's great plays are great because they mean something; and they are able to mean something only because the meaning dictates the form. The surface discrepancies have an aesthetic function: they warn us not to waste time on the surface, and they point to the meaning bene ath it. Of course, this function would hardly be necessary if we were not misled by our naturalistic bias. If, instead of fidgeting about characters and plot, we surrender ourselves to *Phèdre* as acted ,we will never notice any oddities at all. From this viewpoint, they do not exist. The poetry works by its own logic.

'ATHALIE'

I

Much has been written of the reasons for Racine's silence after *Phèdre*. It is hardly possible at this stage to reconstruct his motives, but the most likely view seems to be Picard's: that he felt that, by renouncing the public theatre to further his career at Court, he was passing to a more important and more honourable calling. From the mid-1670s onwards, he followed the trend of the Court towards increasing piety, but in 1677 he cannot have had any religious horror of the theatre. In 1677–83 he worked on opera libretti,[1] and the moralists considered opera far more dangerous than tragedy. Only in the last few years of his life did he become the figure that Pommier has revealed: the leader of the Port-Royalist cabal and the spiritual guide of Madame de Gramont.

I have argued that the acceptance in seventeenth-century France of the neo-classical rules was part of the trend towards naturalism that was to culminate in the naturalism of the middle and late nineteenth-century, and that Racine's work shows a conflict between naturalism and the poetic method to which his temperament inclined him. We can imagine – without any possibility of proof – that in the late 1670s this conflict was particularly acute. The increasing dominance at court of a narrowly dogmatic religion, and the influence of Boileau's moralising naturalism, cast doubt on the value of poetry that was not overtly didactic. At the same time, the success of opera showed the possibilities of an art-form that was frankly decorative. The author of the prefaces of *Iphigénie* and *Phèdre* clearly saw the aesthetic and moral problems which these developments posed.

If Racine had not written *Athalie*, we should have no doubt (despite *Phèdre*) of the trend his art was following – a trend indicated by his flirtations with opera. This is perhaps clearest from two of his late works, *Esther* and *L'Idylle de la Paix*. *Esther* is not bad in the way Corneille's plays sometimes are: it never attempts great things or a difficult synthesis of discordant elements and then falls into clumsiness or bathos. It has that special sweetness which hovers over so much of Racine's verse, but which here attains perfection: a perfection that is all the more readily achieved because the attempt to convey concrete or complex experience is abandoned.

Hélas! si jeune encore,
Par quel crime ai-je pu mériter mon malheur?
Ma vie à peine a commencé d'éclore.
Je tomberai comme une fleur
Qui n'a vu qu'une aurore.

There is no concrete apprehension of death: attention is focused on the sentimental images of the flower and the dawn.

Que ma bouche et mon coeur, et tout ce que je suis,
Rendent honneur au Dieu qui m'a donné la vie.
Dans les craintes, dans les ennuis,
En ses bontés mon âme se confie.
Veut-il par mon trépas que je le glorifie?
Que ma bouche et mon coeur, et tout ce que je suis,
Rendent honneur au Dieu qui m'a donné la vie.

The rigours of faith and martyrdom are here attenuated until they can be fitly expressed by a sweet modulation of 'i'-sounds.

D'un souffle l'aquilon écarte les nuages,
Et chasse au loin la foudre et les orages.
Un roi sage, ennemi du langage menteur,
Ecarte d'un regard le perfide imposteur.

Racine congratulated himself on the 'vérités si utiles aux rois' in the stanzas immediately preceding this one. Perhaps, but this stanza shows the method which made such a dangerous attempt possible. The 'vérités' are couched in the most general form ('un roi sage écarte le perfide imposteur'). Attention is directed onto the imagery, and the imagery suggests the lightness with which the whole subject can be tossed aside ('souffle . . . Écarte d'un regard').

Despite this weakness, *Esther* shows Racine turning around the problem of how to achieve seriousness – the problem which he had presumably failed to solve when planning *Iphigénie en Tauride* and *Alceste* and which he could easily evade in writing his libretti. In *Esther,* the peculiar circumstances of the commission allowed him to approach a solution quite impossible in a normal tragedy. The play has about it an air of 'let's pretend', of fairy-tale, which disarms the severe critic. At the same time, Racine has an excuse which protects him from ridicule and which may have helped to salve his aesthetic conscience: the story is taken from the Bible, and therefore has the authority of literal truth. Also, we can see one result of his long preoccupation with the aesthetics of opera: for the first time in one of his tragedies he includes a strong operatic element. These last two parts of his strategy have often been used since. Most naturalistically-inclined playwrights who want to endow their works with seriousness have relied on the authority of some religious, scientific, or political doctrine as a guarantee of solidity; and even on the most naturalistic stage, sentiments which would cause embarrassment if spoken find sympathetic acceptance when sung.

The *Idylle* shows similar qualities to *Esther*: a virtuosity and grace which, despite a certain air of weakness, give some semblance of interest to a perfectly banal work:

> Un plein repos favorise nos voeux:
> Chantons, chantons la Paix, qui nous rend tous heureux . . .
> De ton retour le laboureur charmé
> Ne craint plus désormais qu'une main etrangère
> Moissonne avant le temps le champ qu'il a semé;
>
> Tu pares nos jardins d'une grâce nouvelle;
> Tu rends le jour plus pur, et la terre plus belle.

As in *Esther*, Racine is not exactly writing poetry without content, but he reduces the content to a level of generality at which it ceases to have much meaning. The ship floats, because the cargo has been thrown overboard.

By 1690 the great days of Louis XIV were over. Politically and economically, France was hard-pressed. The official ideology became more restrictive and sombre. At Court, a rather gloomy piety was now the principal virtue. Racine was the loyal servant of this ideology, which was out of touch with trends already dominant outside France and soon to dominate French intellectual life. (Bayle's *Pensées Diverses sur la Comète* dates from 1682, Fontenelle's *Histoire des Oracles* from 1686.) The theatre was in decline. The classical poetic forms, with their affinities with the primaeval gods, sorted ever more oddly with the rationalising attitudes of writers and critics, yet censorship and the established conventions made very difficult any attempt to infuse new sources of interest compatible with naturalism. We are not far from the insipidly horrendous plays of Crébillon, whose period of greatest success was the last part of the reign of Louis XIV. It was in this darkening atmosphere that France's greatest poet produced his last play for private performance before the king.

2

Athalie stands apart from Racine's other plays, and above all but the greatest of them in quality. Most modern audiences and readers probably feel a slight repugnance to a play of which the preface begins: 'Tout le monde sait que le royaume de Juda etait composé des deux tribus de Juda et de Benjamin, et que les dix autres qui se revoltèrent contre Roboam composaient le royaume d'Israël'. All the world may not be familiar with these things today, but the attitude behind the preface is important. Racine is no longer alleging specious authorities for this or that freedom with history or legend in order to divert attention from the fact that he has adapted his material as high-handedly as he liked. For Racine, the essential features of the material in *Athalie* are that it is both true and important. There is, as we shall see, ambiguity in his attitude, but it is the literal truth and the overwhelming importance of his chosen material which are for him the primary facts.

We can perhaps begin by the risky attempt to imagine the world order as he saw it. The world was finite and stable, but not on that account insignificant or safe: it was surrounded by an infinite spiritual world, ruled over by an omnipotent God who took the thoughts and deeds of men seriously, and could either grant them eternal bliss or thrust them into eternal torment. Man could not change his lot by his own efforts, for God had given Man free-will, and Man had chosen to sin: the flaw was innate in mankind. But God had planned a way out by himself acting as a saviour expiating Man's sins by sacrifice; through this saviour, Man could find grace. Many devout people thought that a man could be foredoomed to eternal punishment anyway. The only hope was in the promised saviour, who had to be born of the royal family of the Jews. If (and nothing could be taken for granted in a system which could be interpreted in terms of both free-will and fate) the royal race died out before the saviour appeared, mankind was indeed doomed. *Athalie* is the story of one of those points of terrible danger in the divine drama. The vital link between mankind and its saviour might be cut; and who could tell whether God would not then weary of Man and refuse redemption after all? On this occasion, God had pursued his purpose, as doctrine proclaimed he would; but the story stood as a paradigm of the ever-present possibility of damnation; in just the same way, at every moment, the soul balanced on the edge of Hell, and only the sure but unbiddable grace of God could save it. On a lower level, the situation reflected that of the courtier before his king. The courtier lived on the edge of disgrace or rewards that depended on the king's inscrutable favour. When the king died, the prosperity of the courtier and of the country could depend on the temperament and ability of his successor. We may imagine that for Racine, with his deepening sympathies for a Jansenism which many considered a damnable heresy, with his devotion to a king who had made him a rich man but hated

Jansenists, with his revulsion from a sinful theatre which still attracted him, may have felt especially acutely the uncertainty inherent in these dilemmas. Whether or not this is so, the material of *Athalie* serves as an expressive myth for all three predicaments: a crisis of the cosmic drama; the daily dilemma of a man's spiritual life; and the moral and social problems of monarchy.

The term 'myth' is chosen deliberately to emphasise the expressive function of the material, without any implication as to its literal truth or otherwise. The happenings depicted in *Athalie*, and the doctrinal superstructure to which they refer, were, for Racine, true in the most literal and factual sense. They also yielded an immediate moral lesson. At the same time, they were true in another sense: they were the best possible formulation of highly significant truths which (because of the inherently ambiguous nature of Jansenist belief and its uncertain relation to the teaching of the Church) could not be fully expressed conceptually. That is, the material of the Bible story had all the advantages of the myth of Phaedra, with the added power of irrefutable moral and factual truth. If we bear in mind the demands implicit in naturalistic criticism that to be serious a work of art should have documentary accuracy and point a moral, we can see why with the support of Biblical material Racine felt able to attempt another, though very different, work of the seriousness of *Phèdre*. The use of a sacred subject may have helped to disarm his religious scruples (though it did not disarm the bigots, who mounted against *Athalie* the most successful of all the cabals against his plays). More important from our point of view, it offered him a way out from the triviality that threatened after *Iphigénie*.

The method has its dangers, however. For the poet's personal belief of the truth of his subject to give him the initial confidence to embark on the work is one thing. For him to place the aesthetic weight of his structure on acceptance of this truth by his audience is another: the literal truth of one age can so easily seem merely quaint to the next. If we are not careful to preserve a critical objectivity we may let our preconceptions lead us to sniff this in *Athalie*: we may, as many have done, side with Athalie and condemn Joad on moral grounds. But to do so can only ruin our appreciation of the play Racine wrote. My approach here will be quite different. I shall take the subject of *Athalie*, as an expressive myth, with the same seriousness as the myth of *Phèdre*. To be sure, it may be found that the substance of the myth in *Athalie* is rather different from that of its façade. I shall also make use of the most reliable guide to the meaning of the play: its verse.

One point to keep well in mind is how far *Athalie* inculcates, or is intended to inculcate, a moral lesson, as the last words of Joad imply:

> Par cette fin horrible, et due à ses forfaits,
> Apprenez, roi des Juifs, et n'oubliez jamais
> Que les rois dans le ciel ont un juge sévère,
> L'innocence un vengeur, et l'orphelin un père.

In his secular tragedies, Racine had learned to circumvent the moralising and naturalistic assumptions of neo-classicism by apparent compliance on the surface and the pursuit of radically different aims underneath. *Athalie* is very different from the secular tragedies. It is not just that the subject-matter is now religious, but that a new attitude to the truth and morality of art has developed (in Racine as well as in his environment) and that this demands a new technique if a serious work of art is to become possible. Whether this new form allows of tragedy we may leave open for the moment. The first point is to examine how far the moral intention is realised.

On the surface, the realisation is perfect. It has been said that the main character in *Athalie* is God. This is evident from the first line:

> Oui, je viens dans son temple adorer l'Eternel

and throughout the play God's omnipotence is stressed:

> Tout l'univers est plein de sa magnificence . . .
> Son empire a des temps précédé la naissance.

On the one hand is the loving God, who cherishes and makes victorious his children, even when they are weak:

> Dieu, qui de l'orphelin protège l'innocence
> Et fait dans la faiblesse éclater sa puissance . . .

On the other hand, God is implacable, and strikes down the ungodly, however powerful:

> Dieu qui hait les tyrans et qui dans Jezraël
> Jura d'exterminer Achab et Jézabel;
> Dieu, qui, frappant Joram, le mari de leur fille,
> A jusque sur son fils poursuivi leur famille;
> Dieu, dont le bras vengeur, pour un temps suspendu,
> Sur cette race impie est toujours étendue . . .

At the end of the play, God through his priest has raised the orphan Joas to the throne and destroyed the wicked Athalie. To all appearances, the pious lesson is complete.

Nevertheless, the moral pattern is clearly more complex than this. As Mme de Mourgues has pointed out, there is a 'double pattern' in the play, a 'powerful ambiguity between fair and foul'.[2] This is not because Racine (as a naturalistic critic might say) is being fair to both sides, holding the balance even, and so on. There is little doubt that Racine considered Joad's attitude, and the values he represents, to be in all essentials right, and the attitude and values represented by Athalie to be in the most literal sense damnable. We may find Joad repulsive and Athalie sympathetic, but if so we are taking these figures of poetic drama at the naturalistic level, rather than responding to the complexities presented by the play as a whole. At the heart of this moral complexity is the presentation of Joas. It is beside the point to complain that he is a mealy-mouthed child who will grow up into a corrupt king ('un perroquet de sacristie, destiné plus tard à devenir un perroquet de cour', to quote Sarcey). From one aspect, we must accept him as a sweet and sympathetic character, because we are told he is a sweet and sympathetic character, by all the other characters and in convincing verse:

> De nos princes hébreux il aura le courage,
> Et déjà son esprit a devancé son âge.
>
> > (Joad)
>
> Cher enfant, que le ciel en vain m'avait rendu
> Hélas! pour vous sauver j'ai fait ce que j'ai pu.
>
> > (Josabeth)
>
> Enfin, Eliacin, vous avez su me plaire;
> Vous n'êtes point sans doute un enfant ordinaire.
>
> > (Athalie)
>
> Quel astre à nos yeux vient de luire?
> Quel sera quelque jour cet enfant merveilleux? . . .
> > Un enfant courageux publie
> > Que Dieu lui seul est éternel.
>
> > (The Chorus)

Despite this, Racine goes out of his way to emphasise that Joas will apostasise and will murder Zacharie, Joad's son and successor as high priest. This outcome is foreshadowed in Joad's forebodings in Act I, ll. 283–6, and is confirmed on the highest authority in Joad's prophecy in Act III, ll. 1142–3. The verse itself carries unmistakable conviction, and Racine (most unusually) confirms by footnotes what is clear enough in the acted text. These future disasters are brought to our minds again in Act IV, Scene iii, when Joad pronounces his famous warning on the corruption that attends on power (ll. 1385–1402). Finally, as a parallel to Joad's ecstasy, in Act V Athalie, in her last imprecations, predicts that Joas will give her her revenge:

> Que dis-je, souhaiter! Je me flatte, j'espère
> Qu'indocile à ton joug, fatigué de ta loi,
> Fidèle au sang d'Achab, qu'il a reçu de moi,
> Conforme à son aïeul, à son père semblable,
> On verra de David l'héritier détestable
> Abolir tes honneurs, profaner ton autel,
> Et venger Athalie, Achab et Jézabel.

One element in the pattern, then, is that Joad in preserving his saviour is preserving the enemy of his family and his beliefs. The paradox is even more agonising in that Joas is in some way a prefiguration of Christ.[3] But the matter is more complex still. Joas is constantly equated with gold and treasure. This equation is sometimes conventional enough ('ce trésor par David caché'; 'ce cher dépôt'; 'cet enfant, ce trésor') but sometimes it is strikingly concrete, as in one of the key lines of the play, from Joad's prophecy:

> Comment en un plomb vil l'or pur s'est-il changé?

This line, coined in an age of alchemy, has lost nothing of its mystery and firmness: a miracle has happened, but instead of the miracle of redemption it is a miracle of degradation. The rôle of Joas is that of destroyer, both for Joad and for Athalie, and it is in the destruction of Athalie that his connection with gold is most emphasised. On the simple plot level, Athalie is lured to her death by greed for gold. Racine weaves this motif into his pattern by linking it with Joas, who is at once the destroyer and saviour, 'l'or pur' and 'un plomb vil'. Athalie, who in Act II entered the temple drawn by a confused attraction towards Joas/Christ, is later drawn by Joas in his aspect of the gold which destroys.[4]

I have stressed the paradox which centres on Joas, but there are others. If God is omnipotent and eternal, Athalie can hardly win, and (to quote another commonplace of naturalistic criticism) there is therefore no drama. Obviously, there is drama in plenty. Racine presents both sides of the paradox. God is indeed eternal and omniscient, and the verse continually evokes his presence. But at the end of Act IV and the beginning of Act V there is undoubtedly suspense of the usual kind. The Chorus expects the worst:

> Triste reste de nos rois,
> Chère et dernière fleur d'une tige si belle,

> Hélas! sous le couteau d'une mère cruelle
> Te verrons-nous tomber une seconde fois?

Zacharie and Salomith believe the Levites may be defeated:

> Peut-être nous touchons à notre heure dernière . . .
> Le temple est-il forcé?

Athalie herself, though trapped, still has good grounds to expect victory:

> Songez, méchants, songez
> Que mes armes encor vous tiennent assiégés.
> J'entends à haute voix tout mon camp qui m'appelle.
> On vient à mon secours. Tremblez, troupe rebelle.

The point is not that Racine is having his cake and eating it, both invoking inevitable Fate and creating melodramatic suspense. The equivocation has a deeper significance which links up with the inevitable but unexpected apostasy of Joas. It is brought out with terrible clarity in Act IV, Scene v, when Josabeth in her despair fears that Athalie will kill Joas after all. Joad replies:

> N'êtes-vous pas ici sur la montagne sainte
> Où le père des Juifs sur son fils innocent
> Leva sans murmurer un bras obéissant,
> Et mit sur un bûcher ce fruit de sa vieillesse,
> Laissant à Dieu le soin d'accomplir sa promesse,
> Et lui sacrifiant, avec ce fils aimé,
> Tout l'espoir de sa race, en lui seul renfermé?

That is the terrible mystery. God's grace is sure, but Man cannot be sure of it:

> Et quand Dieu, de vos bras l'arrachant sans retour,
> Voudrait que de David la maison fut éteinte . . .

It is the agony of faith on the edge of the abyss that gives *Athalie* its piercing intensity.

The knife-edge balance is exemplified in the structure of the piece. Racine's plays are characteristically built on a self-balancing design, by which two, four or six almost equally important characters are grouped round a central poetic theme which cannot be formulated conceptually but which the totality of the play is designed to express. This method is very evident in *Athalie*. Racine's remarks in the preface are interesting, in that (no doubt by design) they both hint at and obscure the truth:

Elle a pour sujet Joas reconnu et mis sur le trône, et j'aurais dû, dans les règles, l'intituler *Joas*; mais la plupart du monde n'en ayant entendu parler que sous le nom d'*Athalie*, je n'ai pas jugé à propos de la leur présenter sous un autre titre, puisque d'ailleurs Athalie y joue un personnage si considérable, et que c'est sa mort qui termine la pièce.

No doubt Joas is the centre of the play, the ambiguous saviour/destroyer placed between Athalie and Joad. Nevertheless, Athalie has an importance out of all proportion to the length of her part. The extraordinary subtlety and complexity of her verse have given critics ample excuse for thinking her rôle central to the play. But, on the face of things, Joad is more important: he has much the longer rôle, his verse is as impressive (though in a very different way), and he controls the action from beginning to end. The parallelism between him and Athalie is striking. Joad sees Joas as the saviour, and learns that he will be the destroyer, yet perseveres in the divine plan of preserving the link with the saviour to come. Athalie sees Joas (in her dream) as her destroyer, then (in her visit to the temple) as a source of comfort ('Je prétends vous traiter comme mon propre fils'), and then, finally, he is indeed the cause of her death (yet she sees that in the future he will avenge her). Both Joad and Athalie are brutally realistic in their methods, yet both are shown the 'real' truth by supernatural rather than rational means, and in the end this 'real' truth does not affect their actions. Joad has no doubt that Joas/Christ is the saviour, yet in his prophetic trance sees that Joas will apostasise and kill Zacharie. Athalie sees in her dream that Joas will destroy her, yet feels a strange tenderness for him, only to find that her dream becomes reality. On close inspection, this parallelism and ambivalence are seen in the motivation of the action. In a sense, Joad conducts the action, and he does so as a direct representative of God.[5] But in fact the motivation comes at least as much from Athalie. She sets the action in motion by coming to the temple, and it is her change of plan, rather than Joad's planned intention,[6] that brings about the dénouement. What is more, Athalie also is driven by the spirit of God:

> J'ignore si de Dieu l'ange se dévoilant
> Est venu lui montrer un glaive étincelant.

> Dans le temple des Juifs un instinct m'a poussée.

> Impitoyable Dieu, toi seul as tout conduit.

The victim no less than the priest is possessed by the divine spirit, and prophesies.

Athalie is far from a placid moral exemplum. There is at its heart a terrible tension, a fundamental opposition but complicity between good and evil, between Joas and Athalie, which gives the play the same disturbing vitality as *Phèdre*. It is only if we regard it as a rich and many-layered expression of this pulsing centre that its full significance can be appreciated.

Act I is apparently simple. Abner comes to the temple, which Athalie is preparing to destroy; Joad hints to Abner that Joas is still alive; Joad tells Josabeth that the time has come to restore Joas to the throne; the Chorus praises God. This simplicity conceals richness. The first speech contrasts the splendour of a just society under God, which is symbolised by the former glory of the temple, with the present poverty and danger. Abner's return itself hints at the return of the nation to its god (and perhaps of Racine to his religion). Against this state of unsatisfied tension Joad sets his calm trust in God:

> Celui qui met un frein à la fureur des flots
> Sait aussi des méchants arreter les complots . . .
> Je crains Dieu, cher Abner, et n'ai point d'autre crainte . . .
> Dieu pourra vous montrer, par d'importants bienfaits,
> Que sa parole est stable et ne trompe jamais.

But side by side with God's goodness is his wrath:

> Sous les pieds des chevaux cette reine foulée,
> Dans son sang inhumain les chiens désaltérés,
> Et de son corps hideux les membres déchirés . . .

which points forward to the cannibalistic motifs prominent in the rest of the play.

When Josabeth enters, Joad comes straight to the point: there is no nonsense about keeping secrets from the audience. What is significant is the paradox of his first speech to her:

> Les temps sont accomplis, Princesse: il faut parler,
> Et votre heureux larcin ne se peut plus celer.

– with its echoes of the Christian doctrine of the saviour ('in the fullness of time'; the redeemer who makes Adam's sin a *felix culpa*). Joad decides to reveal Joas's identity and overthrow Athalie, but the tension of the scene does not come from plot-interest of this kind. Joas is the saviour, but at the same time the wrath of God is feared:

> Qui sait si cet enfant, par leur crime entraîné,
> Avec eux en naissant ne fut pas condamné?
> Si Dieu, le séparant d'une odieuse race,
> En faveur de David voudra lui faire grâce?

Perhaps God will not save mankind; perhaps the 'happy fault' will not turn out to be happy or lucky after all. Joas's apostasy is an essential part of Racine's theme, and he keeps it before us throughout. The climax of this scene between Joad and Josabeth refers to it. Far from trusting cheerfully in Joas's goodness, Joad utters a prayer of terrifying grandeur:

> Grand Dieu, si tu prévois qu'indigne de sa race,
> Il doive de David abandonner la trace,
> Qu'il soit comme le fruit en naissant arraché,
> Ou qu'un souffle ennemi dans sa fleur a séché.

Against this sombre background, the Chorus praises the goodness of God. The songs of the Chorus in *Athalie* are sometimes harder and drier than those of *Esther*, but here they express sweetly enough the sweetness of the love of God:

> Que de raisons, quelle douceur extrême
> D'engager à ce Dieu son amour et sa foi!

This chorus has a double function: it confirms the omnipotence of God and stresses the goodness which is one half of his paradoxical nature.

Act I belongs to Joad, Act II to Athalie. The acts are also contrasted in form. In Act I, we have two long duologues, then the introduction of the Chorus. In Act II, the stage is crowded with characters and there are continual comings and goings. Much has been written about the psychological subtleties and poetic skill of this act. For our present purpose we may note only certain themes which the verse takes up and elaborates. First, the calmness and order which Athalie opposes to the calmness and order of Joad. Many of her lines have an unmistakable firmness:

> Je ne veux point ici rappeler le passé,
> Ni vous rendre raison du sang que j'ai versé.
> Ce que j'ai fait, Abner, j'ai cru le devoir faire.
> Je ne prends point pour juge un peuple téméraire:
> Quoi que son insolence ait osé publier,
> Le Ciel même a pris soin de me justifier.
> Sur d'éclatants succès ma puissance établie
> A fait jusqu'aux deux mers respecter Athalie;
> Par moi Jérusalem goûte un calme profond.[7]

This is contrasted with a second theme: distintegration. Athalie's authority and inner cohesion will dissolve, as the body of Jézabel disintegrates in the dream. This theme is re-echoed in the motifs of dis-

order (ll. 419–20); of uncertainty (l. 487, l. 610); of physical restlessness
(ll. 433–4, l. 436, l. 438); and, above all, of the wavering shapes and
doubtful status of a dream (ll. 501–6).

Athalie is full of references to blood, but in this act they not only occur
more frequently but are also most evidently linked with the motif of
eating:

> Après avoir au Dieu qui nourrit les humains
> De la moisson nouvelle offert les premiers pains . . .

> Des lambeaux pleins de sang et des membres affreux
> Que des chiens dévorants se disputaient entre eux.

> Il me nourrit des dons offerts sur son autel.

This imagery is apparent when Athalie expresses her satisfaction:

> Par moi Jérusalem goûte un calme profond.

> Je jouissais en paix du fruit de ma sagesse.

and also when she expresses her uneasiness:

> Un songe (me devrais-je inquiéter d'un songe?)
> Entretient dans mon coeur un chagrin qui le ronge.

Finally, there is a constant linking together of opposites which refers
to and emphasises the underlying paradoxes of the play. Athalie is rest-
less and vigorous, yet she is one of the characters in Racine who sits
down when under stress (the only others being Bérénice and Phèdre).
There is the paradox of the dream, which is the least realistic yet most
realistic evidence of the situation she is in. The quality of paradox is
present in some of the most famous lines ('Pour réparer des ans l'irré-
parable outrage') but it comes out most strongly in three passages: the
debate between Mathan and Abner (ll. 549–78); the stichomythia between Athalie and Joas (ll. 680–8); and the chorus at the end of the act.
In the first case, Racine is careful to spell out the paradox:

> Moi, nourri dans la guerre, aux horreurs du carnage,
> Des vengeances des rois ministre rigoureux,
> C'est moi qui prête ici ma voix aux malheureux!
> Et vous, qui lui devez des entrailles de père,
> Vous, ministre de paix dans le temps de colère,
> Couvrant d'un zèle faux votre ressentiment,
> Le sang à votre gré coule trop lentement!

In the second passage, contrast is forcibly expressed in the movement
of the verse:

J'ai mon Dieu que je sers; vous servirez le vôtre:
Ce sont deux puissants dieux.
                                        – Il faut craindre le mien;
Lui seul est Dieu, Madame, et le vôtre n'est rien.

The chorus which closes the act takes up this theme of paradox. It
begins with speculation about Joas, then contrasts the righteous with
the unrighteous. So far, this is banal enough. But in the middle of it,
an agonising preoccupation makes itself heard:

Mon Dieu, qu'une vertu naissante
Parmi tant de périls marche à pas incertains!
Qu'une âme qui te cherche et veut être innocent
Trouve d'obstacle à ses desseins!

The way of the just is indeed beset by enemies, but the disturbing
point is that it is difficult to know what the true path is. Finally, the last
stanza and refrain place in sharp juxtaposition the most opposed elements in the play:

De tous ces vains plaisirs où leur âme se plonge,
Que leur restera-t-il? Ce qui reste d'un songe
Dont on a reconnu l'erreur.
A leur réveil, ô réveil plein d'horreur!
Pendant que le pauvre à ta table
Goûtera de ta paix la douceur ineffable,
Il boiront dans la coupe affreuse, inépuisable,
Que tu présenteras, au jour de ta fureur,
A toute la race coupable.

O réveil plein d'horreur!
O songe peu durable!
O dangereuse erreur!

Here the ways of the ungodly are a 'dream', from which they will
awake to the terrible reality; in the scene of Athalie's dream it is the
real political situation ('Par moi Jérusalem goûte un calme profond')
which is an illusion and the dream which presents the reality of divine
judgment. The positive ('Il me nourrit des dons offerts sur son autel')
and the negative ('parmi des loups dévorants') aspects of eating are
fused in an image of the just and unjust at God's table. The fates of the
two are sharply opposed, but there is no doubt where the main accent
falls:

Ils boiront dans la coupe affreuse, inépuisable.

The force of this image of damnation is undeniable, but it contains a
more disturbing inference. The picture of mankind at God's table (re-

inforced by the frequent references to eating and drinking and altars) must have called to the mind of Racine and his first audience the Mass, in which the worshippers (or at least the priests) are given wafers and drink out of a cup, which contains the inexhaustible blood of Christ. It is difficult in this context not to connect the 'inexhaustible cup' of damnation with the chalice of salvation. Once again, the imagery of the play leads back to the central paradox: that the means of salvation is also the means of damnation.

The whole of Act III is given up to this theme, which is given its most extreme expression in the chorus at the end of the act. The first half of the act is centred on Mathan the apostate priest, the second on Joad the true priest. Mathan 'se trouble' and is literally 'égaré'; Joad is possessed by the divine afflatus and prophesies. The prophecy of Joad is the centre of the play, and I analyse its style in more detail later. It is prefaced by another vigorous assertion of the paradoxical nature of God ('Tu frappes et guéris. Tu perds et ressuscites') and falls into two contrasting parts, describing first the apostasy of Joas and the destruction of Jerusalem, and then the establishment of the new Jerusalem by the Messiah. At the end of the prophecy, Racine spends only 10 lines on forwarding the plot (Joad will crown Joas and arm his supporters), and throws the weight of the end of the act onto a further expression of his theme. The Chorus begins by doubting, almost sarcastically, whether God requires human suffering as a sacrifice. Then it reverts to Joad's last words, but only to emphasise their horrible and incongruous aspects:

> Quel spectacle à nos yeux timides!
> Qui l'eût cru, qu'on dût voir jamais
> Les glaives meurtriers, les lances homicides
> Briller dans la maison de paix?

After reflections on the plot (why will Abner not help? how can he?), the tone suddenly changes, and rises to extraordinary violence. Instead of the usual lyrical sweetness, it takes on an abrupt, exclamatory tone. Smooth stanzas give way, for the only time in the play, to short, antithetical cries:

> Je vois tout son éclat disparaître à mes yeux.
>   – Je vois de toutes parts sa clarté répandue.
> – Dans un gouffre profond Sion est descendue.
>   – Sion a son front dans les cieux.
> – Quel triste abaissement!
>   – Quelle immortelle gloire!
> – Que de cris de douleur!
>   – Que de chants de victoire!

After this crisis, the tone is modulated to one of grave earnestness, and then again to sweetness. Faith and hope remain, but the fearful opposites of redemption and damnation still stand on either side.

I have already remarked how in act IV Racine reminds us again of Joas's apostasy by making Joad urge him not to abandon God, and how the chorus to the Act at once plays on the normal dramatic suspense inherent in the plot and again reminds us that God's support (because we never completely know his purpose) is always equivocal. The act is carefully organised to present a whole complex of feelings. In the first scene, Joas thinks he may be sacrificed:

> Est-ce qu'en holocauste aujourd'hui présenté,
> Je dois, comme autrefois la fille de Jephthé,
> Du Seigneur par ma mort apaiser la colère?

The pathos may remind us of *Iphigénie*. But, more important, there is a reminder of two other sacrifices – that of Christ (it is in the chorus to this act that Joas, as the anointed one, will be identified with Christ) and of Zacharie ('dans le lieu saint ce pontife égorgé'). This lends wider significance, as well as a sharper poignancy, to the scene where Joad watches Joas and Zacharie embrace:

> Enfants, ainsi toujours puissiez-vous être unis!

– a significance and poignancy which are increased by the immediate references to blood, killing and salvation:

> Vous savez donc quel sang vous a donné la vie?
> – Et je sais quelle main sans vous me l'eût ravie.

It is in this context that we hear Joad's solemn warning:

> Loin du trône nourri, de ce fatal honneur,
> Hélas! vous ignorez le charme empoisonneur;
> De l'absolu pouvoir vous ignorez l'ivresse,
> Et des lâches flatteurs la voix enchanteresse.
> Bientôt ils vous diront que les plus saintes lois,
> Maîtresses du vil peuple, obéissent aux rois;
> Qu'un roi n'a d'autre frein que sa volonté même;
> Qu'il doit immoler tout à sa grandeur suprême;
> Qu'aux larmes, au travail le peuple est condamné,
> Et d'un sceptre de fer veut être gouverné;
> Que, s'il n'est opprimé, tôt ou tard il opprime:
> Ainsi de piège en piège, et d'abîme en abîme,
> Corrompant de vos moeurs l'aimable pureté,
> Ils vous feront enfin haïr la vérité,
> Vous peindront la vertu sous une affreuse image.
> Hélas! ils ont des rois égaré le plus sage.

We need not look for a reference here to contemporary politics. Louis XIV, the defender of true religion, can hardly have taken these lines as criticism. He, unlike the unjust monarch, did not subvert, but upheld the 'saintes lois'; he did not regard his will as supreme, but as supreme under God. The speech is a reproach to the unjust king, not to the self-disciplined and God-fearing Louis – the king who did at St Cyr indeed 'protect the orphan'. Far more important than any political significance is the speech's expressive function for the main theme of the play. On the level of plot, the evil Athalie is to be replaced by the good Joas: this speech explains how Joas in turn will become bad. On a deeper level, it insinuates a more terrifying mystery: corruption may fasten most insidiously on the best: 'l'or pur' becomes 'un plomb vil'. The speech is long, detailed and concrete because these elements of its meaning are of central importance to the play, and must be borne in on us with complete conviction.

Act V consummates the sacrifice: Athalie is destroyed, but at the price that Joas will avenge her. Joad's deceit in sending Abner to promise Athalie that the temple's hidden treasure will be surrendered has been criticised on moral grounds. There is no justification for criticism on poetic grounds. We should not judge Joad as if he were a real person; we should attend with our minds and ears to the poetic pattern. The trick ('de piège en piège') brings to the fore the motifs of Athalie's blindness to the real situation (Josabeth prays later, 'Puissant maître des cieux, | Remets-lui le bandeau dont tu couvris ses yeux') and of her being attracted to her doom by the gold which is the symbol and means of redemption. The inscrutable divine will may also mislead the just. Joad's realistic appreciation of this is shown as superior to the merely human prudence of Abner, who says:

> Et tout l'or de David, s'il est vrai qu'en effet
> Vous gardiez de David quelque trésor secret,
> Et tout ce que des mains de cette reine avare
> Vous avez pu sauver et de riche et de rare,
> Donnez-le.

Joad's view of the situation is of a more terrifying order:

> Songez qu'autour de vous
> L'ange exterminateur est debout avec nous.

When Athalie comes in, her verse has an earthy, hectic quality:

> Te voilà, séducteur . . .
> Cet enfant, ce trésor qu'il faut qu'on me remette,
> Où sont-ils?

When Joas is revealed, she reacts in a rapid succession of ways: rage ('Perfide!'); self-pity ('ô reine infortunée!'); stinging reproach ('Lâche Abner'); then again this brutal directness:

> Laisse-là ton Dieu, traître,
> Et venge-moi.

Her recourse in this confusion of emotion is an appeal to external reality:

> Lui Joas? lui ton roi? Songez, méchants, songez
> Que mes armes encor vous tiennent assiégés.
> J'entends à haute voix tout mon camp qui m'appelle.
> On vient à mon secours. Tremblez, troupe rebelle.

Against all this, Racine sets the calm authority of the divine world, embodied in the verse of Ismaël's speech:

> Seigneur, le temple est libre et n'a plus d'ennemis.
> L'étranger est en fuite, et le Juif est soumis.
> Comme le vent dans l'air dissipe la fumée,
> La voix du Tout-Puissant a chassé cette armée.

With this, we reach the firm ground of divine authority, with which *Esther* was content. But here, this reassertion of divine law is engulfed by a more terrible revelation. Athalie has a moment of illumination which echoes and completes themes adumbrated in her dream and in Joad's prophecy:

> Voici ce qu'en mourant lui souhaite sa mère:
> Que dis-je, souhaiter? Je me flatte, j'espère
> Qu'indocile à ton joug, fatigué de ta loi,
> Fidèle au sang d'Achab qu'il a reçu de moi,
> Conforme à son aïeul, à son père semblable,
> On verra de David l'héritier detestable
> Abolir tes honneurs, profaner ton autel,
> Et venger Athalie, Achab et Jézabel.

The opposites of damnation and redemption are still dramatically present: Athalie is led off to die, and meanwhile Joas utters a prayer that we know will not be fulfilled:

> Dieu, qui voyez mon trouble et mon affliction,
> Détournez loin de moi sa malédiction,
> Et ne souffrez jamais qu'elle soit accomplie.
> Faites que Joas meure avant qu'il vous oublie.

After this, the play ends quickly. There is no joy, no appeasement.

The righteous have triumphed, but only for a moment. Joad's last words are not ironical, but they do not promise an easy way out. There is no facile hope in *Athalie*, no simple moral recipe for salvation.

I have dwelt on the paradoxicalness, the anguished sense that redemption is needed, and is possible, but cannot be attained with any certainty, because this is the living centre of the play, which does not depend on acceptance of this or that theological doctrine. This is vital for the status of *Athalie*. I have argued that tragedy depends for its existence on the possibility that poetry is regarded as important (i.e. as capable of conveying directly truths felt as irreducible to other terms), not as the elegant presentation of truths revealed by other means. Poetry, to be serious, must depend on experience, not on external theory. The opposites in *Athalie*, like those in *Phèdre*, are based on common and emotionally-charged human experiences. It is because it expresses experience that *Athalie* is able to retain the sense of tragedy. In other words, the achievement is essentially poetic. But it was not achieved without strain, and this strain is evident in the verse.

3

The verse of *Athalie* differs in tone and texture from that of Racine's other plays, and this is a sure indication of a change in his approach. The most obvious difference in technique is the use of the Chorus. *Esther* had shown the way, but only how lyrics could be introduced into a lightweight piece. *Athalie*, like *Phèdre*, has full poetic seriousness, yet a Chorus could hardly have been accommodated in *Phèdre* without changing the nature of the play.

Racine has been praised for introducing into *Athalie* a lyricism rare in the *grand siècle*. But our terms need defining. By lyricism, I think is meant what we may call, for want of a better term, the lyrical element. This covers anything in describing which we are inclined to use words like 'celebration', 'invocation', 'incantation', 'lament'. It is present in many kinds of poetry, perhaps in all great poems. It would include the beginning of *De Rerum Natura*, Enobarbus's description of Cleopatra's arrival at Cydnus, the end of *The Dunciad*. If we bear this in mind, we can perhaps see the significance of the use of a Chorus in *Athalie*. Racinian tragedy, as exemplified in *Bérénice* and *Phèdre*, is not an arid form that needs the lyrical watering-can: it proceeds by an inner law which is only apparently dependent on the formal plot. We can call this method lyrical if we must, but we would be wiser not to: it is simply the method of poetic, as opposed to naturalistic, drama. It certainly embraces, among other things, the lyrical element. What could give more scope for this element than *Phèdre*, where the apparent drama is enveloped and carried along by a deeper dramatic movement which finds expression, for instance, in that delirium in which Phèdre realises her doom? In *Athalie*, a very different method is evident. The verse has a sonority and firmness which some critics have called epic, and rarely displays the hallucinatory sensuousness of the verse in *Phèdre*. The lyrical element is confined to three areas: the choruses, Joad's prophecy, and Athalie's dream. It is precisely in Athalie's dream that we find verse which recalls that of *Phèdre*. The other areas are well fenced-off from the rest of the play, and an effort is made to give them a natural explanation. The presence of the Chorus[8] and two of its songs[9] are carefully motivated, and who, if not a High Priest inspired by his god, can be allowed a lyrical interlude? This separation, far from showing progress towards a form permitting greater lyricism, might be taken as an attempt to retain a lyrical element in a form of drama which increasingly excluded it: what was once part of the main substance is now siphoned off into lyrical interludes. These interludes are 'only poetry', and the characters who indulge in them are given excuses for doing so. Racine is revising his form and flying contrary to the trend of the theatre of his day, but there is in his strategy more than a hint of the manoeuvres adopted by playwrights tied to the conventions of modern naturalism. According to these conventions, intense, fanciful, or even explicit utterance is permitted only in two circumstances: when it comes from drunks, lunatics, artists or professional orators; or when it is sung (which was surely one reason for the vogue of the musical).

What, then, are the characteristics of the style of *Athalie*? Let us take the non-lyrical parts first. Two movements which we have repeatedly found in Racine's verse are the disintegration of a moral value at the moment of formulation, and a revelation of complicity between the character apparently sponsoring the value and the impulses that destroy it. In *Athalie* (except in the speeches of Athalie herself in Act II) there is nothing of this: the verse depends for its effect on the solidity of the values it creates:

> Je crains Dieu, cher Abner, et n'ai point d'autre crainte.
> Viens-tu du Dieu vivant braver la majesté?
> Lieu terrible où de Dieu la majesté repose.

There is here that power to invest an ideal with almost physical substance that we find in Corneille. We also find in *Athalie* (but not in *Phèdre*) that proud irony which is so frequent in Corneille:

Ami, peux-tu penser que d'un zèle frivole
Je me laisse aveugler par une vaine idole,
Pour un fragile bois, que malgré mon secours,
Les vers sur son autel consume tous les jours?
Peuple lâche, en effet, et né pour l'esclavage,
Hardi contre Dieu seul!

With this change in the tone of the verse go two changes in texture.
On the one hand there is a loosening of the rhythm, in the direction of
the flexibility of everyday speech:

> Hé, Madame, excusez
> Un enfant . . .
> Quel père
> Je quitterais! Et pour . . .
> – Hé bien?
> – Pour quelle mère!

On the other hand, there is a tendency to pompousness:

> L'illustre Josabeth porte vers vous ses pas.

Both features can be found together:

> En croirai-je mes yeux,
> Cher Abner? Quel chemin a pu jusqu'en ces lieux
> Vous conduire au travers d'un camp qui nous assiège?
> On disait que d'Achab la fille sacrilège
> Avait, pour assurer ses projects inhumains,
> Chargé d'indignes fers vos généreuses mains.

The periphrasis 'd'Achab la fille' has point, but the ennobling
epithets in the last line have not. We have here a trace of what em-
barrassed Corneille and was to trouble Voltaire: how to express mundane facts in suitably poetical terms.

The lyrical parts of the play also have one disturbing feature. It has
frequently been remarked that in Joad's prophecy the positive elements are weakly presented. The density and force of the lines depicting
disaster –

> Comment en un plomb vil l'or pur s'est-il changé?

> Ton encens à ses yeux est un encens souillé.

– compare strangely with the vague presages of bliss:

> Jérusalem renaît plus charmante et plus belle.

The reason for this (as in other attempts to make heaven convincing) is the lack of experience on which the poet can draw, but the difficulty becomes acute in an age where the framework of thought within which such abstractions carry emotional conviction is ceasing to be fully acceptable. Where a collective and elaborated religious system is failing in this way, the path is open for poets to express their positive mystical feelings in a personal rather than a collective form. (Negative feelings are no problem: everybody has them.) The result, however seriously meant, seems etiolated when compared with the expression of a firmly-established collective myth. In *Athalie*, we have a trace of this personal, mystical approach to religion:

> Au lieu des cantiques charmants
> Où David t'exprimait ses saints ravissements,
> Et bénissait son Dieu, son Seigneur et son père . . .

To sum up, the characteristics of the style of *Athalie* are these: a separation of the lyrical from the non-lyrical; an insistence on the concreteness of abstract values; an occasional approximation to the loose rhythms of speech; a tendency towards empty pomposity; and an intermittent failure to render collective positive values which is partly compensated by hints of a mystical, personal type of faith. We can also note other striking features of the play: the use of spectacle and stage-effects (especially in Act V); the introduction of physical properties (the book, sword and crown at the beginning of Act IV). Taken together, these features point unmistakably to developments in the eighteenth century and later: it is no accident that Voltaire, that supporter of neo-classical pomp allied with the delights of 'philosophical' maxims and spectacle, greatly admired *Athalie*.

The style, in fact, shows evident signs of the naturalistic method that was increasingly to replace the poetic. Poetry was increasingly to retreat to the realm of the lyric; in drama it was to wrap its emptiness in elaborate diction and eke out its failing charms with those of spectacle. *Athalie* is far from succumbing to any of these trends, but we may well believe that Racine, in the depressing climate of the end of the century, felt that the delicate balance that had made possible the poetic drama of *Phèdre* could no longer be maintained. In *Athalie* he sought strength from every quarter to help him erect a serious work of art in an age when criticism was becoming more and more naturalistic in tone. If in *Bérénice* he had achieved a rational tragedy that could live in a world without the supernatural, and if in *Phèdre* he had relied directly on poetry and myth, in *Athalie* he felt unable to turn again to tragedy except under external guarantees of seriousness. The subject of *Athalie* had the sanction of Christianity behind it, and his poetic strategy made concessions to attitudes that did not allow full seriousness to poetry. *Athalie* is a stupendous achievement in the face of great odds. Although Racine was able to win this final victory, the moment for tragedy had passed.

18

CONCLUSION

I have confined myself largely to questions about the form of French classical tragedy, with the aims of finding out what dramatic principles underlay it, and how far the dramatists intended, or were able, to achieve the emotional effect of tragedy. This approach has, I hope, shown its uses, though it cannot by its nature answer all the questions we might wish it to. In this final chapter I shall first summarise the argument and then comment briefly on the light it might throw on other questions.

The conceptual scheme with which we started is that there are two approaches to playwriting which can usefully be distinguished: the poetic, in which the elements of a play are conceived as a means of expressing a meaning inexpressible in any other terms; and the naturalistic, which rests on the assumption that a play is an object which may be skilfully made but is not serious in its own right – its seriousness (if it lays claim to any) can come only from its faithful imitation of real life or its expression of truths established by some other discipline. These definitions are of course intended only to mark two theoretical poles, and in practice matters are not so clear-cut. Nevertheless, terms with the same import are common enough in modern criticism of drama, and have at least an operational usefulness.

I have argued that the neo-classical critical position, as originated by sixteenth-century Italian theorists and elaborated by seventeenth-century critics in France, tended definitely towards the naturalist position. This is above all evident in the way in which the theorists subordinated poetry to external criteria, with the dual imperative that it should teach morality and realistically imitate behaviour. A subordinate imperative, not always insisted on, was that poetry should respect historical truth. In these ways, neo-classicism resembled the naturalism which developed from it in the eighteenth and ninteenth centuries. In some ways, indeed, its theory had already reached the same destination as the nineteenth-century naturalists: it is not hard to find in Chapelain (or Corneille) utterances which reflect faithfully the naturalistic principles of Zola. In reading the neo-classical critics, it is sometimes difficult to see how they could justify such non-representational criteria as the use of verse. With its classical and Renaissance heritage, neo-classicism is obviously a transitional form, and was in fact to lead rapidly as well as logically to the full naturalism of the nineteenth century.

It is in the context of the neo-classical trend towards naturalism that I have tried to interpret the development of Corneille's dramatic technique in his tragedies. My interpretation is that for a time he resisted the trend, but then embraced it and carried its logic very far.

His foreword to *La Veuve* suggests a naturalistic bias, but his early attempts at tragedy show a different attitude. At the time of *Le Cid* he was refractory to the new critical doctrines, and, later, his *Discours*, with their equivocations over poetic justice, their defence of the use of violent and evil characters, and their attempts to use *le vrai* as an escape from *le vraisemblable*, show an awareness of the dilemmas of naturalism. Nevertheless, we can see in his criticism after 1637 a growing reluctance to defend poetic drama as poetry, and an increasing stress on factual accuracy, realistic motivation of the characters, verse close to prose, avoidance of soliloquy and ornate narrations designed for effect, and the use of stage-directions.

Corneille's early comedies suggest a temperamental leaning towards naturalism, but in the mid-1630s he turned towards poetry and tragedy – a development which seems inevitable if we regard him as the poet of *Le Cid* and *Cinna*, but which on a wider view of his work seems to need explanation. At that time, as Tristan's *La Mariane* was to demonstrate, the way was still open not only to poetic drama but to tragedy, and perhaps Corneille was influenced by his fellow-play-wrights. Whatever the cause of this shift towards poetry, we can see the effects of his hesitations in his plays. In *Le Cid*, the uncertainty over the ending is only one sign of his hesitation as to whether he is expressing a tragic meaning through his poetry or decorating a moving but *vraisemblable* story. In *Horace*, he moves towards acceptance of neo-classicism, but the uncertainty over the rôle of the oracle reflects a continuing hesitancy of aim. In *Cinna*, something remarkable happens. He adopts the poetic method wholeheartedly, at the cost of fracturing his plot and characterisation in a very un-naturalistic way. But at the same time he breaks away from tragedy towards a more optimistic, open-ended view of life – one reminiscent of the Renaissance rather than the Counter-Reformation. Then, in *Polyeucte*, there is a reaction against this double heterodoxy: he attempts to reconcile poetry and naturalism in the context of a religious subject. The attempt almost succeeds, but the ending shows that the two methods could not be reconciled within the form he had chosen.

Polyeucte marks a turning-point in Corneille's career. The sharp change in the tone and quality of his plays is hard to explain. We certainly cannot ascribe it, as nineteenth-century critics tended to do, to a general decline in his powers. My explanation is that he recognised the problems posed by naturalism for the poetic and tragic forms he had been attempting, and began consciously to experiment with new solutions.

I believe, then, that by the early 1640s neo-classical drama was set on a course towards naturalism – ultimately in the nineteenth-century sense. If we consider the general effect of this on drama, writers of *tragédies* had two alternatives: to attempt to be serious, or not. After the 1640s, many dramatists turned to lighter forms, and we see the vogue of machine plays and *tragédies galantes* – romantic tragi-comedies under another name.

If a poet chose seriousness, he had again two alternatives. First, he could accept the double convention of basic naturalism allied with neo-classical dignity. Examples of this can be seen in *Le Comte d'Essex* and *Ariane*. I have shown how far Thomas Corneille takes the conventions of naturalism in them – not only in his reliance on the ability of his actors to build their characters, but in his refuge in broken and inarticulate verse. At the same time, his respect for neo-classical decorum inhibits the use of striking effects and hampers the clear development of his plots. The results, though worthy, are a trifle dull: we are not far from the *comédie larmoyante*.

The second option was more exciting, and was the path chosen by the greatest naturalists, in the seventeenth century and later. This was to exploit the new resources of naturalism, and to jettison neo-classical decorum. It was the choice of Pierre Corneille. In his middle period (from *Pompée* to *Pertharite*) he had struggled to break out of the neo-classical impasse. First, he cultivated violent melodrama, with plentiful verbal embroidery; then he experimented with new types of play – a *comédie héroïque* (*Don Sanche*), a *pièce à machines* (*Andromède*), or other remarkable blends (*Nicomède* and *Pertharite*). After *Pertharite*, he retired to think things over. The fruits of his reflection are in his *Examens* and *Discours*. In them he not only carried the implications of naturalism very far, but also reached for some of the ways of evading its dullness: melodrama and the neglect of morality.

The practical results are worked out in his plays from *Oedipe* to *Pulchérie*, and are responsible for some of these plays' unusual features: the mixture of comedy and seriousness, the inclusion of a wide range of unusual characters, the emphasis on local colour and background, and the use of deliberately inflated, precious or confused verse. The style of these plays embraces both naturalism and poetry, both neo-classicism and a more relaxed style. The dangers of the mixture are clear enough, and the faults to which they lead account for the long neglect of the plays of this period. But on the whole these plays are remarkably successful – largely because Corneille throws overboard the attempt at tragic rigour or consistent dignity. All of them are interesting: many of them (*Oedipe*, *Agésilas*, *Tite et Bérénice*, *Pulchérie*) are delightful; two (*Othon* and *Attila*) are near-masterpieces; and *Sertorius* is one of the greatest of his plays. It has not the sobriety of *Horace* or *Cinna*, nor is it tragic: but this is not now what Corneille is after.

Finally, he makes a new departure. *Suréna* is a poetic play, and the meaning it expresses is tragic. Perhaps Racine's first tragic successes inspired him: it is interesting that in *Suréna* he treats in the tragic mode some of the themes of Racine's untragic *Mithridate*.

If we now turn to Racine, I would emphasise the paradoxicalness of his achievement. It has often been remarked that his tragedies, in appearance the logical culmination of French neo-classicism, contrast sharply with the plays of his contemporaries. I would agree that this paradox is real, and is apparent in his critical ideas and his dramatic technique. True, on the face of things, he is the perfect neo-classicist. Yet, if we read his prefaces, we find him constantly under attack for violating neo-classical principles. Certainly, he keeps the rules of the unities, the *liaison des scènes*, and so on, and with a rare docility. But elsewhere there are signs of a profound unorthodoxy: his use of mythological subjects, his retention of soliloquies, his neglect of local colour and background detail, his ambiguous attitude to poetic justice, his emphasis on poetry, his avoidance of naturalistic inarticulacy. This impression is increased if we look at his plays in detail. In some of the greatest of them we find curious gaps between the formal plot and the thematic pattern, and even a lack of concern for imitating probable behaviour.

This leads us to suppose in Racine's dramaturgy something of the ambivalence we find in his attitudes to Port Royal, to the theatre, and to the king: a combination of docility and rebellion. On the surface, there is perfect conformity to neo-classicism and its naturalistic basis. Underneath, there is a concern with poetic and tragic meaning. This underlying concern is connected with his interest in passion, which has always been acknowledged. This passion is not merely sexual, but is linked more generally with what, to use a modern mythologem, we would call the unconscious. His plays are full of references to these sub-rational processes. Nor is this surprising, if we link him with his context. On the one hand, we have the seventeenth-century interest in *le coeur*, which is concerned with just these irrational compulsions. On the other hand, we have that unassimilated element in neo-classicism which Racine was able to use: reliance on the example of the Ancients – including the Greeks, with their amoral and passionate mythology.

In Racine, then, as in Corneille, we find a tension between poetry and naturalism. In Racine, it usually takes the form of a conflict between the poetic substance and the neo-classical façade. In *La Thébaïde*, we see his natural bent in his sense of fatality, his neglect of orthodox morality, his attempts at the poetic method. In *Alexandre* he swings towards a more conventional type of drama: a romanesque play on a naturalistic base, with only touches of poetry. *Andromaque* marks a breakthrough in his technique. We have here the typically Racinian development of an apparently perfect neo-classical plot in conjunction with an inner poetic action. Only on close inspection is the lack of connection between them apparent: the movement of the plot bears little relation to the characters' reactions, and there is a contrast between the relatively static, poetic rôles of Andromaque and Oreste and the more active, naturalistic (even comic) rôles of Hermione and Pyrrhus. In *Britannicus*, Racine moves again towards naturalism. The major part of the play is developed as a Cornelian drama, with only hints of the poetic theme. The main expression of the theme is in the second half of Act V, where it completes the emotional effect but appears divorced from the main action. Finally, Racine achieves a perfect solution in *Bérénice*. By reducing his plot to the simplest, he is able to express his poetic meaning in a form which seems unexceptionably naturalistic: only the lack of political background and the disregard of contemporary conventions in his portrayal of his central characters show that his purpose is not normal psychological drama. The play is a *tour de force*, and the revisions show the trouble it cost him.

Bérénice is the culmination of a stage in Racine's development, and he did not attempt this particular feat again. He turned at once to a further period of experiment. *Bajazet*, *Mithridate* and *Iphigénie* belong to a less strenuous type of drama – a type closer to his audience's expectations, and one which aroused little criticism. The attempt to express a poetic meaning is abandoned, and Racine concentrates on perfecting the dramatic surface. But the tension between his poetic aim and the naturalistic form remained. On my view, in these years he was revolving the problems of achieving seriousness in an *Alceste* or *Iphigénie en Tauride*. The result is *Phèdre*, which shows the conflict in its clearest form. The force of passion in it is more emphatic, more elemental than ever; more obviously than in his other plays, the plot is arbitrary, the surface machinery divorced from the inner progression of the theme.

It has not been part of my purpose to explore the reasons for Racine's retreat. The social pressures described by Picard seem reason enough. It is possible, however, that the aesthetic problems with which he had been struggling were intractable enough to make him glad to turn to the writing of history. Such dramatic or semi-dramatic work as he embarked on between *Phèdre* and *Athalie* – operas, *L'Idylle de la Paix*, *Esther* – show him content with surface prettiness. As he turned back to Jansenism, his aesthetic problems changed their shape, but without changing fundamentally. In *Athalie*, although he takes his sanction from the literal truth of the Bible, in his poetry he expresses an ambiguous meaning: the close kinship between salvation and damnation. The achievement is great, but the form is already beginning to disintegrate: the verse begins to show trends towards the prosaic and the pompous, with lyricism restricted to special interludes.

My approach to Corneille and Racine, though perhaps from an unusual angle, is not far from the views of many modern critics who have approached French classicism from different viewpoints. In the case of Corneille, I would agree with the modern emphasis on the value of the later plays and their resemblance to the early comedies, and in general on his realism and close rendering of contemporary manners and ideals. In the case of Racine, my conclusions are close to those of Vinaver and Butler in particular; but I would also agree with Goldmann to the extent of emphasising the paradoxical nature of Racine's work, and that *Bérénice*, *Phèdre* and *Athalie* are his greatest achievements, each using a different technique and perhaps corresponding to a different underlying attitude. Nor is my overall view very different from the ways in which Corneille and Racine were compared by their contemporaries, if we translate their critical terms into ours. Corneille respected moral virtue – that is, the moral order outside poetry – and the characters of the nationalities he portrayed – that is, the external truths of behaviour; Racine failed in both respects – that is, he turned away from the main concerns of naturalism – and subordinated everything to passion – that is, to the unconscious, the irrational and amoral world of myth.

Beside the power and freshness of the plays themselves, every critical approach seems fragmentary and inadequate, leaving all the important questions unanswered. I will end, therefore, with some speculations – suggested by my conclusions and their congruence with those of other critics – about some of the wider questions which still seek an answer.

The cardinal question is perhaps one I have skirted: why did this trend towards naturalism make itself felt early in the seventeenth century, and eventually come to dominate European literature? Students in many fields have noted that the late sixteenth and the seventeenth centuries saw a shift away from the fluidity and openness of Renaissance culture towards a more schematic and dogmatic attitude in religion, art and intellectual inquiry generally. The critical doctrines of neo-classicism are analogous to the rules laid down for painting by the Council of Trent, and certainly derive from the theorists of Counter-Reformation Italy. Should we see the Counter-Reformation as a factor behind the adoption of the rules, as some have claimed? Would the dogmatism of the Church then be the source in neo-classicism of that naturalistic tendency to subordinate poetry to externally-formulated truth and morality – a source to be replaced in the eighteenth century by the authority of science and rationalism? Some dates are certainly suggestive. Chapelain was not a dogmatic man, and he hated 'les moines', but he was an adolescent when Vanini was burned, and was struggling to make his name during the years when Théophile was in prison and under threat of the stake. Was the emphasis on the morality and truth of poetry in part a prudent insurance, in an age when poets other than Théophile might be suspected of libertinism? Could Corneille's acceptance of the rules have been partly motivated by similar reflections? Should we link the careful reasoning of the *Discours*, so suggestive of a deep uneasiness, not simply with the playwright's pique at d'Aubignac's attacks but also with the pious scruples of the author of *L'Imitation*?

Whatever the answers, they are unlikely to be simple. Modern scholarship has emphasised the conflicting cross-currents in seventeenth-century thought: piety and libertinism, rationalism and superstition. Some have stressed the prevalence of the Renaissance magical and hermetic tradition and its importance in the seventeenth-century rise of science. Corneille was unlikely to be sympathetic to such things, but again some dates are suggestive. Campanella came to Paris in 1634, and in the next few years was high in favour with Richelieu. It is in these years that we find Corneille (at this time closely associated with Richelieu) writing *Médée*, with its magician-heroine, and *L'Illusion*, with its benevolent 'mage' Alcandre. Is this mere coincidence, or did Corneille pick up in Richelieu's circle some of Campanella's ideas, with their mystical insistence on the magic power of poetry? If so, did these ideas play any part in Corneille's movement from the realism of his comedies to the poetic *tragédies* of his early maturity?

Similar questions can be posed of Racine. Butler has linked his early tragedies with the Colbertian policy of opposing to feudal ideas more modern concepts of a centralised secular state allowing freedom of conscience to industrious subjects. There is some evidence – his association with Molière, La Fontaine and Saint-Réal, the suspicious gap in his correspondence from 1665 to 1676 – that Racine may have dabbled in heterodox ideas at this time. Should we see in this a sign of an evasion of dogma which chimes in with his evasion of neo-classic dogma in the period up to the early 1670s? Some have seen in *Bajazet*, *Mithridate* and *Iphigénie* a return to the baroque ideals of the 1620s. Should we see also a parallel between Racine's gradually reawakening piety and his renewed respect for the providential rules of baroque tragedy? Again, the background is unclear. There is perhaps, in the growing friendship of Boileau and Racine, and their growing-together on literary doctrine, an ideological as well as a literary link: Boileau had also flirted with libertinism, but in the 1670s moved towards a severe piety. If so, does this ideological element enter into the quarrel over *Phèdre* – that confrontation in which the two poets were ranged against the free-thinking Madame Deshoulières and the notorious duc de Nevers, who took an interest in black magic and was said to be neither a courtier, nor a warrior nor a Christian? Whatever the answer here, there seems little doubt that there is a connection between Racine's deepening religious seriousness and his concern for moral truth in *Esther* and *Athalie*, which again might be linked with the signs of naturalism in these plays. So much of the inner life of Corneille and Racine is for ever hidden from us; so much of the intellectual history of the *grand siècle* remains to be written.

My argument, therefore, is incomplete, and perhaps in the nature of things must always remain so. At least, in trying to illuminate some of the formal principles behind the great seventeenth-century *tragédies* we have not departed from the main tradition of modern criticism. Corneille and Racine are no longer seen as marble monuments of a timeless classicism, but as men struggling and experimenting in their particular contexts, involved in their own time and its concerns. The form in which they wrote was not fixed, and not isolated from the movement of history. In each play they are struggling to find new aesthetic solutions. In their work as a whole, we can see their place in a long and gradual movement, of which they stand near the beginning: the progression of European dramatic form from poetry towards a greater naturalism; a progression which was to reach its culmination in the late nineteenth century, and then give way to a search for new poetic forms.

NOTES

CHAPTER I

1 S. L. Bethell, *Shakespeare and the Popular Dramatic Tradition* (London, 1948), pp. 22–3.

2 Ronald Gaskell, *Drama and Reality: the European Theatre since Ibsen* (London, 1972), pp. 12–36.

3 'De la Poésie Dramatique', in *Oeuvres Esthétiques*, ed. P. Vernière (Paris, 1968), pp. 198–9.

4 (Paris, 1949), vol. I, p. 31.

5 *Oeuvres Esthétiques, loc. cit.*, p. 196.

6 *La Veuve*, 'Au Lecteur', in *Pierre Corneille: Writings on the Theatre*, ed. H. T. Barnwell (Oxford, 1965), p. 176.

7 'Lettre sur la Règle des Vingt-Quatre Heures', in *Opuscules Critiques*, ed. Alfred C. Hunter (Paris, 1936), p. 115.

8 R. Bray, *La Formation de la Doctrine Classique en France* (Paris, 1963), pp. 206–7.

9 Quoted in *The Oxford Ibsen*, ed. James Walter McFarlane and Graham Orton (Oxford, 1963), vol. IV, p. 606.

10 *Ibid.*, p. 603.

11 There are of course instances of people forgetting this. A famous case is that quoted by Stendhal in which a man in Baltimore shot the actor playing Othello to stop him murdering Desdemona. But our reaction to the anecdote shows how abnormal this complete absorption is. T. J. Reiss, *Toward Dramatic Illusion: Theatrical Technique and Meaning from Hardy to 'Horace'* (New Haven and London, 1971), pp. 144–5, quotes the example of children at a pantomime, and d'Aubignac's reference to a girl at *Pyrame et Thisbé*. Here again, the references are to an abnormal case – that of children unused to plays.

12 'Ce livre, d'un savant dont l'autorité est décisive, va me servir de base solide . . . car je compte, sur tous les points, me retrancher derrière Claude Bernard. Le plus souvent, il me suffira de remplacer le mot "médecin" par le mot "romancier" pour rendre ma pensée claire et lui apporter la rigueur d'une vérité scientifique.' (Quoted in Marc Bernard, *Zola par lui-même* (Paris, 1971), pp. 176–7.)

13 'There is a science of people's social life: a great doctrine of cause and effect in this field. We can find our criteria there.' (*The Messingkauf Dialogues*, trans. John Willett (London, 1965), p. 35.)

14 Quoted from *The Quintessence of Ibsenism* in *Drama from Ibsen to Eliot*

(London, 1952), p. 140. This book by Raymond Williams is especially valuable for its analysis of the implications of naturalism for dramatic form.
15 George Steiner, *The Death of Tragedy* (London, 1961), p. 8.
16 P. J. Yarrow, *Corneille* (London, 1963), pp. 317–18.
17 'Premier Discours', *Writings*, p. 8.
18 'Deuxième Discours', *ibid.*, p. 30.
19 'Premier Discours', *ibid.*, p. 8.
20 'Examen' of *Nicomède*, *ibid.*, p. 152.
21 *Ibid.*
22 Preface to *Iphigénie* (*Oeuvres Complètes*, ed. E. Groos, E. Pilon and R. Picard (Paris, 1950), vol. I, p. 671.)
23 Preface to *Bérénice* (*ibid.*, p. 465).
24 Eugène Vinaver *Racine: Principles de la Tragédie en Marge de la Poetique d'Aristote* (Manchester and Paris, 1951), pp. 59–60.

CHAPTER 2

1 *Writings*, p. 8.
2 *Ibid.*, p. 32.
3 *Ibid.*, pp. 2, 57.
4 *Ibid.*, p. 34.
5 *Ibid.*, p. 21.
6 *Ibid.*, p. 27.
7 *Ibid.*, pp. 5–6.
8 I am not subscribing to the complaint the Corneille's characters are inhuman or unnatural; in my view this is untrue in some of his plays and irrelevant in the others. But the evidence on which it is based certainly increases the difficulty of reconciling Corneille's practice with Aristotle's theory, which clearly recommends a choice of hero 'ni tout à fait bon, ni tout à fait méchant'. (*Ibid.*, p. 31).
9 *Ibid.*, p. 34.
10 *Ibid.*, pp. 33–4.
11 *Ibid.*, p. 14.
12 *Ibid.*, p. 16.
13 *Ibid.*, p. 2.
14 *Ibid.*, pp. 4–5.
15 Another instance is his discussion of narrations, especially in his *Examen* of *Médée*. He emphasises that the characters on the stage must be in a sufficiently patient mood to listen. The stress, that is, is on plausibility – on the presumed emotions of the fictional characters, not on the meaning of the play or the effect on the audience.
16 *Writings*, pp. 147–8.
17 E.g., Bethell, *Shakespeare and Popular Tradition*, p. 22: 'the principles which caused the neo-classicists to fight for the unities are the principles of

naturalism today. So if neo-classicism failed in its directly Aristotelian phase, it did not die, but suffered a quite consistent transformation into the dramatic naturalism characteristic of the late nineteenth and early twentieth centuries.'

18 *Writings*, p. 70.
19 *Ibid.*, p. 26.
20 *Ibid.*, p. 63.
21 *Ibid.*, p. 21.
22 *Ibid.*, p. 64.
23 E.g., Philip Butler, *Classicisme et Baroque dans l'Oeuvre de Racine* (Paris, 1959), p. 36. As Bray long ago demonstrated, the basis of neo-classical doctrine is to be found in the commentators of Counter-Reformation Italy (*La Doctrine Classique*, pp. 47–8).

CHAPTER 3

1 Octave Nadal, *Le Sentiment de l'Amour dans l'Oeuvre de Pierre Corneille* (Paris, 1948).
2 *Clitandre* also, if it deserves to be included among Corneille's tragedies: it ends with the king ordering Clitandre (a homosexual) to try and fall in love with Dorise.
3 William Archer, *Play-making: a Manual of Craftsmanship* (London, 1913), p. 245.
4 *Writings*, p. 152.
5 E.g., Robert J. Nelson: 'Neither tragicomedy nor tragedy, *Le Cid* is a romance.' (*Corneille, His Heroes and Their Worlds* (Philadelphia, 1963), p. 87.)
6 Gustave Lanson, *Corneille* (Paris, 1898), p. 47.
7 *Médée*, ll. 1275–6; *Andromaque*, ll. 1261–4.
8 *Médée*, l. 911; *Bajazet*, l. 538.
9 *Médée*, ll. 259–61, ll. 271–2, l. 380, l. 472, ll. 507–10; *Phèdre*, ll. 169–72, l. 10, l. 1064, ll. 1291–2, ll. 743–9. The verbal resemblances in the French make it unlikely that the parallels are due solely to the common influence of Seneca. It is not chance, however, that Racine comes close to Corneille when Corneille is influenced by Seneca. For the influence of Seneca on Racine, see chapter 16 below.
10 Antoine Adam, *Histoire de la Littérature Française au XVIIe Siècle* (Paris, 1964), vol. 1, p. 547.
11 *Writings*, p. 26.
12 *Ibid.*, pp. 21–2.

CHAPTER 4

1 The pronounced sexual undertones of the imagery may also be intended to suggest the love-motive behind the apparently dominant desire for revenge.

2 Again, we may remark that the images in which the 'duty' and 'vengeance' passages are couched have strong sexual undertones, as especially in the use here of 'surmonte'.

3 Again, we may note the sexual metaphor, with its implied reference to Emilie – the 'beauté' whom both Cinna and Maxime are to find it disconcertingly difficult to possess.

4 'Demain j'attends la haine ou la faveur des hommes.'

5 *La Veuve*, III.vii (1634 text). This domestic and humanised use of the tragic vocabulary foreshadows Corneille's serious but secular use of 'ciel' in *Cinna*. (See pp. 59 and 61.)

6 Cf. the end of *Two Gentlemen of Verona*:
> Know, then, I here forget all former griefs,
> Cancel all grudge, repeal thee home again,
> Plead a new state in thy unrivalled merit,
> To which I this subscribe – Sir Valentine,
> Thou art a gentleman, and well derived;
> Take thou thy Silvia, for thou hast deserved her . . .
> Thou hast prevailed; I pardon them and thee . . .
> Come, Proteus, 'tis your penance but to hear
> The stories of your love discovered.

7 Eugenio Garin, *Moyen Age et Renaissance*, trans. Claude Carme (Paris, 1969), p. 126.

CHAPTER 5

1 The hint that the persecution will be stopped is doubly awkward because it contrasts with the absolute rigour of the divine world, which has been brought out clearly in the exchange between Félix and Polyeucte:
> J'en serai protecteur.
> – Non, non, persécutez,
> Et soyez l'instrument de nos félicités.

2 Jacques Maurens, *La Tragédie Sans Tragique: Le Néo-Stoïcisme dans l'Oeuvre de Pierre Corneille* (Paris, 1966), pp. 304–9, 313.

3 Lawrence E. Harvey, 'Corneille's *Horace*: a Study in Tragic and Artistic Ambivalence', in Jean Jacques Demorest (ed.), *Studies in Seventeenth Century French Literature Presented to Morris Bishop* (New York, 1966), brilliantly analyses this pattern. I agree with his conclusions, and the appropriateness of his method to *Horace*; but in my view the structure of the incidents and the pattern stated by the oracle do not cohere with the pattern emerging from the poetry.

CHAPTER 6

1 Martin Turnell, *The Classical Moment: Studies of Corneille, Molière and Racine* (London, 1947), pp. 23–4.

2 Richard Griffiths, *The Dramatic Technique of Antoine de Montchrestien:*

Rhetoric and Style in French Renaissance Tragedy (Oxford, 1970), especially pp. 75–81 and 106–145; Wolfgang Clemen, *English Tragedy before Shakespeare*, trans. T. S. Dorsch (London, 1961), especially pp. 11–55.
3 *The Classical Moment*, p. 41.

CHAPTER 7

1 See the analysis in Yarrow, *Corneille*, pp. 280–5.
2 Yarrow, *Corneille*, p. 115.
3 *L'Amour dans l'Oeuvre de Corneille*, pp. 226–7.
4 G. Couton, *Corneille* (Paris, 1967), p. 130.

CHAPTER 8

1 In a letter of 3 November 1661 to the Abbé de Pure, he says that both Aristie and Viriate want to marry Sertorius out of ambition, not love. But the letter was written when only half of the play had been drafted. Corneille is exaggerating the similarities between the two women so that he may praise himself for his skill in distinguishing them. Our concern is with the work as written, not with what the author chose to say when he was working on it.
2 *Writings*, p. 8.
3 *Writings, loc. cit.*
4 Hence the tone of the opening speech, with its famous lines:
          Quelque ravage affreux qu'étale ici la peste,
          L'absence aux vrais amants est encor plus funeste.
    Corneille had experience of the ravages of plague. He knew it was sentimental hyperbole to say that a lover's absence was worse. The opening speech warns us not to expect a Sophoclean tragedy, but to sit back and enjoy something more mannered and romantic.

CHAPTER 9

1 See Charles Muller, *Etude de Statistique Lexicale: le Vocabulaire du Théâtre de Pierre Corneille* (Paris, 1967), p. 259. I have picked out those words which occur with unusual frequency and which seem especially significant.
2 Steiner, *Death of Tragedy*, pp. 74–5.

CHAPTER 11

1 Jean Pommier, *Aspects de Racine* (Paris, 1966), p. 177.
2 G. E. Lessing, *Hamburg Dramaturgy*, trans. Helen Zimmern (New York, 1962), no. 25, p. 67.

Notes

CHAPTER 12

1 Adam, *Histoire*, vol. IV, p. 301.
2 *Ibid.*, p. 302.
3 Raymond Picard, *La Carrière de Jean Racine* (rev. ed., Paris, 1961), pp. 101–2.
4 Michael Edwards, '*La Thébaïde*' de Racine: clé d'une nouvelle interprétation de son théâtre.
5 Jacques Schérer, *La Dramaturgie Classique en France* (Paris n.d. [1950]), appendix IV.
6 H. C. Lancaster, *A History of French Dramatic Literature in the Seventeenth Century* (Baltimore, 1929–42), part V, p. 88.
7 References are to the 1664 text, reprinted in Edwards, '*La Thébaïde*'. I have modernised the spelling and punctuation.

CHAPTER 13

1 Eugène Vinaver, *Racine et la Poésie Tragique* (rev. ed., Paris, 1963), pp. 43–4.
2 See the discussion in Schérer, *La Dramaturgie Classique*, especially pp. 219–20.
3 A. Bailly, *Racine* (Paris, 1949), p. 118.
4 In the final text. But her reappearance in Act V in the 1668 text does not show her making any decisions.
5 *Classicisme et Baroque*, pp. 223–4.
6 *Racine: Principes* and *Racine et la Poésie Tragique*.

CHAPTER 14

1 Examples abound in *Bérénice* (ll. 89–98, 771–814) and in Racine's other plays e.g. *Phèdre*, ll. 349–50). The convention is universal. Viriate, for example, states it to her confidante in set terms: 'L'apparence t'abuse' (*Sertorius*, l. 674).
2 The significance of this motif of self-destruction in *Bérénice* and in Racine's work generally is brought out by Butler, *Classicisme et Baroque*, pp. 242–4.
3 Schérer, *La Dramaturgie Classique*, p. 195.
4 *Playmaking*, p. 290.
5 *Ibid.*, pp. 290–1.
6 *Ibid.*, pp. 251–2.
7 *The Art of Jean Racine* (Chicago and London, 1963), pp. 156–7.
8 Butler, *Classicisme et Baroque*, p. 242.

CHAPTER 15

1 *Racine et la Poésie Tragique*, p. 70.
2 Roland Barthes, *Sur Racine* (Paris, 1967), p. 109.
3 Martin Turnell, *Jean Racine – Dramatist* (London, 1972), p. 13.

4 C. G. Jung, *Collected Works*, ed. Sir Herbert Read, Michael Fordham and Gerhard Adler, trans. R. F. C. Hull (London, 1960), vol. 8, pp. 349–50.
5 John C. Lapp, *Aspects of Racinian Tragedy* (Toronto, 1955), pp. 156, 159.
6 *Ibid.*, p. 158.
7 G. M. A. Grube, *The Drama of Euripides* (London, 1961), pp. 41–2.
8 Paul Bénichou, *Morales du Grand Siècle* (Paris, 1967), pp. 169–70.
9 W. G. Moore's brilliant discussion (*La Rochefoucauld, His Mind and Art* (Oxford, 1969), pp. 34–46) is relevant here, though his emphasis is rather different.
10 *Maximes*, ed. J. Truchet (Paris, 1967), pp. 283–5.
11 *Ibid.*, p. 291.
12 *Ibid.*, pp. 206–7.
13 Adam, *Histoire*, vol. IV, p. 111.
14 *Ibid.*, p. 110.
15 *Ibid.*, p. 112.
16 Geoffrey Brereton, *A Short History of French Literature* (London, 1954), p. 149.
17 J. Isaacs, *An Assessment of Twentieth Century Literature* (London, 1951), p. 159.
18 *Racine et la Poésie Tragique*, p. 69.
19 *Andromaque*, Act V, Scene iii; *Britannicus*, the scene at the beginning of Act III preserved by Louis Racine and the scene between the present V.v and V.vi; *Bérénice*, the last scene of Act IV and the reading of Bérénice's letter in Act V; *Phèdre*, Thésée's (lost) soliloquy between IV.i and IV.ii.
20 *Racine et la Poésie Tragique*, pp. 84–5.

CHAPTER 16

1 Jean-Louis Barrault, '*Phèdre*', Collections '*Mises en Scène*' (Paris, 1946), p. 16.
2 *Ibid.*, p. 21.
3 See Pommier's *Aspects de Racine*, pp. 207–11. He concludes that Phèdre is a good deal older than Hippolyte, but agrees that some evidence in the text points the other way.
4 See the examples of the ages of tragic characters in Schérer, *La Dramaturgie Classiques*, pp. 20–1.
5 R. C. Knight, *Racine et la Grèce* (Paris, 1951), pp. 262–3.
6 Racine, *Oeuvres Complètes*, vol. II, p. 846 (note on l. 1 of Sophocles's *Electra*).
7 *Ibid.*, p. 855 (note on l. 334 of *Oedipus Rex*).
8 *Ibid.*, p. 872 (note on l. 57 of *Medea*).
9 *Ibid.*, p. 876 (note on l. 119 of *The Phoenician Women*).
10 *Ibid.*, p. 878 (note on ll. 469–70 of *The Phoenician Women*).
11 *Ibid.*, p. 879 (note on ll. 991–2 of *The Phoenician Women*).
12 *Ibid.*, p. 879 (note on ll. 1532–3 of *Iphigenia in Aulis*).
13 *Ibid.*, p. 880 (note on ll. 1177–80 of Euripides's *Electra*).
14 *Ibid.*, p. 875 (note on ll. 296–7 of *The Bacchae*).
15 *Racine et la Grèce*, p. 333.

Notes

16 Lapp, *Racinian Tragedy*, p. 153.
17 *Hercules Oetaeus*, ll. 706–7.
18 *Hercules Oetaeus*, ll. 847–8.
19 *Ibid.*, ll. 1003–15. Knight, *Racine et la Grèce*, p. 347, has drawn attention to this passage.
20 E.g., ll. 16–30, 79–96, 256–62, 282–4, 848–52, 878–9, 980–1, 998–9.
21 ll. 986 and 996–9.
22 *Jean Racine*, pp. 239–40.
23 Butler, *Classicisme et Baroque*, especially pp. 217–26.
24 Oldisworth, quoted by Johnson in his 'Life of Edmund Smith' (*Lives of the Poets* (Everyman edition, London, 1925), vol. 1, p. 284).
25 *The Interpretation of Dreams*, trans. James Strachey (London, 1954), pp. 340–1.
26 *Classicisme et Baroque*, p. 288.

CHAPTER 17

1 Picard, *Jean Racine*, pp. 354–5; Pommier, *Aspects de Racine*, pp. 78–81.
2 Odette de Mourgues, *Racine, or, The Triumph of Relevance* (Cambridge, 1967), pp. 123–6.
3 This is in part due to the idea that saviour/victim figures in the Old Testament prefigured the saviour in the New. In Racine's text we have numerous associative links between Joas and Christ. Joas is 'votre unique espérance' and 'ce fils de David' (l. 213). There is an emphasis on his being 'nourri' in the temple which links with the Christian sentiment of 'Il nous nourrit de lui-même.' There is one obvious link in the reference to 'le Christ' – both Joas (the anointed one) and Christ.
4 The psychoanalytical interpretation of gold as faeces is perhaps relevant. The play contains a great deal of imagery referring to urination and defaecation: 'Vous cachez des *trésors* par David amassés'; 'Comme si dans le *fond* de ce vaste édifice'; 'Celui qui met *un frein à la fureur des flots*'; 'Les cieux par lui *fermés* et devenu d'airain, | Et la terre trois ans sans *pluie* et sans *rosée*'; 'Des *mers* pour eux il entr'ouvrit les *eaux*, | D'un *aride rocher* fit sortir les ruisseaux'; 'Vient-il *infecter l'air* qu'on respire en ces lieux?'; 'Ton encens à ses yeux est un encens souillé'. The first speech is especially full of this symbolism: ('La *trompette* sacrée'; 'Le peuple saint en foule *inondait* les portiques'), and of ideas related to anal symbolism: ornament ('Ornés partout de festons magnifiques'); ritual ('L'usage antique et solennel'); order ('Avec ordre introduits'); and of faeces as gifts ('De leurs champs dans leurs mains portant les nouveaux fruits'). The play also contains a good deal of cannibalistic imagery: this double determination perhaps helped Racine to decide, in most unclassical fashion, to retain the 'chiens dévorants' he found in the Bible. If these Freudian views have any validity, the anal symbolism is especially relevant to an understanding of *Athalie*: it points to the underlying ambivalence which is important to the play.

317

5 The virtual identification of Joad and God is evident from the text. God is 'Celui qui met un frein à la fureur des flots'; Athalie says, 'Que Joad mette un frein à son zèle sauvage.' The last words of the play make plain that God is the 'father' of the 'orphan'. In the rest of the play, Joad is the 'father' of the orphan Joas.

6 Joad had planned a sortie (see ll. 1530–6).

7 This contradicts Joad's view of Abner as 'l'un des soutiens de ce tremblant Etat'. There is no need to debate the political situation and whether Joad is mistaken or Athalie is lying. Their statements are both true, because both are stated authoritatively – another sign of the paradoxical meaning that Racine is expressing in the play.

8 ll. 299–301.

9 ll. 309–10, l. 1462.

SELECT BIBLIOGRAPHY

EDITIONS OF FRENCH SEVENTEENTH-CENTURY WRITERS

Corneille

There is no fully satisfactory collected edition. The standard edition is by Charles Marty-Laveaux, 12 vols., Paris, 1862–8. It is dated in its critical approach and by modern standards over-punctuates the text, but gives all Corneille's variants, which modern collected editions do not. For Corneille's critical writings, I have used:
Pierre Corneille: Writings on the Theatre, ed. H. T. Barnwell, Oxford, 1965.

Racine

The best edition is that by E. Groos, E. Pilon and R. Picard, 2 vols., Paris, 1950. The major plays have often been published separately, in excellent editions, but special mention should be made of two illuminating critical editions of minor works:
Edwards, Michael, *'La Thébaïde' de Racine: clé d'une nouvelle interprétation de son théâtre*, Paris, 1965
Vinaver, Eugène, *Racine: Principes de la Tragédie en Marge de la Poétique d'Aristote*, Manchester and Paris, 1951

Although not a scholarly edition, Jean-Louis Barrault's *Phèdre* in the *Collection 'Mises en Scène'* (Paris, 1946) is outstanding.

Other Writers

Tristan, *La Mariane*, ed. Jacques Madeleine, Paris, 1939.
Chapelain, *Opuscules Critiques*, ed. Alfred C. Hunter, Paris, 1936.
Thomas Corneille, *Ariane* and *Le Comte d'Essex* in *Oeuvres Complètes de P. Corneille, suivies des Oeuvres Choisies de Thomas Corneille*, ed. Charles Lahure, 5 vols., Paris, 1857.
La Rochefoucauld, *Maximes*, ed. J. Truchet, Paris, 1967.
Boileau, *Oeuvres Complètes*, ed. Antoine Adam and Françoise Escal, Paris, 1966.

Note. In all quotations, I have modernised the spelling where necessary, and have on occasion slightly modified the punctuation.

OTHER WORKS

References to all works quoted are given in the notes. The following list includes only those which are useful for the general background or which I have found especially valuable for the particular aspects covered in this book. Those of the latter whose relevance to Corneille and Racine may not be immediately apparent are listed separately in section 4.

General Works

Adam, Antoine, *Histoire de la Littérature Française au XVIIe Siècle*. 5 vols., Paris, 1964 (original ed. 1948–56). The standard history. Comprehensive, scholarly and lively.

Bray, R., *La Formation de la Doctrine Classique en France*. Paris, 1963 (original ed. 1927). Somewhat over-schematic in its presentation of neo-classicism as a coherent doctrine, but essential for the information it contains.

Lancaster, H. C., *A History of French Dramatic Literature in the Seventeenth Century*, 9 vols., Baltimore, 1929–42. An indispensable collection of information.

Schérer, Jacques, *La Dramaturgie Classique en France*. Paris, n.d. [1950]. A detailed and thoroughly-documented examination of the formal and technical aspects of neo-classical drama. Especially good on the unities.

Corneille

Couton, G., *Corneille*. Paris, 1967. A scholarly account of the life and works, with heavy emphasis on the relevance of the plays to seventeenth-century events.

Yarrow, P. J., *Corneille*. London, 1963. To date, the only full-length survey by an English critic of the plays and their background.

Racine

Butler, Philip, *Classicisme et Baroque dans l'Oeuvre de Racine*. Paris, 1959. A penetrating, controversial study of Racinian tragedy and its relation to seventeenth-century ideas.

Knight, R. C., *Racine et la Grèce*, Paris, 1951. A detailed study of Racine's knowledge of Greek and Greek literature and its influence on his work.

Lapp, John C., *Aspects of Racinian Tragedy*, Toronto, 1955. A brilliant critical study, more fundamental than its modest title suggests.

Picard, Raymond, *La Carrière de Jean Racine*. Rev. ed., Paris, 1961. A thoroughly-documented biography, emphasising the material aspects of Racine's career.

Pommier, Jean, *Aspects de Racine*. Paris, 1966. Biographical and critical essays, the former containing much important information.

Vinaver, Eugène, *Racine et la Poésie Tragique*. Rev. ed., Paris, 1963. Approaches Racine through his poetry, with profound and suggestive insights into his tragic vision and dramatic method.

History of Ideas and Critical Approaches

Adam, Antoine, *Les Libertins au XVIIe Siècle*, Paris, 1964. Mainly an anthology, but with helpful introduction and commentaries. Demonstrates the strength and variety of free-thought in seventeenth-century France, and the significance of some minor figures encountered in the biographies of the great writers.

Bethell, S. L., *Shakespeare and the Popular Dramatic Tradition*. London, 1948. A brisk (sometimes over-brisk) demonstration of the irrelevance of many of the conventions of naturalistic criticism to the work of Shakespeare, with some interesting remarks on the relationship between neo-classicism and naturalism.

Griffiths, Richard, *The Dramatic Technique of Antoine de Montchrestien: Rhetoric and Style in French Renaissance Tragedy*. Oxford, 1970. A thorough examination of the effects a Renaissance tragic poet was aiming at, and how they differ from the concerns of most dramatists since the beginning of the seventeenth century.

Spink, J. S., *French Free-Thought from Gassendi to Voltaire*. London, 1959. An analysis of the various currents of free-thought in seventeenth-century France, with valuable sidelights on the intellectual milieu of the great age of classical poetry and tragedy.

Williams, Raymond, *Drama from Ibsen to Eliot*. London, 1952. Valuable for its critique of the bases and limits of naturalism as a theatrical form.

Yates, Frances A., *Giordano Bruno and the Hermetic Tradition*, London, 1964. A seminal contribution to intellectual history. Discusses the rôle of the Renaissance revival of magic in the rise of science and in Renaissance poetry. Important as a corrective to the usual exclusive emphasis on Cartesianism and rationalism in accounts of the seventeenth-century revolution in thought.

'The Hermetic Tradition in Renaissance Science', in *Art, Science and History in the Renaissance*, ed. Charles S. Singleton, Baltimore, 1967. A short and wide-ranging summary of the author's views.

INDEX

Adam, Antoine, 2, 37, 166, 229, 312, 315, 316, 320, 321
Aeschylus, 11, 12, 84; *Oresteia*, 8, 99; *Prometheus Bound*, 90, 153
alchemy, 286
Archer, William, 211–12, 312, 315
Aristotle, 13, 17–20, 261, 311
Arnauld, Antoine, 260
Aubignac, François Hédelin, abbé d', 17, 24, 155, 261, 308, 310

Bailly, Auguste, 182, 315
Barrault, Jean-Louis, 237, 316, 319
Barthes, Roland, 223, 315
Bayle, Pierre, 281
Beckett, Samuel, 3; *En Attendant Godot*, 153
Bellessort, André, 36
Bénichou, Paul, 228, 316
Bernard, Claude, 9, 310
Bernard, Marc, 310
Bethell, S. L., 2, 9, 310, 311, 321
Beuchat, Charles, 4, 310
Boileau, Nicolas Despréaux, 158, 166, 279, 319; critical principles, 160–1, 220; and Racine, 160–1, 309; *L'Art Poétique*, 160–1, 219; *Epître VII*, 219; *Ode sur la Prise de Namur*, 254
Boyer, Claude, 166
Bray, René, 310, 312, 320
Brecht, Bertolt, 3, 7, 9, 11, 310
Brereton, Geoffrey, 230, 316
Brunetière, Ferdinand, 260
Butler, Philip, 189, 208, 215, 260, 278, 307, 309, 312, 315, 317, 320

Campanella, Tomaso, 308
Castelvetro, Ludovico, 20
catharsis, 13, 17–18, 19–20
Chapelain, Jean, 5, 6, 22, 155, 158, 160, 161, 302, 308, 310, 319
Chekhov, Anton, 3, 9
Christianity; and tragedy, 64–5; Corneille and, 59, 63, 115, 308; Racine and, 161, 170, 172, 282–3, 300–1, 309
Clagett, Marshall, 2

Clemen, Wolfgang, 85, 314
Colbert, Jean-Baptiste, 309
comedy, Corneille's view of, 13, 17
comedy, thought in, 4
Condé, Louis de Bourbon, Prince de, 30, 117
Corneille, Pierre, 3, 5, 14, 26–7, 39, 158, 159, 162, 188, 213, 218, 229, 233, 298, 302, 307, 309, 312, 319; career, 15–16; and Christianity, 59, 63, 115, 308; comic elements in tragedies, 56, 95–7, 139, 156, 157, 304–5, 307; contrasted with Racine, 1, 79, 159, 178, 192, 197, 200, 211, 278, 279, 298, 307; and 'Cornelian' verse, 78–9, 81–2; and morality in tragedy, 18–21, 26, 155–6, 308; and naturalism, 1, 22, 24–7, 29–30, 33–4, 37, 39, 70, 72–3, 75, 76, 89, 93, 96, 105–6, 112–13, 115–16, 117, 128–30, 131, 136, 138–40, 155–6, 192–3, 278, 303–5, 307; and neo-stoicism, 76; and the poetic method, 21, 23, 24–5, 27, 35–7, 39, 51–2, 59, 62–3, 70, 75–7, 83–4, 117, 125, 128–31, 138–40, 150–1, 153, 155, 156, 303, 305, 308; and seventeenth-century jargon, 68, 113, 128–9, 143, 149–50, 276; and tragedy in the modern sense, 13, 31, 34–5, 125, 151–4, 156, 167, 305; treatment of character, 18–20, 50, 58, 65–6, 73–4, 83–4, 93, 103–8, 113–15, 116, 128–9, 132–3, 145, 148, 156–7, 311; of plot, 23–4, 33, 36, 40, 51–2, 99, 103, 116, 120, 137–8, 141, 143–5, 148, 150, 153, 156, 157; and unity of action, 23; and unity of place, 56, 149; use of melo-dramatic effects, 24–5, 100, 155–6, 304; variations in his verse, 78–9, 90–8, 108–13; views, on comedy, 13, 17, on tragedy, 13
works: *Agésilas*, 17, 90, 91, 97, 118, 139, 305; *Andromède*, 15, 22, 117, 304; *Attila*, 16, 90–3, 97, 98, 118, 139, 213, 305; *Le Cid*, 15, 17, 28–9, 31–7, 39,

323

Index

in the plays of, 214, 232–3, 276, 278, 305–7; and Greek tragedy, 166, 172, 220, 227–8, 239–40; and Jansenism, 159, 166, 172, 233, 279, 282–3, 305, 307; and myth, 167, 220–3, 233, 260–1, 283, 305, 306, 307; and naturalism, 188, 189, 199–200, 201, 204–5, 224, 225, 227, 279, 305–6; and neo-classicism, 159, 190, 192, 197 199, 220, 227, 230–1, 259, 261–2, 305–6; and opera, 279, 280, 307; and poetic justice, 189, 190, 260, 305; and poetic method, 169, 170, 176–7, 187–8, 194–5, 201, 204–5, 213–14, 225, 230, 244–5, 247, 273–8, 279, 305, 306, 307; as a psychologist, 211–12, 216; sense of tragedy in, 169–73, 186, 190, 193–6, 197, 214–15, 227, 228–9, 278, 297, 305; and seventeenth-century jargon, 239, 256, 276–8; soliloquies in, 167, 176–7, 192, 197–8, 305; treatment, of character, 182–6, 188–9, 199–200, 201, 204–5, 211–12, 214, 216, 217, 223, 225, 237–9, 248, 254–7, 259–60, 274–6, 285, 305–6, of plot; 168–9, 170, 172, 177, 179–82, 184, 188, 191–3, 204, 214, 217, 219, 223, 224, 237, 258–9, 274–5, 286–7, 289, 305–7; and the unconscious, 194–5, 225–9, 233, 239, 248, 249–57, 305–6, 307; view of tragedy, 13

works: *Alceste*, 235, 236, 280, 306; *Alexandre*, 159, 173–7, 178, 186, 188, 192, 306; *Amasie*, 166; *Les Amours d'Ovide*, 166, 167, 234; *Andromaque*, 37, 177, 178–90, 191, 192, 214, 219, 225, 232, 234, 235, 239, 240, 241, 243, 260, 278, 306, 312, 315, 316; *Athalie*, 159, 208, 219, 230, 232, 279, 281–301, 307, 309, 317, 318; *Bajazet*, 37, 85, 192, 216, 217, 218–19, 223, 224, 234, 237, 243, 306, 309, 312; *Bérénice*, 84, 85, 143, 192, 193, 196, 197–215, 223, 225, 230, 234, 235, 246, 278, 297, 300, 306, 307, 311, 315, 316; *Britannicus*, 178, 190, 191–6, 214, 225, 232, 234, 306, 316; *Esther*, 159, 279–81, 296, 297, 307, 309; *L'Idylle de la Paix*, 279, 281, 307; *Iphigénie*, 192, 216, 217–18, 219–23, 224, 225, 229, 232, 233, 234, 235, 236, 237, 239, 240, 261, 278, 279, 283, 294, 306, 309, 311; *Iphigénie en Tauride*, 234, 235, 236, 280, 306; *Mithridate*, 192, 216, 217, 218, 219, 223, 224, 229, 232, 234, 235, 237, 240,

278, 305, 306, 309; *Phèdre*, 37, 90, 117, 159, 160, 192, 206, 208, 219, 229, 230, 232, 233, 234, 235, 236, 237–78, 279, 283, 297, 298, 300, 306–7, 309, 312, 315, 316; *Théagène et Chariclée*, 166, 167; *La Thébaïde*, 159, 166–73, 175, 189, 192, 214, 239, 275, 306

Racine, Louis, 234, 235, 316
Rationalism and the decline of poetry, 2
Reiss, T. J., 310
Renaissance, 2, 11, 62–3, 82, 303, 308
Renaissance tragedy, 35–6, 83, 85, 214
Richelieu, Armand Jean du Plessis, duc de, Cardinal, 76, 308
Rossi, Paolo, 2
Rostand, Edmond, 87
Rotrou, Jean, 36, 168, 240
rules, the, 16–17, 24, 25–6, 155–6, 160, 232–3, 305, 308

Saint-Réal, César Vichard, abbé de, 229, 309
Saint-Simon, Louis de Rouvroy, duc de, 122
Sarcey, François, 285
Schérer, Jacques, 167, 315, 316, 320
Schlegel, August Wilhelm, 99, 244
science and the rise of naturalism, 2, 9, 308
Scribe, Eugène, 24, 39
Seneca, 37, 39, 85, 240–2, 251, 312; *Hercules Oetaeus*, 186, 241–2, 317; *Phaedra*, 241–2; *Troades*, 241
Sévigné, Marie de Rabutin-Chantal, marquise de, 160
Shakespeare, William, 11; *Antony and Cleopatra*, 297; *As You Like It*, 118; *Hamlet*, 8, 104; *King Lear*, 8, 101; *Macbeth*, 115; *Richard III*, 7, 115; *Troilus and Cressida*, 86; *Two Gentlemen of Verona*, 313; *The Winter's Tale*, 8
Shaw, G. B.: and Shakespeare, 9; *The Apple Cart*, 87
Shelley, P. B., 8
Smith, Edmund, 317; *Phaedra and Hippolytus*, 261–2
Sophocles: *Electra*, 316; *Oedipus at Colonus*, 186; *Oedipus Rex*, 12, 316
Spink, J. S., 2, 321
Steele, Sir Richard, 3
Steiner, George: *The Death of Tragedy*, 141, 152, 311, 314
Stendhal (Marie Henri Beyle), 310
Strindberg, Johan August, 11, 39; *Miss Julie*, 7, 238